Mike Holt's Illustrated Guide to

CHANGES TO THE NATIONAL ELECTRICAL CODE®

BASED ON THE
2023 NEC®

Mike Holt Enterprises
MikeHolt.com • 888.632.2633

NOTICE TO THE READER

The text and commentary in this book is the author's interpretation of the 2023 Edition of NFPA 70®, National Electrical Code®. It shall not be considered an endorsement of or the official position of the NFPA® or any of its committees, nor relied upon as a formal interpretation of the meaning or intent of any specific provision or provisions of the 2023 edition of NFPA 70, National Electrical Code.

The publisher does not warrant or guarantee any of the products described herein or perform any independent analysis in connection with any of the product information contained herein. The publisher does not assume, and expressly disclaims, any obligation to obtain and include information other than that provided to it by the manufacturer.

The reader is expressly warned to consider and adopt all safety precautions and applicable federal, state, and local laws and regulations. By following the instructions contained herein, the reader willingly assumes all risks in connection with such instructions.

Mike Holt Enterprises disclaims liability for any personal injury, property or other damages of any nature whatsoever, whether special, indirect, consequential or compensatory, directly or indirectly resulting from the use of this material. The reader is responsible for relying on his or her personal independent judgment in determining safety and appropriate actions in all circumstances.

The publisher makes no representation or warranties of any kind, including but not limited to, the warranties of fitness for particular purpose or merchantability, nor are any such representations implied with respect to the material set forth herein, and the publisher takes no responsibility with respect to such material. The publisher shall not be liable for any special, consequential, or exemplary damages resulting, in whole or part, from the reader's use of, or reliance upon, this material.

Mike Holt's Illustrated Guide to Changes to the National Electrical Code®, based on the 2023 NEC® in Partnership with the NFPA

First Printing: September 2022
Author: Mike Holt
Technical Illustrator: Mike Culbreath
Cover Design: Bryan Burch
Layout Design and Typesetting: Cathleen Kwas
COPYRIGHT © 2022 Charles Michael Holt
ISBN 978-1-950431-69-4

All rights reserved. No part of this work covered by the copyright hereon may be reproduced or used in any form or by any means graphic, electronic, or mechanical, including photocopying, recording, taping, or information storage and retrieval systems without the written permission of the publisher.

For more information, or to request permission to use material from this text, e-mail Info@MikeHolt.com.

 Produced and Printed in the USA

 This logo is a registered trademark of Mike Holt Enterprises, Inc.

 NEC®, NFPA 70®, NFPA 70E® and National Electrical Code® are registered trademarks of the National Fire Protection Association.

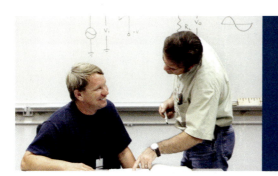

Are you an instructor?

You can request an examination copy of this or other Mike Holt Publications:

888.632.2633 • Training@MikeHolt.com

Download a sample PDF of all our publications by visiting MikeHolt.com/Instructors

I dedicate this book to the
Lord Jesus Christ, *my mentor and teacher.*
Proverbs 16:3

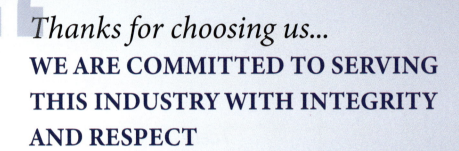

" Thanks for choosing us...
WE ARE COMMITTED TO SERVING THIS INDUSTRY WITH INTEGRITY AND RESPECT

Since 1975, we have worked hard to develop products that get results, and to help individuals in their pursuit of success in this exciting industry.

From the very beginning we have been committed to the idea that customers come first. Everyone on my team will do everything they possibly can to help you succeed. I want you to know that we value you and are honored that you have chosen us to be your partner in training.

You are the future of this industry and we know that it is you who will make the difference in the years to come. My goal is to share with you everything that I know and to encourage you to pursue your education on a continuous basis. I hope that not only will you learn theory, *Code*, calculations, or how to pass an exam, but that in the process, you will become the expert in the field and the person others know to trust.

To put it simply, we genuinely care about your success and will do everything that we can to help you take your skills to the next level!

We are happy to partner with you on your educational journey.

God bless and much success,

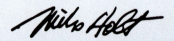

TABLE OF CONTENTS

About This Textbook..xi

Additional Products to Help You Learn.............................xv

How to Use the *National Electrical Code*.............................1

Global Changes in the 2023 *National Electrical Code*.......7
Global Changes...7

Article 90—Introduction to the *National Electrical Code*...9
90.1 Scope...9
90.2 Use and Application..10
90.4 Enforcement...14
90.5 Mandatory Rules, Permissive Rules, and Explanatory Material, (C) Explanatory Material..16

CHAPTER 1—GENERAL RULES 19

Article 100—Definitions..21
Article 100 Global Summary..21

Article 110—General Requirements for Electrical Installations...33
110.3 Use and Product Listing (Certification) of Equipment.................33
110.8 Wiring Methods..34
110.12 Mechanical Execution of Work............................35
110.16 Arc-Flash Hazard Warning....................................36
110.17 Servicing and Maintenance of Equipment..........37
110.20 Reconditioned Equipment....................................37
110.22 Identification of Disconnecting Means...............38
110.26 Spaces About Electrical Equipment....................38

CHAPTER 2—WIRING AND PROTECTION 49

Article 200—Use and Identification of Grounded Conductors...51
200.6 Means of Identifying Grounded Conductors.....51

Article 210—Branch Circuits....................................53
210.1 Scope...53
210.4 Multiwire Branch Circuits.....................................54
210.5 Identification for Branch Circuits........................55
210.8 Ground-Fault Circuit-Interrupter Protection for Personnel.........57
210.11 Branch Circuits Required.....................................66
210.12 Arc-Fault Circuit-Interrupter Protection...........68
210.17 Guest Rooms and Guest Suites............................71
210.19 Conductors—Minimum Ampacity and Size......71
210.23 Multiple-Outlet Branch Circuits..........................75
210.52 Dwelling Unit Receptacle Outlets........................75
210.62 Show Windows...80
210.65 Meeting Rooms..80
210.70 Lighting Outlets Required....................................81

Article 215—Feeders..87
215.2 Conductor Sizing..87
215.15 Barriers..88
215.18 Surge Protection..89

Article 220—Branch-Circuit, Feeder, and Service Load Calculations..91
220.1 Scope...91
220.5 Calculations...92
220.53 Appliance Load—Dwelling Unit(s)......................93
220.57 Electric Vehicle Supply Equipment (EVSE) Load.....94
220.60 Noncoincident Loads..95
220.70 Energy Management Systems (EMSs)................96
220.87 Determining Existing Loads.................................96
220.120 Receptacle Loads..96

Table of Contents

Article 225—Outside Branch Circuits and Feeders 99
- 225.1 Scope 99
- 225.27 Raceway Seal 100
- 225.41 Emergency Disconnects 100
- 225.42 Surge Protection 101

Article 230—Services 103
- 230.1 Scope 103
- 230.7 Service Conductors Separate from Other Conductors 104
- 230.8 Raceway Seal 104
- 230.24 Clearances 105
- 230.43 Wiring Methods for 1000V, Nominal, or Less 106
- 230.62 Service Equipment—Enclosed or Guarded 107
- 230.67 Surge Protection 107
- 230.71 Maximum Number of Disconnects 109
- 230.85 Emergency Disconnects 110

Article 240—Overcurrent Protection 113
- 240.4 Protection of Conductors 113
- 240.6 Standard Ampere Ratings 116
- 240.24 Location of Overcurrent Protective Devices 117

Article 242—Overvoltage Protection 119
- 242.9 Indicating 120

Article 250—Grounding and Bonding 121
- 250.36 Impedance Grounded Systems—480V to 1000V 121
- 250.53 Grounding Electrode Installation Requirements 122
- 250.64 Grounding Electrode Conductor Installation 124
- 250.66 Sizing Grounding Electrode Conductors 127
- 250.68 Grounding Electrode Conductor and Bonding Jumper Connection to Grounding Electrodes 128
- 250.70 Grounding Electrode Conductor Termination Fittings 129
- 250.92 Bonding Metal Parts Containing Service Conductors 131
- 250.94 Bonding for Communications Systems 133
- 250.102 Neutral Conductor, Main Bonding Jumper, System Bonding Jumper, Supply-Side Bonding Jumper, Load-Side Bonding Jumper 135
- 250.109 Metal Enclosures 136
- 250.140 Frames of Ranges, Ovens, and Clothes Dryers 137
- 250.148 Continuity of Equipment Grounding Conductors and Attachment in Boxes 138

CHAPTER 3—WIRING METHODS AND MATERIALS 141

Article 300—General Requirements for Wiring Methods and Materials 145
- 300.3 Conductors 145
- 300.4 Protection Against Physical Damage 148
- 300.5 Underground Installations 149
- 300.6 Protection Against Corrosion 150
- 300.12 Mechanical Continuity—Raceways and Cables 151
- 300.14 Length of Free Conductors at Outlets, Junctions, and Switch Points 152
- 300.15 Boxes or Fittings 153
- 300.25 Exit Stair Towers 154

Article 310—Conductors for General Wiring 157
- 310.10 Uses Permitted 157

Article 312—Cabinets, Cutout Boxes, and Meter Socket Enclosures 161
- 312.5 Cabinets, Cutout Boxes, and Meter Socket Enclosures 161
- 312.8 Overcurrent Device Enclosures 162
- 312.10 Screws or Other Fasteners 163

Article 314—Boxes, Conduit Bodies, and Handhole Enclosures 165
- 314.5 Screws or Other Fasteners 165
- 314.17 Conductors and Cables Entering Boxes, Conduit Bodies, or Fittings 166
- 314.23 Supports 166
- 314.25 Covers and Canopies 167
- 314.29 Boxes, Conduit Bodies, and Handhole Enclosures to be Accessible 168

Article 320—Armored Cable (Type AC) 171
- 320.23 In Accessible Attics 171
- 320.30 Securing and Supporting 171

Article 330—Metal-Clad Cable (Type MC) 175
- 330.10 Uses Permitted 175
- 330.30 Securing and Supporting 176

Table of Contents

Article 334—Nonmetallic-Sheathed Cable: Types NM and NMC 179
- 334.10 Uses Permitted 179
- 334.15 Exposed Work 181
- 334.19 Cable Entries 182
- 334.40 Boxes and Fittings 183

Article 352—Rigid Polyvinyl Chloride Conduit (PVC) 185
- 352.10 Uses Permitted 185
- 352.44 Expansion Fittings 187

Article 356—Liquidtight Flexible Nonmetallic Conduit (LFNC) 189
- 356.10 Uses Permitted 189

Article 358—Electrical Metallic Tubing (EMT) 191
- 358.10 Uses Permitted 191

Article 362—Electrical Nonmetallic Tubing (ENT) 193
- 362.10 Uses Permitted 193

Article 376—Metal Wireways 197
- 376.60 Equipment Grounding Conductor 197

CHAPTER 4—EQUIPMENT FOR GENERAL USE 199

Article 404—Switches 201
- 404.1 Scope 201
- 404.14 Rating and Use of Switches 201

Article 406—Receptacles, Attachment Plugs, and Flanged Inlets 203
- 406.3 Receptacle Rating and Type 203
- 406.4 General Installation Requirements 204
- 406.6 Receptacle Faceplates 207
- 406.9 Receptacles in Damp or Wet Locations 208
- 406.12 Tamper-Resistant Receptacles 211

Article 408—Switchboards, Switchgear, and Panelboards 215
- 408.4 Circuit Directory and Descriptions of Circuit Source 215
- 408.9 Replacement Panelboards 216
- 408.43 Panelboard Orientation 217

Article 410—Luminaires, Lampholders, and Lamps 219
- 410.10 Luminaires in Specific Locations 219
- 410.42 Luminaire(s) with Exposed Conductive Surfaces 221
- 410.71 Disconnecting Means for Fluorescent or LED Luminaires that Utilize Double-Ended Lamps 221
- 410.184 Ground-Fault Circuit-Interrupter (GFCI) Protection and Special Purpose Ground-Fault Circuit-Interrupter (SPGFCI) Protection 223

Article 422—Appliances 225
- 422.5 GFCI Protection 225
- 422.13 Storage-Type Water Heaters 227
- 422.16 Flexible Cords 228
- 422.18 Ceiling-Suspended (Paddle) Fans 230
- 422.33 Disconnection of Cord-and-Plug-Connected or Attachment Fitting-Connected Appliances 231

Article 424—Fixed Electric Space-Heating Equipment 233
- 424.4 Branch Circuits 233

Article 430—Motors 235
- 430.1 Scope 235
- 430.6 Conductor Ampacity and Motor Rating Determination 236
- 430.31 General 237
- 430.83 Ratings 238

Article 440—Air-Conditioning and Refrigerating Equipment 241
- 440.8 Single Machine and Location 241
- 440.11 General 241
- 440.14 Location 242
- 440.22 Application and Selection 243

Article 445—Generators 245
- 445.11 Marking 245
- 445.19 Emergency Shutdown of Prime Mover 245

Table of Contents

Article 450—Transformers and Transformer Vaults (Including Secondary Ties) 247
- 450.1 Scope 247
- 450.10 Grounding and Bonding 248

Article 480—Stationary Standby Batteries 249
- Article 480—Article Analysis 249
- 480.4 Battery and Cell Terminations 249
- 480.10 Battery Locations 250

CHAPTER 5—SPECIAL OCCUPANCIES 251

Article 500—Hazardous (Classified) Locations, Classes I, II, and III, Divisions 1 and 2 253
- 500.1 Scope 254
- 500.4 Documentation 254
- 500.5 Classifications of Locations 255

Article 501—Class I Locations 257
- 501.1 Scope 257
- 501.10 Wiring Methods 257
- 501.15 Sealing and Drainage 260
- 501.30 Grounding and Bonding 265
- 501.135 Utilization Equipment 266
- 501.145 Receptacles and Attachment Plugs, Class I, Division 1 and Division 2 267

Article 502—Class II Locations 269
- 502.10 Wiring Methods 269
- 502.15 Sealing 271
- 502.30 Grounding and Bonding 272

Article 511—Commercial Garages, Repair and Storage 275
- 511.3 Area Classification 275
- 511.7 Wiring and Equipment Installed Above Hazardous (Classified) Locations 276
- 511.8 Underground Wiring Hazardous (Classified) Locations 277

Article 514—Motor Fuel Dispensing Facilities 279
- 514.7 Wiring and Equipment Above Hazardous (Classified) Locations 279

Article 517—Health Care Facilities 281
- 517.1 Scope 282
- 517.10 Applicability 282
- 517.13 Equipment Grounding Conductor for Receptacles and Fixed Electrical Equipment in Patient Care Spaces 283

Article 518—Assembly Occupancies 287
- 518.2 General Classification 287

Article 547—Agricultural Buildings 289
- 547.20 Wiring Methods 290
- 547.25 Flexible Connections 290
- 547.26 Physical Protection 290
- 547.44 Equipotential Planes and Bonding of Equipotential Planes 291

Article 555—Marinas, Boatyards, Floating Buildings, and Commercial and Noncommercial Docking Facilities 293
- 555.4 Location of Service Equipment 293
- 555.15 Replacement of Equipment 293
- 555.30 Electrical Equipment and Connections 294
- 555.34 Wiring Methods and Installation 295
- 555.35 Ground-Fault Protection of Equipment (GFPE) and Ground-Fault Circuit Interrupter 296
- 555.36 Shore Power Receptacle Disconnecting Means 298
- 555.37 Equipment Grounding Conductor 299
- 555.38 Luminaires 300

CHAPTER 6—SPECIAL EQUIPMENT 301

Article 600—Electric Signs and Outline Lighting 303
- 600.5 Branch Circuits 303
- 600.6 Disconnects 304

Article 620—Elevators, Dumbwaiters, Escalators, Moving Walks, Platform Lifts, and Stairway Chairlifts 307
- 620.6 Ground-Fault Circuit-Interrupter Protection for Personnel 307
- 620.22 Branch Circuits for Car Lighting, Receptacle(s), Ventilation, Heating, and Air-Conditioning 308

Table of Contents

Article 625—Electric Vehicle Power Transfer System 311
- 625.6 Listed 311
- 625.40 Electric Vehicle Branch Circuit 312
- 625.43 Disconnecting Means 312
- 625.49 Island Mode 312

Article 630—Electric Welders 315
- 630.8 Ground-Fault Circuit-interrupter Protection for Personnel 315

Article 680—Swimming Pools, Fountains, and Similar Installations 317
- 680.5 Ground-Fault Circuit-Interrupter (GFCI) and Special Purpose Ground-Fault Circuit-Interrupter (SPGFCI) Protection 317
- 680.7 Grounding and Bonding 318
- 680.10 Electric Water Heaters and Heat Pumps 318
- 680.14 Corrosive Environment 319
- 680.21 Pool Pump Motors 320
- 680.22 Receptacles, Luminaires, and Switches 321
- 680.26 Equipotential Bonding 324
- 680.32 Ground-Fault Circuit-Interrupter (GFCI) and Special Purpose Ground-Fault Circuit-Interrupter (SPGFCI) Protection 328
- 680.43 Indoor Installations 329
- 680.44 Ground-Fault Circuit-Interrupter (GFCI) and Special Purpose Ground-Fault Circuit-Interrupter (SPGFCI) Protection 330
- 680.50 General 331
- 680.54 Connection to an Equipment Grounding Conductor 331
- 680.58 GFCI or SPGFCI Protection of Receptacles 332
- 680.59 Ground-Fault Protection for Permanently Installed Nonsubmersible Pumps 332
- 680.74 Bonding 333

Article 690—Solar Photovoltaic (PV) Systems 335
- 690.4 General Requirements 335
- 690.7 Maximum PV System Direct-Current Circuit Voltage 336
- 690.12 Rapid Shutdown of PV Systems on Buildings 338
- 690.15 PV Equipment Disconnect or Isolating Device 340
- 690.31 Wiring Methods 342
- 690.43 Equipment Grounding and Bonding 348
- 690.56 Identification of Power Sources 349

Article 691—Large-Scale Photovoltaic (PV) Electric Supply Systems 351
- 691.4 Special Requirements for Large-Scale PV Electric Supply Stations 351

Article 695—Fire Pumps 353
- 695.1 Scope 353
- 695.6 Power Wiring 354
- 695.7 Fire Pump Controller Voltage Drop 354

CHAPTER 7—SPECIAL CONDITIONS 357

Article 700—Emergency Systems 359
- 700.1 Scope 359
- 700.3 Tests and Maintenance 360
- 700.4 Capacity and Rating 361
- 700.6 Signals 361
- 700.8 Surge Protection 361
- 700.11 Wiring, Class-2-Powered Emergency Lighting Systems 362
- 700.12 General Requirements 362
- 700.27 Class 2 Powered Emergency Lighting Systems 365

Article 701—Legally Required Standby Systems 367
- 701.3 Commissioning and Maintenance 367
- 701.4 Capacity and Rating 368

Article 702—Optional Standby Systems 369
- 702.4 Capacity and Rating 369
- 702.5 Interconnection or Transfer Equipment 370
- 702.12 Portable Outdoor Generators 371

Article 705—Interconnected Electric Power Production Sources 373
- 705.6 Equipment Approval 373
- 705.11 Source Connections to a Service 373
- 705.13 Energy Management Systems (EMS) 375
- 705.28 Circuit Sizing and Current 375
- 705.30 Overcurrent Protection 377
- 705.82 Single 120-Volt Supply 378

Article 706—Energy Storage Systems 379
- 706.7 Commissioning and Maintenance 380
- 706.15 Disconnecting Means 380
- 706.31 Overcurrent Protection 381

Article 710—Stand-Alone Systems 383
- 710.1 Scope 383
- 710.6 Equipment Approval 384

Table of Contents

Article 722—Cables for Power-Limited Circuits and Fault-Managed Power Circuits 387
Article 722—Article Analysis 387
722.1   Scope 387
722.3   Other Articles 388
722.24 Mechanical Execution of Work 388
722.179 Listing and Marking of Cables 390

Article 724—Class 1 Power-Limited Circuits and Class 1 Power-Limited Remote-Control and Signaling Circuits 393
Article 724—Article Analysis 393
724.40 Class 1 Circuits 393

Article 725—Class 2 and Class 3 Power-Limited Circuits 395
Article 725—Article Analysis 395

Article 726—Class 4 Fault-Managed Power Systems 397
Article 726—Article Analysis 397

Article 750—Energy Management Systems 399
750.6   Listing 399
750.30 Load Management 399

Article 760—Fire Alarm Systems 401
760.33 Supply-Side Overvoltage Protection 401

CHAPTER 8—COMMUNICATIONS SYSTEMS 403

Article 800—General Requirements for Communications Systems 405
800.3   Other Articles 405
800.24   Mechanical Execution of Work 406
800.133 Installation of Coaxial Cables and Equipment 407
800.170 Plenum Cable Ties 408

Article 810—Antenna Systems 409
Article 810—Article Analysis 409
810.3   Other Articles 409

2023 NATIONAL ELECTRICAL CODE CHANGES REVIEW QUIZ 411

About the Author 423

About the NFPA Review Team 424

About the Illustrator 425

About the Mike Holt Team 426

ABOUT THIS TEXTBOOK

A Unique Partnership

The National Fire Protection Association® (NFPA®) and Mike Holt Enterprises have partnered for the first time, bringing together two recognized electrical leaders to advance safety. This book, *Changes to the National Electrical Code*, 2023 edition, explains the key updates to the next edition of NFPA 70®, *National Electrical Code*® (*NEC*®). It highlights the latest updates with full-color illustrations, insightful commentary, technical clarifications, and a general review of the *Code*. Electrical professionals, including electricians, electrical contractors, engineers, and inspectors, will find it to be a valuable resource for understanding the *NEC*.

"Today's world is increasingly complex when it comes to all things electrical," said NFPA President and CEO Jim Pauley. "The *NEC* remains the essential resource to ensure all those who work in this field have the latest safety information to address existing and emerging issues. We are extremely excited to partner with Mike to bring this information to life for those who rely on the *NEC* to do their jobs."

"Joining with NFPA for this project allows us to bring top *NEC* resources together to explain the changes in the most important standard in the industry, the *NEC*. Our book provides the information and illustrations that electrical professionals need to understand and apply the *NEC* in the field. This partnership will truly advance electrical safety and an understanding of what changed in the *Code*." said Holt. "This is a unique and special collaboration for me, and I am thrilled that together we will be able to provide the best possible *NEC* changes resource."

Mike Holt's Illustrated Guide to Changes to the National Electrical Code, based on the 2023 NEC, in Partnership with the NFPA

This textbook provides insight on how the 2023 *NEC* changes impact work in the field.

There were 4,006 Public Inputs, 1,805 First Revisions, 1,956 Public Comments, 900 Second Revisions, 164 Correlating Revisions, and 55 Certified Amending Motions. As a result, there were significant changes and reorganizations throughout the *Code*, including a few new articles and quite a few new sections.

The theme for this cycle seemed to be "global" updates to the style and the reorganization of large blocks of text into list formats or subdivisions. All in all, this is easily one of the best efforts ever put forward by the *NEC* team, and they have produced a document that will make life easier for all of us.

The goal of this textbook is to focus on the most significant changes to the *Code*, and to provide explanations and analyses to help you understand the impact of the changes and how they apply in the field.

Mike's writing style is informative, practical, easy to comprehend, and applicable for today's electrical professional. Just like all of Mike Holt's textbooks, this one is built around hundreds of full-color illustrations and photographs that show the requirements of the *National Electrical Code* in real world scenarios so you can visualize *Code* rules as they apply to your electrical installations.

It's possible that even with explanation, some rules might seem unclear or leave you wondering why they were changed in the first place! We can't eliminate confusing, conflicting, or controversial *Code* requirements, but our goal is to put them into perspective and help you understand their intended purpose so that you can remain compliant in the field. Sometimes it may be hard to understand the actual application of a requirement. We want to help you and the industry understand the current *NEC* as best as possible, point out areas that need refinement, and encourage *Code* users to be a part of the change process that creates a better *NEC* for the future.

About This Textbook

Keeping up with the ever-changing requirements of the *Code* is a must. Whether you're an installer, contractor, inspector, engineer, or instructor, understanding these changes is essential. Using this textbook along with the video series and your *Code* book will allow you to do just that.

The Scope of This Textbook

This textbook, *Mike Holt's Illustrated Guide to Changes to the National Electrical Code, based on the 2023 NEC*, in Partnership with the NFPA, covers those installation requirements that we consider to be of critical importance and is based on the following conditions:

1. Power Systems and Voltage. All power-supply systems are assumed to be one of the following nominal ac voltages, unless identified otherwise:

- 2-wire, single-phase, 120V
- 3-wire, single-phase, 120/240V
- 4-wire, three-phase, 120/240V Delta High-Leg
- 4-wire, three-phase, 208Y/120V or 480Y/277V Wye

2. Electrical Calculations. Unless the question or example specifies three-phase, they're based on a single-phase ac power supply. In addition, all amperage calculations are rounded to the nearest ampere in accordance with Section 220.5(B).

3. Conductor Material/Insulation. All conductors are insulated copper THWN-2, unless otherwise indicated.

4. Conductor Sizing.

Circuits Rated 100A or Less. Conductors are sized to the 60°C column of Table 310.16 [110.14(C)(1)(a)(2)]. Where equipment is listed and identified for use with conductors having at least a 75°C temperature rating, the conductors can be sized to the 75°C column of Table 310.16 [110.14(C)(1)(a)(3)].

Circuits Rated Over 100A. Conductors are sized to the 75°C column of Table 310.16 [110.14(C)(1)(b)(2)].

5. Overcurrent Protective Device. The term "overcurrent protective device" refers to a molded-case circuit breaker, unless specified otherwise. Where a fuse is specified, it's a single-element type fuse, also known as a "onetime fuse," unless the text specifies otherwise.

How to Use this Textbook

This textbook is to be used along with the *NEC* and not as a replacement for it. Be sure to have a copy of the *2023 National Electrical Code* handy. Compare what's being explained in this textbook to what the *Code* book says and get with others who are knowledgeable about the *NEC* to discuss any topics that you find difficult to understand.

We carefully select what is covered in Mike Holt's textbooks to include content that represents the most common installations.

This textbook follows the *NEC* format, but it doesn't cover every *Code* requirement.

For example, it doesn't include every Article, Section, Subsection, Exception, or Informational Note. So don't be concerned if you see the textbook cover Exception No. 1 and Exception No. 3, but not Exception No. 2. It's true that you may find a question on an exam that isn't covered in one of those sections, but you will have built the necessary skills while studying the provided content to easily handle those certain cases.

Cross-References. *NEC* cross-references to other related *Code* requirements are included to help you develop a better understanding of how the *NEC* rules relate to one another. These cross-references are indicated by *Code* section numbers in brackets, an example of which is "[90.4]."

Informational Notes. Informational Notes contained in the *NEC* will be identified in this textbook as "Note."

Exceptions. Exceptions contained in this textbook will be identified as "Ex" and not spelled out.

As you read through this textbook, allow yourself sufficient time to review the text along with the detailed graphics and examples, which will be invaluable to your understanding of the *NEC*.

Answer Keys

Digital answer keys are provided for all your purchases of Mike Holt textbooks, and can be found in your online account at Mike Holt Enterprises. Go to MikeHolt.com/MyAccount and log in to your account, or create one if you haven't already. If you are not currently a Mike Holt customer, you can access your answer key at MikeHolt.com/MyAK23CC.

About This Textbook

Watch the Videos That Accompany This Textbook

Mike, along with an expert panel, recorded videos to accompany this textbook. These videos contain explanations and additional commentary that expound on the topics covered in this textbook. Watching these videos will complete your learning experience and explain the nuances behind some of these changes that just can't be properly conveyed in a written format.

To watch a few video clips, scan this QR *Code* with a smartphone app or visit MikeHolt.com/23CCvideos for a sample selection. To get the complete video library that accompanies this book, call 888.632.2633 and let them know you want to upgrade your purchase to add the videos.

Technical Questions

As you progress through this textbook, you might find that you don't understand every explanation, example, calculation, or comment. If you find some topics difficult to understand, they are discussed in detail in the videos that correlate to this book. You may also find it helpful to discuss your questions with instructors, co-workers, other students, or your supervisor—they might have a perspective that will help you understand more clearly. Don't become frustrated, and don't get down on yourself. If you have additional questions that aren't covered in this material, visit MikeHolt.com/forum, and post your question on the *Code* Forum for help.

Textbook Errors and Corrections

We're committed to providing you the finest product with the fewest errors and take great care to ensure our textbooks are correct. But we're realistic and know that errors might be found after printing. If you believe that there's an error of any kind (typographical, grammatical, technical, etc.) in this textbook or in the Answer Key, please visit MikeHolt.com/Corrections and complete the online Textbook Correction Form.

Textbook Format

The layout and design of this textbook incorporate special features and symbols that were designed for Mike Holt textbooks to help you easily navigate through the material, and to enhance your understanding of the content.

Caution and Warning Icons

These icons highlight areas of concern.

CAUTION: An explanation of possible damage to property or equipment.

WARNING: An explanation of possible severe property damage or personal injury.

Formulas

$$P = I \times E$$

Formulas are easily identifiable in green text on a gray bar.

About This Textbook

Key Features

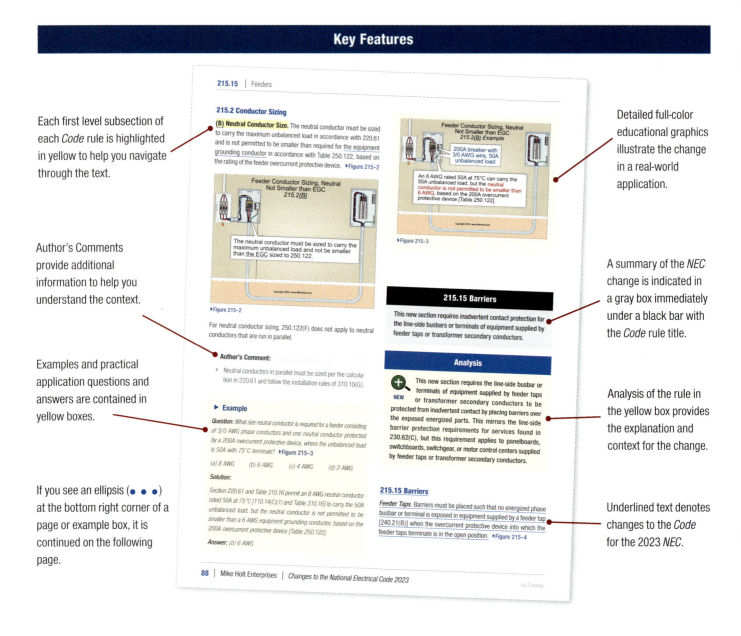

Each first level subsection of each *Code* rule is highlighted in yellow to help you navigate through the text.

Author's Comments provide additional information to help you understand the context.

Examples and practical application questions and answers are contained in yellow boxes.

If you see an ellipsis (• • •) at the bottom right corner of a page or example box, it is continued on the following page.

Detailed full-color educational graphics illustrate the change in a real-world application.

A summary of the *NEC* change is indicated in a gray box immediately under a black bar with the *Code* rule title.

Analysis of the rule in the yellow box provides the explanation and context for the change.

Underlined text denotes changes to the *Code* for the 2023 *NEC*.

Code Change Icons

A *Code* Change icon signifies whether the rule is new, deleted, edited, reduced, clarified, expanded, reorganized, or moved.

 Clarified—A change that clarifies the requirements of a rule that wasn't clear in the previous *Code* cycle.

 Edited—An editorial revision that doesn't change the requirement; but it gives us the opportunity to review the rule.

 Expanded—A change where a previous requirement(s) was expanded to cover additional applications.

 New—A new requirement which could be an entirely new section, subsection, exception, table, and/or Informational Note.

 Reduced—A change that's reduced the requirements from the previous edition of the *NEC*.

 Relocated—This identifies a rule that was relocated from one section of the *Code* to another without a change in the requirement(s).

 Reorganized—A change made to place the existing requirements in a more logical order or list.

ADDITIONAL PRODUCTS TO HELP YOU LEARN

Upgrade Your Textbook with the *Changes to the 2023 NEC* Videos

One of the best ways to get the most out of this textbook is to use it in conjunction with the corresponding videos. These videos showcase dynamic discussions as Mike and his video team of industry experts deep-dive into the topics in this book. They analyze each rule, its purpose, and its application in the field.

Whether you're a visual or an auditory learner, watching the videos as you work through the textbook will enhance your knowledge and provide additional in-depth insight into each topic. Upgrade your program today, and you will broaden your understanding of the changes and their impact on your work. All upgrade purchases include the corresponding videos plus a digital copy of the textbook.

Upgrade Package includes:

- ***Changes to the 2023 NEC* videos**
- Digital copy of the textbook

 Ready to get started? To add the videos that accompany this textbook, scan the QR code or call our office at 888.632.2633.

Have questions? You can e-mail info@MikeHolt.com.

Understanding the *NEC* Complete Video Library

Do you want a comprehensive understanding of the *Code*? Then you need Mike's best-selling Understanding the *NEC* Complete Video Library. This program has helped thousands of electricians learn the *Code* because of its easy-to-use format. Mike guides students through the most utilized rules and breaks them down in a complete and thorough way. The full-color instructional graphics in the textbooks help students visualize and understand the concepts being taught; the videos provide additional reinforcement with Mike and the panel discussing each article, its meaning and its application in the real world. When you need to know the *Code*, this program is the best tool you can use to start building your knowledge—there's no other product quite like it.

This program includes:

- ***Understanding the National Electrical Code—Volume 1*** textbook and videos
- ***Understanding the National Electrical Code—Volume 2*** textbook and videos
- ***Bonding and Grounding*** textbook and videos
- ***Understanding the National Electrical Code Workbook***, Articles 90-480
- Plus, digital versions of the textbooks and digital answer keys

To order visit MikeHolt.com/Code, or call 888.632.2633.

Additional Products to Help You Learn

Understanding Electrical Theory Program

Do you know how to keep yourself safe from the dangers of electricity? Do you know where electricity comes from, why wires get hot, why breakers trip or why lights sometimes blink? This textbook explains the theory behind these questions and gives you the knowledge to understand the answers.

If you don't understand how and why these things are happening, you're at a big disadvantage when it comes to understanding the why and how to apply the *NEC* on your jobs. You may unintentionally place yourself or someone else in danger. This makes it important for every electrical professional to take the time to learn Theory so they can understand even the most complex situations.

This full-color textbook provides hundreds of illustrated graphics, detailed examples, practice questions, and a comprehensive practice final exam. The videos provide additional explanation and expansion of the concepts.

This program includes:

▶ ***Understanding Electrical Theory*** textbook and videos
▶ Plus, a digital version of the textbook and digital answer keys

To order, visit MikeHolt.com/Theory.

2023 *Code* Books and Tabs

The easiest way to use your copy of the *NEC* correctly is to tab it for quick reference. Mike's best-selling tabs make organizing your *Code* book easy. Please note that if you're using it for an exam, you'll need to confirm with your testing authority that a tabbed *Code* book is allowed into the exam room.

To order your *Code* book and tabs, visit MikeHolt.com/Code.

HOW TO USE THE *NATIONAL ELECTRICAL CODE*

The original *NEC* document was developed in 1897 as a result of the united efforts of various insurance, electrical, architectural, and other cooperative interests. The National Fire Protection Association (NFPA) has sponsored the *National Electrical Code* since 1911.

The purpose of the *Code* is the practical safeguarding of persons and property from hazards arising from the use of electricity. It isn't intended as a design specification or an instruction manual for untrained persons. It is, in fact, a standard that contains the minimum requirements for an electrical installation that's essentially free from hazard. Learning to understand and use the *Code* is critical to you working safely; whether you're training to become an electrician, or are already an electrician, electrical contractor, inspector, engineer, designer, or instructor.

The *NEC* was written for qualified persons; those who understand electrical terms, theory, safety procedures, and electrical trade practices. Learning to use the *Code* is a lengthy process and can be frustrating if you don't approach it the right way. First, you'll need to understand electrical theory and if you don't have theory as a background when you get into the *NEC*, you're going to struggle. Take one step back if necessary and learn electrical theory. You must also understand the concepts and terms in the *Code* and know grammar and punctuation in order to understand the complex structure of the rules and their intended purpose(s). The *NEC* is written in a formal outline which many of us haven't seen or used since high school or college so it's important for you to pay particular attention to this format. Our goal for the next few pages is to give you some guidelines and suggestions on using your *Code* book to help you understand that standard, and assist you in what you're trying to accomplish and, ultimately, your personal success as an electrical professional!

Language Considerations for the *NEC*

Terms and Concepts

The *NEC* contains many technical terms, and it's crucial for *Code* users to understand their meanings and applications. If you don't understand a term used in a rule, it will be impossible to properly apply the *NEC* requirement. Article 100 defines those that are used generally in two or more articles throughout the *Code*; for example, the term "Dwelling Unit" is found in many articles. If you don't know the *NEC* definition for a "dwelling unit" you can't properly identify its *Code* requirements. Another example worth mentioning is the term "Outlet." For many people it has always meant a receptacle—not so in the *NEC*!

Article 100 contains the definitions of terms used throughout the *Code*. Where a definition is unique to a specific article, the article number is indicated at the end of the definition in parenthesis (xxx). For example, the definition of "Pool" is specific to Article 680 and ends with (680) because it applies ONLY to that article. Definitions of standard terms, such as volt, voltage drop, ampere, impedance, and resistance are not contained in Article 100. If the *NEC* does not define a term, then a dictionary or building code acceptable to the authority having jurisdiction should be consulted.

Small Words, Grammar, and Punctuation

Technical words aren't the only ones that require close attention. Even simple words can make a big difference to the application of a rule. Is there a comma? Does it use "or," "and," "other than," "greater than," or "smaller than"? The word "or" can imply alternate choices for wiring methods. A word like "or" gives us choices while the word "and" can mean an additional requirement must be met.

An example of the important role small words play in the *NEC* is found in 110.26(C)(2), where it says equipment containing overcurrent, switching, "or" control devices that are 1,200A or more "and" over 6 ft wide require a means of egress at each end of the working space. In this section, the word "or" clarifies that equipment containing any of the three types of devices listed must follow this rule. The word "and" clarifies that 110.26(C)(2) only applies if the equipment is both 1,200A or more and over 6 ft wide.

Grammar and punctuation play an important role in establishing the meaning of a rule. The location of a comma can dramatically change the requirement of a rule such as in 250.28(A), where it says a main bonding jumper shall be a wire, bus, screw, or similar suitable conductor. If the comma between "bus" and "screw" was removed, only a "bus screw" could be used. That comma makes a big change in the requirements of the rule.

Slang Terms or Technical Jargon

Trade-related professionals in different areas of the country often use local "slang" terms that aren't shared by all. This can make it difficult to communicate if it isn't clear what the meaning of those slang terms are. Use the proper terms by finding out what their definitions and applications are before you use them. For example, the term "pigtail" is often used to describe the short piece of conductor used to connect a device to a splice, but a "pigtail" is also used for a rubberized light socket with pre-terminated conductors. Although the term is the same, the meaning is very different and could cause confusion. The words "splice" and "tap" are examples of terms often interchanged in the field but are two entirely different things! The uniformity and consistency of the terminology used in the *Code*, makes it so everyone says and means the same thing regardless of geographical location.

NEC Style and Layout

It's important to understand the structure and writing style of the *Code* if you want to use it effectively. The *National Electrical Code* is organized using twelve major components.

1. Table of Contents
2. Chapters—Chapters 1 through 9 (major categories)
3. Articles—Chapter subdivisions that cover specific subjects
4. Parts—Divisions used to organize article subject matter
5. Sections—Divisions used to further organize article subject matter
6. Tables and Figures—Represent the mandatory requirements of a rule
7. Exceptions—Alternatives to the main *Code* rule
8. Informational Notes—Explanatory material for a specific rule (not a requirement)
9. Tables—Applicable as referenced in the *NEC*
10. Annexes—Additional explanatory information such as tables and references (not a requirement)
11. Index
12. Changes to the *Code* from the previous edition

1. Table of Contents. The Table of Contents displays the layout of the chapters, articles, and parts as well as the page numbers. It's an excellent resource and should be referred to periodically to observe the interrelationship of the various *NEC* components. When attempting to locate the rules for a specific situation, knowledgeable *Code* users often go first to the Table of Contents to quickly find the specific *NEC* rule that applies.

2. Chapters. There are nine chapters, each of which is divided into articles. The articles fall into one of four groupings: General Requirements (Chapters 1 through 4), Specific Requirements (Chapters 5 through 7), Communications Systems (Chapter 8), and Tables (Chapter 9).

- Chapter 1—General
- Chapter 2—Wiring and Protection
- Chapter 3—Wiring Methods and Materials
- Chapter 4—Equipment for General Use
- Chapter 5—Special Occupancies
- Chapter 6—Special Equipment
- Chapter 7—Special Conditions
- Chapter 8—Communications Systems (Telephone, Data, Satellite, Cable TV, and Broadband)
- Chapter 9—Tables–Conductor and Raceway Specifications

3. Articles. The *NEC* contains approximately 160 articles, each of which covers a specific subject. It begins with Article 90, the introduction to the *Code* which contains the purpose of the *NEC*, what is covered and isn't covered, along with how the *Code* is arranged. It also gives information on enforcement, how mandatory and permissive rules are written, and how explanatory material is included. Article 90 also includes information on formal interpretations, examination of equipment for safety, wiring planning, and information about formatting units of measurement. Here are some other examples of articles you'll find in the *NEC*:

- Article 110—General Requirements for Electrical Installations
- Article 250—Grounding and Bonding
- Article 300—General Requirements for Wiring Methods and Materials
- Article 430—Motors, Motor Circuits, and Motor Controllers
- Article 500—Hazardous (Classified) Locations
- Article 680—Swimming Pools, Fountains, and Similar Installations
- Article 725—Class 2 and Class 3 Power-Limited Circuits
- Article 800—General Requirements for Communications Systems

4. Parts. Larger articles are subdivided into parts. Because the parts of a *Code* article aren't included in the section numbers, we tend to forget to what "part" an *NEC* rule is relating. For example, Table 110.34(A) contains working space clearances for electrical equipment. If we aren't careful, we might think this table applies to all electrical installations, but Table 110.34(A) is in Part III, which only contains requirements for "Over 1,000 Volts, Nominal" installations. The rules for working clearances for electrical equipment for systems 1,000V, nominal, or less are contained in Table 110.26(A)(1), which is in Part II—1,000 Volts, Nominal, or Less.

5. Sections. Each *NEC* rule is called a "*Code* Section." A *Code* section may be broken down into subdivisions; first level subdivision will be in parentheses like (A), (B),..., the next will be second level subdivisions in parentheses like (1), (2),..., and third level subdivisions in lowercase letters such as (a), (b), and so on.

For example, the rule requiring all receptacles in a dwelling unit bathroom to be GFCI protected is contained in Section 210.8(A)(1) which is in Chapter 2, Article 210, Section 8, first level subdivision (A), and second level subdivision (1).

Note: According to the *NEC Style Manual*, first and second level subdivisions are required to have titles. A title for a third level subdivision is permitted but not required.

Many in the industry incorrectly use the term "Article" when referring to a *Code* section. For example, they say "Article 210.8," when they should say "Section 210.8." Section numbers in this textbook are shown without the word "Section," unless they're at the beginning of a sentence. For example, Section 210.8(A) is shown as simply 210.8(A).

6. Tables and Figures. Many *NEC* requirements are contained within tables, which are lists of *Code* rules placed in a systematic arrangement. The titles of the tables are extremely important; you must read them carefully in order to understand the contents, applications, and limitations of each one. Notes are often provided in or below a table; be sure to read them as well since they're also part of the requirement. For example, Note 1 for Table 300.5(A) explains how to measure the cover when burying cables and raceways and Note 5 explains what to do if solid rock is encountered.

7. Exceptions. Exceptions are *NEC* requirements or permissions that provide an alternative method to a specific rule. There are two types of exceptions—mandatory and permissive. When a rule has several exceptions, those exceptions with mandatory requirements are listed before the permissive exceptions.

Mandatory Exceptions. A mandatory exception uses the words "shall" or "shall not." The word "shall" in an exception means that if you're using the exception, you're required to do it in a specific way. The phrase "shall not" means it isn't permitted.

Permissive Exceptions. A permissive exception uses words such as "shall be permitted," which means it's acceptable (but not mandatory) to do it in this way.

8. Informational Notes. An Informational Note contains explanatory material intended to clarify a rule or give assistance, but it isn't a *Code* requirement.

9. Tables. Chapter 9 consists of tables applicable as referenced in the *NEC*. They're used to calculate raceway sizing, conductor fill, the radius of raceway bends, and conductor voltage drop.

10. Informative Annexes. Annexes aren't a part of the *Code* requirements and are included for informational purposes only.

 Annex A. Product Safety Standards
 Annex B. Application Information for Ampacity Calculation
 Annex C. Conduit, Tubing, and Cable Tray Fill Tables for Conductors and Fixture Wires of the Same Size
 Annex D. Examples
 Annex E. Types of Construction
 Annex F. Availability and Reliability for Critical Operations Power Systems (COPS), and Development and Implementation of Functional Performance Tests (FPTs) for Critical Operations Power Systems
 Annex G. Supervisory Control and Data Acquisition (SCADA)
 Annex H. Administration and Enforcement
 Annex I. Recommended Tightening Torque Tables from UL Standard 486A-486B
 Annex J. ADA Standards for Accessible Design
 Annex K. Use of Medical Electrical Equipment in Dwellings and Residential Board-and-Care Occupancies

11. Index. The Index at the back of the *NEC* is helpful in locating a specific rule using pertinent keywords to assist in your search.

12. Changes to the *Code*. Changes in the *NEC* are indicated as follows:

▸ Rules that were changed since the previous edition are identified by shading the revised text.

▸ New rules aren't shaded like a change, instead they have a shaded "N" in the margin to the left of the section number.

▸ Relocated rules are treated like new rules with a shaded "N" in the left margin by the section number.

- Deleted rules are indicated by a bullet symbol " • " located in the left margin where the rule was in the previous edition. Unlike older editions the bullet symbol is only used where one or more complete paragraphs have been deleted.
- A "Δ" represents partial text deletions and or figure/table revisions somewhere in the text. There's no specific indication of which word, group of words, or a sentence was deleted.

How to Locate a Specific Requirement

How to go about finding what you're looking for in the *Code* book depends, to some degree, on your experience with the *NEC*. Experts typically know the requirements so well that they just go to the correct rule. Very experienced people might only need the Table of Contents to locate the requirement for which they're looking. On the other hand, average users should use all the tools at their disposal, including the Table of Contents, the Index, and the search feature on electronic versions of the *Code* book.

Let's work through a simple example: What *NEC* rule specifies the maximum number of disconnects permitted for a service?

Using the Table of Contents. If you're an experienced *Code* user, you might use the Table of Contents. You'll know Article 230 applies to "Services," and because this article is so large, it's divided up into multiple parts (eight parts to be exact). With this knowledge, you can quickly go to the Table of Contents and see it lists the Service Equipment Disconnecting Means requirements in Part VI.

> **Author's Comment:**
> - The number "70" precedes all page numbers in this standard because the *NEC* is NFPA Standard Number 70.

Using the Index. If you use the Index (which lists subjects in alphabetical order) to look up the term "service disconnect," you'll see there's no listing. If you try "disconnecting means," then "services," you'll find that the Index indicates the rule is in Article 230, Part VI. Because the *NEC* doesn't give a page number in the Index, you'll need to use the Table of Contents to find it, or flip through the *Code* book to Article 230, then continue to flip through pages until you find Part VI.

Many people complain that the *NEC* only confuses them by taking them in circles. Once you gain experience in using the *Code* and deepen your understanding of words, terms, principles, and practices, you'll find it much easier to understand and use than you originally thought.

With enough exposure in the use of the *NEC*, you'll discover that some words and terms are often specific to certain articles. The word "solar" for example will immediately send experienced *Code* book users to Article 690—Solar Photovoltaic (PV) Systems. The word "marina" suggests what you seek might be in Article 555. There are times when a main article will send you to a specific requirement in another one in which compliance is required in which case it will say (for example), "in accordance with 230.xx." Don't think of these situations as a "circle," but rather a map directing you to exactly where you need to be.

Customizing Your *Code* Book

One way to increase your comfort level with your *Code* book is to customize it to meet your needs. You can do this by highlighting and underlining important *NEC* requirements. Preprinted adhesive tabs are also an excellent aid to quickly find important articles and sections that are regularly referenced. However, understand that if you're using your *Code* book to prepare to take an exam, some exam centers don't allow markings of any type. For more information about tabs for your *Code* book, visit MikeHolt.com/tabs.

Highlighting. As you read through or find answers to your questions, be sure you highlight those requirements in the *NEC* that are the most important or relevant to you. Use one color, like yellow, for general interest and a different one for important requirements you want to find quickly. Be sure to highlight terms in the Index and the Table of Contents as you use them.

Underlining. Underline or circle key words and phrases in the *Code* with a red or blue pen (not a lead pencil) using a short ruler or other straightedge to keep lines straight and neat. This is a very handy way to make important requirements stand out. A short ruler or other straightedge also comes in handy for locating the correct information in a table.

Interpretations

Industry professionals often enjoy the challenge of discussing, and at times debating, the *Code* requirements. These types of discussions are important to the process of better understanding the *NEC* requirements and applications. However, if you decide you're going to participate in one of these discussions, don't spout out what you think without having the actual *Code* book in your hand. The professional way of discussing a requirement is by referring to a specific section rather than talking in vague generalities. This will help everyone involved clearly understand the point and become better educated. In fact, you may become so well educated about the *NEC* that you might even decide to participate in the change process and help to make it even better!

Become Involved in the *NEC* Process

The actual process of changing the *Code* takes about two years and involves hundreds of individuals trying to make the *NEC* as current and accurate as possible. As you advance in your studies and understanding of the *Code*, you might begin to find it very interesting, enjoy it more, and realize that you can also be a part of the process. Rather than sitting back and allowing others to take the lead, you can participate by making proposals and being a part of its development. For the 2023 cycle, there were over 4,000 Public Inputs and 1,956 Public Comments. This resulted in several new articles and a wide array of revised rules to keep the *NEC* up to date with new technologies and pave the way to a safer and more efficient electrical future.

Here's how the process works:

STEP 1—Public Input Stage

Public Input. The revision cycle begins with the acceptance of Public Input (PI) which is the public notice asking for anyone interested to submit input on an existing standard or a committee-approved new draft standard. Following the closing date, the committee conducts a First Draft Meeting to respond to all Public Inputs.

First Draft Meeting. At the First Draft (FD) Meeting, the Technical Committee considers and provides a response to all Public Input. The Technical Committee may use the input to develop First Revisions to the standard. The First Draft documents consist of the initial meeting consensus of the committee by simple majority. However, the final position of the Technical Committee must be established by a ballot which follows.

Committee Ballot on First Draft. The First Draft developed at the First Draft Meeting is balloted. In order to appear in the First Draft, a revision must be approved by at least two-thirds of the Technical Committee.

First Draft Report Posted. First revisions which pass ballot are ultimately compiled and published as the First Draft Report on the document's NFPA web page. This report serves as documentation for the Input Stage and is published for review and comment. The public may review the First Draft Report to determine whether to submit Public Comments on the First Draft.

STEP 2—Public Comment Stage

Public Comment. Once the First Draft Report becomes available, there's a Public Comment period during which anyone can submit a Public Comment on the First Draft. After the Public Comment closing date, the Technical Committee conducts/holds their Second Draft Meeting.

Second Draft Meeting. After the Public Comment closing date, if Public Comments are received or the committee has additional proposed revisions, a Second Draft Meeting is held. At the Second Draft Meeting, the Technical Committee reviews the First Draft and may make additional revisions to the draft Standard. All Public Comments are considered, and the Technical Committee provides an action and response to each Public Comment. These actions result in the Second Draft.

Committee Ballot on Second Draft. The Second Revisions developed at the Second Draft Meeting are balloted. To appear in the Second Draft, a revision must be approved by at least two-thirds of the Technical Committee.

Second Draft Report Posted. Second Revisions which pass ballot are ultimately compiled and published as the Second Draft Report on the document's NFPA website. This report serves as documentation of the Comment Stage and is published for public review.

Once published, the public can review the Second Draft Report to decide whether to submit a Notice of Intent to Make a Motion (NITMAM) for further consideration.

STEP 3—NFPA Technical Meeting (Tech Session)

Following completion of the Public Input and Public Comment stages, there's further opportunity for debate and discussion of issues through the NFPA Technical Meeting that takes place at the NFPA Conference & Expo®. These motions are attempts to change the resulting final Standard from the committee's recommendations published as the Second Draft.

STEP 4—Council Appeals and Issuance of Standard

Issuance of Standards. When the Standards Council convenes to issue an NFPA standard, it also hears any related appeals. Appeals are an important part of assuring that all NFPA rules have been followed and that due process and fairness have continued throughout the standards development process. The Standards Council considers appeals based on the written record and by conducting live hearings during which all interested parties can participate. Appeals are decided on the entire record of the process, as well as all submissions and statements presented.

After deciding all appeals related to a standard, the Standards Council, if appropriate, proceeds to issue the Standard as an official NFPA Standard. The decision of the Standards Council is final subject only to limited review by the NFPA Board of Directors. The new NFPA standard becomes effective twenty days following the Standards Council's action of issuance.

Temporary Interim Amendment—(TIA)

Sometimes, a change to the *NEC* is of an emergency nature. Perhaps an editing mistake was made that can affect an electrical installation to the extent it may create a hazard. Maybe an occurrence in the field created a condition that needs to be addressed immediately and can't wait for the normal *Code* cycle and next edition of the standard. When these circumstances warrant it, a TIA or "Temporary Interim Amendment" can be submitted for consideration.

The NFPA defines a TIA as, "tentative because it has not been processed through the entire standards-making procedures. It is interim because it is effective only between editions of the standard. A TIA automatically becomes a Public Input of the proponent for the next edition of the standard; as such, it then is subject to all of the procedures of the standards-making process."

Author's Comment:

▶ Proposals, comments, and TIAs can be submitted for consideration online at the NFPA website, www.nfpa.org. From the homepage, look for "Codes & Standards," then find "Standards Development," and click on "How the Process Works." If you'd like to see something changed in the *Code*, you're encouraged to participate in the process.

GLOBAL CHANGES IN THE 2023 *NATIONAL ELECTRICAL CODE*

Introduction to Global Changes in the 2023 *National Electrical Code*

Global Changes

The 2023 *NEC* cycle was very active with 4,006 Public Inputs, 1,805 First Revisions, 1,956 Public Comments, 900 Second Revisions, 164 Correlating Revisions, and 55 Certified Amending Motions. This resulted in several new articles and a wide array of new and revised rules. In addition to all this activity, it was a busy year for the correlating committee who eliminated "subjective terms," and tasked the Code-Making Panels with reorganizing many of the rules that were long paragraphs into list formats. Long terms were replaced with acronyms where possible. Redundant language was removed, and definitions were consolidated with nearly all being relocated to Article 100. Many of these changes were made to bring the existing *NEC* text in line with the *NEC* Style Manual requirements.

New Medium Voltage Articles

Several new articles were created to address the growing number of medium voltage installations that are being installed under the purview of the *NEC*. Some proposed medium voltage articles were also rejected. This will be worked out in the second revision of the *Code*.

The medium voltage articles that are in the 2023 *NEC* are:

- Article 235. Branch Circuits, Feeders, and Services Over 1000V ac, 1500V dc, Nominal.
- Article 245. Overcurrent Protection for Systems Rated Over 1000V ac, 1500V dc.
- Article 305. General Requirements for Wiring Methods and Materials for Systems Rated Over 1000V ac, 1500V dc, Nominal. This article replaces Article 399 because Article 305 is a more logical location for the information.
- Article 315. Medium Voltage Conductors, Cable, Cable Joints, and Cable Terminations. This article replaces Article 311 in a more logical location for the information.
- Article 495. Equipment Over 1000V ac, 1500V dc, Nominal. This article replaces Article 490 in the 2020 *NEC*.

Other New Articles Found in the 2023 *NEC*

- Article 369. Insulated Bus Pipe (IBP)/Tubular Covered Conductors (TCC) Systems. A cylindrical solid or hollow conductor with a solid insulation system, having conductive grading layers and a grounding layer embedded in the insulation, and provided with an overall covering of insulating or metallic material.

...

- **Article 371. Flexible Bus Systems.** This is an engineered product like cable bus systems but is instead using thin pieces of copper bus covered with insulation. It is installed in a support system much like cable tray but is specifically designed for the flexible bus.

- **Article 722. Cables for Power-Limited Circuits, Fault-Managed Power Circuits, and Optical Fiber.** This new article creates a common set of cabling rules for Articles 725, 760, and 770 to avoid repeating many of the common general requirements in each of those articles.

- **Article 724. Class 1 Power-Limited Circuits and Class 1 Power-Limited Remote-Control and Signaling Circuits.** A new article was created for Class 1 power-limited circuits to separate them from Class 2 and Class 3 power-limited circuits. This revision adds clarity and better usability to the *Code*. Historically, Class 1 circuits were either nonpower-limited or power limited. But now Chapter 7 only addresses Class 1 power-limited circuits with a power limitation of 30V and 1000 VA. Nonpower-limited remote control and signaling circuits will be covered by the first four chapters of the *NEC*.

- **Article 726. Class 4 Fault-Managed Power Systems.** This article covers a new class of power systems that provide excellent protection for people by limiting exposure times (short pulses or fast shut-off times) and eliminating repetitive impulses. In addition to increased personnel safety, they utilize sophisticated monitoring and control systems providing better equipment monitoring and protection rather than a traditional OCPD.

ARTICLE 90
INTRODUCTION TO THE *NATIONAL ELECTRICAL CODE*

Introduction to Article 90—Introduction to the *National Electrical Code*

Article 90 states that the *National Electrical Code* (*NEC/Code*) is not intended as a design specification or instruction manual for untrained persons. The *Code* has one purpose only, and that is the "practical safeguarding of persons and property from hazards arising from the use of electricity." That does not necessarily mean the installation will be efficient, convenient, or able to accommodate future expansion; just that it is as safe as possible.

The need to carefully study the *NEC* cannot be overemphasized, and the step-by-step explanatory design of this material will help in the undertaking of understanding the *Code*. Grasping where to find the requirements in the *NEC* that apply to a given installation is important.

Article 90 describes when the *NEC* applies, when it does not, and the arrangement of the *Code* book. The other requirements in this article provide the reader with information essential to understanding the scope of the *NEC* and other important rules that set the tone for using other rules in the *Code*.

Most electrical installations require you to understand the first four chapters of the *NEC* (which apply generally) and have a working knowledge of the Chapter 9 tables. That understanding begins with this article. Chapters 5, 6, and 7 make up a large portion of the *Code* book, but they apply to special occupancies, special equipment, or special conditions. Chapters 5, 6, and 7 may modify or supplement the rules in the first four chapters.

Chapter 8 contains the requirements for communications systems such as hard-wired telephone systems, radio and television antennas, and coaxial cable wiring. Communications systems are not subject to the general requirements of Chapters 1 through 4, or the special requirements of Chapters 5 through 7, unless there is a specific reference to a rule in the previous chapters.

90.1 Scope

This section was renamed from "Purpose" to "Scope" and contains new text to clarify the function of the section and provide a clear description of the scope of Article 90.

Analysis

NEW

Rules that govern how the *Code* is written are based on the *NEC* Style Manual. It requires all xxx.1 sections to contain the scope of each article. The scope defines the conditions or installations to which the rules in the article apply. In the case of Article 90, the "Scope" tells us in broad terms how the *Code* works and how it should be applied.

90.2 | Introduction to the *National Electrical Code*

90.1 Scope

Article 90 covers the use, application, arrangement, and enforcement of this Code. It also covers the expression of mandatory, permissive, and nonmandatory text, provides guidance on the examination of equipment and on wiring planning, and specifies the use and expression of measurements.

90.2 Use and Application

What was 90.1 is now 90.2 with some editorial revisions to improve the usability of the NEC.

Analysis

RELOCATED The content for subdivisions (A), (B), and (E) were relocated here from 90.1 and added to the existing list in 90.2. Doing so consolidated the information related to the "Use and Application" of the *NEC* into a list format. Subdivisions (C) and (D) added the word "Installations" to the title to clearly indicate what the *Code* does and does not cover.

90.2 Use and Application

(A) Purpose of the *NEC*. The purpose of the *National Electrical Code* is to ensure electrical systems are installed in a manner that protects people and property by minimizing the risks associated with the use of electricity. ▶Figure 90-1

The *NEC* is not a design specification standard nor is it an instruction manual for the untrained and unqualified.

Author's Comment:

▸ The *Code* is intended to be used by those who are skilled and knowledgeable in electrical theory, electrical systems, building and electrical construction, and the installation and operation of electrical equipment.

(B) Essentially Safe Installation.

Considered Safe. The *NEC* contains the requirements considered necessary for safety.

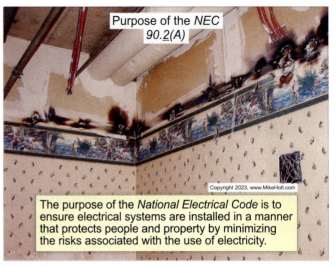

▶Figure 90-1

Essentially Free from Hazards. Installations that comply with the *Code* and are properly maintained are considered essentially free from electrical hazards. ▶Figure 90-2

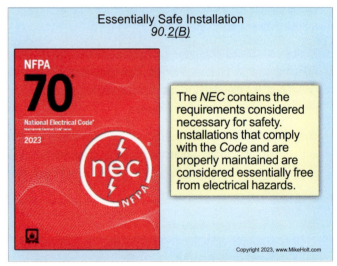

▶Figure 90-2

NEC Rules not Intended. The requirements contained in the *NEC* are not intended to ensure an electrical installation will be efficient, convenient, adequate for good service, or suitable for future expansion. ▶Figure 90-3

Note: Hazards often occur because the initial wiring did not provide for increases in the use of electricity resulting in wiring systems becoming overloaded. ▶Figure 90-4

Introduction to the *National Electrical Code* | **90.2**

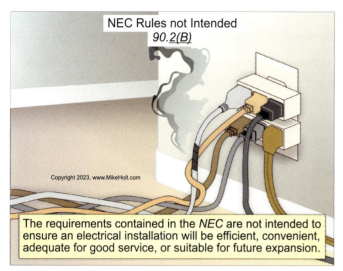
▶Figure 90–3

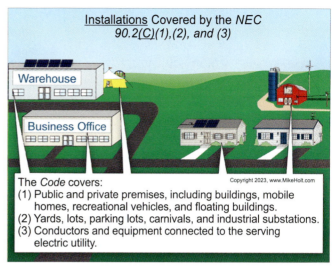
▶Figure 90–5

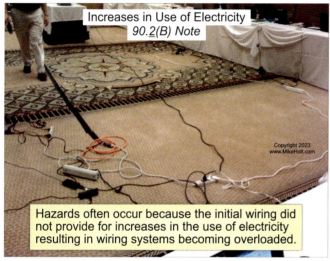
▶Figure 90–4

Author's Comment:

▸ The *NEC* does not require electrical systems to be designed or installed to accommodate future loads. However, consideration should be given not only to ensuring electrical safety (*Code* compliance), but also that the electrical system meets the customers' needs, both for today and in the coming years.

(C) Installations Covered by the *NEC*. The *Code* covers the installation and removal of electrical conductors, equipment, and raceways; limited-energy and communications conductors, equipment, and raceways; and optical fiber cables for the following: ▶Figure 90–5

(1) Public and private premises including buildings, mobile homes, recreational vehicles, and floating buildings.

(2) Yards, lots, parking lots, carnivals, and industrial substations.

(3) Conductors and equipment connected to the serving electric utility.

(4) Installations used by a serving electric utility such as office buildings, warehouses, garages, machine shops, recreational buildings, and other electric utility buildings that are not an integral part of a utility's generating plant, substation, or control center.
▶Figure 90–6

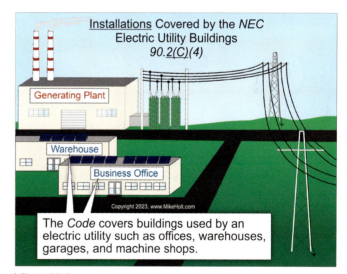
▶Figure 90–6

(5) Installations supplying shore power to ships and watercraft in marinas and boatyards, including the monitoring of leakage current.
▶Figure 90–7

90.2 | Introduction to the *National Electrical Code*

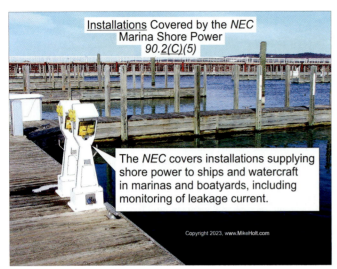
▶Figure 90–7

Author's Comment:

▸ The text in 555.35(D) requires leakage detection equipment to detect leakage current from boats and applies to the load side of the supplying receptacle.

(6) Installations used to export power or for bidirectional current flow from vehicles to premises wiring. ▶Figure 90–8

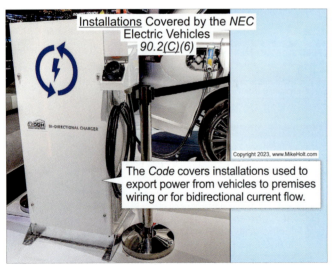
▶Figure 90–8

Author's Comment:

▸ The battery power supply of an electric vehicle can be used "bidirectionally" which means it can be used as a backup or alternate power source to supply premises wiring circuits in the event of a power failure. The rules for this application can be found in Article 625.

(D) Installations Not Covered by the *NEC*. The *Code* does not cover installations of electrical or communications systems for:

(1) Transportation Vehicles. The *NEC* does not cover installations in ships, watercraft other than floating buildings, aircraft, or automotive vehicles other than mobile homes and recreational vehicles.

Author's Comment:

▸ An automotive vehicle is any vehicle that may be transported upon a public highway. The wiring of food trucks is not required to comply with *NEC*, since they are considered an automotive vehicle.

(2) Mining Equipment. The *Code* does not cover installations in underground mines, or self-propelled mobile surface mining machinery and its attendant electrical trailing cable.

(3) Railways. The *NEC* does not cover installations for railway power, energy storage, and communications wiring.

(4) Communications Utilities. The *Code* does not apply to communications equipment under the exclusive control of the communications utility located outdoors or in building spaces used exclusively for these purposes. ▶Figure 90–9

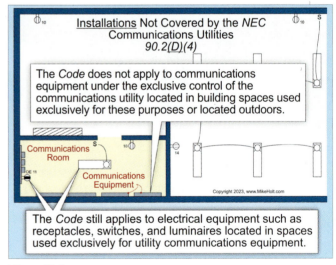
▶Figure 90–9

Author's Comment:

▸ The *Code* still applies to electrical equipment such as receptacles, switches, and luminaires located in spaces used exclusively for utility communications equipment.

Introduction to the *National Electrical Code* | **90.2**

(5) Electric Utilities. The *NEC* does not cover installations under the exclusive control of a serving electric utility where such installations:

a. Consist of service drops or service laterals and associated metering, or ▶Figure 90–10

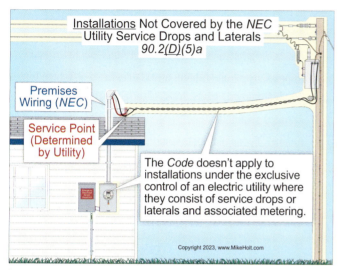
▶Figure 90–10

b. Are on property owned or leased by the utility for the purpose of communications, metering, generation, control, transformation, transmission, energy storage, or distribution of electrical energy, or ▶Figure 90–11

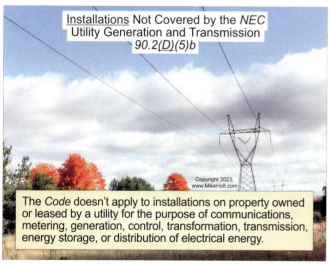
▶Figure 90–11

c. Are in legally established easements or rights-of-way. ▶Figure 90–12

▶Figure 90–12

(E) Relation to International Standards. The requirements of the *NEC* address the fundamental safety principles contained in the International Electrotechnical Commission (IEC) Standard IEC 60364-1, *Low-Voltage Electrical Installations—Part 1: Fundamental Principles, Assessment of General Characteristics, Definitions.*

Note: IEC 60364-1, *Low-Voltage Electrical Installations—Part 1: Fundamental Principles, Assessment of General Characteristics, Definitions, Section 131*, contains fundamental principles of protection for safety that encompass protection against electric shock, protection against thermal effects, protection against overcurrent, protection against fault currents, and protection against overvoltage. All these potential hazards are addressed by the requirements in this *Code*. ▶Figure 90–13

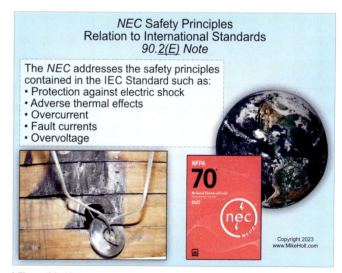
▶Figure 90–13

90.3 Code Arrangement

General Requirements. The NEC consists of an introduction and nine chapters followed by informative annexes. The requirements contained in Chapters 1, 2, 3, and 4 apply generally to all electrical installations.
▸Figure 90–14

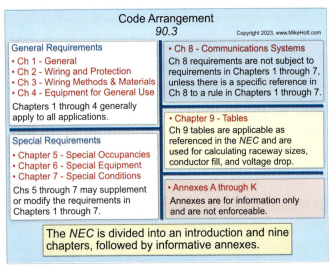

▸Figure 90–14

The requirements contained in Chapters 5, 6, and 7 apply to special occupancies, special equipment, or other special conditions, which may supplement or modify the requirements contained in Chapters 1 through 7; but not Chapter 8. Chapter 7 wiring systems covered in this material include:

- Article 722—Cables for Power-Limited Circuits and Optical Fiber
- Article 724—Class 1 Power-Limited Circuits
- Article 725—Class 2 Power-Limited Circuits
- Article 760—Fire Alarm Circuits
- Article 770—Optical Fiber Circuits

Chapter 8 covers communications systems and is not subject to the requirements contained in Chapters 1 through 7 unless specifically referenced in Chapter 8.

Chapter 8 wiring systems covered in this material include:

- Article 800—General Requirements for Communications Systems
- Article 810—Radio and Television Antennas

Chapter 9 consists of tables that apply as referenced in the NEC. The tables are used to calculate raceway sizing, conductor fill, the radius of raceway bends, and conductor voltage drop.

Annexes are not part of the requirements of the *Code* but are included for informational purposes only. There are eleven annexes:

- Annex A. Product Safety Standards
- Annex B. Application Information for Ampacity Calculation
- Annex C. Conduit, Tubing, and Cable Tray Fill Tables for Conductors and Fixture Wires of the Same Size
- Annex D. Examples
- Annex E. Types of Construction
- Annex F. Availability and Reliability for Critical Operations Power Systems (COPS), and Development and Implementation of Functional Performance Tests (FPTs) for Critical Operations Power Systems
- Annex G. Supervisory Control and Data Acquisition (SCADA)
- Annex H. Administration and Enforcement
- Annex I. Recommended Tightening Torque Tables from UL Standard 486A-486B
- Annex J. ADA Standards for Accessible Design
- Annex K. Use of Medical Electrical Equipment in Dwellings and Residential Board-and-Care Occupancies

90.4 Enforcement

Along with the rest of Article 90, this section was reorganized for ease of use. That's a plus for all of us.

Analysis

REORGANIZED There were no changes to the text or its meaning in this section. However, the section was reorganized into four subdivisions with titles for improved usability.

90.4 NEC Enforcement

(A) Suitable for Application. The NEC is intended to be adopted for mandatory application by governmental bodies that exercise legal jurisdiction over electrical installations. ▸Figure 90–15

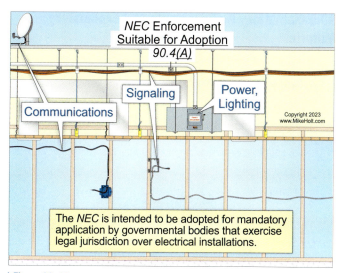
▶Figure 90–15

Author's Comment:

▸ Once adopted (in part, wholly, or amended), the *National Electrical Code* becomes statutory law for the adopting jurisdiction and is thereby considered a legal document.

(B) AHJ Responsibility. The enforcement of the *NEC* is the responsibility of the authority having jurisdiction, who is responsible for interpreting *NEC* requirements, approving equipment and materials, and granting special permission. ▶Figure 90–16

▶Figure 90–16

Author's Comment:

▸ "Authority Having Jurisdiction" is defined in Article 100 as the organization, office, or individual responsible for approving equipment, materials, an installation, or a procedure. See 90.4 and 90.7 for more information.

▸ "Approved" is defined in Article 100 as acceptable to the authority having jurisdiction, usually the electrical inspector.

▸ The authority having jurisdiction's decisions must be based on a specific *Code* requirement. If an installation is rejected, the AHJ is legally responsible for informing the installer of the specific *NEC* rule that was violated.

(C) Waiving Requirements and Alternate Methods. By special permission, the authority having jurisdiction may waive *NEC* requirements or approve alternate methods where equivalent safety can be achieved and maintained. ▶Figure 90–17

▶Figure 90–17

Author's Comment:

▸ "Special Permission" is defined in Article 100 as the written consent of the AHJ.

▸ According to the *90.4(B)*, the authority having jurisdiction determines the approval of equipment. This means he or she can reject an installation of listed equipment and can approve the use of unlisted equipment. Given our highly litigious society, approval of unlisted equipment is becoming increasingly difficult to obtain.

90.5 | Introduction to the *National Electrical Code*

(D) Waiver of Product Requirements. If the *Code* requires products, constructions, or materials that are not yet available at the time the *NEC* is adopted, the authority having jurisdiction can allow products that were acceptable in the previous *Code* that was adopted in the jurisdiction to continue to be used.

Author's Comment:

▸ Typically, the AHJ will approve equipment listed by a product testing organization such as Underwriters Laboratories, Inc. (UL). The *NEC* does not require all equipment to be listed, but many state and local authorities having jurisdictions do. See 90.7, 110.2, and 110.3 and the definitions for "Approved," "Identified," "Labeled," and "Listed" in Article 100.

▸ Sometimes it takes years for testing laboratories to establish product standards for new *NEC* product requirements; then it takes time before manufacturers can design, manufacture, and distribute those products to the marketplace.

90.5 Mandatory Rules, Permissive Rules, and Explanatory Material, (C) Explanatory Material

This change clarifies that references to other standards are not required to indicate the date if the most current reference is to be used. Another revision clarifies that the Informative Annex material is not enforceable as a requirement.

Analysis

CLARIFIED

Historically, standards other than the *NEC* were referenced throughout the *Code*. These references usually included the date or edition of the reference. A jurisdiction may, however, adopt a newer edition of that standard than the one referenced in the *NEC* which caused confusion. To resolve this issue, it is now optional to include the date, and the absence of a date indicates the latest edition of the reference.

Another clarification that is sure to cause waves is the language indicating that the annex materials are not enforceable requirements. This unenforceability was not clear prior to this *Code* cycle and has therefore caused problems.

90.5 Mandatory Requirements and Explanatory Material

(A) Mandatory Requirements. The words "shall" or "shall not" indicate a mandatory requirement.

Author's Comment:

▸ For greater ease in reading this material, we will use the word "must" instead of "shall," and "must not" will be used instead of "shall not."

(B) Permissive Requirements. The phrases "shall be permitted" or "shall not be required" indicates the action is permitted, but not required, or that there are other options or alternatives permitted. Permissive rules are often contained in exceptions to the general requirement.

Author's Comment:

▸ For greater ease in reading, the phrase "shall be permitted" (as used in the *NEC*) has been replaced in this material with "is permitted" or "are permitted."

(C) Explanatory Material. Explanatory material referencing other standards, referencing related sections to an NEC rule, or just providing information related to a rule, is included in this *Code* in the form of informational notes <u>or informative annexes</u> and are not enforceable as *NEC* requirements. <u>Unless the standard reference includes a date, the reference is to be considered as the latest edition of the standard.</u>

Author's Comment:

▸ A Note, while not enforceable itself, may reference an enforceable *Code* rule elsewhere in the *NEC*.

▸ For convenience and ease in reading this material, "Informational Notes" will simply be identified as "Note."

> **Caution**
> ⚠ **CAUTION:** Informational notes are not enforceable but notes to tables are. Within this material, we will call notes contained in a table a "Table Note."

(D) Informative Annexes. Nonmandatory information relative to the use of the *NEC* is provided in informative annexes. These annexes are not enforceable as requirements of the *NEC* but are included for informational purposes only.

90.7 Examination of Equipment for Safety

Product evaluation for *Code* compliance, approval, and safety is typically performed by a qualified electrical testing laboratory (QETL) in accordance with the listing standards.

Except to detect alterations or damage, listed factory-installed internal wiring of equipment does not need to be inspected for *NEC* compliance at the time of installation. ▶Figure 90–18

Note 1: The requirements contained in Article 300 do not apply to the integral parts of electrical equipment [300.1(B)]; see 110.3 for guidance on safety examinations.

Note 2: "Listed" is defined in Article 100 as equipment or materials included in a list published by an organization acceptable to the authority having jurisdiction. The listing organization must periodically inspect the production of listed equipment or material to ensure it meets appropriate designated standards and is suitable for a specified purpose.

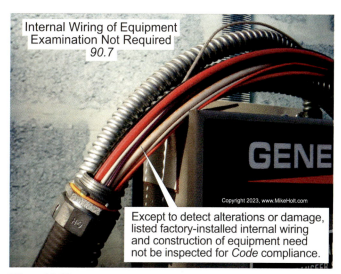

▶Figure 90–18

Notes

CHAPTER 1

GENERAL RULES

Introduction to Chapter 1—General Rules

Before you can make sense of the *NEC*, you must become familiar with its general rules, concepts, definitions, and requirements. Chapter 1 consists of two topics; Article 100 which provides definitions that help ensure consistency when *Code*-related matters are the topic of discussion, and Article 110 which supplies the general requirements for electrical installations.

After gaining an understanding of Chapter 1, some of the *Code* requirements that might be confusing to many, will become increasingly clear to you. *NEC* requirements will make more sense to you because you will have the foundation from which to build upon your understanding and application of the rules.

- **Article 100—Definitions.** Article 100 contains the definitions of terms used throughout the *Code*. Where a definition is unique to a specific article, the article number is indicated at the end of the definition in parenthesis (xxx). For example, the definition of "Pool" is specific to Article 680 and ends with (680) because it applies ONLY to that article. Definitions of standard terms, such as volt, voltage drop, ampere, impedance, and resistance are not contained in Article 100. If the *NEC* does not define a term, then a dictionary or building code acceptable to the authority having jurisdiction should be consulted.

- **Article 110—General Requirements for Electrical Installations.** This article contains general requirements applicable to all electrical installations.

Notes

ARTICLE 100 DEFINITIONS

Introduction to Article 100—Definitions

Have you ever had a conversation with someone only to discover that what you meant and what they understood were completely different? This often happens when people have different definitions or interpretations of the words being used, and that is why the definitions of key *NEC* terms are located at the beginning of the *Code* in Article 100. If we can all agree on important definitions, then we speak the same language and avoid misunderstandings. Words taken out of context have created more than their fair share of problems. Because the *NEC* exists to protect people and property, it is important for you to be able to convey and comprehend the language used. Review and study Article 100 until you are confident you know the definitions presented.

Article 100 Global Summary

Definitions across the entire Code were moved from the individual articles to Article 100 with some being revised and a number of new definitions being added. There are several that are worth mention and they are covered in the following material.

Analysis

EDITED — *Accessible (as applied to wiring methods).* The previous definition did not prohibit electrical or mechanical equipment from blocking access to electrical equipment. Now there is some level of clarity. There is still more work to be done here.

100 Definitions

Scope. This article contains definitions essential to the application of this *Code*. It does not include general or technical terms from other codes and standards.

An article number in parentheses following the definition indicates that the definition only applies to that article.

Accessible (as applied to wiring methods). Capable of being removed or exposed without damaging the building structure or finish or not permanently closed in or blocked by the building structure, other electrical equipment, other building systems (piping, ducts, drains, or other mechanical systems), or the building finish. ▶Figure 100-1

Author's Comment:

- Wiring methods above a suspended ceiling or below a raised floor with removable panels designed to permit access are examples of accessible as applied to wiring methods.

- A junction box above a suspended ceiling blocked by mechanical duct work is an example of a violation of this requirement.

100 | Definitions

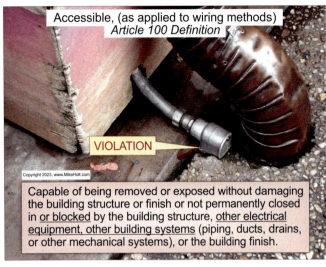
▶Figure 100–1

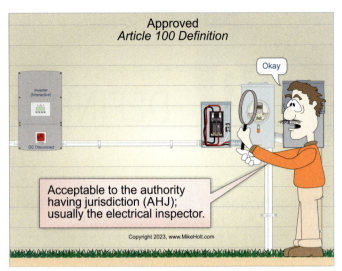
▶Figure 100–2

Analysis

CLARIFIED

Appliance. This change clarifies that appliances can be fastened in place, stationary, or portable to allow easier application of rules that have specific requirements for appliances.

Analysis

CLARIFIED

Bonding Conductor (Bonding Jumper). This change removed the unenforceable term "reliable" and replaced it with "ensures" to more clearly state what a bonding conductor does.

Appliance. Electrical equipment, other than industrial equipment, which is fastened in place, stationary, or portable, and normally built in a standardized size or type. Examples of appliances are ranges, ovens, cooktops, refrigerators, drinking water coolers, and beverage dispensers.

Approved. Acceptable to the authority having jurisdiction; usually the electrical inspector. ▶Figure 100–2

Author's Comment:

▸ Product listing does not mean the product is approved, but it can be a basis for approval. See 90.4, 90.7, and 110.2 and the definitions in this article for "Authority Having Jurisdiction," "Identified," "Labeled," and "Listed."

▸ There is not general definition for "fastened in place." However, the definition for "fastened in place" for the application of Article 625 states that the equipment 'mounting means are specifically designed to permit removal without the use of a tool.

Bonding Conductor (Bonding Jumper). A conductor that ensures electrical conductivity between metal parts that are required to be electrically connected. ▶Figure 100–3

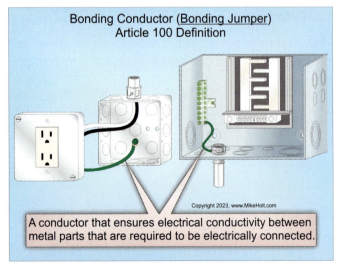
▶Figure 100–3

Definitions | 100

Analysis

REDUCED

Clothes Closet Storage Space. The definition that was in Article 410 included many measurements which were requirements. The *NEC* Style Manual does not permit definitions to contain requirements. Those requirements are now found in 410.16(A).

Clothes Closet Storage Space. The area within a clothes closet in which combustible materials can be kept (Article 410).

Analysis

NEW

Commissioning. This is a new definition in the *NEC* but not a new on in the industry. It was added to support various rules in Chapter 7.

Commissioning. The process, procedures, and testing used to set up and verify the initial performance, operational controls, safety systems, and sequence of operation of electrical devices and equipment prior to them being placed into active service.

Author's Comment:

▸ This term is used in Emergency Power Systems 700.3, Legally Required Standby Power Systems 701.3, Energy Storage Systems 706.7(A), and Critical Operations Power Systems 708.8.

Cord Set. A length of flexible cord having an attachment plug at one end and a cord connector at the other end. ▸Figure 100–4

▸Figure 100–4

Analysis

NEW

Corrosive Environment. This is an example of a term that appears in one form or another in many *Code* articles, but this definition is specific to Article 680. This definition makes it possible to correctly enforce the requirements for corrosive environments in Article 680 instead of using a vague dictionary definition.

Corrosive Environment. Areas or enclosures without adequate ventilation where electrical equipment is located and pool sanitation chemicals are stored, handled, or dispensed (Article 680). ▸Figure 100–5

▸Figure 100–5

100 | Definitions

Note 1: Sanitation chemicals and pool water pose a risk of corrosion (gradually damaging or destroying materials) due to the presence of oxidizers (for example, calcium hypochlorite, sodium hypochlorite, bromine, and chlorinated isocyanurates) and chlorinating agents that release chlorine when dissolved in water.

Analysis

 Counter (Countertop). There are many rules in Articles 210 and 406 that reference the term "countertop." This definition makes it clear exactly what makes a surface a countertop.

Counter (Countertop). A surface intended for food preparation and serving, or a surface that presents a routine risk of spillage of large quantities of water. ▶Figure 100–6

▶Figure 100–6

Author's Comment:

▸ A countertop pop-up receptacle assembly is expected to withstand a routine risk of spillage of large quantities of water.

Analysis

 Energized, Likely to Become. This term has long been used throughout the *Code* without a definition. The new definition was previously found in the *NEC* Style Manual, but is now located here. This makes it clear that if there are not electrical conductors or equipment attached to the item, it is not likely to be energized.

Energized, Likely to Become. Conductive material that could become energized because of the failure of electrical insulation or electrical spacing. ▶Figure 100–7

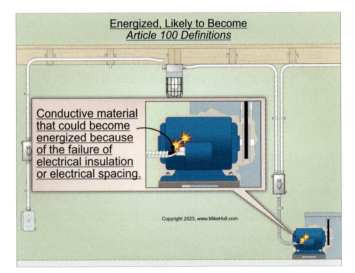

▶Figure 100–7

Analysis

 Generator. I'm not sure we were confused on this term, but now it's in Article 100.

Generator. A machine that converts mechanical energy into electrical energy by means of a prime mover or inverter. ▶Figure 100–8

Author's Comment:

▸ Article 445 contains the primary requirements for Generators.

Definitions | 100

▶Figure 100–8

Author's Comment:

▸ Special purpose GFCIs are engineered to interrupt leakages of 20 mA to reduce the likelihood of electrocution [UL 943C].

Analysis

 EDITED *Ground-Fault Current Path, Effective.* This isn't a new term but it was re-arranged to make electronic searching easier. By placing, the word "effective" at the end, the alphabetic sorting places this term with other terms that include the words "ground-fault."

Ground-Fault Current Path, Effective. An intentionally constructed low-impedance conductive path designed to carry ground-fault current during a ground fault event to the power source. The purpose of the effective ground-fault current path is to assist in opening the circuit overcurrent protective device in the event of a ground fault. ▶Figure 100–10

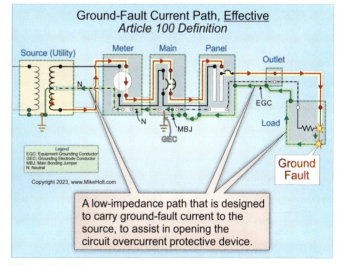
▶Figure 100–10

Analysis

NEW *Ground-Fault Circuit Interrupter, Special Purpose (SPGFCI).* This term has been added to accommodate new rules in Articles 410 and 680 requiring the use of these devices.

Ground-Fault Circuit Interrupter, Special Purpose (SPGFCI). A device intended for the detection of 277/480V ground-fault currents that de-energizes a circuit when the ground-fault current exceeds the values established for Class C device. ▶Figure 100–9

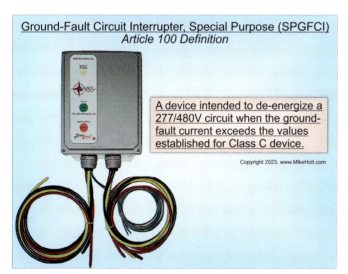
▶Figure 100–9

Changes to the National Electrical Code 2023 | MikeHolt.com

100 | Definitions

Analysis

CLARIFIED

In Sight From (Within Sight From). This definition was rewritten to remove any requirements from the definition and to make it clear what the term actually means. The requirements for "In Sight From" are now found in 110.29. There is no technical change

In Sight From (Within Sight From). Equipment that is visible and not more than 50 ft away from and in sight from the other equipment.
▶Figure 100–11

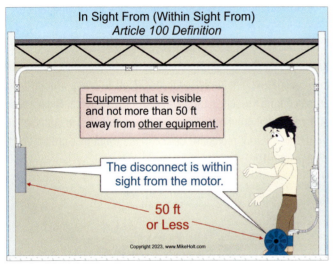
▶Figure 100–11

Analysis

RELOCATED

Interactive Mode. This definition identifies the only operational mode for an interactive system or inverter. Equipment that has more than one operational mode are multi-mode systems or inverters which have two modes, interactive and island.

Interactive Mode. The operating mode for power production equipment or microgrids that operate in parallel with and can deliver power to the serving electric utility. ▶Figure 100–12

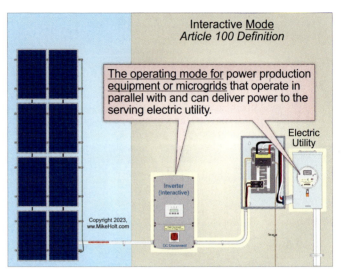
▶Figure 100–12

Note: Interactive mode is an operational mode of both interactive systems and of equipment such as interactive inverters.

Author's Comment:

▶ A listed interactive inverter automatically stops exporting power upon loss of utility voltage and cannot be reconnected until the voltage has been restored. Interactive inverters can automatically or manually resume exporting power to the utility once the utility source is restored.

Analysis

RELOCATED

Inverter, Interactive. This one is pretty obvious, but it's good to have clarity in the *NEC*.

Inverter, Interactive. Inverter equipment having the capability to operate only in interactive mode. ▶Figure 100–13

Definitions | 100

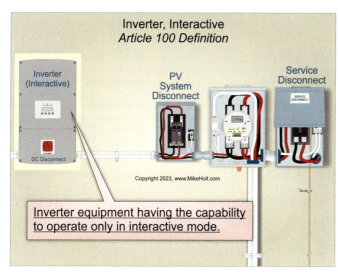
▶Figure 100-13

Analysis

 RELOCATED *Inverter, Stand-Alone.* This term was relocated here and is only used with Article 710 installations.

Inverter, Stand-Alone. Inverter equipment having the capabilities to operate only in island mode.

Inverter Input Circuit. Conductors connected to the direct-current input of an inverter. ▶Figure 100-15

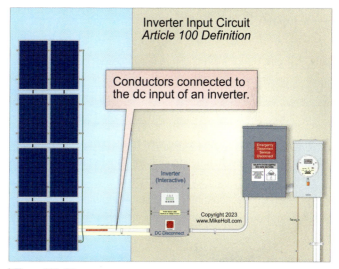
▶Figure 100-15

Analysis

 RELOCATED *Inverter, Multimode.* This term was relocated here and is only used with Article 705 installations.

Inverter, Multimode. Inverter equipment capable of operating in both interactive and island modes. ▶Figure 100-14

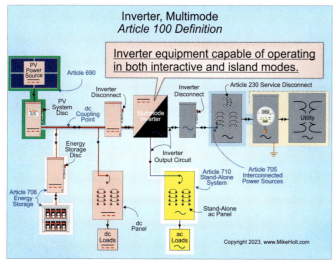
▶Figure 100-14

Analysis

 NEW *Microgrid.* This new definition is a general definition for the term microgrid that doesn't specify ac or dc like the previous definitions. Previously the definitions related to microgrids were located in Article 705.

Microgrid. An electric power system capable of operating in island mode and capable of being interconnected to an electric power production and distribution network or other primary source while operating in interactive mode, which includes the ability to disconnect from and reconnect to a primary source and operate in island mode. ▶Figure 100-16

100 | Definitions

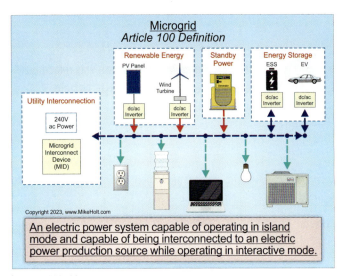

▶Figure 100-16

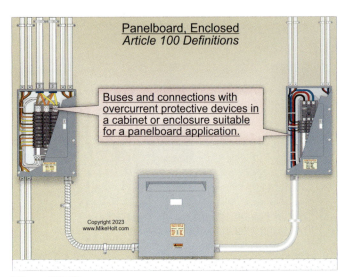

▶Figure 100-17

Note 2: Examples of microgrid power sources include photovoltaic systems, generators, fuel cell systems, wind electric systems, energy storage systems, electric vehicles that are used as a source of supply, and electrical power conversion from other energy sources.

Normal High-Water Level (as applies to electrical datum plane distances). An elevation delineating the highest water level that has been maintained for a sufficient period of time to leave evidence upon the landscape, commonly the point where the natural vegetation changes from predominantly aquatic to predominantly terrestrial.

Author's Comment:

▸ Article 555 contains important information on the use of the term Normal High-Water Level.

Panelboard, Enclosed. Buses and connections with overcurrent protective devices in a cabinet or enclosure suitable for a panelboard application. ▶Figure 100-17

Author's Comment:

▸ For the purpose of this material, we will use the term "Panelboard" instead of "Enclosed Panelboard."

Pool, Permanently Installed. Pools constructed or installed in the ground or partially in the ground, and pools installed inside of a building [Article 680]. ▶Figure 100-18

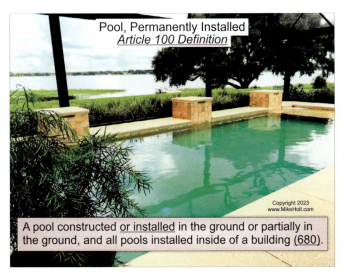

▶Figure 100-18

Analysis

 REDUCED

Pool, Storable. This term had a little change with some big implications. The removal of the depth criteria has included many above ground pools in this definition that were previously not included. It is only use in Article 680.

Pool, Storable. A pool installed entirely on or above the ground designed for ease of relocation regardless of water depth (Article 680).
▶Figure 100-19

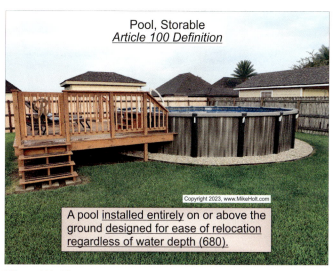
▶Figure 100–19

Analysis

NEW
Power-Supply Cord. This term has been misused over the years. Adding it to Article 100 makes it easier to understand the requirements that apply to these cords.

Power-Supply Cord. An assembly consisting of an attachment plug and a length of flexible cord connected to utilization equipment.

Author's Comment:

▸ Article 400 contains information on the use of Power-Supply Cords.

Analysis

NEW
Primary Source. While there wasn't a great deal of confusion in the energy sector on this term, there was some misunderstanding that this definition will clear up. This is especially true for those new to Chapter 6 and Chapter 7 installations.

Primary Source. An electric utility or another source of power that acts as the main forming and stabilizing source in an electric power system.

Analysis

RELOCATED
PV DC Circuit, Source. (PV Source Circuit). This term is one of many that are now in Article 100 to clarify the application of the rules contained in Article 690.

PV DC Circuit, Source. (PV Source Circuit). The PV source dc circuit consists of the dc circuit conductors between modules in a PV string and from PV string circuits to dc combiners, electronic power converters, or the PV system dc disconnect (Article 690). ▶Figure 100–20

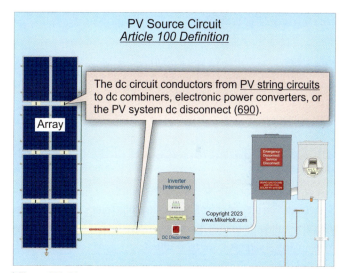
▶Figure 100–20

PV DC Circuit, String. (PV String Circuit). The PV source circuit conductors of one or more series-connected PV modules. (Article 690)

Sealed [as applied to hazardous (classified) locations]. Constructed such that equipment is sealed effectively against entry of an external atmosphere and is not opened during normal operation or for any maintenance activities.

Author's Comment:

▸ Articles 501, 502, 503 contains information on the use of the term Sealed as it relates to hazardous (classified) locations.

100 | Definitions

Analysis

EDITED — **Service-Entrance Conductors.** This definition combines what was two definitions into a single definition, by including both overhead and underground installations.

Service-Entrance Conductors. The conductors between the terminals of the service equipment and the service drop, overhead service conductors, service lateral, or underground service conductors. ▶Figure 100-21

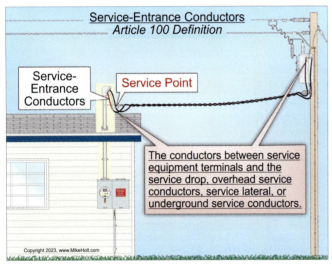

▶Figure 100-21

Servicing. The process of following a manufacturer's instructions or industry standards to analyze, adjust, or perform maintenance and repair of the equipment. ▶Figure 100-22

Note: Servicing often encompasses maintenance and repair activities.

Author's Comment:
- See 110.17 on the use of the term "servicing."

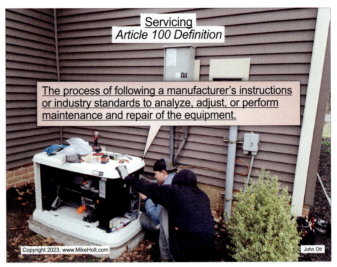

▶Figure 100-22

Analysis

 NEW — **Short Circuit.** If you've ever wondered what this term really means, your question has been answered by the addition of this definition.

Short Circuit. An abnormal connection of relatively low impedance, whether made accidentally or intentionally, between two or more points of different potential. ▶Figure 100-23

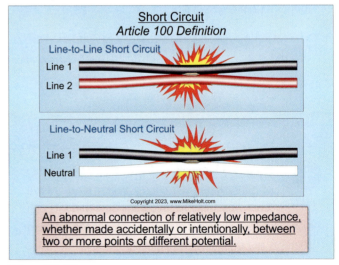

▶Figure 100-23

Authors Comment:

▸ A short circuit occurs when there is an unintentional electrical connection between two phase conductors, or a phase conductor and neutral conductor.

Splash Pad. A fountain intended for recreational use by pedestrians with a water depth of 1 in. or less. This definition does not include showers intended for hygienic rinsing prior to use of a pool, spa, or other water feature (Article 680). ▸Figure 100-24

▸Figure 100-24

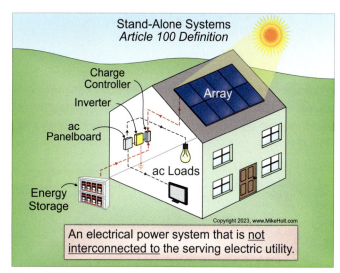

▸Figure 100-25

Analysis

 Stand-Alone System. This definition now clarifies that stand-alone systems are NOT connected to any other system.

Stand-Alone System. An electrical power system that is not interconnected to the electric utility power system. ▸Figure 100-25

Author's Comment:

▸ Although stand-alone systems can operate independently of the serving electric utility, they may include a connection to the serving electric utility for use when not operating in stand-alone mode ("island mode").

Analysis

 Transformer. I'm not sure we were confused on this one, but it's a great definition and it found a home in Article 100.

Transformer. Equipment, either single-phase or polyphase, that uses electromagnetic induction to convert current and voltage in a primary circuit into current and voltage in a secondary circuit. ▸Figure 100-26

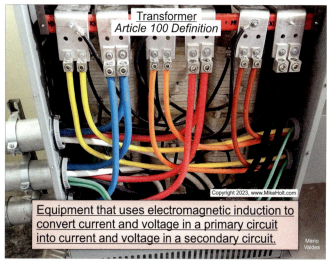

▸Figure 100-26

100 | Definitions

Author's Comment:

- Article 450 contains the primary requirements for Transformers.

Wireless Power Transfer Equipment (WPTE). Equipment for the purpose of transferring energy between premises wiring and the electric vehicle without physical electrical contact (Article 625).
▶Figure 100–27

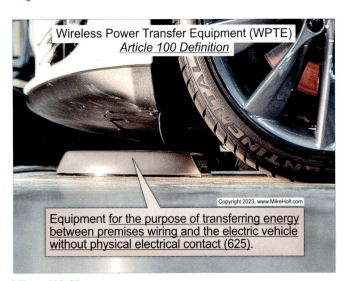

▶Figure 100–27

Wireway, Metal. A sheet metal trough with hinged or removable covers for housing and protecting electrical conductors and cable, and in which conductors are placed after the raceway has been installed.
▶Figure 100–28

▶Figure 100–28

ARTICLE 110 — GENERAL REQUIREMENTS FOR ELECTRICAL INSTALLATIONS

Introduction to Article 110—General Requirements for Electrical Installations

Article 110 sets the stage for how the rest of the *NEC* is implemented. It is critical for you to completely understand all aspects of this article since it is the basis for much of the *Code*. As you read and master Article 110, you are building your foundation for correctly applying the *NEC*. While the purpose of the *National Electrical Code* is to provide a safe installation, this article is perhaps focused a little more on providing an installation that is safe for the installer and maintenance electrician, so time spent here is a good investment.

110.3 Use and Product Listing (Certification) of Equipment

A new list item (A)(8) was added to address cybersecurity for network-connected life safety equipment and QR codes. In addition, a few other improvements were made to 110.3(B).

EXPANDED As technology progresses, so have the means to communicate information. Product manufacturers can now provide much better instructions for products using digital media and save a tree or two in the process. To reflect this shift in technology, a new Note allows the manufacturer's instructions to be printed material, a QR code, or a hyperlink on or provided with the product.

Analysis

NEW A specific requirement was added by list item (A)(8) requiring network-connected life safety equipment be able to withstand unauthorized updates and malicious attacks while continuing to perform its intended safety function.

EXPANDED The rule in 110.3(B) was expanded to include equipment that is not just listed, labeled, or both, but also identified for use in accordance with the manufacturer's instructions. Previously you only had to follow the instructions provided with listed and labeled products.

110.3 Use and Product Listing (Certification) of Equipment

(A) Guidelines for Approval. The authority having jurisdiction must approve equipment. In doing so, consideration must be given to the following:

(1) Suitability for installation and use in accordance with the *NEC*

Note 1: Equipment may be new, reconditioned, refurbished, or remanufactured.

Note 2: Suitability of equipment use may be identified by a description marked on, or provided with, a product to identify the suitability of the product for a specific purpose, environment, or application. Special conditions of use or other limitations may be marked on the equipment, in the product instructions, or included in the appropriate listing and labeling information. Suitability of equipment may be evidenced by listing or labeling.

110.8 | General Requirements for Electrical Installations

(2) Mechanical strength and durability

(3) Wire-bending and connection space

(4) Electrical insulation

(5) Heating effects under all conditions of use

(6) Arcing effects

(7) Classification by type, size, voltage, current capacity, and specific use

(8) Cybersecurity for network-connected life safety equipment to address its ability to withstand unauthorized updates and malicious attacks while continuing to perform its intended life safety functionality.

Note: See the IEC 62443 series of standards for industrial automation and control systems, the UL 2900 series of standards for software cybersecurity for network connectible products, and UL 5500, *Standard for Remote Software Updates*, which are standards that provide frameworks to mitigate current and future security cybersecurity vulnerabilities and address software integrity in systems of electrical equipment.

(9) Other factors contributing to the practical safeguarding of persons using or in contact with the equipment

(B) Installation and Use. Equipment that is listed, labeled, or both, or identified for a use must be installed in accordance with any instructions included in the listing, labeling, or identification. ▶Figure 110–1

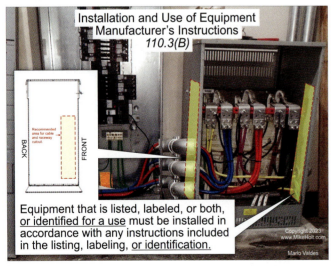

▶Figure 110–1

Note: The installation instructions can be provided in the form of printed material, quick response (QR) code, or the address on the Internet where users can download the required instructions. ▶Figure 110–2

▶Figure 110–2

Author's Comment:

▸ Many electricians simply throw away installation instructions, however that excuse is now becoming less valid since manufactures are starting to use QR codes on electrical equipment, so the instructions are always readily available.

110.8 Wiring Methods

The words "or premises wiring system" were added to clarify that the covered wiring methods are not limited to installation on or in buildings.

Analysis

CLARIFIED The *NEC* is a legal document and must identify exactly what is covered by a rule. In this case the language was revised so that a literal reading of the rule makes it clear that this one applies to wiring systems either in, on, or outside of a structure. The phrase "occupancy, or premises wiring system" was added to clarify that scope of the rule is not limited to installations on or in buildings.

110.8 Suitable Wiring Methods

The only wiring methods permitted to be installed in buildings, occupancies, <u>or premises</u> are those recognized by the *NEC* in Chapter 3.
▶Figure 110-3

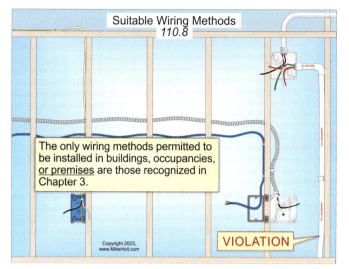
▶Figure 110-3

▶Figure 110-4

Note: For information on accepted industry practices, see ANSI/NECA 1, *Standard for Good Workmanship in Electrical Construction*, and other ANSI-approved installation standards. ▶Figure 110-5

110.12 Mechanical Execution of Work

The *Code* recognizes the importance of quality installations in this section. Some editorial changes were made to clarify how to recognize "quality."

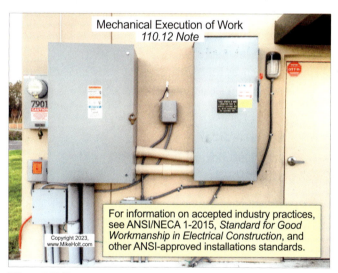
▶Figure 110-5

Analysis

CLARIFIED The subjective term "neat" was replaced with a less subjective term "professional," and "workmanlike" was replaced with "skillful" to better communicate what this rule is about. While the changes in these terms may not provide more enforceability than those used previously, the attention to this section reminds us how important it is to be a professional.

Author's Comment:

▸ This rule is perhaps one of the most subjective of the entire *Code* and its application is still ultimately a judgment call made by the authority having jurisdiction

110.12 Mechanical Execution of Work

Electrical equipment must be installed in a <u>professional</u> and <u>skillful</u> manner. ▶Figure 110-4

110.16 Arc-Flash Hazard Warning

The title and rule of 110.16(B) were updated to expand the arc-flash marking requirements from only service equipment to include feeder-supplied equipment. Furthermore, the ampacity threshold requirement was changed from 1200A to 1000A.

Analysis

EXPANDED

As awareness has increased as to the dangers of injury or death from arc-flash and arc-blast events, the industry has identified the need to expand this rule. Arc-flash label requirements in this rule previously applied to service equipment rated 1200A or larger. In this *Code* cycle, the requirements were expanded to include both feeders and service equipment with a rating of 1000A or more. Other changes in this section removed some of the specific marking requirements for the labels instead requiring them to include the date the label was applied and be created in accordance with acceptable industry practices (NFPA 70E, *Standard for Electrical Safety in the Workplace*) as indicated in Note 2.

110.16 Arc-Flash Hazard Warning, Other Than Dwelling Units

(B) Service and Feeder Equipment. In other than dwelling units, service and feeder equipment rated 1000A or more must have an arc-flash label in accordance with applicable industry practices that includes the date the label was applied and have sufficient durability to withstand the environment. ▶Figure 110–6

Note 2: NFPA 70E, *Standard for Electrical Safety in the Workplace* provides applicable industry practices for developing arc-flash labels that include nominal system voltage, incident energy levels, arc-flash boundaries, and selecting personal protective equipment. ▶Figure 110–7

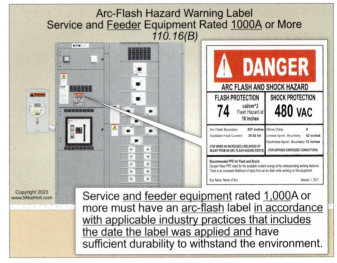
▶Figure 110–6

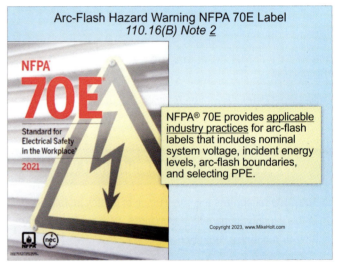
▶Figure 110–7

Author's Comment:

▸ The information required by 110.16(B) is necessary to determine the incident energy and arc-flash boundary distance by using of an app or computer software to ensure the label complies with NFPA 70E, *Standard for Electrical Safety in the Workplace* to increase safety during future work on service and feeder equipment.

General Requirements for Electrical Installations | 110.20

110.17 Servicing and Maintenance of Equipment

A new section was added to address the servicing and maintenance of equipment

Analysis

NEW This new rule was added to clarify the differences between servicing and maintenance of equipment, and reconditioning equipment. However, it has requirements as to who and how servicing and maintenance can be performed.

110.17 Servicing and Maintenance of Equipment

Equipment servicing and maintenance is required to be performed by a qualified person trained in servicing and maintenance of equipment and comply with the following: ▶Figure 110–8

▶Figure 110–8

(1) Standards. Servicing and maintenance must be performed in accordance with the equipment manufacturer's instructions, applicable industry standards, or as approved by the authority having jurisdiction.

(2) Replacement Parts. Servicing and maintenance replacement parts must:

a. Be provided by the original equipment manufacturer

b. Be designed by an engineer experienced in the design of replacement parts for the type of equipment being serviced or maintained

c. Be approved by the authority having jurisdiction

Note 2: See NFPA 70B, *Recommended Practice for Electrical Equipment Maintenance*, for information related to preventive maintenance for electrical equipment.

110.20 Reconditioned Equipment

This new section identifies the general requirements for reconditioned equipment.

Analysis

NEW As more equipment ages out and becomes harder to replace, it has become increasingly popular to recondition equipment to prolong the service life of an existing installation. This new section and its three subdivisions tell us what equipment can be reconditioned and what reconditioning includes. Subdivisions (A) and (B) cover listed and unlisted equipment, while subdivision (C) provides a method for the AHJ to approve reconditioned equipment.

110.20 Reconditioned Equipment

Equipment that is restored to operating condition must be reconditioned with identified replacement parts, verified under applicable standards, which are either provided by the original equipment manufacturer or that are designed by an engineer experienced in the design of replacement parts for the type of equipment being reconditioned.

(A) Equipment Required to Be Listed. Equipment that is reconditioned and required by this *Code* to be listed must be listed or field labeled as reconditioned using available instructions from the original equipment manufacturer.

110.22 | General Requirements for Electrical Installations

(B) Equipment Not Required to Be Listed. Equipment that is reconditioned and not required by this *Code* to be listed must comply with one of the following:

(1) Be listed or field labeled as reconditioned

(2) Have the reconditioning performed in accordance with the original equipment manufacturer instructions

(C) Approved Equipment. If the options specified in 110.20(A) or (B) are not available, the authority having jurisdiction can approve reconditioned equipment, and the reconditioner must provide the authority having jurisdiction with documentation of the changes to the product.

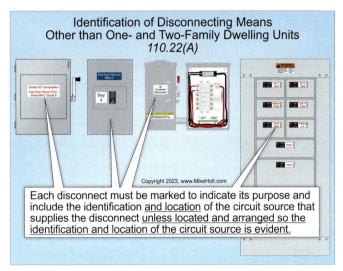

▶Figure 110–9

Author's Comment:

▸ See 408.4 for additional requirements for identification markings on circuit directories for switchboards and panelboards.

110.22 Identification of Disconnecting Means

Additional language was added to clarify the identification of the disconnect supply source.

Analysis

CLARIFIED This change makes it clear that where the purpose of the disconnect and the location of the circuit source for the disconnect is not evident, identification of the purpose and the supply circuit location must be provided at the disconnect. This clarifies that where the disconnect is a circuit breaker installed in a panelboard, one need not identify the source of the supply to the disconnect as it would be evident.

110.22 Identification of Disconnecting Means

(A) General. Each disconnect must be legibly marked to indicate its purpose unless located and arranged so the purpose is evident.

In other than one- or two-family dwelling units, the disconnect marking must include the identification and location of the circuit source that supplies the disconnect unless located and arranged so the identification and location of the circuit source is evident. The marking must be of sufficient durability to withstand the environment involved. ▶Figure 110–9

110.26 Spaces About Electrical Equipment

Several requirements for equipment doors that open into the path of egress were relocated within this section and now apply to all electrical installations—not just large equipment. Standing areas of working space are now required to be relatively flat. In addition, "service equipment" now requires dedicated equipment space.

Analysis

RELOCATED A requirement from 110.26(C)(2) in 2020 was relocated to the parent text. It prohibits open doors from impeding the entry or egress path. The relocation makes it apply to all electrical installations—not just large equipment. This rule now specifies that when open equipment doors result in an egress path that is less than 24 in. wide or 6 ft 6 in. high, the opening must be increased to prevent the equipment doors from impeding the egress path.

General Requirements for Electrical Installations | 110.26

RELOCATED The requirement from 110.26(C)(2) that open equipment doors not impede access to and egress from the working space was relocated to 110.26(A)(4). Revisions clarify that the space in front of equipment must be unobstructed by fixed cabinets, walls, or partitions. A weight-bearing ceiling structural member is permitted if it does not result in a side reach of more than 6 in. to access the equipment.

NEW New 110.26(A)(6) requires the standing surface of the work area required by (A)(1), (A)(2), and (A)(3) to be level and as flat as practical for the entire required depth and width of the working surface. This addresses the required working space or attic installations where there are no floorboards to establish a surface for the electrical equipment.

CLARIFIED Revisions in 110.26(C)(2)(2) clarify that large equipment includes multiple individual service disconnects where the combined width of the multiple disconnects exceeds 6 ft. It also changed the reference from 230.71 to the more specific reference of 230.71(B).

EXPANDED Changes to 110.26(C)(3) require egress doors to open at least 90 degrees in the direction of egress to provide a safe and effective egress path. A door that does not open at least 90 degrees could impede a safe exit in case of an emergency.

EXPANDED Revisions to 110.26(E) add "service equipment" to the list of equipment that requires dedicated equipment space. The intent is to provide dedicated space for a required emergency disconnect [230.85] which was not covered in previous requirements and needs to remain accessible in case of an emergency.

110.26 Spaces Around Electrical Equipment

Working space, access to and egress from working space must be provided and maintained around equipment to permit safe operation and maintenance of equipment. ▶Figure 110–10

▶Figure 110–10

Open equipment doors must not impede access to and egress from the working space. Access or egress to working space is considered impeded if one or more simultaneously opened equipment doors restrict working space access to less than 24 in. wide and 6½ ft high. ▶Figure 110–11

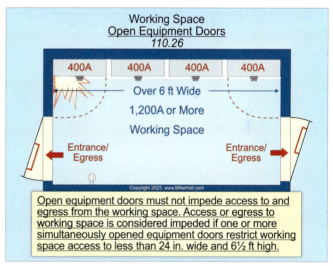

▶Figure 110–11

(A) Working Space. Equipment that may need examination, adjustment, servicing, or maintenance while energized must have working space provided in accordance with 110.26(A)(1), (2), (3), and (4).

Author's Comment:

▶ The phrase "while energized" is the root of many debates. As always, check with the authority having jurisdiction to see what equipment he or she believes needs a clear working space.

110.26 | General Requirements for Electrical Installations

Note: For guidance in determining the severity of potential exposure, planning safe work practices including establishing an electrically safe work condition, arc-flash labeling, and selecting personal protective equipment, see NFPA 70E, *Standard for Electrical Safety in the Workplace*. ▶Figure 110-12

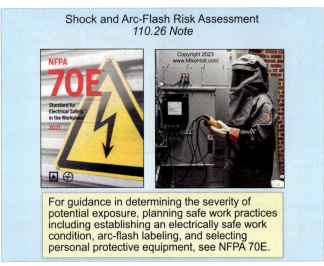

▶Figure 110-12

(1) Depth of Working Space. The depth of working space, which is measured from the enclosure front, cannot be less than the distances contained in Table 110.26(A)(1), which are dependent on voltage-to-ground and three different conditions. ▶Figure 110-13

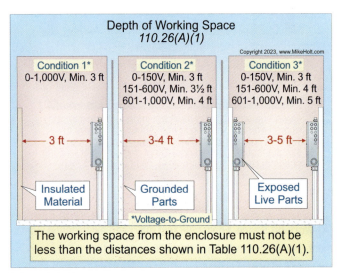

▶Figure 110-13

Depth of working space must be measured from the enclosure front, not the live parts. ▶Figure 110-14

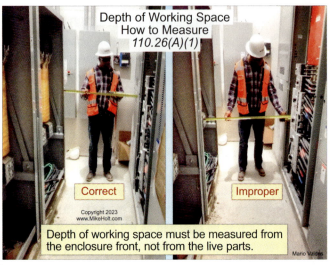

▶Figure 110-14

Table 110.26(A)(1) Working Space

Voltage-to-Ground	Condition 1	Condition 2	Condition 3
0–150V	3 ft	3 ft	3 ft
151–600V	3 ft	3½ ft	4 ft
601–1000V	3 ft	4 ft	5 ft

▶Figure 110-15, ▶Figure 110-16, and ▶Figure 110-17

Table Note:

Condition 1: Exposed live parts on one side of the working space and no live or grounded parts (including concrete, brick, or tile walls) on the other side of the working space.

Condition 2: Exposed live parts on one side of the working space and grounded parts on the other. Concrete, brick, tile, and similar surfaces are considered grounded.

Condition 3: Exposed live parts on both sides of the working space.

General Requirements for Electrical Installations | 110.26

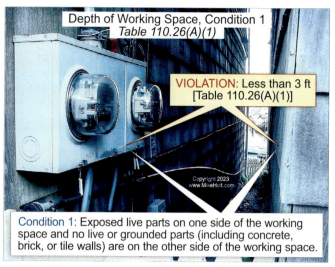
▶Figure 110–15

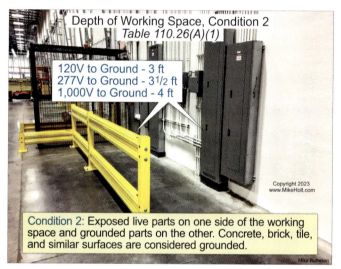
▶Figure 110–16

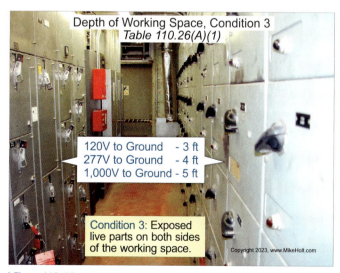
▶Figure 110–17

(a) Rear and Sides of Dead-Front Equipment. Working space is not required at the back or sides of equipment where all connections and all renewable, adjustable, or serviceable parts are accessible from the front. ▶Figure 110–18

▶Figure 110–18

Author's Comment:

▸ Sections of equipment that require rear or side access to make field connections must be marked by the manufacturer on the front of the equipment. See 408.18(C).

(c) Existing Buildings. If electrical equipment is being replaced, Condition 2 working space is permitted between dead-front switchboards, switchgear, panelboards, or motor control centers located across the aisle from each other where conditions of maintenance and supervision ensure that written procedures have been adopted to prohibit equipment on both sides of the aisle from being open at the same time, and only authorized, qualified persons will service the installation.

(2) Width of Working Space. The width of the working space must be a minimum of 30 in., but in no case less than the width of the equipment.
▶Figure 110–19

Author's Comment:

▸ The width of the working space can be measured from left-to-right, from right-to-left, or simply centered on the equipment and can overlap the working space for other electrical equipment.
▶Figure 110–20 and ▶Figure 110–21

110.26 | General Requirements for Electrical Installations

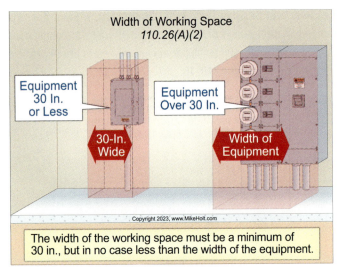

▶Figure 110–19

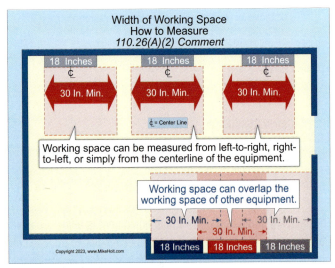

▶Figure 110–20

▶Figure 110–21

The working space must be of sufficient width, depth, and height to permit equipment doors to open at least 90 degrees. ▶Figure 110–22

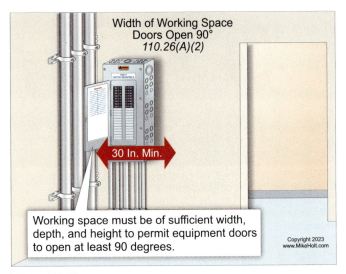

▶Figure 110–22

(3) Height of Working Space. The height of the working space must be clear and extend from the grade, floor, or platform to a height of 6½ ft or the height of the equipment, whichever is greater. ▶Figure 110–23 and ▶Figure 110–24

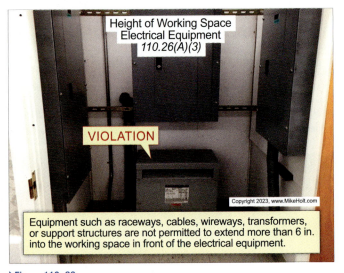

▶Figure 110–23

General Requirements for Electrical Installations | 110.26

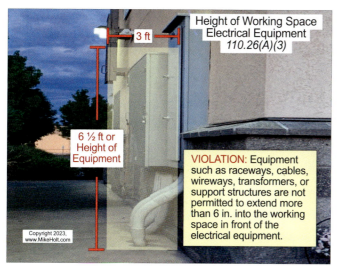
▸Figure 110-24

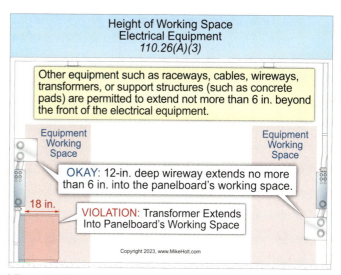
▸Figure 110-26

Other equipment such as raceways, cables, wireways, transformers, or support structures (such as concrete pads) are not permitted to extend more than 6 in. into the working space in front of the electrical equipment. ▸Figure 110-25, ▸Figure 110-26, and ▸Figure 110-27

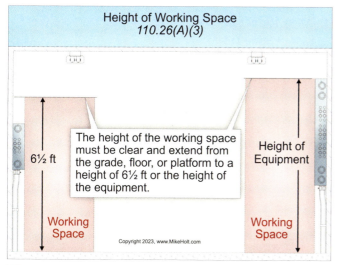
▸Figure 110-25

Ex 2: *The minimum height of working space does not apply to a service disconnect or panelboards rated 200A or less located in an existing dwelling unit.*

Ex 3: *Meters are permitted to be installed in the required working space.*

(4) Limited Access. Where equipment is likely to require examination, adjustment, servicing, or maintenance while energized is located above a suspended ceiling or crawl space, all the following conditions apply:

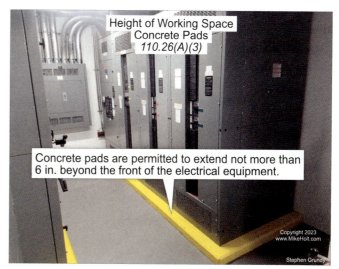
▸Figure 110-27

(1) Equipment installed above a suspended ceiling must have an access opening not smaller than 22 in. × 22 in., and equipment installed in a crawl space must have an accessible opening not smaller than 22 in. × 30 in.

(2) The width of the working space must be a minimum of 30 in., but in no case less than the width of the equipment.

(3) The working space must permit equipment doors to open 90°.

(4) The working space in front of equipment must comply with the depth requirements of Table 110.26(A)(1) and be unobstructed to the floor by fixed cabinets, walls, or partitions. Horizontal ceiling structural members are permitted in this space provided the location of weight-bearing structural members does not result in a side reach of more than 6 in. to work within the enclosure.

110.26 | General Requirements for Electrical Installations

(6) Grade, Floor, or Working Platform. The grade, floor, or platform for working space must be as level and flat as practical for the required depth and width of the working space. ▶Figure 110–28 and ▶Figure 110–29

▶Figure 110–28

▶Figure 110–29

(C) Entrance to and Egress from Working Space.

(1) Minimum Required. At least one entrance large enough to give access to and egress from the working space must be provided. ▶Figure 110–30

Author's Comment:

▸ Check to see what the authority having jurisdiction considers "large enough." Building codes contain minimum dimensions for doors and openings for personnel travel.

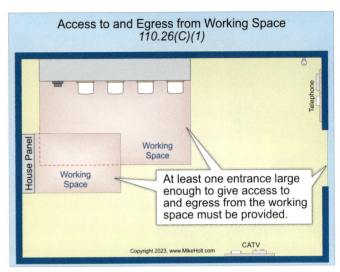

▶Figure 110–30

(2) Large Equipment. For large equipment containing overcurrent, switching, or control devices, an entrance to and egress from the required working space not less than 24 in. wide and 6½ ft high is required at each end of the working space. This requirement applies for either of the following conditions:

(1) Where feeder equipment is rated 1200A or more and over 6 ft wide. ▶Figure 110–31

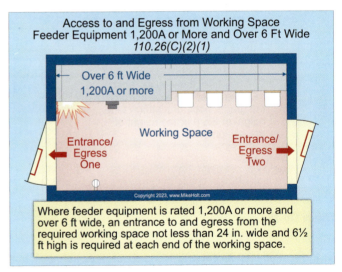

▶Figure 110–31

(2) Where the service disconnect installed in accordance with 230.71(B) has a combined rating of 1200A or more and where the combined width is over 6 ft. ▶Figure 110–32

General Requirements for Electrical Installations | 110.26

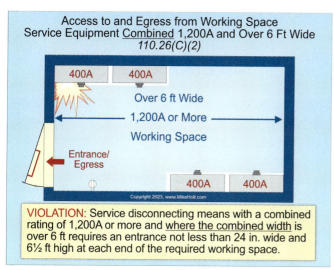
▶Figure 110-32

A single entrance for access to and egress from the required working space is permitted where either of the following conditions are met:

(a) Unobstructed Egress. Where the location permits a continuous and unobstructed way of egress travel. ▶Figure 110-33

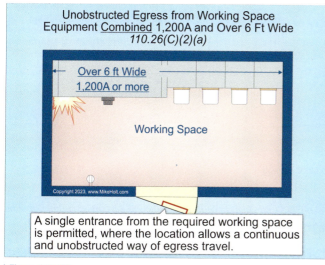
▶Figure 110-33

(b) Double Working Space. Where the required working space depth is doubled, and the equipment is located so the edge of the entrance is no closer than the required working space distance required by 110.26(A)(1). ▶Figure 110-34

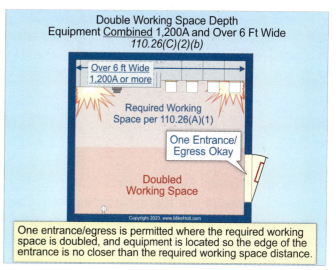
▶Figure 110-34

(3) Fire Exit Hardware on Personnel Doors. Where equipment rated 800A or more contains overcurrent, switching, or control devices is installed and there is a personnel door(s) intended for entrance to and egress from the working space less than 25 ft from the nearest edge of the working space, the door(s) are required to open at least 90 degrees in the direction of egress and be equipped with listed panic or listed fire exit hardware. ▶Figure 110-35

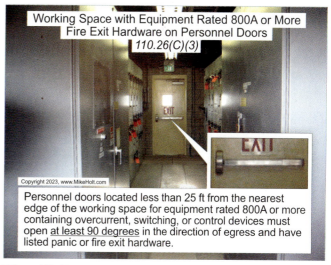
▶Figure 110-35

Author's Comment:

▸ History has shown that electricians who suffer burns on their hands in electrical arc flash or arc blast events often cannot open doors equipped with knobs that must be turned or doors that must be pulled open.

Changes to the National Electrical Code 2023 | MikeHolt.com | 45

110.26 | General Requirements for Electrical Installations

▸ Since this requirement is in the *NEC*, electrical contractors are responsible for ensuring fire exit hardware is installed where required. Some are surprised at being held liable for nonelectrical responsibilities, but this rule is designed to save the lives of electricians. For this and other reasons, many construction professionals routinely hold "pre-construction" or "pre-con" meetings to review potential opportunities for miscommunication—before the work begins.

(E) Dedicated Electrical Equipment Space. Service equipment, switchboards, panelboards, and motor control centers must have dedicated electrical equipment space and be protected from damage that could result from condensation, leaks, breaks in the foreign systems, and vehicular traffic as follows:

(1) Indoors. Service equipment, switchboards, panelboards, and motor control centers installed indoors must comply with the following:

(a) Equipment Space. The footprint space of the dedicated electrical space extending from the floor to a height of 6 ft above the equipment or to the structural ceiling, whichever is lower, must be dedicated for the electrical equipment. ▸Figure 110–36

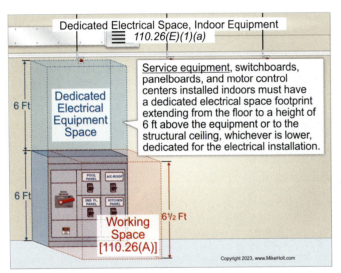
▸Figure 110–36

No piping, ducts, or other equipment foreign to the electrical system can be installed in this dedicated electrical equipment space. ▸Figure 110–37

Author's Comment:

▸ Electrical equipment such as raceways and cables not associated with the electrical equipment can be installed within the dedicated electrical space. ▸Figure 110–38

▸Figure 110–37

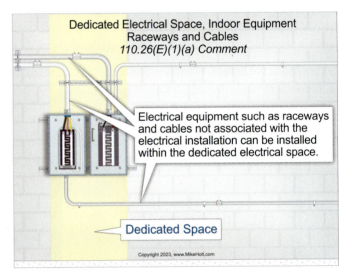
▸Figure 110–38

Ex: Suspended ceilings with removable panels can be within the dedicated space [6 ft zone].

(b) Foreign Systems. Foreign systems can be located above the dedicated space if protection is installed to prevent damage to the electrical equipment from condensation, leaks, or breaks in the foreign systems. Such protection can be as simple as a drip-pan. ▸Figure 110–39

(c) Sprinkler Protection. Sprinkler protection piping is not permitted in the dedicated space, but the *NEC* does not prohibit sprinklers from spraying water on electrical equipment.

(d) Suspended Ceilings. A dropped, suspended, or similar ceiling is not considered a structural ceiling. ▸Figure 110–40

General Requirements for Electrical Installations | 110.26

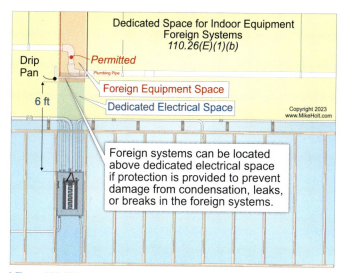
▶Figure 110–39

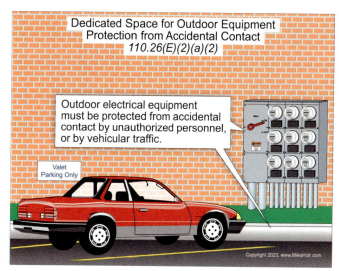
▶Figure 110–41

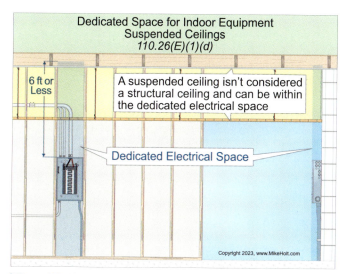
▶Figure 110–40

(2) Outdoor. Outdoor installations for switchboards and panelboard must comply with the following:

(a) Installation Requirements.

(1) Installed in identified enclosures

(2) Protected from accidental contact by unauthorized personnel or by vehicular traffic. ▶Figure 110–41

(3) Protected from accidental spillage or leakage from piping systems

(b) Working Space. The working clearance space includes the zone described in 110.26(A). Architectural appurtenances or other equipment are not permitted within this zone.

(c) Dedicated Equipment Space Outdoors. The footprint space (width and depth of the equipment) of the outdoor dedicated space extending from grade to a height of 6 ft above the equipment must be dedicated for electrical installations. No piping, ducts, or other equipment foreign to the electrical installation can be installed in this dedicated space. ▶Figure 110–42

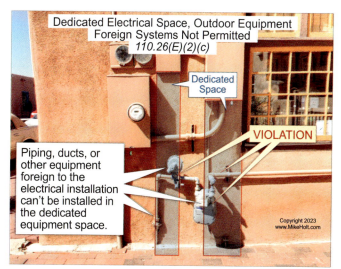
▶Figure 110–42

Ex: Structural overhangs and roof extensions are permitted in this zone.

Notes

CHAPTER 2
WIRING AND PROTECTION

Introduction to Chapter 2—Wiring and Protection

Chapter 2 provides the general rules for wiring and sizing circuits, overcurrent protection of conductors, overvoltage protection of equipment, as well as the proper bonding and grounding of electrical circuits and systems. The rules in this chapter apply to all electrical installations covered by the *NEC*—except as modified in Chapters 5, 6, 7, or specifically referenced in Chapter 8 [90.3].

As you go through Chapter 2, remember that it is primarily focused on correctly sizing and protecting circuits. Every article in this chapter deals with a different aspect of providing a safe installation.

- **Article 200—Use and Identification of Neutral and Grounded-Phase Conductors.** This article contains the requirements for the use and identification, of the grounded conductor, which (in most cases) is the neutral conductor.

- **Article 210—Branch Circuits.** Article 210 contains the requirements for branch circuits, such as conductor sizing, identification, AFCI and GFCI protection, as well as receptacle and lighting outlet requirements.

- **Article 215—Feeders.** This article covers the requirements for the installation, minimum size protection and ampacity of feeders.

- **Article 220—Branch-Circuit, Feeder, and Service Calculations.** Article 220 provides the requirements for calculating the sizes required for branch circuits, feeders, and services. It also provides guidance in determining such things as the mandatory number of branch circuits and the number of receptacles on each.

- **Article 225—Outside Feeders.** This article covers the requirements for wiring methods outside (both overhead and underground). It includes feeders that run on or between buildings, poles, and other structures which may be present on the premises and used to feed equipment.

- **Article 230—Services.** Article 230 covers the installation requirements for service conductors and equipment. It is very important to know where the service begins and ends when applying Article 230.

- **Article 240—Overcurrent Protection.** This article provides the requirements for overcurrent protection and overcurrent protective devices.

- **Article 242—Overvoltage Protection.** Part I of this article covers the general installation and connection requirements for surge-protective devices (SPDs) permanently installed on both the line side and load side of service disconnects. Part II covers SPDs permanently installed on wiring systems 1000V and less.

- **Article 250—Bonding and Grounding.** Article 250 covers the grounding requirements for providing a path to the Earth to reduce overvoltage from lightning, and the bonding requirements for the low-impedance fault current path necessary to facilitate the operation of overcurrent protective devices in the event of a ground fault.

Notes

ARTICLE 200 — USE AND IDENTIFICATION OF GROUNDED CONDUCTORS

Introduction to Article 200—Use and Identification of Grounded Conductors

This article contains the requirements for the identification of grounded conductors and their terminals. There are two types of grounded conductors: neutral conductors and grounded-phase conductors. ▶Figure 200-1 and ▶Figure 200-2

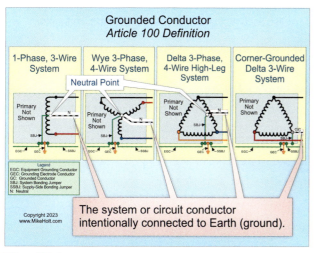
▶Figure 200-1

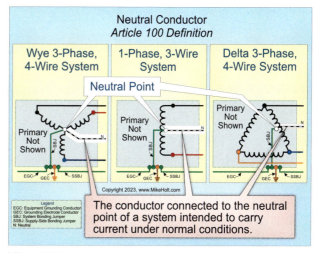
▶Figure 200-2

200.6 Means of Identifying Grounded Conductors

Editorial revisions were made throughout 200.6(A) to remove the repetitive phrase "insulated grounded conductor." An incorrect reference to 690.41 was updated. In addition, 200.6(D) was clarified by adding the words "nominal voltage" before the word "system."

Analysis

CLARIFIED The phrase "nominal voltage" was added before the word "system" throughout 200.6(D). This provides clarification that the marking requirements only apply when there are multiple system voltages. The previous language was not clear that multiple systems of the same voltage can use the same grounded conductor identification method. This was only a clarification—not a technical change.

200.6 | Use and Identification of Grounded Conductors

200.6 Identification of Neutral and Grounded Conductors

(D) Neutral Conductors of Different Nominal Voltage Systems.
When neutral conductors of different nominal voltage systems are installed in the same raceway, cable, or enclosure each nominal voltage system neutral conductor must be identified by: ▶Figure 200–3

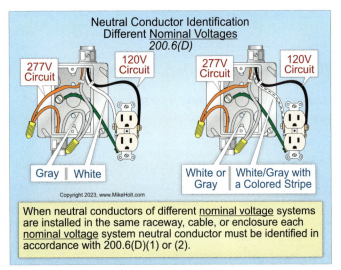

▶Figure 200–3

(1) One neutral conductor of a nominal voltage system installed in the same raceway, cable, or enclosure must have a continuous white or gray outer finish along its entire length in accordance with 200.6(A) and 200.6(B).

(2) The neutral conductor of the other nominal voltage systems installed in the same raceway, cable, or enclosure must have an outer covering of white or gray along its entire length in accordance with 200.6(A) and 200.6(B) or have an outer covering of white or gray with a readily distinguishable color stripe (other than green) along its entire length.

Author's Comment:

▸ There are several possible combinations but where neutral conductors of different nominal voltage systems are installed together, a common practice is to use white for 120V systems [200.6(A)(1)] and gray for 277V systems [200.6(A)(2)].

(3) Other identification allowed by 200.6(A) or 200.6(B) that will distinguish each nominal voltage system neutral conductor.

Author's Comment:

▸ The requirement to identify the neutrals by nominal voltage system only applies where there are neutrals from more than one nominal voltage system in a raceway, cable, or enclosure.

ARTICLE 210 BRANCH CIRCUITS

Introduction to Article 210—Branch Circuits

This article contains branch-circuit requirements such as those for conductor sizing and identification, GFCI, AFCI and overcurrent protection, and receptacle and lighting outlet requirements. It consists of three parts:

- Part I. General Provisions
- Part II. Branch-Circuit Ratings
- Part III. Required Outlets

210.1 Scope

Article 210 provides the general requirements for branch circuits not over 1000V ac or 1500V dc, such as conductor sizing, overcurrent protection, identification, GFCI and AFCI protection, as well as receptacle outlet and lighting outlet requirements.

Analysis

CLARIFIED This change clarifies that the rules in this article only apply to the lower voltage circuits and was made because the new Article 235 covers the requirements for branch circuits operating at higher voltages.

NEW A new Informational Note was added calling attention to Part II of the new Article 235 for installations with branch circuits of over 1000V ac and over 1500V dc.

210.1 Scope

Article 210 provides the general requirements for branch circuits not over 1000V ac or 1500V dc, such as conductor sizing, overcurrent protection, identification, GFCI and AFCI protection, as well as receptacle outlet and lighting outlet requirements. ▶Figure 210-1

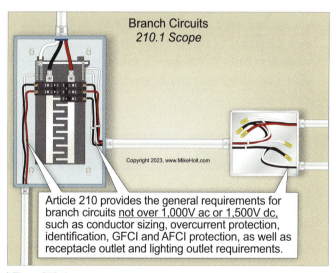

▶Figure 210-1

210.4 | Branch Circuits

Author's Comment:

▸ According to Article 100 a "Branch Circuit" consists of the conductors between the final overcurrent protective device and the receptacle outlets, lighting outlets, or other outlets. ▸Figure 210–2

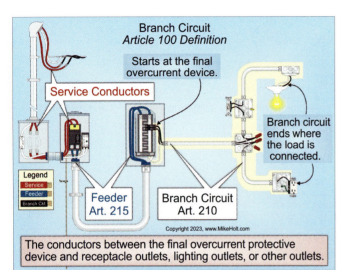

▸Figure 210–2

 An editorial change was made to (C) Exception 1 and Exception 2 clarifying that line-to-line loads can be connected to a multiwire branch circuit for an individual piece of utilization equipment, or where the ungrounded conductors of that circuit are opened simultaneously by the branch-circuit overcurrent device.

210.4 Multiwire Branch Circuits

(A) General. Except as permitted in 300.3(B)(4), all conductors of a multiwire branch circuit must originate from the same equipment containing the branch-circuit overcurrent protective devices. ▸Figure 210–3

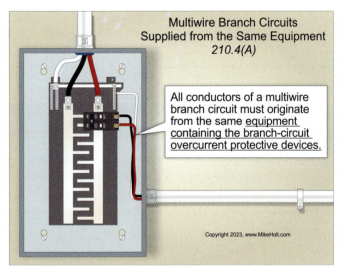

▸Figure 210–3

All conductors of a circuit (including the neutral and equipment grounding conductors) must be installed together in the same raceway, cable, trench, cord, or cable tray [300.3(B)], except as permitted by 300.3(B)(1) through (4).

Note 2: For the requirements relating to the continuity of the neutral conductor on multiwire branch circuits, see 300.13(B). ▸Figure 210–4

Author's Comment:

▸ According to Article 100, a "Multiwire Branch Circuit" consists of two or more circuit phase conductors with a common neutral conductor. This type of circuit has a voltage between the phase conductors and an equal difference of voltage from each phase conductor to the common neutral conductor. ▸Figure 210–5

210.4 Multiwire Branch Circuits

An editorial change was made to 210.4(A) which clarifies what the source of the multiwire branch circuit is, and revisions to 210.4(C) Exception 1 and Exception 2 clarify when a line-to-line load may be connected to a multiwire branch circuit.

Analysis

 The 2020 text in (A) that required all conductors of a multiwire branch circuit to be from the "same distribution equipment" now says, "equipment containing the branch-circuit overcurrent protective device." This clarifies that the rule applies to all types of equipment containing OCPD(s), not to just panelboards and distribution equipment. A reference to 300.3(B)(4) also clarifies that column-width panelboards may use a neutral that does not originate in the enclosure that contains the OCPD. There is no technical change here, but it is much easier to read and understand.

Branch Circuits | 210.5

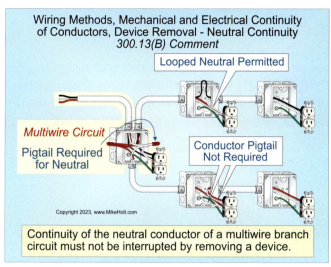

▶Figure 210-4

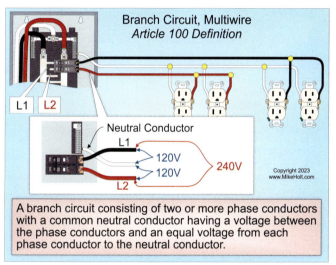

▶Figure 210-5

(C) Line-to-Neutral Loads. Multiwire branch circuits must supply only line-to-neutral loads.

Ex 1: A multiwire branch circuit can supply an individual utilization equipment with line-to-line and line-to-neutral loads for such as a range or dryer.

Ex 2: A multiwire branch circuit can supply both line-to-line and line-to-neutral loads if the circuit is protected by a circuit breaker with a common internal trip that opens phase conductors of the multiwire branch circuit simultaneously under a fault condition.

210.5 Identification for Branch Circuits

The phrase "voltage class" was replaced with "nominal voltage" in (C) to clarify the identification requirements for branch-circuit phase conductors.

Analysis

CLARIFIED

The phrase "system voltage class" was replaced with the defined term "nominal voltage system" in (C)(1) making it clear that different systems of the same nominal system voltage are permitted to have the same identification. The term "voltage class" is used by IEEE to identify different system voltages and does not make sense in the *NEC*. Changing "voltage class" to the defined term "nominal voltage" matches the language used in other areas of the *Code* which makes the language easier to understand and enforce.

210.5 Identification for Branch Circuits

(C) Identification of Phase Conductors. Circuit phase conductors must be identified as follows:

(1) More Than One Nominal Voltage System. Where premises wiring is supplied from more than one nominal voltage system, the phase conductors of branch circuits must be identified by phase or line and by nominal voltage system at termination, connection, and splice points in accordance with 210.5(C)(1)(a) and (b). Different systems within the premises with the same nominal voltage can use the same method of identification.

(a) Means of Identification. Identification of the branch-circuit phase conductors from more than one nominal voltage system can be by color coding, marking tape, tagging, or other means approved by the authority having jurisdiction. ▶Figure 210-6

(b) Posting of Identification. The method of identification must be readily available or permanently posted at each branch-circuit panelboard or similar equipment, not be handwritten, and be sufficiently durable to withstand the environment involved. ▶Figure 210-7

Ex: Where a different voltage system is added to an existing installation, branch-circuit identification is only required for the new one. Each voltage system distribution equipment must have a label with the words "other unidentified systems exist on the premises." ▶Figure 210-8

210.5 | Branch Circuits

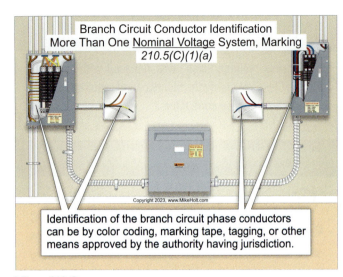
▶Figure 210–6

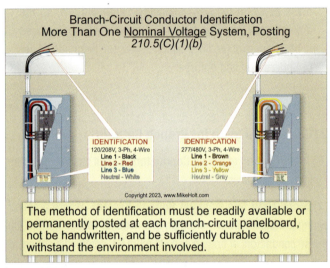
▶Figure 210–7

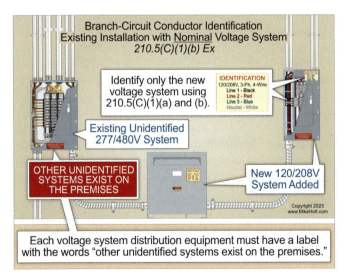
▶Figure 210–8

Author's Comment:

▸ When a premises has more than one voltage system supplying branch circuits, the phase conductors must be identified by phase and system. This can be done by permanently posting an identification legend that describes the method used, such as color-coded marking tape or color-coded insulation.

▸ Although the *NEC* does not require a specific color code for phase conductors, electricians often use the following system:
▶Figure 210–9

▶Figure 210–9

▸ 120/240V, single-phase—black, red, and white

▸ 120/208V, three-phase—black, red, blue, and white

▸ 120/240V, three-phase (high-leg)—black, orange, blue, and white

▸ 277/480V, three-phase—brown, orange, yellow, and gray; or, brown, purple, yellow, and gray

▸ Whichever color scheme is used, it is important for it to remain consistent wherever phase conductors are terminated or accessible throughout the entire premises. This is especially important when identifying different system voltages and neutrals.

210.8 Ground-Fault Circuit-Interrupter Protection for Personnel

For over 30 years GFCI requirements have been added to the *NEC*, and this *Code* cycle continues that trend. The term "listed Class A GFCI" replaced "ground-fault circuit-interrupter" throughout the rule. It is now clear that the path of measurement for a power-supply cord is related to the receptacle and not the appliance from which it came. An interesting Exception was added for exhaust fans, nondwelling GFCI requirements have taken over in food service areas, and protection is required for all outlets in garages, accessory buildings, boathouses, and aquariums. These rules now basically say that where there is water you need a GFCI!

Analysis

CLARIFIED The term "ground-fault circuit-interrupter" throughout this section was changed to "listed Class A GFCI" because acronyms are now permitted to be used in the *NEC*. The addition of "Class A" to GFCI clarifies that the device must trip at the nominal 5 mA (± 1 mA) required for the protection of personnel. In addition, the words "of an appliance" were removed from the charging text clarifying that the measurement applies to all power-supply cords plugged into a receptacle—not just appliance cords. Furthermore, the phrase "shortest path without passing through a window" was removed to alleviate confusion resulting from a cord passing through an interior opening similar to a window.

EXPANDED The specific mention in 210.8(A) and (B) of the list items included in those first level subdivisions was replaced with a general reference to the "following locations."

EXPANDED List item (A)6 was expanded to address GFCI protection for any cord-and-plug-connected appliance in kitchens by deleting the reference to the receptacles serving the countertop.

NEW A new list item (A)7 requires areas with sinks and permanent provisions for food preparation, beverage preparation, or cooking to have GFCI-protected receptacles. The remaining list items became 8 through 12.

RELOCATED The Exceptions that previously followed the list items in 210.8(A) were relocated to follow the last list item and clarifications were made as to when the Exception(s) applies, but there were no technical changes.

NEW A new Exception No. 4 to 210.8(A) was added to say that the internal receptacle in a bathroom exhaust fan does not require GFCI protection, unless required by the installation or listing instructions. This receptacle is not accessible and not used as a convenience receptacle, so this rule makes sense.

EXPANDED In 210.8(B), the word "kitchens" was added as list item (2) and removed from list item (3) clarifying that all areas with permanent provisions for food serving, beverage service, or cooking must be protected.

List item (4) was added to include buffet areas and beverage serving areas in the GFCI requirements. This is kind of an open-ended rule using the term "area" instead of a specific distance, as is used in list item (7), and may cause some problems with enforcement. Only time will tell.

List item (7) expands the requirement in other than dwellings to protect electric appliances and not just receptacles located within 6 ft of a sink. This lets us know that the rule is about the hazard from both the appliance and its supplying receptacle.

A new rule in (13) requires GFCI protection for receptacles within 6 ft of the top inside edge or conductive support framing of aquariums, bait wells, and similar aquatic vessels.

RELOCATED All the Exceptions that previously followed the list items in 210.8(B) were relocated to follow the last list item, and clarifications were made as to when the Exception(s) applies, but there were no technical changes.

• • •

210.8 | Branch Circuits

EXPANDED Changes in 210.8(D) now require GFCI protection to be provided for the branch circuit or the outlet supplying listed appliances rated 150V to ground and 60A or less. This rule previously referenced others to determine if protection was required—now you can just read the list here.

Five more appliances have been added in addition to the seven that were in the Article 422 appliances requiring GFCI protection and inserted here in (D) They include electric ranges, wall-mounted ovens, counter-mounted cooking units, clothes dryers, and microwave ovens. This expansion of the GFCI requirements applies to both cord-and-plug-connected and hardwired equipment.

EXPANDED The rule in 210.8(F) for outdoor outlets was new last cycle and caused a big problem with air-conditioning units in areas outside of dwelling units. This battle continued during the 2023 revision and four new items were added to the list. Dwelling unit receptacles rated 50A or less in garages, accessory buildings, outdoors, and in boathouses already had GFCI protection requirements, but this change requires the outlet to be protected and GFCI protection must be added for unprotected existing equipment that is replaced.

210.8 GFCI Protection

A listed ground-fault circuit interrupter (GFCI) must provide protection as required in 210.8(A) through (F). The GFCI protective device must be in a readily accessible location. ▶Figure 210–10

> **Author's Comment:**
> ▸ According to Article 100, a "Ground-Fault Circuit Interrupter" (GFCI) is a device intended to protect people by opening a circuit when a current imbalance is 6 mA or higher and does not open when the current to ground is less than 4 mA. ▶Figure 210–11

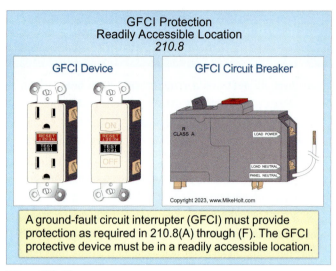
▶Figure 210–10

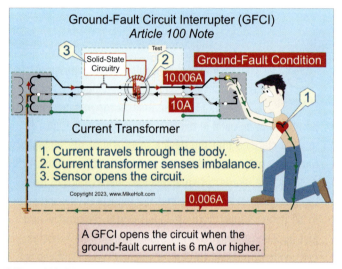
▶Figure 210–11

▸ The GFCI protection required by 210.8(A) and (B) can be provided using either a breaker with GFCI protection or a receptacle with GFCI protection. However, the use of a GFCI receptacle is somewhat limited by the requirement that the GFCI must be readily accessible.

▸ According to Article 100, "Readily Accessible" means capable of being reached quickly without having to climb over or remove obstacles, or resort to the use of portable ladders. ▶Figure 210–12

For the application of 210.8(A)(8), 210.8(A)(10), 210.8(B)(7), 210.8(B)(13), and 210.8(B)(15), the distance (from the sink or bathtub/shower) is measured as the shortest path the power-supply cord connected to the receptacle will follow without piercing a floor, wall, ceiling, or fixed barrier. ▶Figure 210–13

Branch Circuits | 210.8

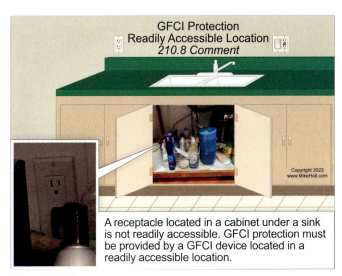
▶Figure 210-12

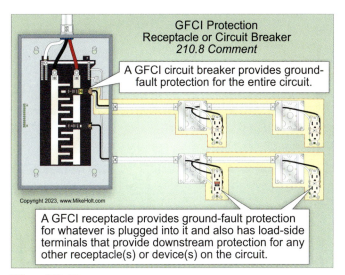
▶Figure 210-14

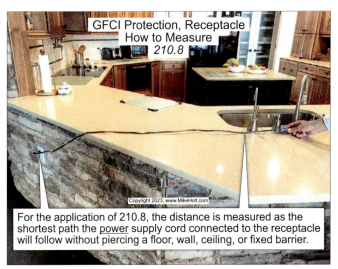
▶Figure 210-13

Author's Comment:

▸ The reference to windows and doors was removed to ensure receptacles within the measured distance as required in 210.8, even if passing through a window or door, are afforded GFCI protection.

▸ The GFCI circuit breaker provides ground-fault protection starting at the breaker, so the entire circuit has ground-fault protection. A GFCI receptacle provides ground-fault protection for whatever is plugged into it and also has load-side terminals that provide downstream protection for any other receptacle(s) or device(s) on the circuit. ▶Figure 210-14

(A) Dwelling Units. Receptacles installed in the following dwelling unit locations must be GFCI protected. ▶Figure 210-15

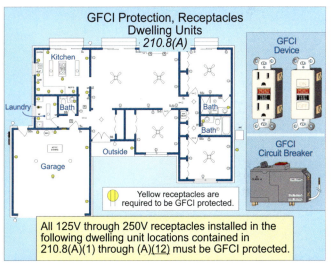
▶Figure 210-15

(1) Bathrooms. GFCI protection is required for receptacles in dwelling unit bathroom areas. ▶Figure 210-16

Author's Comment:

▸ According to Article 100, a "Bathroom Area" is an area that includes a sink (basin) and one or more of the following: a toilet, urinal, tub, shower, bidet, or similar plumbing fixture.

210.8 | Branch Circuits

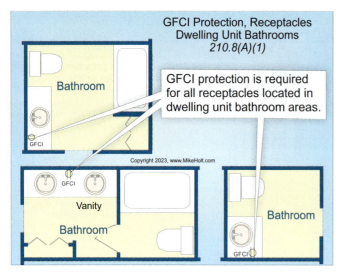

▶Figure 210–16

▶Figure 210–18

(2) Garages and Accessory Buildings. GFCI protection is required for receptacles in dwelling unit garages and dwelling unit accessory buildings not intended as habitable rooms and limited to storage areas, work areas, and areas of similar use. ▶Figure 210–17

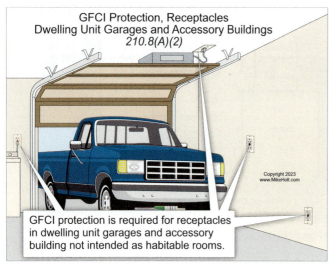

▶Figure 210–17

(3) Outdoors. GFCI protection is required for receptacles located outdoors of a dwelling unit. ▶Figure 210–18

(4) Crawl Spaces. GFCI protection is required for receptacles in dwelling unit crawl spaces at or below grade. ▶Figure 210–19

(5) Basements. GFCI protection is required for receptacles in dwelling unit basements. ▶Figure 210–20

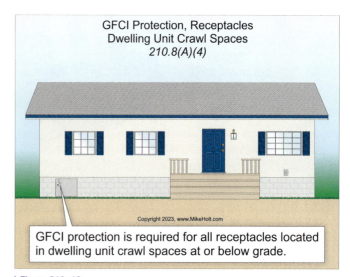

▶Figure 210–19

▶Figure 210–20

(6) Kitchens. GFCI protection is required for receptacles in dwelling unit kitchens. ▶Figure 210–21

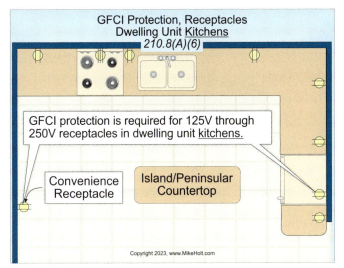
▶Figure 210–21

▶Figure 210–22

Author's Comment:

▸ Traditionally this requirement only applied to kitchen countertop receptacles, now any cord-and-plug-connected appliance in the kitchen such as the range receptacle, refrigerator receptacle, disposal receptacle, and microwave receptacles will require GFCI protection.

(7) Food Preparation Areas. GFCI protection is required for receptacles in areas with sinks with permanent provisions for food preparation, beverage preparation, or cooking.

(8) Sinks. GFCI protection is required for receptacles within 6 ft of the top inside edge of the bowl of a dwelling unit sink.

(9) Boathouses. GFCI protection is required for receptacles in a boathouse for a dwelling unit. ▶Figure 210–22

Author's Comment:

▸ The *Code* does not require a receptacle to be installed in a boathouse, but if any are then they must be GFCI protected.

(10) Bathtubs or Shower Stalls. GFCI protection is required for receptacles within 6 ft of the outside edge of a bathtub or shower stall not installed within a bathroom as defined in Article 100. ▶Figure 210–23

▶Figure 210–23

(11) Laundry Areas. GFCI protection is required for receptacles installed in the laundry area of a dwelling unit. ▶Figure 210–24

(12) Damp and Wet Locations Indoors. GFCI protection is required for receptacles installed in indoor damp and wet locations.

Ex 1: GFCI protection is not required for a receptacle dedicated to fixed electric snow-melting equipment if the receptacle is not readily accessible and ground-fault protection of equipment (GFPE) is provided as required by 426.28 and 427.22. ▶Figure 210–25

210.8 | Branch Circuits

▶Figure 210–24

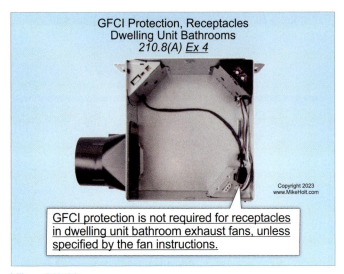
▶Figure 210–26

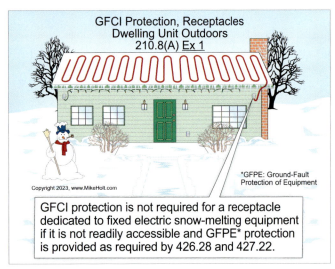
▶Figure 210–25

Ex 2: A receptacle supplying only a permanently installed premises security system is permitted to omit ground-fault circuit-interrupter protection.

Ex 4: GFCI protection is not required for receptacles in dwelling unit bathroom exhaust fans, unless specified by the fan instructions.
▶Figure 210–26

Author's Comment:

▸ The receptacle for exhaust fans is internal to the exhaust fan and is not accessible as a convenience cord-and-plug receptacle, therefore GFCI protection is not required.

Author's Comment:

▸ In accordance with the UL GPWX guide information, exhaust fans installed in the area directly above the footprint of the bathtub or shower must be GFCI protected.

(B) Other Than Dwellings. GFCI protection is required for 125V through 250V receptacles supplied by single-phase branch circuits 50A or less, and receptacles supplied by three-phase branch circuits 100A or less installed in the following locations:

(1) Bathrooms. GFCI protection is required for receptacles in bathroom areas. ▶Figure 210–27

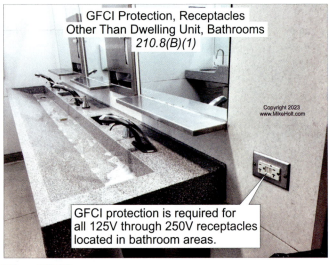
▶Figure 210–27

62 | Mike Holt Enterprises | *Changes to the National Electrical Code 2023* | 1st Printing

Author's Comment:

▸ According to Article 100, a "Bathroom Area" is one that includes a sink (basin) and one or more of the following: a toilet, urinal, tub, shower, bidet, or similar plumbing fixture.

(2) Kitchens. GFCI protection is required for 125V through 250V receptacles in kitchens. ▸Figure 210-28

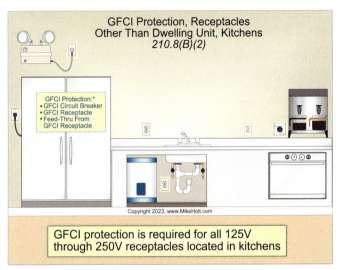
▸Figure 210-28

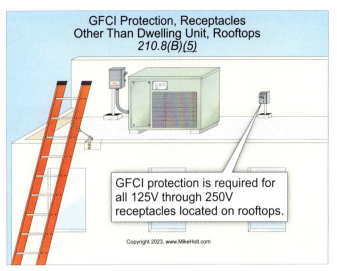
▸Figure 210-29

(3) Food Preparation Areas. GFCI protection is required for 125V through 250V receptacles in areas with sinks with permanent provisions for food preparation, beverage preparation, or cooking.

(4) Buffet Serving Areas. GFCI protection is required for 125V through 250V receptacles in buffet serving areas with permanent provisions for food serving, beverage serving, or cooking.

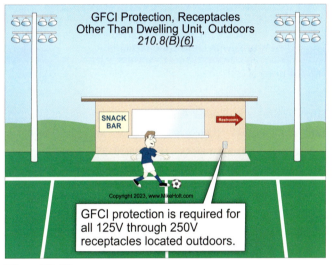
▸Figure 210-30

Author's Comment:

▸ This requires GFCI protection for receptacles in the break area of a commercial occupancy.

(5) Rooftops. GFCI protection is required for 125V through 250V receptacles on rooftops. ▸Figure 210-29

(6) Outdoors. GFCI protection is required for 125V through 250V receptacles outdoors. ▸Figure 210-30

(7) Sinks. GFCI protection is required for 125V through 250V receptacles and receptacles used for cord-and-plug-connected appliances located within 6 ft from the top inside edge of the bowl of a sink. ▸Figure 210-31

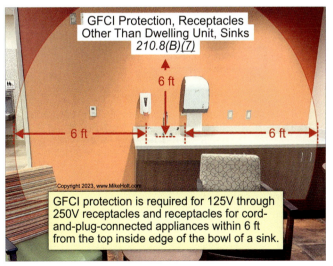
▸Figure 210-31

210.8 | Branch Circuits

(8) Indoor Damp or Wet Locations. GFCI protection is required for 125V through 250V receptacles in indoor damp or wet locations.

(9) Locker Rooms. GFCI protection is required for 125V through 250V receptacles in locker rooms with showering facilities. ▶Figure 210-32

▶Figure 210-32

(10) Garages and Similar Areas. GFCI protection is required for 125V through 250V receptacles in garages, accessory buildings, service bays, and similar areas. ▶Figure 210-33

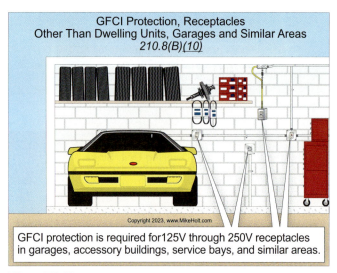

▶Figure 210-33

Author's Comment:

▸ According to Article 100, a "Garage" is a building or portion of a building in which one or more self-propelled vehicles can be kept for use, sale, storage, rental, repair, exhibition, or demonstration.

(11) Crawl Spaces. GFCI protection is required for 125V through 250V receptacles in crawl spaces at or below grade level.

(12) Unfinished Areas of Basements. GFCI protection is required for 125V through 250V receptacles in the unfinished areas of basements.

(13) Aquatic Tanks or Bowls. GFCI protection is required for 125V through 250V receptacles within 6 ft from the top inside edge or rim from the conductive support framing of the vessel or container for aquariums, bait wells, and similar open aquatic vessels or containers, such as tanks or bowls.

(14) Laundry Areas. GFCI protection is required for 125V through 250V receptacles in laundry areas.

(15) Bathtubs and Shower Stalls. GFCI protection is required for 125V through 250V receptacles installed within 6 ft of the outside edge of a bathtub or shower stall not installed in a bathroom as defined in Article 100.

Ex 2: Rooftop GFCI receptacles are only required to be readily accessible from the rooftop itself. ▶Figure 210-34

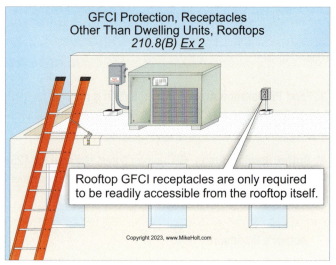

▶Figure 210-34

(C) Crawl Space Lighting Outlets. GFCI protection is required for 120V lighting outlets in crawl spaces.

Author's Comment:

▸ A lighting outlet is not required for a dwelling unit crawl space unless the space is used for storage or has equipment requiring servicing [210.70(C)].

(D) Specific Appliance. GFCI protection is required for the outlet supplying the following appliances rated 150V or less to ground, 60A or less, single- or three-phase:

(1) Automotive vacuum machines

(2) Drinking water coolers and bottle fill stations

(3) High-pressure spray washing machines

(4) Tire inflation machines

(5) Vending machines

(6) Sump pumps

(7) Dishwashers

(8) Electric ranges

(9) Wall-mounted electric ovens

(10) Counter-mounted electric cooking units

(11) Clothes dryers

(12) Microwave ovens

Author's Comment:

▸ The appliances in list items 210.8(D)(8) through (12) are commonly installed as hardwired outlets and the GFCI protection requirements of 210.8(A) and (B) only apply to receptacles. The shock hazards exist whether appliances are hardwired, or cord-and-plug-connected and therefore GFCI protection must be provided for the appliance branch circuit or outlet.

(E) Equipment Requiring Servicing.

Air-Conditioning Equipment. GFCI protection is required for air-conditioning equipment 125V, 15A or 20A service receptacle outlets installed within 25 ft of the equipment as specified in 210.63(A).
▸Figure 210-35

Indoor Service Equipment. GFCI protection must be provided for indoor service equipment 125V, 15A or 20A service receptacle outlets as required by 210.63(B)(1). ▸Figure 210-36

Indoor Switchboards, Switchgear, Panelboards, and Motor Control Centers. GFCI protection must be provided for 125V, 15A or 20A service receptacles as required by 210.63(B)(2) for indoor switchboards, switchgear, panelboards, and motor control centers.

(F) Outdoor Dwelling Unit Outlets. GFCI protection is required for outdoor outlets rated 50A or less and outlets in the following dwelling unit areas:
▸Figure 210-37

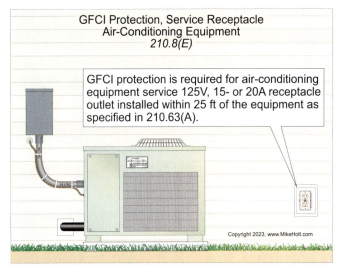
▸Figure 210-35

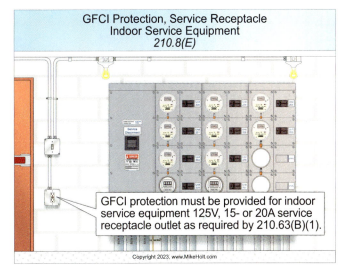
▸Figure 210-36

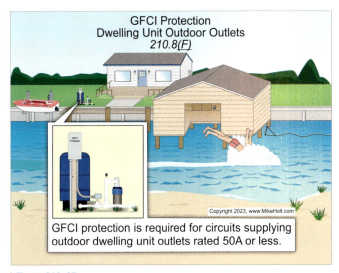
▸Figure 210-37

210.11 | Branch Circuits

(1) Garages. GFCI protection is required for outdoor outlets rated 50A or less in dwelling unit garages.

(2) Accessory Buildings. GFCI protection is required for outlets rated not over 150V to ground, 50A or less in dwelling unit accessory buildings.

(3) Boathouses. GFCI protection is required for outlets rated not over 150V to ground, 50A or less in dwelling unit boathouses.

If equipment connected to any of the above outlets is replaced, the circuit to the outlet must be GFCI protected.

Ex 1: GFCI protection is not required on lighting outlets other than those covered in 210.8(C).

Ex 2: GFCI protection is not required for listed HVAC equipment.
▶Figure 210–38

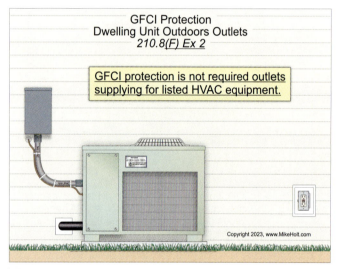
▶Figure 210–38

210.11 Branch Circuits Required

There has been some confusion about what this section required in a garage. Language was added to clarify the intent of these rules.

Analysis

CLARIFIED The rule in (C)(4) for dwelling garage receptacle outlets requires at least one 20A branch circuit supplying no other outlets. This clarification permits this branch circuit to supply other receptacle outlets within the garage, including those required by 210.52(G)(1) for each vehicle bay.

NEW A new sentence in (C)(4) permits additional branch circuits rated 15A or greater to serve outlets other than those required by 210.52(G)(1). This clears up any confusion about installing extra circuits in a garage once the required circuits have been provided.

NEW This new Exception 2 allows a single 20A branch circuit for a single vehicle bay garage to supply outlets for other equipment in the garage in accordance with 210.23(B)(1) and (2).

210.11 Branch Circuits Required

(C) Dwelling Unit.

(1) Small-Appliance Receptacle Outlet Circuits. At least two 20A, 120V branch circuits are required to supply receptacle outlets in a dwelling unit kitchen, dining room, breakfast room, pantry, or similar areas as required by 210.52(B). ▶Figure 210–39

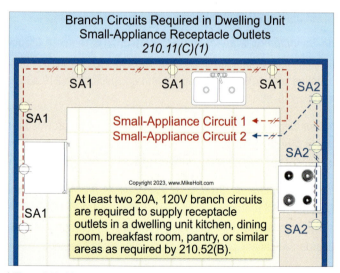
▶Figure 210–39

Author's Comment:

▸ The two 20A small-appliance branch circuits can be supplied by one 3-wire multiwire circuit or by two separate 120V circuits [210.4(A)].

(2) Laundry Receptacle Outlet Circuit. One 20A, 120V branch circuit is required to supply the receptacle outlet for dwelling unit laundry equipment as required by 210.52(F). This circuit is permitted to supply other receptacles in the laundry area, but not lighting outlets or receptacle outlets outside the laundry area. ▶Figure 210–40

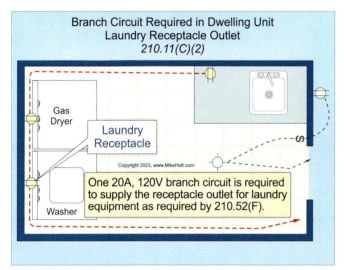

▶Figure 210–40

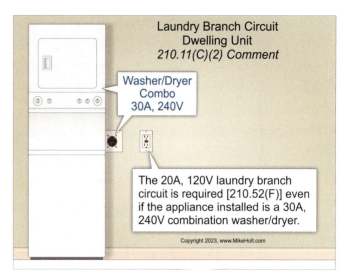

▶Figure 210–41

Author's Comment:

▸ The laundry receptacle circuit is permitted to supply more than one receptacle outlet in the laundry area if the laundry equipment (washing machine) does not exceed 80 percent of the branch-circuit ampere rating [210.23(B)(1)].

▸ The laundry receptacle circuit is required even if the laundry appliance is a 30A, 240V combination washer/dryer. ▶Figure 210–41

(3) Bathroom Receptacle Outlet Circuit. At least one 20A, 120V branch circuit is required to be installed to supply dwelling unit bathroom sink receptacle outlets required by 210.52(D). This bathroom sink receptacle circuit is not permitted to supply lighting outlets or any other receptacle outlets. ▶Figure 210–42

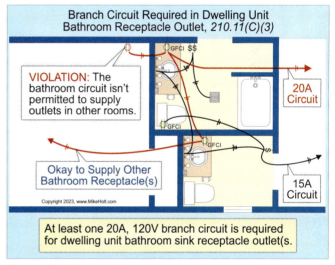

▶Figure 210–42

Author's Comment:

▸ The 20A, 120V bathroom circuit is only permitted to supply the required bathroom sink receptacle outlets [210.52(D)] in one or more bathrooms. This circuit is not permitted to supply lighting, fans, heaters, or other receptacle outlets used for any other purpose. ▶Figure 210–43

210.12 | Branch Circuits

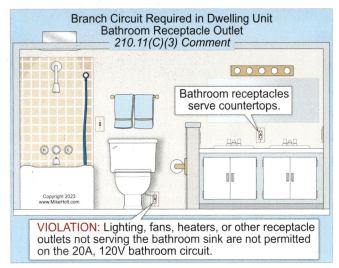
▶Figure 210-43

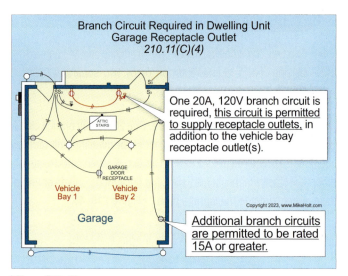
▶Figure 210-45

Ex: A single 20A, 120V branch circuit can supply all the outlets in a single bathroom area. ▶Figure 210-44

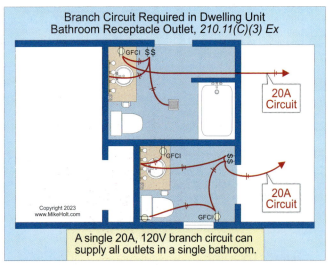
▶Figure 210-44

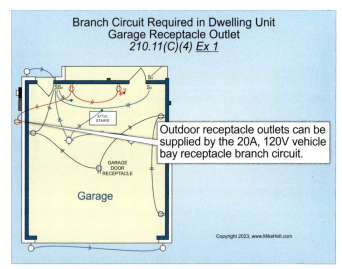
▶Figure 210-46

Ex 2: The 20A circuit for a single vehicle bay garage can supply outlets for other equipment within the garage in accordance with 210.23(B)(1) and (B)(2).

(4) Garage Receptacle Outlet Circuits. In dwelling unit garages with electric power, at least one 20A, 120V branch circuit is required to supply the vehicle bay receptacle outlets required by 210.52(G)(1). ▶Figure 210-45

A branch circuit rated 15A or greater is permitted in addition to the required 20A, 120V garage vehicle bay branch circuit.

Ex 1: Outdoor receptacle outlets can be supplied by the 20A, 120V vehicle bay receptacle branch circuit. ▶Figure 210-46

210.12 Arc-Fault Circuit-Interrupter Protection

There were no big changes here, but the panel did a great job organizing and editing this section to address over 50 public inputs while making the whole thing easier to read and use.

Branch Circuits | 210.12

Analysis

EDITED The global changes made in this section are not technical in nature but were a massive improvement from a usability standpoint. One change that stands out is changing the phrase "arc-fault circuit interrupter" to "AFCI" throughout the section.

REORGANIZED The rules for dwelling unit AFCIs were moved to subdivision (B), dormitory units were moved to (C), and the coverage requirements were converted into simple numbered lists. Rules about AFCI protection for branch-circuit extensions or modifications were moved to (E), and all the associated references within 210.12 were updated to match.

EXPANDED The requirement to provide 15A and 20A branch circuits with AFCI protection was expanded to include the new allowance for 10A branch circuits in (B) through (D).

NEW Subdivision (C) became (D) and was retitled as Other Occupancies. The requirements were reorganized into a list format which includes a list item 3 to clear up any confusion about AFCI protection requirements for branch circuits in the sleeping rooms of fire houses, rescue squads, police departments, and similar locations.

210.12 Arc-Fault Circuit-Interrupter Protection

Arc-fault circuit-interrupter protection (AFCI), in a readily accessible location, is required in accordance with 210.12(B) through (C).

Author's Comment:

▸ According to Article 100, an "Arc-Fault Circuit Interrupter (AFCI)" is a device intended to de-energize the circuit when it detects the current waveform characteristics unique to an arcing fault. ▸Figure 210-47

(B) Dwelling Units. AFCI protection is required for 15A or 20A, 120V branch circuits supplying outlets or devices in the following dwelling unit locations: ▸Figure 210-48

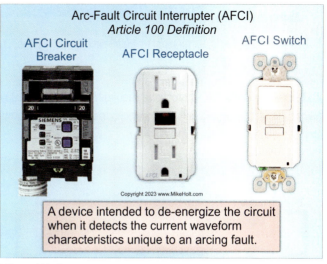
▸Figure 210-47

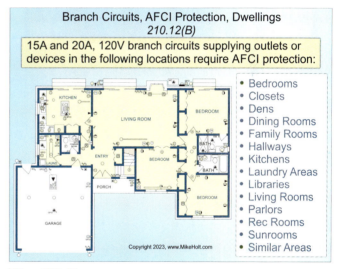
▸Figure 210-48

(1) Kitchens
(2) Family rooms
(3) Dining rooms
(4) Living rooms
(5) Parlors
(6) Libraries
(7) Dens
(8) Bedrooms
(9) Sunrooms
(10) Recreation rooms
(11) Closets
(12) Hallways
(13) Laundry areas
(14) Similar areas

210.12 | Branch Circuits

Author's Comment:

▸ AFCI protection is not required for outlets in bathroom areas, garages, or outside.

(C) Dormitory Units. AFCI protection is required for 15A or 20A, 120V branch circuits supplying outlets or devices in the following dormitory unit locations: ▸Figure 210-49

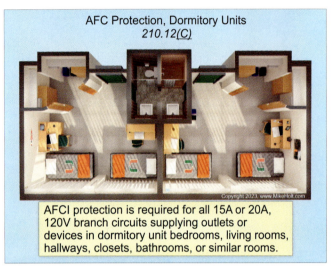

▸Figure 210-49

(1) Bedrooms

(2) Living rooms

(3) Hallways

(4) Closets

(5) Bathrooms

(6) Similar rooms

(D) Other Occupancies. AFCI protection is required for 15A and 20A, 120V branch circuits supplying outlets or devices in the following other occupancy locations:

(1) Guest rooms and guest suites of hotels and motels. ▸Figure 210-50

(2) Areas used exclusively as patient sleeping rooms in nursing homes and limited care facilities.

(3) Areas designed for use exclusively as sleeping quarters in fire stations, police stations, ambulance stations, rescue stations, ranger stations, and similar locations. ▸Figure 210-51

▸Figure 210-50

▸Figure 210-51

(E) Branch-Circuit Wiring Extensions, Modifications, or Replacements. If 15A or 20A, 120V branch-circuit wiring is extended, modified, or replaced in any of the areas specified in 210.12(B), (C), or (D), the wiring must be AFCI protected by one of the following.

(1) An AFCI circuit breaker

(2) An AFCI receptacle installed at the first receptacle outlet of the existing branch circuit.

Ex: AFCI protection is not required for extension wiring that is less than 6 ft in length (raceway or cable) if no outlets or devices, other than splicing devices, are added. This measurement does not include the conductors inside an enclosure, cabinet, or junction box.

210.17 Guest Rooms and Guest Suites

You need to sit up and take notice of this change. Assisted living facilities with permanent provisions for cooking were added to the list of guest rooms and guest suites that must have branch circuits installed to meet the dwelling unit requirements.

Analysis

EXPANDED This rule was reorganized into a list and the new list item (3) "Assisted living facilities" lets us know that if guest rooms or guest suites in hotels, motels, and assisted living facilities include permanent provisions for cooking, then the dwelling unit branch-circuit rules must be met! A new Informational Note directs us to NFPA 101, *Life Safety Code*, for the definition an "assisted living facility."

210.17 Guest Rooms and Guest Suites

Guest rooms and guest suites with permanent provisions for cooking located in the following areas, must have branch circuits installed to meet the rules for dwelling units:

(1) Hotels

(2) Motels

(3) Assisted living facilities

Note 2: For the definition of assisted living facilities, see NFPA 101, *Life Safety Code*.

Authors Comment:

▸ In accordance with NFPA 101, Life Safety Code, section 3.3.198.12(5), an assisted living facility is defined as an occupancy used for the lodging and boarding of four or more residents for the purposes of providing personal care services.

210.19 Conductors—Minimum Ampacity and Size

This section had no technical change. It was simply reorganized for readability.

Analysis

REORGANIZED The information that was in (A)(1)(a) and (A)(1)(b) became list items (1) and (2) without change.

210.19 Conductor Sizing

Branch Circuits. Branch circuits must be sized in accordance with 210.19(A) through (D).

Note: The *NEC* recommends that branch-circuit conductors be sized to prevent a voltage drop of not more than 3 percent. In addition, it recommendations that the total voltage drop on both feeders and branch circuits should not exceed 5 percent. ▸Figure 210–52

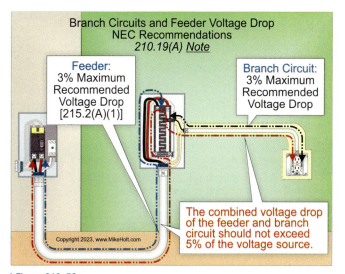

▸Figure 210–52

Author's Comment:

▸ Sizing conductors to accommodate the voltage drop percentages indicated in the *NEC*'s Informational Note is not a *Code* requirement because Informational Notes contain information only and are not enforceable [90.5(C)].

▸ See 695.7 for fire pump controller voltage-drop requirements.

210.19 | Branch Circuits

(A) General. Branch-circuit conductors must be sized to carry the largest of the following: ▶Figure 210-53

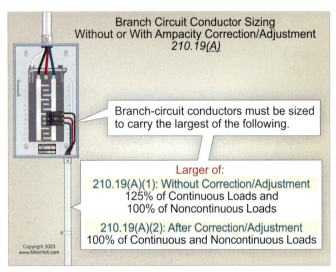

▶Figure 210-53

(1) Without Conductor Ampacity Correction/Adjustment. Branch-circuit conductors must be sized to carry 125 percent of the continuous loads, plus 100 percent of the noncontinuous loads, based on the temperature rating of equipment in accordance with 110.14(C)(1) and Table 310.16, prior to conductor ampacity correction and/or adjustment.
▶Figure 210-54

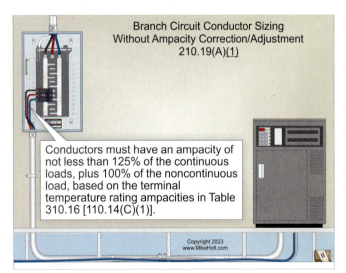

▶Figure 210-54

▶ **Example**

Question: What size conductors rated 90°C are required for a circuit supplying a 44A continuous load where the equipment is rated 75°C?
▶Figure 210-55

(a) 8 AWG (b) 6 AWG (c) 4 AWG (d) 3 AWG

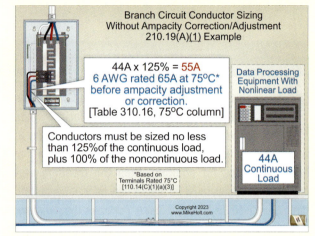

▶Figure 210-55

Solution:

Step 1: *Conductor Ampacity.* The conductor must have an ampacity of not less than 55A (44A × 125%).

Step 2: Size conductors in accordance with 110.14(C)(1)(a)(3) and Table 310.16.

6 AWG is rated 65A and is suitable to be used [Table 310.16, 75°C column].

Answer: (b) 6 AWG

(2) With Conductor Ampacity Correction/Adjustment. Branch-circuit conductors must be sized to carry 100 percent of the continuous loads, plus 100 percent of the noncontinuous loads in accordance with Table 310.16, based on the temperature rating of equipment in accordance with 110.14(C)(1), after conductor ampacity correction and/or adjustment in accordance with Table 310.15(B)(1)(1) and Table 310.15(C)(1).
▶Figure 210-56

> **Author's Comment:**
>
> ▸ The temperature ampacity correction of 310.15(B)(1)(1) and adjustment ampacity factors of 310.15(C)(1) are applied to the ampacities listed in Table 310.16, based on the conductor insulation temperature rating [310.15(A)].

Branch Circuits | 210.19

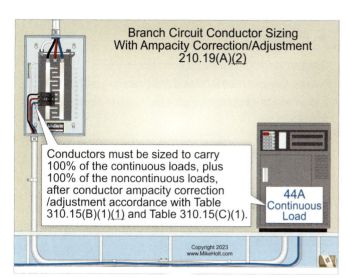

▶ Figure 210–56

▶ Example

Question: What size conductors rated 90°C are required for a circuit containing four current-carrying conductors supplying a 44A continuous load in an ambient temperature of 100°F where the equipment is rated 75°C? ▶Figure 210–57

(a) 10 AWG (b) 8 AWG (c) 6 AWG (d) 4 AWG

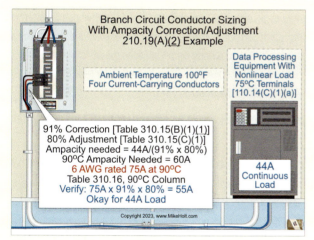

▶ Figure 210–57

Solution:

Step 1: The circuit conductors must have an ampacity of 44A after conductor ampacity temperature correction [Table 310.15(B)(1)(1)] and adjustment [Table 310.15(C)(1)], based on the conductor insulation rating of 90°C [110.14(C)(1)(a)(3)]. One way to find the conductor size is to determine the conductor ampacity required to supply a 44A load at 100 percent after correction and adjustment.

Conductor Ampacity at 90°C = Actual Load/(Correction × Adjustment)

Actual Load = 44A

Correction [Table 310.15(B)(1)(1)] = 91% (100°F with 90°C Conductor)

Adjustment [Table 310.15(C)(1)] = 80% (four current-carrying conductors)

Conductor Ampacity at 90°C Column = 44A/(91% × 80%)
Conductor Ampacity at 90°C Column = 44A/73%
Conductor Ampacity at 90°C Column = 60A

Step 2: Select the conductors from the 90°C column of Table 310.16.

6 AWG is suitable because it has an ampacity of 75A at 90°C before any correction and adjustment. In addition, 6 AWG is the minimum conductor size allowed according to 210.19(A)(1).

Step 3: Verify that the ampacity of 6 AWG after correction and adjustment is capable of carrying 100 percent of the 44A continuous load at 90°C.

Conductor Ampacity after Correction and Adjustment = Conductor Ampacity × Correction × Adjustment

Conductor Ampacity at 90°C = 75A (from Step 2.)

Correction = 91%
Adjustment = 80%

Conductor Ampacity after Correction and Adjustment =
 75A × 91% × 80%

Conductor Ampacity after Correction and Adjustment = 55A

6 AWG has an ampere rating of 55A which is more than enough for the 44A continuous load.

Step 4: Verify that the ampacity of 6 AWG at 75°C without correction and adjustment is capable of carrying 125 percent of the 44A continuous load in accordance with 210.19(A)(1).

Conductor Ampacity at 125% = 44A × 125%
Conductor Ampacity at 125% = 55A

According to Table 310.16, 6 AWG is suitable because it is rated 65A at 75°C. ▶Figure 210–58

The branch-circuit conductors cannot be sized less than determined using 210.19(A)(1). In this case, based on the conditions specified in this example, 6 AWG is the minimum permitted size.

210.19 | Branch Circuits

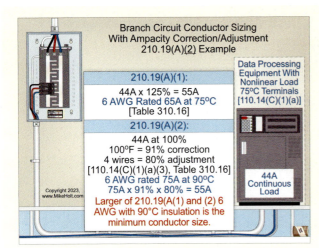
▶Figure 210–58

The conductor cannot be sized less than the load at 100 percent based on the 75°C terminals specified in the question (60°C when not specified [110.14(C)(1)(a)]). In this case, the minimum conductor size for a 44A circuit using the 75°C column of Table 310.16 is 8 AWG but, since 210.19(A)(1) only permits a minimum of 6 AWG, the 8 AWG cannot be used.

Answer: *(c) 6 AWG*

Ex to (1) and (2): A section of conductors that terminates in a junction box at both ends to separate pressure connectors in accordance with 110.14(C)(2) can have an ampacity of 100 percent of the continuous and 100 percent of the noncontinuous loads based on the 90°C column of Table 310.16 for 90°C conductor insulation. ▶Figure 210–59

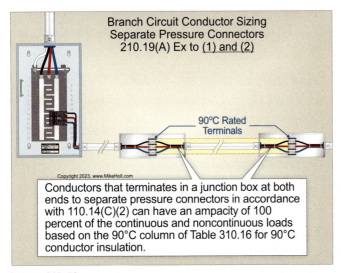
▶Figure 210–59

▶ Example

Question: *What size branch-circuit conductors rated 90°C are required between terminals rated 90°C for a circuit supplying a 44A continuous load, where the conductors are protected by a 60A breaker?* ▶Figure 210–60

(a) 10 AWG (b) 8 AWG (c) 6 AWG (d) 4 AWG

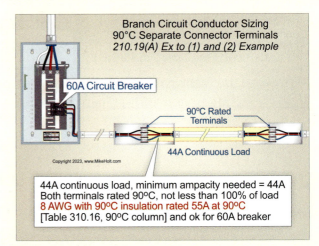
▶Figure 210–60

Solution:

Step 1: Conductor Ampacity. Size the conductors between the 90°C terminals to carry 100 percent of the 44A continuous load. Where terminals of separately installed connectors at each end of a conductor are rated 90°C, the branch circuit between the 90°C terminals can be sized to the 90°C column of Table 310.16 [210.19(A)(1) and (2) Ex]. 8 AWG is rated 55A at 90°C.

Step 2: Size conductors in accordance with 110.14(C)(2) and Table 310.16.

When terminals at each end of a conductor have different terminal temperature ratings, use the lower temperature rating when sizing conductors from Table 310.16. In this case the terminals are both rated 90°C, so the conductors are selected in accordance with the 90°C column of Table 310.16. Based on the 44A load at 100 percent, 8 AWG is rated 55A at 90°C, and is permitted to be protected by a 60A overcurrent protective device [240.4(B)].

Answer: *(b) 8 AWG*

Branch Circuits | **210.52**

210.23 Multiple-Outlet Branch Circuits

This section was expanded to accommodate 10A branch circuits and provides some rules for their use.

Analysis

EXPANDED

Here is another place we see copper-clad aluminum making its mark. The new subdivision (A) provides rules for 10A branch circuits in dwelling units. Locations permitted include lighting outlets, exhaust fans, and gas fireplaces. Receptacle outlets, fixed appliances, garage door openers, and laundry equipment are not yet permitted on this size circuit. I think it is only a matter of time until we see many more applications of this rebooted wiring method.

210.23 Multiple-Outlet Branch Circuits

(B) 15A and 20A Branch Circuits. A 15A or 20A branch circuit can supply lighting, equipment, or any combination in accordance with 210.23(B)(1) and (B)(2). ▶Figure 210-61

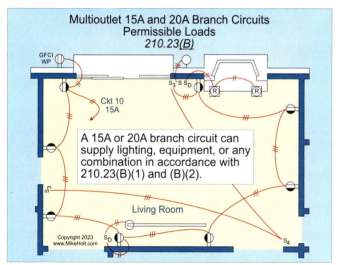
▶Figure 210-61

(1) Cord-and-Plug Equipment. Cord-and-plug-connected equipment not fastened in place with other outlets is not permitted to exceed 80 percent of the branch-circuit rating.

(2) Equipment Fastened in Place. Equipment fastened in place with other outlets is not permitted to exceed 50 percent of the branch-circuit rating. ▶Figure 210-62

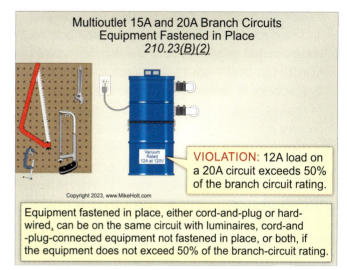
▶Figure 210-62

210.52 Dwelling Unit Receptacle Outlets

The phrase "stationary appliance" was added to the list of things in subdivision (A) that do not count as wall space, subdivision (C) has some impactful technical changes, and subdivision (D) was edited for clarity and usability.

Analysis

EXPANDED

The phrase "stationary appliance" was added to the list of things that do not count as wall space for the purposes of locating the required receptacles. The rule previously listed doorways, similar openings, fireplaces, and fixed cabinets as not counted as wall space. This means the appliance does not have to be bolted down for the space to qualify. Comments during the changes to this rule use cord-connected range equipment as an example of a "portable appliance." This may need more attention in the future, but it is a great start.

•••

210.52 | Branch Circuits

 DELETED The parent text in 210.52(C)(2), Island and Peninsular Countertops and Work Surfaces, was revised to make the installation of receptacles in those locations optional. If a receptacle is not installed at the time of construction, provisions must be made for future installation. This change was based on information obtained from the Consumer Product Safety Commission indicating that incidents of appliances being pulled off islands and peninsulas began after receptacles were required to be provided in those locations by the 1990 *Code*.

 REDUCED The permission to install a receptacle below the countertop or work surface was removed from the *Code*, and 210.52(C)(3) lists three permitted locations for receptacles that serve countertops or work surfaces.

 EXPANDED New text in (G) prohibits a receptacle supplying a permanently installed premises security system from being used to meet any of the requirements of this section.

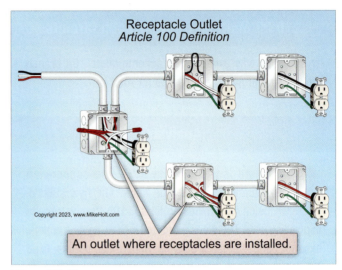

▶Figure 210–63

(C) Countertop and Work Surface Requirements. In kitchens, pantries, breakfast rooms, dining rooms, and similar areas of dwelling units, receptacle outlets for countertop and work surfaces 12 in. or wider must be installed in accordance with 210.52(C)(1) through (C)(3) and are not permitted to be used to meet the receptacle outlets for wall space required by 210.52(A).

Two or more receptacles in each 1 ft section of an multioutlet assembly, are considered a single receptacle outlet.

(1) Countertop Wall Spaces, Receptacle Outlets. A receptacle outlet must be installed so no point along the countertop or work surface wall space is more than 2 ft, measured horizontally, from a receptacle outlet. ▶Figure 210–64

210.52 Dwelling Unit Receptacle Outlet Requirements

This section provides the requirements for 15A and 20A, 125V receptacle outlets in dwelling units. Receptacles or receptacle outlets located in the following locations do not count as the required 15A and 20A, 125V receptacle outlets under this section.

(1) Receptacles that are part of a luminaire or appliance,

(2) Receptacles controlled by a listed wall-mounted control device in accordance with 210.70(A)(1) Ex 1,

(3) Receptacle outlets located within cabinets or cupboards, or

(4) Receptacle outlets located more than 5½ ft above the floor.

> **Author's Comment:**
> ▸ According to Article 100, a "Receptacle Outlet" is an outlet where receptacles are installed. ▶Figure 210–63

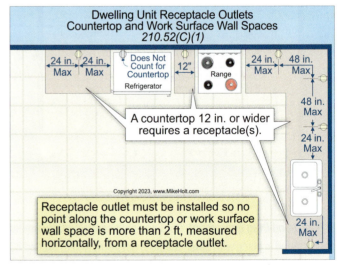

▶Figure 210–64

Branch Circuits | 210.52

Ex 1: A receptacle outlet is not required directly behind a range, counter-mounted cooking unit, or sink in accordance with Figure 210.52(C)(1) in the NEC. ▶Figure 210–65

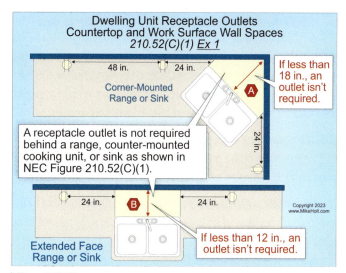
▶Figure 210–65

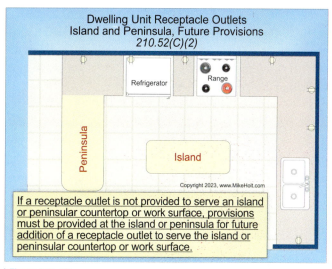
▶Figure 210–66

Author's Comment:

▸ If the countertop space behind a range or sink is larger than the dimensions noted in Figure 210.52(C)(1) of the *Code* book, then a GFCI-protected receptacle must be installed in that space. This is because (for all practical purposes) if there is enough space for an appliance, it is assumed one will be placed there.

Ex 2: Where a required receptacle outlet cannot be installed in the wall areas shown in Figure 210.52(C)(1) of the NEC, the required receptacle outlet is permitted to be installed as close as practicable to the countertop area to be served. The total number of receptacle outlets serving the countertop must not be less than the number needed to satisfy 210.52(C)(1). These outlets must be in accordance with 210.52(C)(3).

(2) Island and Peninsular Countertops and Work Surfaces. If a receptacle outlet is not provided to serve an island or peninsular countertop or work surface, provisions must be provided at the island or peninsula for the future addition of a receptacle outlet to serve the island or peninsular countertop or work surface. ▶Figure 210–66

(3) Countertop and Work Surface Receptacle Location. The required receptacle outlets must be installed in one or more of the following locations:

(1) On or Above Countertops or Work Surfaces. The required receptacle outlets can be installed on or not more than 20 in. above the countertop or work surface. ▶Figure 210–67

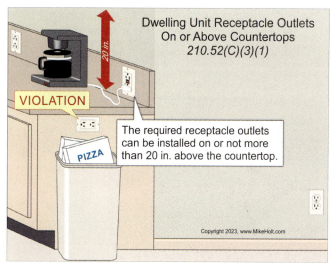
▶Figure 210–67

Author's Comment:

▸ Receptacle outlets installed at islands and peninsulas must be located on or above the countertop or work surface. ▶Figure 210–68

210.52 | Branch Circuits

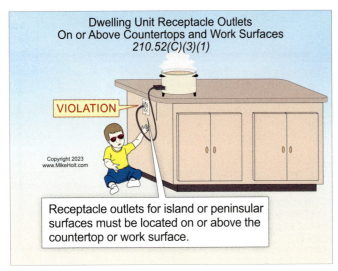
▶Figure 210-68

(2) In Countertops. The required receptacle outlets can in the countertop with a receptacle outlet assemblies listed for use in countertops are permitted. ▶Figure 210-69

▶Figure 210-69

(3) The required receptacle outlets can be in the countertop with a receptacle outlet assembly listed for use in work surfaces or listed for use in countertops.

Receptacle outlets rendered not readily accessible by appliances fastened in place, in an appliance garage, behind sinks, ranges, or cooktops [210.52(C)(1) Ex 1], or supplying appliances that occupy assigned spaces do not count as the required countertop surface receptacle outlets.

Author's Comment:

▸ An "Appliance Garage" is an enclosed area on the countertop where an appliance can be stored and hidden from view when not in use. Receptacles installed inside an appliance garage do not count as a required countertop receptacle outlet.

Note 1: For the installation of receptacles in countertops, see 406.5(E). For installation of receptacles in work surfaces see 406.5(F), and for the installation of multioutlet assemblies in work surfaces see 380.10.

(D) Bathroom Sink Receptacle Outlet(s). At least one 15A or 20A, 125V receptacle outlet must be installed within 3 ft of the outside edge of each bathroom sink.

The receptacle outlet must be on a wall or partition adjacent to the sink counter surface, or on the side or face of the sink cabinet. In no case can the receptacle outlet be more than 12 in. below the top of the sink or sink countertop. ▶Figure 210-70

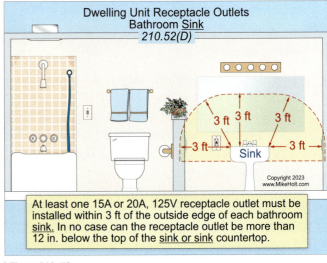
▶Figure 210-70

Author's Comment:

▸ One bathroom receptacle outlet can serve two sinks to meet this requirement if it is within 3 ft of the outside edge of each sink. ▶Figure 210-71

Receptacle outlet assemblies listed for use in countertops are permitted to be installed in the bathroom sink countertop surface.

Note 1: For the installation of receptacles in countertops, see 406.5(E) and 406.5(G).

Branch Circuits | 210.52

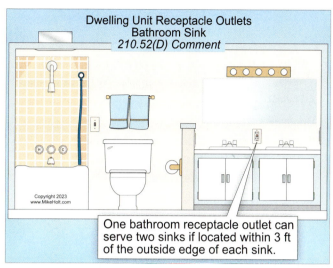
▶Figure 210–71

(G) Garage, Basement, and Accessory Building Receptacle Outlet(s). For one- and two-family dwellings, and multifamily dwellings, at least one receptacle outlet must be installed in accordance with (1) through (3). Receptacles supplying only a permanently installed premises security system are not considered as meeting these requirements.

(1) Garages. A receptacle outlet is required in each vehicle bay of a garage with electric power and must be installed no higher than 5 ft 6 in. above the floor. ▶Figure 210–72

▶Figure 210–72

Ex: A receptacle outlet is not required in a garage space not attached to an individual dwelling unit of a multifamily dwelling.

(2) Accessory Building Receptacle Outlets. A receptacle outlet is required in each accessory building with electric power. ▶Figure 210–73

▶Figure 210–73

(3) Basements. Each unfinished portion of a basement must have a receptacle outlet. ▶Figure 210–74

▶Figure 210–74

Changes to the National Electrical Code 2023 | MikeHolt.com

210.62 Show Windows

This rule was clarified to specify that the required receptacles must be located to service the entire window area.

Analysis

CLARIFIED The language was clarified to say that no point along the top of the show window can be more than 6 ft from a receptacle outlet. This could impact the number of required receptacles and where they are located.

210.62 Show Window Receptacles

At least one 125V, single-phase, 15A or 20A rated receptacle outlet must be installed within 18 in. of the top of each show window and no point along the top of the window can be further than 6 ft from a receptacle outlet. ▶Figure 210–75

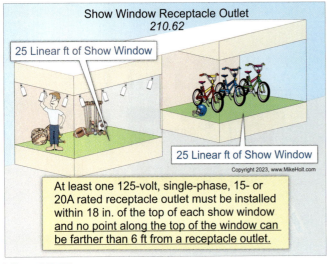
▶Figure 210–75

210.65 Meeting Rooms

New wording was added to require additional meeting room floor outlets.

Analysis

EXPANDED The language in 210.65(B)(2) was changed to require one floor receptacle for each 215 square feet of floor area or fraction thereof. The previous language said each 215 square feet or major portion of floor space. That could be read as saying that you did not need two floor receptacles until you had over 322.50 square feet of floor area, but now, a second receptacle is required at 216 square feet of floor area.

210.65 Meeting Rooms

(A) General. Meeting rooms of 215 sq ft and larger, but not larger than 1000 sq ft, must have receptacle outlets for 15A or 20A, 125V receptacles in accordance with 210.65(B). ▶Figure 210–76

▶Figure 210–76

Where a room or space is provided with a movable partition(s), the room size must be determined with the partition(s) in the position that results in the smallest size meeting room.

Note 1: Meeting rooms are typically designed or intended for the gathering of seated occupants for conferences, deliberations, or similar purposes where portable electronic equipment such as computers, projectors, or similar equipment is likely to be used. ▶Figure 210–77

Note 2: Examples of rooms that are not meeting rooms within the scope of 210.65 include auditoriums, school rooms, and coffee shops. ▶Figure 210–78

Branch Circuits | 210.70

▶Figure 210-77

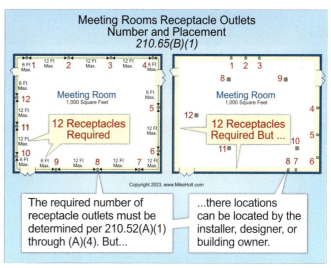
▶Figure 210-79

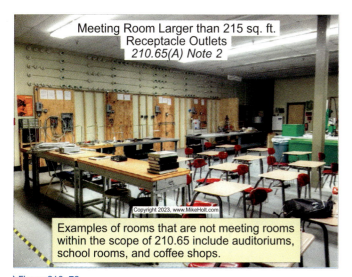
▶Figure 210-78

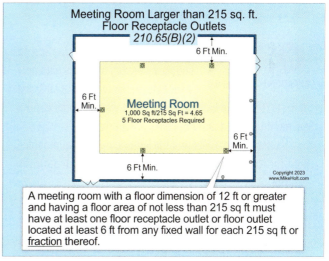
▶Figure 210-80

(B) Meeting Room Outlet Requirements. For meeting rooms of 215 sq ft and larger, but not larger than 1000 sq ft, the total number of wall receptacle outlets, floor receptacle outlets, floor outlets, and receptacle outlets in fixed furniture, must not be less than as determined in 210.65(B)(1) and (B)(2).

(1) Receptacle Outlets in Fixed Walls. The required number of receptacle outlets must be determined in accordance with 210.52(A)(1) through (A)(4). Their location can be determined by the installer, designer, or building owner. ▶Figure 210-79

(2) Floor Outlets. A meeting room with a floor dimension of 12 ft or greater and having a floor area of not less than 215 sq ft must have at least one floor receptacle outlet or floor outlet at least 6 ft from any fixed wall for each 215 sq ft or fraction thereof. ▶Figure 210-80

Note 1: For requirements on floor boxes used for receptacles in the floor, see 314.27(B).

210.70 Lighting Outlets Required

A new sentence clarifies that a switch or wall-mounted control device must not rely exclusively on a battery, that a lighting outlet for the laundry area must be provided, that accessory buildings with power are required to have a lighting outlet, and that required exterior lighting outlets must be located on the exterior of the building.

Analysis

 EDITED A new last sentence tells us that a wall-mounted control device (think of a wireless remote for a fan light) that relies solely on a battery to operate must automatically energize the lighting outlet on battery failure. Makes sense!

 EXPANDED The 2020 *Code* did not require a lighting outlet in a laundry area. Changes in (A)(1) add that requirement and specify that lighting outlets cannot be a switch-controlled receptacle. Laundry areas can be small, and lighting is often provided by lighting adjacent to, and outside, the laundry area. Do not be caught by this—add a lighting outlet in the laundry area. The rule title was also updated to include laundry areas.

  EXPANDED CLARIFIED In some areas it is a practice to supply accessory buildings with only a receptacle. Now 210.70(A)(2) list item (1) requires a lighting outlet and a wall-mounted control device if the accessory building has power.

List item (2) clarifies that the lighting outlet that provides light for the exterior of entrances must be located on the exterior.

NEW A new Exception to List item (2) permits a lighting outlet inside a basement within 5 ft of the stairs to provide the exterior lighting where the entrance is a grade level, sloped bulkhead door with stair access to the basement.

Finally, the Exception to list items (1), (2), and (3) added permission to use remote control for the required exterior lighting in hallways, stairways, and outdoor entrances.

210.70 Lighting Outlet Requirements

The switch or wall-mounted control device must not rely exclusively on a battery to energize the lighting outlet unless a means is provided for automatically energizing the lighting outlets upon battery failure. ▶Figure 210–81

▶Figure 210–81

(A) Dwelling Unit Lighting Outlets. Lighting outlets must be installed in:

(1) Habitable Rooms, Kitchens, Laundry Areas, and Bathrooms. At least one lighting outlet controlled by a listed wall-mounted control device must be installed in every habitable room, kitchen, laundry area and bathroom area of a dwelling unit. The wall-mounted control device must be on a wall near an entrance to the room. ▶Figure 210–82

▶Figure 210–82

Author's Comment:

▸ See the definition of "Lighting Outlet" in Article 100.
▸ See the definition of "Habitable Room" in Article 100.

Ex 1: In other than kitchens, laundry areas, and bathrooms, a receptacle controlled by a listed wall-mounted control device can be used instead of a lighting outlet. ▶Figure 210–83

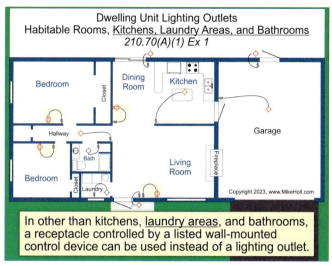
▶Figure 210–83

Author's Comment:

▸ The *Code* specifies the location of the lighting outlet, but it does not specify the wall-mounted control device's location. You would naturally not want to install a switch behind a door or other inconvenient location, but the *NEC* does not require you to move the switch to suit the swing of the door. When in doubt as to the best location to place a light switch, consult the job plans or ask the customer. ▶Figure 210–84

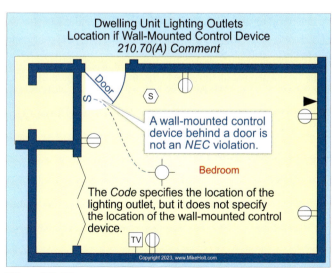
▶Figure 210–84

(2) Additional Locations.

(1) Hallways, Stairways, Garages, and Accessory Buildings. At least one lighting outlet controlled by a listed wall-mounted control device must be installed in hallways, stairways, garages, and accessory buildings with electric power. ▶Figure 210–85

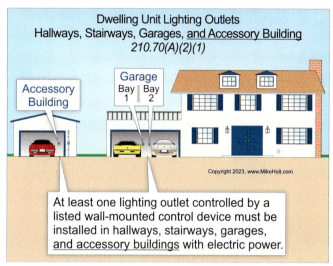
▶Figure 210–85

(2) Exterior Entrance. For dwelling units having attached and/or detached garages with electric power, at least one exterior lighting outlet controlled by a listed wall-mounted control device must provide illumination on the exterior side of outdoor entrances with grade-level access. A garage vehicle door is not considered an outdoor entrance or exit. ▶Figure 210–86

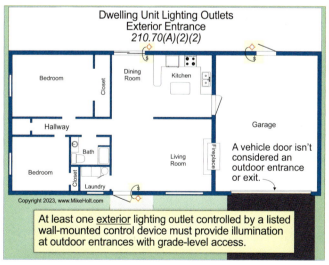
▶Figure 210–86

Ex to 2: For an outdoor grade-level stairway access to a basement, the lighting outlet that provides illumination on the stairway steps is permitted to be in the basement interior within 5 ft horizontally of the bottommost stairway riser. This lighting outlet is permitted to be controlled by a listed wall-mounted control device or a switch on the luminaire or lampholder.

(3) Stairways. Where a lighting outlet(s) is installed in interior stairways having six risers or more between floor levels, a listed wall-mounted control device for the lighting outlet(s) must be at each floor level and at each landing level that includes a stairway entry to control the lighting outlets. ▶Figure 210–87

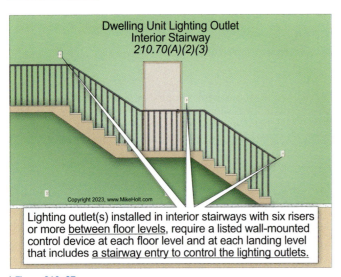

▶Figure 210–87

Ex to (A)(1), (2), and (3): Remote, central, or automatic control of hallway lighting, stairway lighting, and exterior entrance lighting is permitted. ▶Figure 210–88

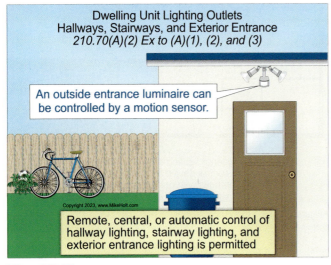

▶Figure 210–88

(4) Dimmer Control. Lighting outlets in stairways [210.70(A)(2)(3)] can be controlled by a listed wall-mounted control device where dimming control can provide a maximum brightness at each control location for the interior stairway illumination.

(B) Guest Rooms or Guest Suites. At least one lighting outlet controlled by a listed wall-mounted control device must be installed in every habitable room and bathroom area of a guest room or guest suite of hotels, motels, and similar occupancies.

Ex 1: In other than bathroom areas and kitchens, a receptacle controlled by a listed wall-mounted control device is permitted. ▶Figure 210–89

▶Figure 210–89

(C) Storage and Equipment Spaces. At least one lighting outlet that contains a switch or is controlled by a wall switch, or listed wall-mounted control device, must be installed in attics, underfloor spaces, utility rooms, and basements used for storage or containing equipment that requires servicing. The switch or wall-mounted control device must be at the usual point of entrance to these spaces. ▶Figure 210–90

The lighting outlet must be at each entry that permits access to the attic and underfloor space, utility room, or basement. Where a lighting outlet is installed for equipment requiring service, it must be installed at or near that equipment.

Branch Circuits | 210.70

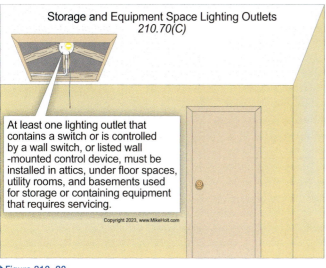

▶Figure 210-90

Notes

ARTICLE 215 FEEDERS

Introduction to Article 215—Feeders

Article 215 covers the rules for the installation, protection, and ampacity of feeders. It is important to understand the distinct differences between these circuits to correctly apply the *Code* requirements.

Feeders are the conductors between the service disconnect, the separately derived system, or other supply source, and the final branch-circuit overcurrent protective device. Conductors past the final overcurrent protective device protecting the circuit and the outlet are branch-circuit conductors and fall within the scope of Article 210 [Article 100 Definitions]. ▶Figure 215–1

It is easy to be confused between feeder, branch-circuit, and service conductors so it is important to evaluate each installation carefully using the Article 100 definitions to be sure the correct *NEC* rules are followed.

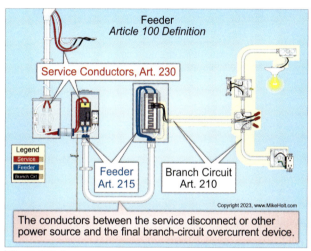
▶Figure 215–1

215.2 Conductor Sizing

This section was reorganized for readability without technical changes. Changes to (B) clarify that the feeder grounded conductor cannot be smaller than the EGC.

Analysis

REORGANIZED The information that was in (1)(a) and (1)(b) became list items (1) and (2) without change. Section 215.2(A)(2), grounded conductors, became 215.52(B). Section 215.52(A)(3) is now (C) and the former (B) was deleted as that is now covered in Part III of Article 235.

CLARIFIED The requirements for the feeder grounded conductor in 215.2(A)(2) now clearly state that it cannot be smaller than the equipment grounding conductor size required by 250.122. The rule previously referenced 250.122 but did not specify "the equipment grounding conductor size."

REORGANIZED This section has been reorganized with 215.2(A)(2) and (A)(3) becoming 215.2(B) and 215.2(C). There were no technical changes with the reorganization but the rules for feeders over 1000V were moved to Article 235.

215.2 Conductor Sizing

(B) Neutral Conductor Size. The neutral conductor must be sized to carry the maximum unbalanced load in accordance with 220.61 and is not permitted to be smaller than required for the equipment grounding conductor in accordance with Table 250.122, based on the rating of the feeder overcurrent protective device. ▶Figure 215-2

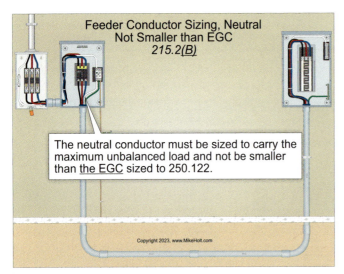

▶Figure 215-2

For neutral conductor sizing, 250.122(F) does not apply to neutral conductors that are run in parallel.

Author's Comment:

▸ Neutral conductors in parallel must be sized per the calculation in 220.61 and follow the installation rules of 310.10(G).

▶ **Example**

Question: What size neutral conductor is required for a feeder consisting of 3/0 AWG phase conductors and one neutral conductor protected by a 200A overcurrent protective device, where the unbalanced load is 50A with 75°C terminals? ▶Figure 215-3

(a) 8 AWG   (b) 6 AWG   (c) 4 AWG   (d) 2 AWG

Solution:

Section 220.61 and Table 310.16 permit an 8 AWG neutral conductor rated 50A at 75°C [110.14(C)(1) and Table 310.16] to carry the 50A unbalanced load, but the neutral conductor is not permitted to be smaller than a 6 AWG equipment grounding conductor, based on the 200A overcurrent protective device [Table 250.122].

Answer: (b) 6 AWG

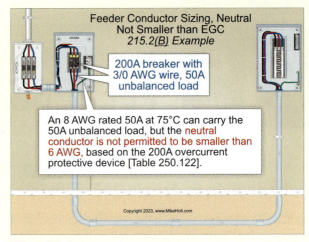

▶Figure 215-3

215.15 Barriers

This new section requires inadvertent contact protection for the line-side busbars or terminals of equipment supplied by feeder taps or transformer secondary conductors.

Analysis

NEW This new section requires the line-side busbar or terminals of equipment supplied by feeder taps or transformer secondary conductors to be protected from inadvertent contact by placing barriers over the exposed energized parts. This mirrors the line-side barrier protection requirements for services found in 230.62(C), but this requirement applies to panelboards, switchboards, switchgear, or motor control centers supplied by feeder taps or transformer secondary conductors.

215.15 Barriers

Feeder Taps. Barriers must be placed such that no energized phase busbar or terminal is exposed in equipment supplied by a feeder tap [240.21(B)] when the overcurrent protective device into which the feeder taps terminate is in the open position. ▶Figure 215-4

Feeders | 215.18

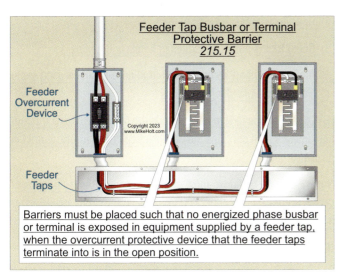

▶Figure 215-4

Secondary Conductors. Barriers must be placed such that no energized phase busbar or terminal is exposed in equipment supplied by transformer secondary conductors [240.21(C)] when the overcurrent protective device into which the secondary conductors terminate is in the open position. ▶Figure 215-5

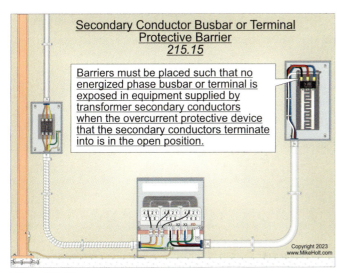

▶Figure 215-5

Author's Comment:

▸ During maintenance and servicing it is very likely an electrical worker can be exposed to inadvertent contact with energized parts on the line side of a feeder tap or secondary conductor disconnect, even if the disconnect is in the open position. Barriers on feeder tap and transformer secondary conductor disconnects reduce the hazards that exist and create an electrically safe work condition.

215.18 Surge Protection

New rules were added to require surge protection for distribution equipment that supplies feeders.

Analysis

NEW Surge protection is now required to be installed for new or replaced distribution equipment where a feeder supplies dwelling units, dormitory units, guest rooms and suites of hotels or motels, and patient sleeping areas of nursing homes and limited care facilities. Surge protection is already required for dwelling unit services to protect appliances and safety devices such as AFCIs, GFCIs, and smoke alarms. This new requirement adds protection for equipment located at an extended distance from the service. If you struggle with this requirement, read up on how surge protection works, and you will understand the need for this change.

215.18 Surge Protection

(A) Surge-Protective Device (SPD). Where a feeder supplies any of the following occupancies, a surge-protective device must be provided:

(1) Dwelling units ▶Figure 215-6 and ▶Figure 215-7

▶Figure 215-6

Changes to the National Electrical Code 2023 | MikeHolt.com | 89

215.18 | Feeders

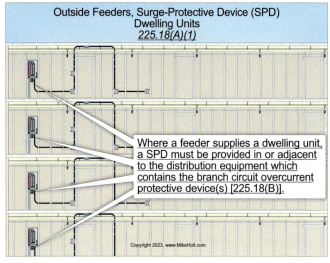
▶Figure 215-7

(2) Dormitory units

(3) Guest rooms and guest suites of hotels and motels

(4) Areas of nursing homes and limited care facilities used exclusively as patient sleeping rooms

(B) Location. The SPD must be installed in or adjacent to distribution equipment which contains the branch-circuit overcurrent protective device(s).

Note: Surge protection is most effective when closest to the branch circuit. Surges can be generated from multiple sources including, but not limited to, lightning, the electric utility, or utilization equipment.

(C) Type. The SPD must be either Type 1 or Type 2.

(D) Replacement. Where the distribution equipment supplied by the feeder is replaced, all the requirements of this section apply.

(E) Ratings. SPDs must have a nominal discharge current rating (In) of not less than 10 kA.

ARTICLE 220
BRANCH-CIRCUIT, FEEDER, AND SERVICE LOAD CALCULATIONS

Introduction to Article 220—Branch-Circuit, Feeder, and Service Load Calculations

This article focuses on the requirements for calculating demand loads (including demand factors) to size branch circuits [210.19(A)], feeders [215.2(A)(1)], and service conductors [230.42(A)].

Part I describes the layout of Article 220 and provides a table showing where other types of load calculations can be found in the *NEC*. Part II provides requirements for branch-circuit calculations and for specific types of branch circuits. Part III covers the requirements for feeder and service calculations using what is commonly called the "Standard Method of Calculation." Part IV provides optional calculations that can be used in place of the standard calculations [Parts II and III]. "Farm Load Calculations" are discussed in Part V of this article.

In some cases, the *Code* provides an optional method [Part IV] for feeder and service calculations in addition to the standard method [Part III], however they do not yield identical results. In fact, the optional method of calculation will often result in a smaller feeder or service. The neutral conductor must be calculated using the standard method [220.61]. As you work through Article 220, be sure to study the illustrations to help you fully understand this article's requirements. Also, be sure to review the examples in Annex D of the *NEC* to gain more practice with these calculations. The *Code* recognizes that not all demand for power will occur at the same time and it is because of this load diversity that certain demand factors are able to be applied.

220.1 Scope

The scope was edited to reflect the addition of Parts VI and VII.

Analysis

EXPANDED Part VI for health care facilities and Part VII for marinas were added to the article, and the scope was revised to include those new Parts.

220.1 Scope

This article contains the requirements necessary for calculating demand loads for branch circuits, feeders, and services. ▶Figure 220–1

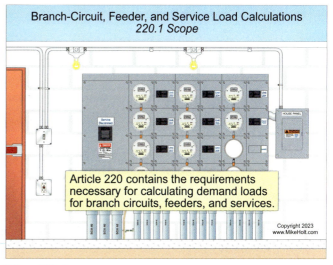
▶Figure 220–1

220.5 | Branch-Circuit, Feeder, and Service Load Calculations

- Part II provides the calculation method for branch circuits
- Parts III and IV provide the calculation for feeder and service loads
- Part VII provides the calculation methods for marinas, boatyards, floating buildings, and docking facilities

Note 2: See *NEC* Figure 220.1 for information on the organization of Article 220. ▶Figure 220-2

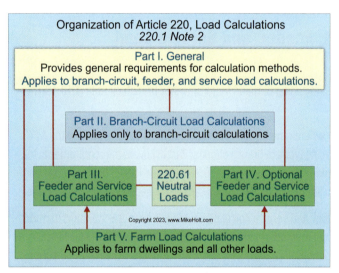

▶Figure 220-2

220.5 Calculations

The floor area calculation was relocated and was expanded to include the floor area of garages

Analysis

  This rule was relocated here from 220.11 because it is a general calculation and belongs in Part I, General, instead of in Part II with the branch-circuit calculations. The floor area included in the calculations was expanded to include everything except open porches, and spaces that are not adaptable to being used as a habitable room or occupiable space, in recognition that some lighting loads are in almost every area.

RELOCATED **EXPANDED**

220.5 Calculations

(A) Voltage Used for Calculations. Unless other voltages are specified, branch-circuit, feeder, and service loads must be calculated on nominal system voltages such as 120V, 120/240V, 120/208V, 240V, 277/480V, or 480V. ▶Figure 220-3

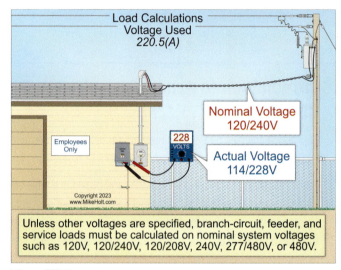

▶Figure 220-3

Author's Comment:

- According to Article 100, "Nominal System Voltage" is defined as a nominal value assigned to a circuit for convenient circuit identification. The actual voltage at which a circuit operates can vary from the nominal within a range that permits satisfactory operation of equipment.

(B) Rounding Fractions of Amperes. Calculations for branch-circuit, feeder, and service loads resulting in a decimal fraction 0.50 of an ampere can be rounded to the nearest whole number. ▶Figure 220-4

(C) Floor Area.

Commercial. For commercial buildings, the floor area for general lighting load calculations is based on the outside floor dimensions of the building. ▶Figure 220-5

Dwelling Units. For dwelling units, the floor area for general lighting load calculations is based on the outside floor dimensions of the building or other area involved, but does not include open porches or unfinished areas not adaptable for future use as a habitable room or occupiable space. ▶Figure 220-6

Branch-Circuit, Feeder, and Service Load Calculations | 220.53

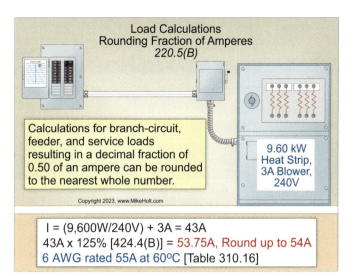
▶Figure 220–4

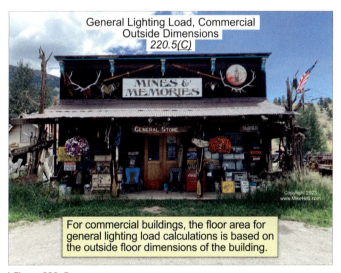
▶Figure 220–5

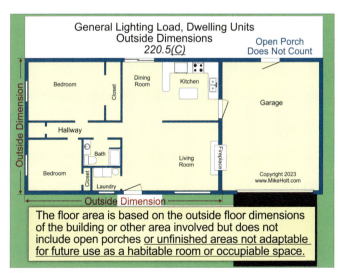
▶Figure 220–6

220.53 Appliance Load—Dwelling Unit(s)

Editorial changes were made in this section to clarify to what the rule applies.

Analysis

EXPANDED **EDITED**

There were a few editorial changes made in this section to improve its usability with no real technical change. Electric vehicle supply equipment (EVSE) was added as list item 5 to identify that these loads are significant, and no reduction is permitted.

220.53 Appliance Demand Load, Dwelling

A demand factor of 75 percent can be applied to the total connected load of four or more appliances rated ¼ hp or greater, or 500W or greater, that are fastened in place. ▶Figure 220–7

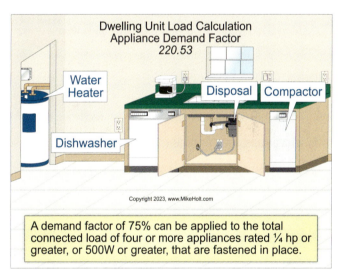
▶Figure 220–7

This demand factor does not apply to:

(1) Household electric cooking equipment that is fastened in place

(2) Clothes dryers

(3) Space-heating equipment

(4) Air-conditioning equipment

(5) Electric vehicle supply equipment (EVSE)

Changes to the National Electrical Code 2023 | MikeHolt.com | 93

220.57 | Branch-Circuit, Feeder, and Service Load Calculations

▶ **Not more than Four Appliances, Example**

Question: The conductor demand load for a dwelling unit containing a 1000 VA waste disposal, a 1500 VA dishwasher, and a 4500 VA water heater is _____. ▶Figure 220–8

(a) 6000 VA   (b) 7000 VA   (c) 8000 VA   (d) 9000 VA

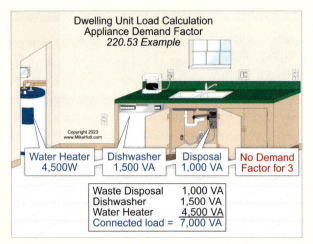

▶Figure 220–8

Solution:

Total Connected Load = 1000 VA + 1500 VA + 4500 VA
Total Connected Load = 7000 VA

Answer: *(b) 7000 VA*

▶ **More than four Appliances, Example**

Question: The conductor demand load for a dwelling unit containing a 1000 VA waste disposal, a 1500 VA dishwasher, a 1800 VA microwave, and a 4500 VA water heater is _____.

(a) 6600 VA   (b) 10,400 VA   (c) 11,250 VA   (d) 12,450 VA

Solution:

Step 1: Determine the total connected appliance nameplate load.

Total Connected Load = 1000 VA + 1500 VA + 1800 VA + 4500 VA
Total Connected Load = 8800 VA

Step 2: Determine the total demand load: Four units at 75 percent

Total Demand Load = 8800 VA × 75%
Total Demand Load = 6600 VA

Answer: *(a) 6600 VA*

220.57 Electric Vehicle Supply Equipment (EVSE) Load

This new section specifies the load that must be included for electric vehicle supply equipment.

Analysis

NEW As electric vehicles have grown in popularity, the rules for EVSEs are being updated to ensure the power needs for this equipment are met. This new section specifies that a load of 7200 VA or the nameplate rating of the equipment, whichever is larger, must be included for electric vehicle supply equipment. The continuous load from 625.42 is already taken into account when using the nameplate rating and no additional 125 percent demand factor is required for the calculation.

220.57 Electric Vehicle Supply Equipment Load

The load for electric vehicle supply equipment must be calculated at the larger of 7200 VA or the nameplate rating of the equipment.
▶Figure 220–9

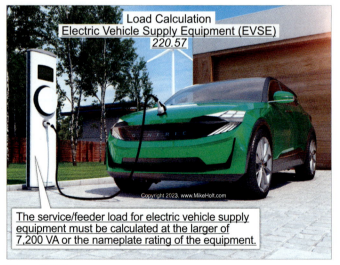

▶Figure 220–9

▶ **Example**

Question: What is the load for ten 9600W EVSEs?

(a) 56,000 VA   (b) 76,000 VA   (c) 86,000 VA   (d) 96,000 VA

Solution:

EVSE Load = 9600 VA x 10
EVSE Load = 96,000 VA

Answer: (d) 96,000 VA

220.60 Noncoincident Loads

Revisions in this section clarify that an air-conditioning load can be considered a noncoincident load.

Analysis

CLARIFIED Revisions to this section are intended to clarify that when determining the largest noncoincident load where the air-conditioning unit itself is the largest motor, you must use the air-conditioning load as the largest motor for the service calculation as well as the largest noncoincident load (which is usually the heat). This language is still a brain bender but if you take your time reading the rule, it makes sense.

220.60 Noncoincident Loads

If two or more loads are unlikely to be used at the same time, only the largest load is used for load calculations. The load must be the larger of the air-conditioning load at 125 percent [220.50(B)] as compared to the heating load at 100 percent [220.51].

▶ **Example**

Question: What is the demand load for one 16.70A, 240V air-conditioning unit and one 6 kW, 240V electric space heater? ▶Figure 220-10

(a) 5 kW   (b) 6 kW   (c) 11 kW   (d) none of these

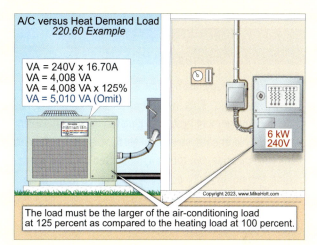

▶Figure 220-10

Solution:

Step 1: Determine the air-conditioning load at 125 percent in accordance with 220.50(B).

Air-Conditioning VA Load = 240V × 16.70A × 125%
Air-Conditioning VA Load = 4008 VA × 125%
Air-Conditioning VA Load = 5010 VA

Step 2: Determine the electric space heating load at 100 percent in accordance with 220.51.

Heat Load = 6000W

Step 3: Determine the larger of air-conditioning load at 125 percent as compared to heat load at 100 percent in accordance with 220.60.

Heat Load = 6000W

Answer: (b) 6 kW

220.70 Energy Management Systems (EMSs)

A new section was added for energy management systems that can control the maximum load of a service.

Analysis

NEW — Technology has become a big part of our electrical systems. This new section allows an energy management system to limit the maximum current used by the electrical system. I am sure there will be growing pains with this rule, but this is a major step forward in integrating technology with power systems on a large scale.

220.70 Energy Management Systems

If an energy management system is used to limit the current to a feeder or service in accordance with 750.30(C)(1)(2), the maximum ampere setpoint of the energy management system can be used in load calculations. The setpoint value of the energy management system is considered a continuous load.

220.87 Determining Existing Loads

The general Exception text was moved into the list item (1) Exception to indicate that it only applies to the one-year maximum demand data limiting its use with renewable energy systems.

Analysis

CLARIFIED — There is no significant change here, but it reminds us that the actual measured load of an existing installation can be used instead of a calculated load if you can meet the requirements of the rule. The general Exception text was moved into the Exception as list item (1) limiting the use of one year's maximum demand data to systems without solar PV, wind electric, or peak load shaving systems in use. This allows list items (2) and (3) to be used with such systems and so clarifies the intent of the rule.

220.87 Determining Existing Loads

The feeder or service calculated load for an existing building must be in accordance with all the following:

(1) The maximum demand data for a one-year period.

Ex: If the maximum demand data for a one-year period is not available, the calculated load is permitted to be based on the highest average kW for a 15-minute period over a period of 30 days. This calculation is not permitted if the occupancy has a renewable energy system (solar PV) or uses any form of peak load shaving. ▶Figure 220–11

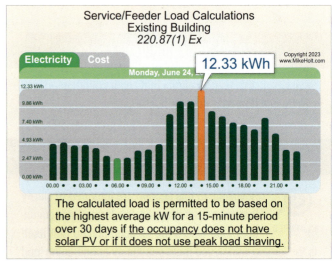

▶Figure 220–11

(2) The maximum demand at 125 percent plus the new load does not exceed the ampacity of the feeder or rating of the service.

(3) The feeder has overcurrent protection in accordance with 240.4, and the service has overload protection in accordance with 230.90.

220.120 Receptacle Loads

This is a relocated requirement from 555.6 for marina receptacle loads.

Branch-Circuit, Feeder, and Service Load Calculations | 220.120

Analysis

RELOCATED Part VII, Marinas, Boatyards, Floating Buildings, and Commercial and Noncommercial Docking Facilities, was added to this section and is the only section in this new Part VII. It was relocated (without technical change) from 555.6.

220.120 Shore Power Receptacle Loads

When calculating service and/or feeder ampacities for boat shore power receptacles, the demand factors shown in Table 220.120 can be applied.

Table 220.120 Demand Factors

Number of Shore Power Receptacles	Sum of the Rating of the Receptacles %
1–4	100
5–8	90
9–14	80
15–30	70
31–40	60
41–50	50
51–70	40
71 and Over	30

Note 1: Where shore power accommodations provide two receptacles specifically for an individual boat slip and these receptacles have different voltages (for example, one 30A, 125V and one 50A, 125/250V), only the receptacle with the larger kilowatt demand is required to be calculated. ▶Figure 220-12

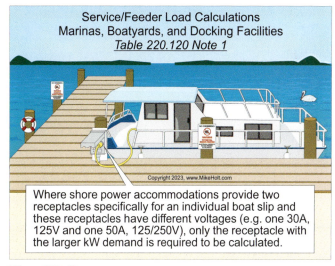

▶Figure 220-12

Notes

ARTICLE 225 — OUTSIDE BRANCH CIRCUITS AND FEEDERS

Introduction to Article 225—Outside Branch Circuits and Feeders

This article covers the installation requirements for equipment, including overhead and underground branch-circuit and feeder conductors outdoors on or between buildings, poles, and other structures on the premises. Conductors installed outdoors can serve many purposes such as area lighting, power for outdoor equipment, or for providing power to separate buildings or structures. It is important to remember that the power supply for buildings is not always a service conductor but may be feeder or branch-circuit conductors originating in another building. Never just assume that the conductors supplying power to a building are service conductors until you have identified where the service point is [Article 100] and have reviewed the Article 100 definitions for feeders, branch circuits, and service conductors. If you have correctly determined the conductors are service conductors, then use Article 230.

Part II of this article limits the number of feeders plus branch circuits to a building and provides rules regarding their disconnects. These requirements include the disconnect rating, construction characteristics, labeling, where to locate the disconnect, and the grouping of multiple disconnects.

225.1 Scope

The scope was revised to say this article does not apply to outside branch circuits and feeders over 1000V ac or 1500V dc

Analysis

EDITED

The new Article 235 was added to address installations of these higher voltage systems, so this one is limited to voltages that are not greater than 1000V ac or 1500V dc. The Informational Note directs users to Part IV of Article 235 for the higher voltage systems.

225.1 Scope

Article 225 contains the installation requirements for outside branch circuits and feeders installed on or between buildings, structures, or poles. ▶Figure 225–1

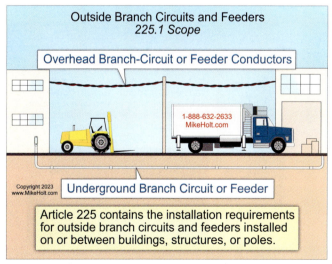

▶Figure 225–1

225.27 | Outside Branch Circuits and Feeders

Author's Comment:

▸ Review the following in Article 100:
  ▸ "Branch Circuit"
  ▸ "Building"
  ▸ "Feeder"
  ▸ "Structure"

225.27 Raceway Seal

Two references were added to clarify the requirements for sealing raceways.

Analysis

CLARIFIED References to 300.7(A) and 300.5(G) were added in this section to provide more guidance on how to seal raceways.

225.27 Raceway Seals

Where a raceway enters a building or structure from outside, it must be sealed in accordance with 300.5(G) and 300.7(A). Sealants must be identified for use with cable insulation, conductor insulation, bare conductor, shield, or other components. ▸Figure 225–2

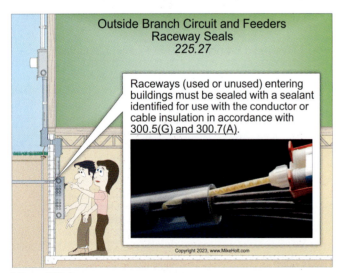
▸Figure 225–2

225.41 Emergency Disconnects

This new section requires outside emergency disconnects for feeders supplied to one- and two-family dwelling units, and mirrors the requirements in 230.85 for service-supplied dwelling units.

Analysis

NEW This new section requires outside emergency disconnects for feeders supplied to one- and two-family dwelling units. This mirrors the requirements in 230.85 for service-supplied dwelling units so first responders are always able to shut off the power on the exterior of a dwelling regardless of how it is supplied.

Section 225.41(B) requires the identification of the location of other isolation disconnects for other power sources where those disconnects are not located adjacent to the emergency disconnect.

225.41 Emergency (Shutoff) Disconnects

For one- and two-family dwelling units, an emergency disconnect must be installed for first responders and others.

(A) General.

(1) Location. The emergency disconnect must be installed in a readily accessible outdoor location on or within sight of the dwelling unit. ▸Figure 225–3

(2) Rating. The emergency disconnect must have a short-circuit current rating equal to or greater than the available fault current.

(3) Grouping. If more than one emergency disconnect is provided, they must be grouped.

(B) Identification of Other Disconnects. Where disconnects for other energy source systems are not adjacent to the emergency disconnect, a plaque or directory identifying the location of other energy source disconnects must be adjacent to the emergency disconnect.

Note: See 445.18, 480.7, 705.20, and 706.15 for examples of other energy source system isolation means.

(C) Marking. The emergency disconnect must be marked "EMERGENCY DISCONNECT."

225.42 Surge Protection

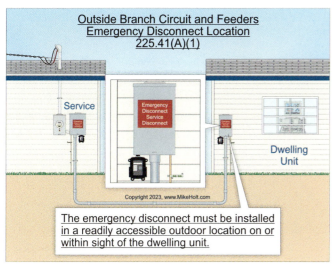
▶Figure 225–3

Markings must be permanently affixed and be sufficiently durable to withstand the environment involved in accordance with 110.21(B) and comply with following:

(1) The emergency disconnect marking or label must be on the outside front of the disconnect with a red background and white text.

(2) The letters must be at least ½ in. high.

225.42 Surge Protection

This new section requires surge protection for various occupancies supplied by feeders.

Analysis

 NEW Surge protection requirements have expanded for the last few *Code* cycles. This new rule requires surge protection for dwellings, dormitories, guest rooms and guest suites of hotels and motels, and areas of nursing homes and limited care facilities. This revision is sure to catch many people off guard, and mirrors the same expansion of SPD requirements for services that we will see in 230.67.

The SPD must be located in or adjacent to the distribution equipment at the second building.

225.42 Surge Protection

(A) Surge-Protective Device (SPD). Where a feeder supplies any of the following occupancies, a surge-protective device must be provided:

(1) Dwelling units ▶Figure 225–4

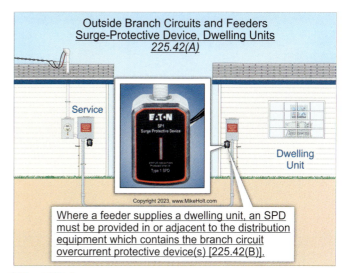
▶Figure 225–4

(2) Dormitory units

(3) Guest rooms and guest suites of hotels and motels

(4) Areas of nursing homes and limited care facilities used exclusively as patient sleeping rooms

(B) Location. The SPD must be installed in or adjacent to distribution equipment connected to the load side of the feeder, which contains the branch-circuit overcurrent protective device(s).

Note: Surge protection is most effective when closest to the branch circuit. Surges can be generated from multiple sources including, but not limited to, lightning, the electric utility, or utilization equipment.

(C) Type. The SPD must be either Type 1 or Type 2.

(D) Replacement. Where the distribution equipment supplied by the feeder is replaced, an SPD must be installed in or adjacent to the distribution equipment.

(E) Ratings. SPDs must have a nominal discharge current rating (In) of not less than 10 kA.

Note: Lead lengths of conductors to the SPD should be kept as short as possible to reduce let-through voltages.

Notes

ARTICLE 230 SERVICES

Introduction to Article 230—Services

This article covers the installation requirements for service conductors and their first means of disconnect. It consists of seven parts:

- Part I. General
- Part II. Overhead Service Conductors
- Part III. Underground Service Conductors
- Part IV. Service-Entrance Conductors
- Part V. Service Disconnect
- Part VI. Disconnecting Means
- Part VIII. Overcurrent Protection

230.1 Scope

The scope was revised to limit the application of this article to systems not greater than 1000V ac or 1500V dc.

Analysis

EDITED With the addition of the new Article 235, the requirements for services over 1000V ac or 1500V dc are now found in Part V of that article.

230.1 Scope

Article 230 covers the installation requirements for service conductors and service disconnects not over 1000V ac or 1500V dc. ▶Figure 230–1

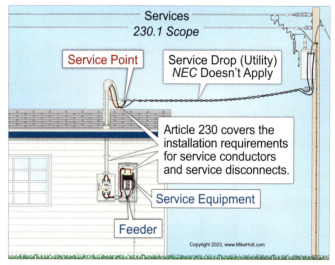

▶Figure 230–1

230.7 Service Conductors Separate from Other Conductors

Handholes and underground boxes were added to the items that must not contain both service conductors and other conductors.

Analysis

EXPANDED

The intent of this rule is to limit exposure to the dangers of unfused service conductors. Previously, unfused service conductors could not occupy the same raceway or cable with other conductors. Deleting "raceway or cable" from the title and adding "handholes and underground boxes" to the rule text expands this rule to include all the scenarios exposing the end user to unnecessary dangers from these conductors. If they add junction or pull boxes in 2026, they will have a home run.

230.7 Service Conductors Separate from Other Conductors

Feeder and branch-circuit conductors are not permitted to be installed in the same raceway, cable, handhole enclosure, or underground box with service conductors. ▶Figure 230-2

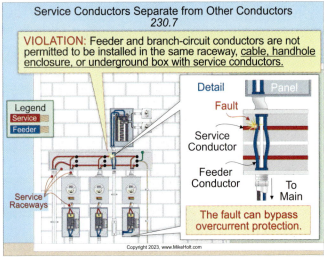

▶Figure 230-2

Ex 1: Grounding electrode conductors or supply-side bonding jumpers can be in a service raceway with service conductors.

Warning

⚠️ **WARNING:** If service, feeder, and/or branch-circuit conductors are installed in the same raceway, and a short-circuit occurs between the service and feeder or branch-circuit conductors, the feeder or branch-circuit overcurrent protection will be bypassed.

Author's Comment:

▸ Service, feeder, and branch-circuit conductors are permitted in the service disconnect enclosure.

▸ Feeders and branch-circuit conductors can be in the same raceway or enclosure. ▶Figure 230-3

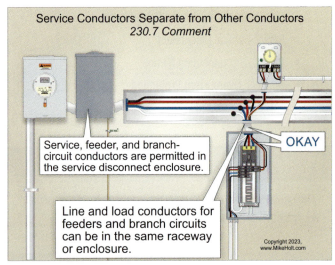

▶Figure 230-3

230.8 Raceway Seal

This section was expanded to include a requirement to seal service raceways anywhere they enter a building or structure.

Services | 230.24

Analysis

EXPANDED The requirements here were expanded to include all locations where a service raceway enters a building or structure. The 2020 *Code* only required those raceways entering from underground locations to be sealed.

A reference was added to 300.7(A) requiring a seal where there is a temperature difference between the inside and outside of the raceway that could cause condensation.

The sealing material must now be identified for use with the cable insulation or the bare conductor, which was not required in the 2020 *Code* cycle.

230.8 Raceway Seals

Where a raceway enters a building or structure from outside, it must be sealed in accordance with 300.5(G) and 300.7(A). Sealants must be identified for use with cable insulation, conductor insulation, bare conductor, shield, or other components. ▶Figure 230-4

▶Figure 230-4

230.24 Clearances

This rule was intended to apply to all Article 680 installations, so the title in (D) was updated to reflect this intent.

Analysis

CLARIFIED The term "swimming pools" in the title was intended to apply to all Article 680 installations. Adding the phrase "Fountains, and Similar Installations" to the title in (D) clarified the intent of the rule.

230.24 Vertical Clearance for Overhead Service Conductors

Overhead service conductor spans must maintain vertical clearances as follows:

(A) Above Roofs. A minimum of 8 ft <u>6 in.</u> above the surface of a roof for a minimum distance of 3 ft in all directions from the edge of the roof.

Ex 2: If the slope of the roof exceeds 4 in. of vertical rise for every 12 in. of horizontal run, 120/208V or 120/240V overhead service conductor clearances can be reduced to 3 ft over the roof.

Ex 3: If no more than 6 ft of conductors pass over no more than 4 ft of roof overhang, 120/208V or 120/240V overhead service conductor clearances over the roof overhang can be reduced to 18 in. ▶Figure 230-5

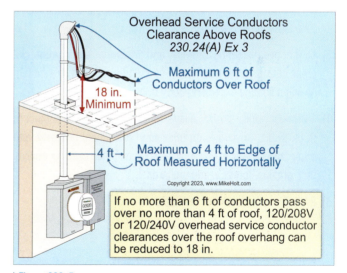
▶Figure 230-5

Ex 4: The 3-ft vertical clearance for overhead service conductors that extends from the roof does not apply when the point of attachment is on the side of the building below the roof.

Ex 5: If the voltage between conductors does not exceed 300V and the roof area is guarded or isolated, the clearance can be reduced to 3 ft.

(B) Vertical Clearance for Overhead Service Conductors. Overhead service conductor spans must maintain the following vertical clearances: ▶Figure 230-6

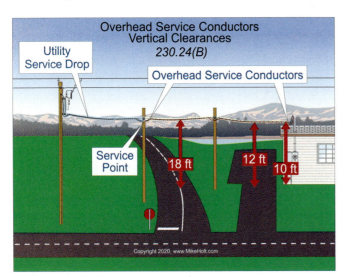

▶Figure 230-6

(1) 10 ft above finished grade, sidewalks, platforms, or projections that permit personal contact for circuits supplied by 120/208V or 120/240V.

(2) 12 ft above residential property and driveways, and commercial areas not subject to truck traffic, for circuits supplied by 120/208V, 120/240V, or 277/480V.

(3) 15 ft above residential property and driveways, and commercial areas not subject to truck traffic for circuits supplied by a system having a voltage exceeding 300V to ground.

(4) 18 ft over public streets, alleys, roads, parking areas subject to truck traffic, driveways on other than residential property, and other areas traversed by vehicles such as those used for cultivation, grazing, forestry, and orchards.

(5) 24 ft 6 in. over tracks of railroads.

230.43 Wiring Methods for 1000V, Nominal, or Less

The use of properly identified Type TC-ER cable was expanded, and flexible bus systems are now an option as service-entrance conductors.

Analysis

CLARIFIED   EXPANDED

List item (20) permitted the use of Type TC-ER cable as service-entrance conductors in the 2020 *Code*. The product standard does not require that type of cable to be evaluated for use as service-entrance conductors so the language now clarifies that TC-ER used for service conductors must be identified for that use.

NEW

List item (21) for the flexible bus systems found in the new Article 371 was added here to correlate with 371.10(1) which permits flexible bus systems to be used for services.

230.43 Wiring Methods

Service-entrance conductors can be installed with any of the following wiring methods:

(1) Open wiring on insulators

(3) Rigid metal conduit

(4) Intermediate metal conduit

(5) Electrical metallic tubing

(6) Electrical nonmetallic tubing

(7) Service-entrance cables

(8) Wireways

(11) PVC conduit

(13) Type MC cable

(15) Flexible metal conduit or liquidtight flexible metal conduit in lengths not longer than 6 ft

(16) Liquidtight flexible nonmetallic conduit ▶Figure 230-7

(17) High-density polyethylene conduit

(18) Nonmetallic underground conduit with conductors

(19) Reinforced thermosetting resin conduit

(20) Type TC-ER cable <u>identified for use as service-entrance conductors</u>

(21) <u>Flexible bus system</u>

Services | 230.67

▶Figure 230-7

(B) Guarded. Energized parts that are not enclosed must be installed on a switchboard, panelboard, or control board and guarded in accordance with 110.18 and 110.27. Where energized parts are guarded as provided in 110.27(A)(1) and (A)(2), a means for locking or sealing doors providing access to energized parts must be provided.

(C) Barriers. Barriers must be placed on energized uninsulated phase service busbar or service terminals exposed to inadvertent contact when the service disconnect is in the open position. ▶Figure 230-8

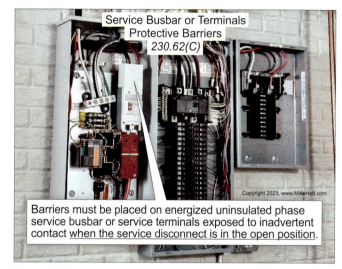

▶Figure 230-8

230.62 Service Equipment— Enclosed or Guarded

Language was added to clarify where line-side terminal barriers are required.

Analysis

CLARIFIED The rule in 230.62(C) was changed to clarify that protective barriers are required for any uninsulated exposed parts on the line side of the service disconnect when in the open position. This was always the intent of the rule, but the language was not completely clear.

Author's Comment:

▸ The line-side of the service disconnect will have energized parts even with the disconnect in the open position. Barriers provide some measure of safety against inadvertent contact with line-side energized parts.

230.67 Surge Protection

This section was expanded to cover occupancies other than dwellings and to establish a minimum nominal discharge current for surge-protective devices.

230.62 Service Equipment—Enclosed or Guarded

Energized parts of service equipment must be enclosed as specified in 230.62(A) or guarded as specified in 230.62(B).

(A) Enclosed. Energized parts must be enclosed so they will not be exposed to accidental contact or must be guarded in accordance with 230.62(B).

1st Printing | Changes to the National Electrical Code 2023 | MikeHolt.com | 107

230.67 | Services

Analysis

EXPANDED — Changes to 230.67(A) now require surge protection for dwelling units, dormitory units, guest rooms and guest suites of hotels and motels, and areas of nursing homes and limited care facilities used exclusively as patient sleeping rooms.

NEW — The new subdivision (E) now requires a minimum nominal discharge rating of 10 kA for the surge-protective devices recognized in this section.

▶Figure 230–10

230.67 Surge Protection

(A) Surge-Protective Device. Where a service supplies any of the following occupancies, a surge-protective device must be provided:

(1) Dwelling units ▶Figure 230–9

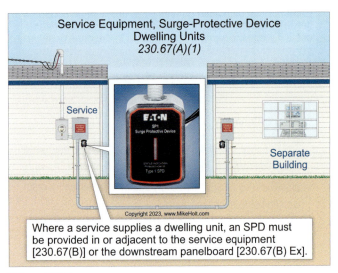

▶Figure 230–9

(2) Dormitory units

(3) Guest rooms and guest suites of hotels and motels

(4) Areas of nursing homes and limited care facilities used exclusively as patient sleeping rooms

(B) Location. The surge-protective device must be an integral part of the service disconnect or be immediately adjacent to the service disconnect. ▶Figure 230–10

Ex: The surge-protective device is permitted to be at the downstream panelboard.

Author's Comment:

▸ An example of the application of this exception is where there is an exterior meter main that feeds an interior panel. The SPD could be installed at the interior panel using the exception.

▸ See Parts I and II of Article 242 for installation requirements that apply to SPDs.

(C) Type. The surge-protective device must be a Type 1 or Type 2 SPD.

(D) Replacement. Where service equipment is replaced, surge protection must be installed.

(E) Rating. SPDs must have a nominal discharge current rating of not less than 10 kA.

Author's Comment:

▸ Lead lengths of conductors to the SPD should be kept as short as possible to reduce let-through voltages.

Services | 230.71

230.71 Maximum Number of Disconnects

This section caused a lot of stir in the 2020 *Code* cycle by requiring a physical barrier between each of the sections of a meter pack or switchgear without a main disconnecting means. Several revisions here aim to solve some of the field issues created by the rules last cycle while preserving the intended added safety.

Analysis

CLARIFIED The revision to 230.71(B)(3) clarifies that the vertical barriers between the sections of switchboards must maintain the inadvertent contact protective barriers between adjacent sections.

EXPANDED Section 230.71(B)(4) was expanded to require each have a separate compartment for multiple service disconnects in transfer switches.

NEW Section 230.71(B)(5) is new and permits meter centers with a main service disconnecting means upstream of the metering center in a separate compartment to be used to meet the intent of this rule.

NEW Section 230.71(B)(6) is also new and adds MCCs to the types of service disconnecting equipment covered under this rule. The previous Informational Note said that MCCs are one of the types of equipment covered by this rule, but this revision now places it in enforceable text. Up to two service disconnects in an MCC are permitted, provided each is in its own unit and there are barriers to prevent inadvertent contact between the units.

NEW A new Exception was added to 230.71(B) permitting the use of spare service disconnect spaces in equipment installed prior to the adoption of the 2020 *NEC*.

230.71 Number of Service Disconnects

Each service must have only one service disconnect except as permitted in 230.71(B). ▶Figure 230–11

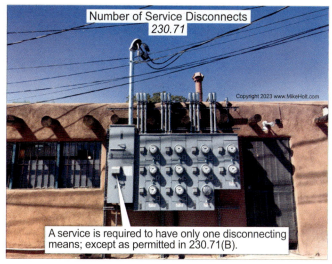

▶Figure 230–11

(B) Two to Six Service Disconnecting Means. Each service can have up to six service disconnects in accordance with 230.71(B)(1) through (5). ▶Figure 230–12

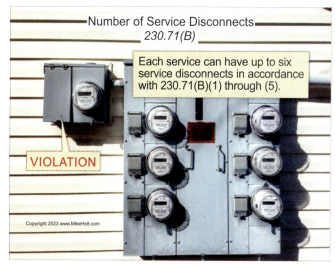

▶Figure 230–12

Caution

⚠ **CAUTION:** This rule limits six disconnects for each service or set of service-entrance conductors. For example, if the building has more than one service as permitted by 230.2, then there can be more than six service disconnects at the building. ▶Figure 230–13

Changes to the National Electrical Code 2023 | MikeHolt.com | 109

230.85 | Services

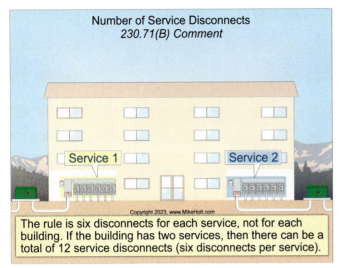
▶Figure 230-13

The two to six service disconnects can consist of a combination of any of the following:

(1) Separate enclosures with a service disconnect in each enclosure.

(2) Panelboards with a service disconnect in each panelboard.

(3) Switchboard(s) where there is only one service disconnect in each separate vertical section with barriers provided between each vertical section from the adjacent section.

(4) Switchgear, transfer switches, or metering centers where each service disconnect is in a separate compartment.

(5) Metering centers with a service disconnect upstream in a separate compartment of each metering center.

Ex: Existing service equipment in compliance with previous editions of this Code that permitted multiple service disconnects is permitted to contain a maximum of six service disconnects.

230.85 Emergency Disconnects

This section was editorially revised into parent text and second level subdivisions with some technical changes.

Analysis

CLARIFIED   REORGANIZED

Section 230.85(A)(1) clarifies that emergency disconnects not attached to a dwelling unit must be installed at a readily accessible location on or within sight of the dwelling unit. This means you now must be able to see the emergency disconnect from the dwelling unit, and it must be within 50 ft.

An Exception was added to 230.85(A)(1) where the dwelling unit is supplied by a feeder and a feeder emergency disconnect has been installed.

REORGANIZED

Part of the reorganization of this rule is the new second level subdivision in 230.85(A)(2) requiring the emergency disconnect to have a short-circuit rating equal to or greater than the available fault current.

A requirement to group multiple disconnects together was relocated to (A)(3) from the main rule, and the types of emergency disconnects permitted for this rule were relocated to (B).

NEW

A new Informational Note 1 tells us the conductors between the disconnects permitted in (B)(2) and (B)(3) are service conductors and Informational Note 2 advises us that equipment marked "suitable for use only as service equipment" is not appropriate for use as the disconnect permitted in (B)(3).

NEW

A new rule 230.85(C) requires an emergency disconnect to be installed when the service equipment is replaced. A new Exception indicates that if you only replace the meter socket or the service-entrance conductors, the requirements of this section do not apply.

NEW

A new requirement in (D) requires installing a plaque or directory adjacent to the emergency disconnect required for the service that identifies the locations of emergency disconnects for other sources or systems.

RELOCATED

The labeling requirements for emergency disconnects were relocated into 230.85(E) and specify that labels must be red in color with white text at least ½ in. high.

230.85 Emergency (Shutoff) Disconnect

For one- and two-family dwelling units, an emergency disconnect must be installed for first responders and others in accordance with (A) through (E).

(A) General.

(1) Location. The required emergency disconnect must be installed at a readily accessible outdoor location within sight of the dwelling unit.

Ex: Where the requirements of 225.41 are met, this section does not apply.

(2) Rating. The emergency disconnect must have a short-circuit current rating equal to or greater than the available fault current.

(3) Grouping. If more than one emergency disconnect is provided, they must be grouped.

(B) Type. Each emergency disconnect must be one of the following types:

(1) The emergency disconnect can be the service disconnect required by 230.70.

Author's Comment:

▸ An automatic transfer switch that is rated for service equipment can be used to meet the service disconnect requirements of 230.70 and the emergency disconnect requirement.

(3) The emergency disconnect can be a switch or circuit breaker, installed on the supply side of each service disconnect, marked "suitable for use as service equipment," but not marked as "suitable only for use as service equipment." ▸Figure 230–14

Note 1: Conductors between the emergency disconnect and the service disconnect in 230.85(2) and 230.85(3) are service conductors.

Note 2: Equipment marked "Suitable only for use as service equipment" has a factory marking "Service Disconnect."

Author's Comment:

▸ The emergency disconnect in 230.85(3) cannot be marked "Suitable only for use as service equipment" because it would require the equipment to be modified after leaving the factory by removing the marking "Service Disconnect" and by removing the factory installed main bonding jumper.

(C) Replacement. Where a service disconnect is replaced, all the requirements of this section apply.

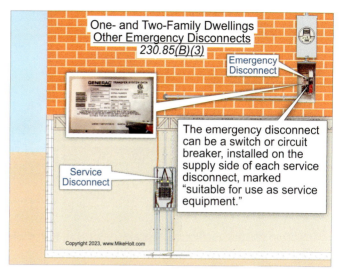

▸Figure 230–14

Ex: Where only meter sockets, service-entrance conductors, or related raceways and fittings are replaced, an emergency disconnect is not required.

(D) Identification of Other Isolation Disconnects. Where disconnects for other energy source systems are not adjacent to the emergency disconnect, a plaque or directory identifying the location of all other energy source disconnects must be adjacent to the emergency disconnect.

Note: For examples of other energy source system disconnecting means, see 445.19, 480.7, 705.20, and 706.15.

(E) Marking.

(1) Marking Text. The disconnect must be marked as follows:

(1) Service conductors terminating in an outdoor service disconnect must be marked: EMERGENCY DISCONNECT, SERVICE DISCONNECT. ▸Figure 230–15

(3) Service conductors terminating in a switch or circuit breaker on the load side of the meter and supply side of the service disconnect must be marked: EMERGENCY DISCONNECT, NOT SERVICE EQUIPMENT. ▸Figure 230–16

230.85 | Services

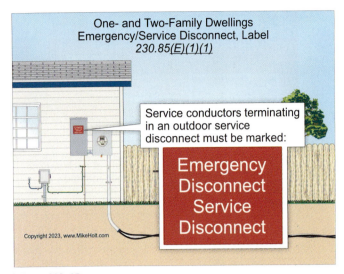

▶Figure 230–15

▶Figure 230–16

Author's Comment:

▸ List item (3) permits, when replacing a service, to replace the interior service equipment and install an "EMERGENCY DISCONNECT, NOT SERVICE EQUIPMENT" on the outside of the building without having to change the location of the existing service bonding and grounding requirements contained in 250.24.

(2) Marking Location and Size. Markings must be permanently affixed and be sufficiently durable to withstand the environment involved in accordance with 110.21(B) and comply with following:

(1) The marking or labels must be on the outside front of the disconnect with a red background and white text.

(2) The letters must be at least ½ in. high.

ARTICLE 240 — OVERCURRENT PROTECTION

Introduction to Article 240—Overcurrent Protection

This article provides the requirements for overcurrent protection and selecting and installing overcurrent protective devices—typically circuit breakers or fuses.

240.4 Protection of Conductors

There was a laundry list of revisions in this section. Here is the rundown.

- Overcurrent protective device requirements for 800A or less were clarified.
- The word "wire" was replaced with "conductor."
- Type CF fuses are now permitted.
- A reference to Article 440 Part IV was added to Table 240.4(G).
- A new (D)(3) was added to address 14 AWG copper-clad aluminum conductors.
- A new (H) was added to correlate dwelling unit service and feeder conductors with the general requirements.

Whew!

Analysis

CLARIFIED New language in 240.4(B) clarifies that an overcurrent protective device rated 800A or less may be set to a value greater than the ampacity of the conductors but must be equal to or less than the next standard size OCPD. This was not clear previously and this change clarifies that adjustable trip circuit breakers are permitted.

EDITED   EXPANDED The word "wire" was replaced with "conductor" to comply with the requirements in the *NEC* Style Manual. Class CF fuses were added to the types of fuses permitted for the conductors in (D)(1) and (D)(2).

Comment: Class CF fuses have let-through current values that are equivalent to Class J fuses and will provide equivalent protection.

NEW The new (D)(3) specifies that the overcurrent protection for 14 AWG copper-clad aluminum is 10A, provided the continuous load does not exceed 8A and the branch-circuit OCPD is a breaker or fuse listed and marked for use with 14 AWG copper-clad aluminum.

NEW   CLARIFIED The table was revised to include Part IV of Article 440 for air-conditioning and refrigeration equipment circuit conductors. Without that reference we do not know we are permitted to size the conductors for an air-conditioning unit differently than we would normally size branch-circuit conductors. This issue goes back to the 1971 *Code* cycle when Article 440 first appeared in the *NEC*. This change in the 2023 *Code* corrects this long-standing oversight.

NEW Nothing in 240.4 allowed dwelling unit service and feeder conductors to be sized at 83 percent of the overcurrent device rating. A new first level subdivision (H) was finally added to permit this.

240.4 Overcurrent Protection of Conductors

Overcurrent protection for conductors is required in accordance with their ampacities as specified in 310.14, except as permitted by (A) through (H). ▶Figure 240-1 and ▶Figure 240-2

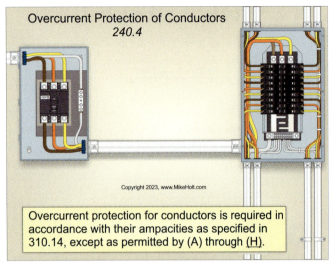

▶Figure 240-1

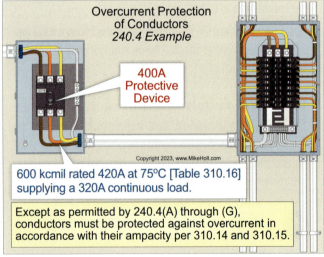

▶Figure 240-2

Author's Comment:

▸ Table 310.16 contains conductor ampacities based on up to three current-carrying conductors in a raceway and in an ambient temperature of 86°F or 30°C at up to 2000V. If any other conditions apply such as more than three current-carrying conductors, or a different ambient temperature, the ampacities found in Table 310.16 must be corrected in accordance with 310.15(B) and adjusted in accordance with 310.15(C).

▸ Overcurrent protection of conductors is a critical safety component to ensure an electric circuit will fail properly. Bypassing overcurrent protection is extremely dangerous to persons and property. ▶Figure 240-3

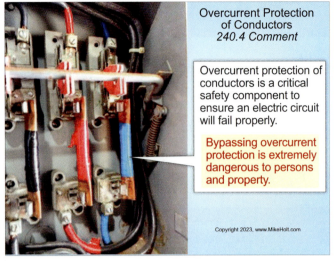

▶Figure 240-3

▸ Overcurrent protection of flexible cords, flexible cables, and fixture wires must be provided in accordance with 240.5.

(B) Overcurrent Protective Devices Rated 800A or Less. The next higher standard overcurrent device rating (above the ampacity of the phase conductors being protected) is permitted, provided conditions (1) through (3) are met:

(1) The conductors are not part of a branch circuit supplying more than one receptacle for cord-and-plug-connected loads.

(2) The ampacity of a conductor, after the application of ambient temperature correction [Table 310.15(B)(1)(1)], conductor bundling adjustment [Table 310.15(C)(1)], or both, does not correspond with the standard rating of a fuse or circuit breaker in accordance with 240.6(A).

(3) The next higher standard overcurrent protective device rating from 240.6(A) does not exceed 800A.

If the overcurrent protective device is an adjustable trip device in accordance with 240.4(B)(1), it is permitted to be set to a value that does not exceed the next higher standard value above the ampacity of the conductors being protected when in compliance with 240.6(C).

▶ **Example**

Question: According to Table 310.16, what is the maximum size overcurrent protective device that can be used to protect 500 kcmil conductors where each conductor has an ampacity of 380A at 75°C?
▶Figure 240-4

(a) 300A (b) 350A (c) 400A (d) 500A

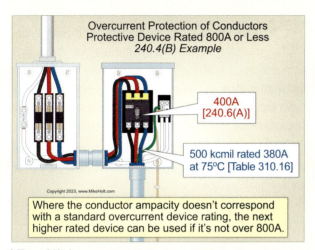
▶Figure 240-4

Answer: (c) 400A [240.6(A)]

(C) Overcurrent Protective Devices Rated Over 800A. If the circuit's overcurrent protective device exceeds 800A, the conductor ampacity, after the application of ambient temperature correction [310.15(B)(1)(1)], conductor spacing adjustment [Table 310.15(C)(1)], or both, must have an ampere rating or setting of not less than the rating of the overcurrent protective device defined in 240.6.

▶ **Example**

Question: What is the minimum size of conductors, paralleled in three conductors per phase, allowed to be protected by a 1200A overcurrent protective device? ▶Figure 240-5

(a) 400 kcmil (b) 500 kcmil (c) 600 kcmil (d) 750 kcmil
Solution:

The total ampacity of the three parallel conductor sets must be equal to or greater than 1200A [240.4(C)]. The ampacity for each conductor within the parallel set must be equal to or greater than 400A (1200A/3 raceways).

Conductor Size = 600 kcmil conductors per phase rated 420A at 75°C [110.14(C)(1)(b)(2) and Table 310.16]

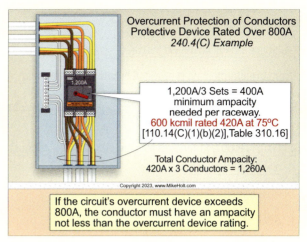
▶Figure 240-5

Total Conductor Ampacity = 420A × 3 conductors
Total Conductor Ampacity = 1260A, okay for a 1200A overcurrent protective device

Answer: (c) 600 kcmil

(D) Small Conductors. Unless permitted in 240.4(E) or (G), overcurrent protection for conductors is not permitted to exceed the following:
▶Figure 240-6

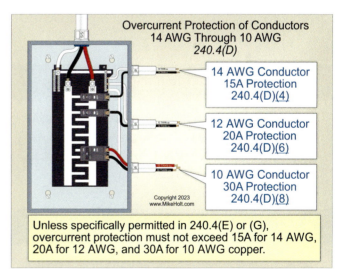
▶Figure 240-6

(1) 18 AWG Copper—7A.

(2) 16 AWG Copper—10A.

240.6 | Overcurrent Protection

(3) 14 AWG Copper-Clad Aluminum. 10A, provided all the following conditions are met:

(1) Continuous loads do not exceed 8A.

(2) Overcurrent protection is provided by one of the following:

   a. Circuit breakers listed and marked for use with 14 AWG copper-clad aluminum conductors.

   b. Fuses listed and marked for use with 14 AWG copper-clad aluminum conductors

(4) 14 AWG Copper—15A.

(5) 12 AWG Aluminum and Copper-Clad Aluminum—15A.

(6) 12 AWG Copper—20A.

(7) 10 AWG Aluminum and Copper-Clad Aluminum—25A.

(8) 10 AWG Copper—30A.

(E) Tap Conductors. Tap conductors must have overcurrent protection in accordance with the following:

(1) Household Ranges, Cooking Appliances, and Other Loads [210.19(D)].

(2) Fixture Wire [240.5(B)(2)].

(3) Location in Circuit [240.21].

240.6 Standard Ampere Ratings

A 10A standard rating was added to the fuse and circuit-breaker table, and a need for cybersecurity awareness was addressed in a new Informational Note for remotely accessible adjustable trip circuit breakers.

Analysis

EXPANDED To accommodate the new 10A branch circuits used with 14 AWG copper-clad aluminum conductors, 10A was added to Table 240.6(A). Another win for CCA!

NEW Cybersecurity is a concern in every area of society. Because the number of remotely accessible adjustable trip circuit breakers have increased, the word "local" was added to the title for (C) to differentiate it from the new (D) for remotely accessible adjustable trip circuit breakers.

NEW Section 240.6(D) permits circuit breakers to have remote access to the current settings by either connecting directly to the breaker through a non-networked interface or via a network interface if the software is identified as evaluated for cybersecurity and a cybersecurity assessment is completed and made available to those who inspect, operate, and maintain the system.

Comment: The Informational Notes in this rule reference standards and documents that can be used for the assessment process.

240.6 Standard Ampere Ratings

(A) Fuses and Fixed-Trip Circuit Breakers. The standard ratings in amperes for fuses and inverse time circuit breakers are shown in Table 240.6(A). Additional standard ampere ratings for fuses are 1A, 3A, 6A, and 601A.

Table 240.6(A) Standard Ampere Ratings for Fuses and Inverse Time Circuit Breakers Standard Ampere Ratings

10	15	20	25	30
35	40	45	50	60
70	80	90	100	110
125	150	175	200	225
250	300	350	400	450
500	600	700	800	1000
1200	1600	2000	2500	3000

(B) Adjustable Trip Circuit Breakers, Without Restricted Access. The ampere rating of an adjustable trip circuit breaker without restricted access is equal to its maximum long-time pickup current setting.

Overcurrent Protection | 240.24

(C) Adjustable Trip Circuit Breakers, Local Restricted Access. The ampere rating of adjustable trip circuit breakers with restricted access to the adjusting means is equal to the adjusted long-time pickup current settings. Restricted access is achieved by one of the following methods:

(1) Locating behind removable and sealable covers over the adjusting means

(2) Locating behind bolted equipment enclosure doors

(3) Locating behind locked doors accessible only to qualified personnel

(4) Being password protected with the password only accessible to qualified personnel

Author's Comment:

▸ According to Article 100, an adjustable circuit breaker permits the circuit breaker to be set to trip at various values of current, time (or both), within a predetermined range. ▶Figure 240–7

▶Figure 240–7

(D) Adjustable-Trip Circuit Breakers, Remotely Accessible. A circuit breaker(s) that can be adjusted remotely to modify the adjusting means is permitted to have an ampere rating(s) that is equal to the adjusted current setting (long-time pickup setting).

Remote access must be achieved by one of the following methods:

(1) Connected directly through a local nonnetworked interface.

(2) Connected through a networked interface complying with one of the following methods:

a. The circuit breaker and associated software for adjusting the settings are identified as being evaluated for cybersecurity.

b. A cybersecurity assessment of the network is completed. Documentation of the assessment and certification must be made available to those authorized to inspect, operate, and maintain the system.

Note 3: Cybersecurity is a specialized field requiring constant, vigilant attention to security vulnerabilities that could arise due to software defects, system configuration changes, or user interactions. Installation of devices that can be secured is an important first step but not sufficient to guarantee a secure system.

240.24 Location of Overcurrent Protective Devices

Revisions to this rule clarify that OCPDs are no longer permitted in any bathroom or area with showers.

Analysis

CLARIFIED The term "overcurrent devices" was changed to "overcurrent protective devices" throughout this section for clarity and to correlate with the Article 100 definitions.

EXPANDED In the 2020 *Code*, dwelling units, dormitory units, or guest suites were not permitted to have OCPDs located in bathrooms. The list of locations in (E) was deleted this cycle and the rule was expanded to apply to all bathrooms, showering facilities, and locker rooms with showering facilities.

240.24 Location of Overcurrent Protective Devices

(E) Not in Bathroom Areas. Overcurrent protective devices are not permitted to be installed in bathroom areas, showering facilities, or locker rooms with showering facilities. ▶Figure 240–8

240.24 | Overcurrent Protection

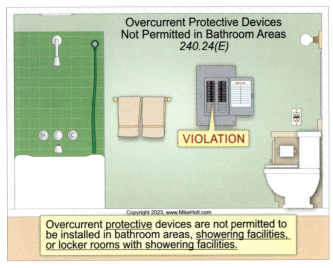

▶Figure 240-8

Author's Comment:

▶ The service disconnect switch is not permitted to be installed in a bathroom area even in commercial or industrial facilities [230.70(A)(2)].

ARTICLE 242
OVERVOLTAGE PROTECTION

Introduction to Article 242—Overvoltage Protection

Part I of this article provides the general installation and connection requirements for overvoltage protection and overvoltage protective devices (surge-protective devices or SPDs). Part II covers SPDs rated 1 kV or less that are permanently installed on premises wiring systems.

Surge-protective devices are designed to reduce transient voltages present on premises power distribution wiring and load-side equipment, particularly electronic equipment such as computers, telecommunications equipment, security systems, and electronic appliances.

These transient voltages can originate from several sources, including anything from lightning to laser printers. Voltage spikes and transients caused by the switching of utility power lines, power factor correction capacitors, or lightning can reach thousands of volts and amperes. ▶Figure 242–1

Voltage spikes and transients produced by premises equipment such as photocopiers, laser printers, and other high reactive loads cycling off and on can be in the hundreds of volts. ▶Figure 242–2

The best line of defense for all types of electronic equipment may be the installation of surge-protective devices at the electrical service and source of power, as well as at the location of the utilization equipment.

The intent of a surge-protective device is to limit transient voltages by diverting or limiting surge current and preventing continued flow of current while remaining capable of repeating these functions [Article 100]. ▶Figure 242–3 and ▶Figure 242–4

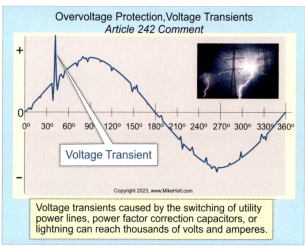

▶Figure 242–1

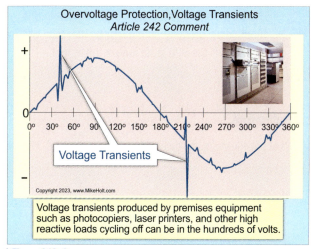

▶Figure 242–2

242.9 | Overvoltage Protection

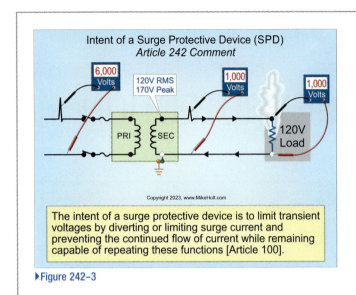
▶Figure 242-3

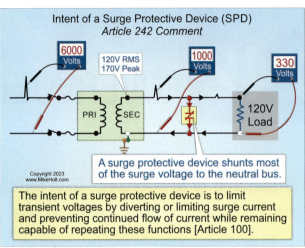
▶Figure 242-4

242.9 Indicating

A new section was added requiring an SPD to indicate that it is functioning properly.

Analysis

NEW — This new section requires an SPD to indicate it is functioning properly. Without this, the user will not know if the SPD is no longer functional.

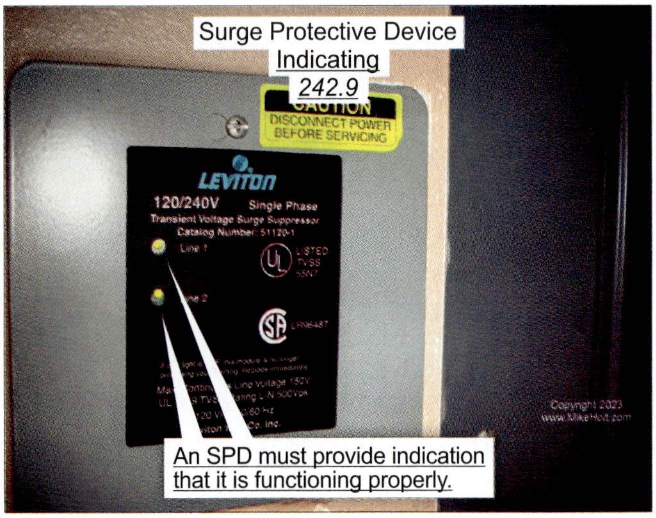

▶Figure 242-5

242.9 Indicating

An SPD must provide indication that it is functioning properly. ▶Figure 242-5

ARTICLE 250 GROUNDING AND BONDING

Introduction to Article 250—Grounding and Bonding

No other article can match this one for misapplication, violation, and misinterpretation. The terminology used in Article 250 has been a source of much confusion but has been improved during the last few Code revisions. It is very important for you to understand the difference between bonding and grounding to correctly apply the provisions of this article. Pay careful attention to the definitions of important terms in Article 100 that apply to bonding and grounding. Article 250 covers the grounding requirements for providing a path to the Earth through a conductive body that extends the ground connection to reduce overvoltage from lightning strikes, and the bonding requirements that establish a low-impedance fault current path back to the source of the electrical supply to facilitate the operation of overcurrent protective devices in the event of a ground fault.

This article is arranged in a logical manner as illustrated in Figure 250.1 in the NEC. It may be a good idea for you to just read through the entire article first to get a big picture overview. Then, study Article 250 closely so you understand the details and remember to check Article 100 for the definitions of terms that may be new to you. The illustrations that accompany the text in this material will help you better understand the key points.

250.36 Impedance Grounded Systems—480V to 1000V

The title of this section was edited to reflect the actual type of system being referenced. In addition, terms throughout the section were revised to match those defined in Article 100 with no technical change.

Analysis

 CLARIFIED These systems are out of the ordinary and can be confusing to talk about. To address this, the title was revised and the newly defined term "impedance grounding conductor" was used to clarify how the grounding impedance device is to be connected to the transformer.

The title and text of (E) were also updated to "impedance bonding jumper" to be consistent with 250.36(B) and (D), and to avoid confusion with the term "equipment bonding jumper" used throughout the *Code*.

250.36 Impedance Grounded Systems—480V to 1000V

To limit ground-fault current to a low value, an impedance grounded system with a grounding impedance device, typically a resistor, is permitted to be installed on three-phase systems of 480V up to 1000V where all the following conditions are met: ▶Figure 250–1

(1) Conditions of maintenance and supervision ensure that only qualified persons service the installation.

(2) Ground detectors are installed on the system.

(3) Only line-to-line loads are served.

250.53 | Grounding and Bonding

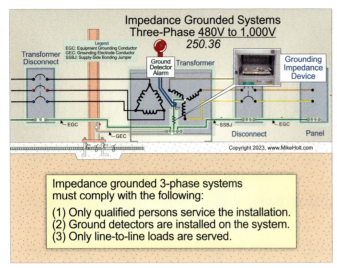
▶ Figure 250–1

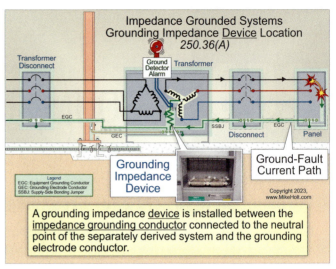
▶ Figure 250–2

Note: Impedance grounding is an effective tool for reducing arc-flash hazards see Annex O of NFPA 70E, *Standard for Electrical Safety in the Workplace*.

Author's Comment:

▸ Impedance grounded systems are generally referred to as "high-resistance grounded systems" in the industry. These systems are generally used where sudden interruption of power will create increased hazards and where a reduction of incident energy is needed for worker safety.

▸ High-resistance grounding will insert an impedance in the ground return path and will typically limit the fault current to 10A or less, leaving insufficient fault energy and thereby reducing the arc-flash hazard level. High-resistance grounding will not affect arc-flash energy for line-to-line faults [Annex O.2.3(7) NFPA 70E, *Standard for Electrical Safety in the Workplace*].

(A) Grounding Impedance Device Location. A grounding impedance device must be installed between the impedance grounding conductor and the neutral point of the separately derived system. ▶ Figure 250–2

250.53 Grounding Electrode Installation Requirements

The requirement for electrode surfaces to be free from nonconductive coatings was relocated to (A) and the title and text of (E) were updated to more accurately reflect the content of the rule and permission to use copper-clad aluminum as a bonding jumper.

Analysis

EDITED It is important for an electrode to make good contact with the earth. This means it must have surfaces that are free from nonconductive coatings. This requirement was relocated to (A) where it belongs instead of in the subdivision on the moisture level.

CLARIFIED The rule in 250.53(E) applies to the size and type of the bonding jumper connecting the supplemental grounding electrode to the grounding electrode system. Copper-clad aluminum is now listed as a permitted bonding jumper conductor and was added here along with copper and aluminum.

250.53 Grounding Electrode Installation

(A) Ground Rods. Ground rods, pipes, and plate electrodes must be free from nonconductive coatings such as paint or enamel. ▶Figure 250-3

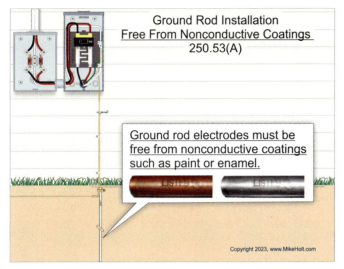
▶Figure 250-3

(1) Below Permanent Moisture Level. If practicable, rod, pipe, and plate electrodes must be embedded below the permanent moisture level.

(2) Supplemental Electrode. A single ground rod must be supplemented by an additional electrode. The supplemental electrode must be bonded to: ▶Figure 250-4

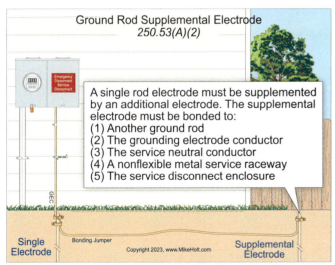
▶Figure 250-4

(1) Another ground rod

(2) The grounding electrode conductor

(3) The service neutral conductor

(4) A nonflexible metal service raceway

(5) The service-disconnect enclosure

Ex: A single ground rod electrode having a contact resistance to the earth of 25 ohms or less is not required to have a supplemental electrode. ▶Figure 250-5

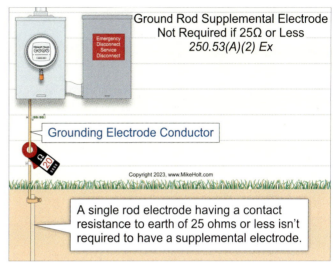
▶Figure 250-5

(3) Supplemental Ground Rod, Spacing. The supplemental electrode must be installed not less than 6 ft from the ground rod. ▶Figure 250-6

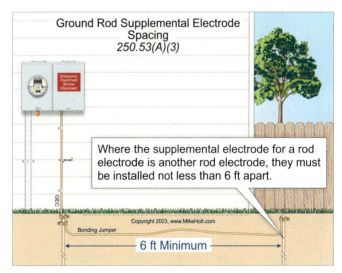
▶Figure 250-6

(4) Rod and Pipe Electrodes. The electrode must be driven to a depth of not less than 8 ft in the earth. Where rock bottom is encountered, the electrode can be driven at an angle not to exceed 45° from the vertical. Where rock bottom is encountered at 45°, the electrode can be placed in a trench that is at least 30 in. deep.
▶Figure 250–7

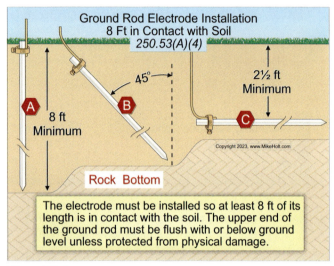

▶Figure 250–7

The upper end of the ground rod must be flush with or below ground level unless the grounding electrode conductor attachment is protected against physical damage as specified in 250.10. ▶Figure 250–8

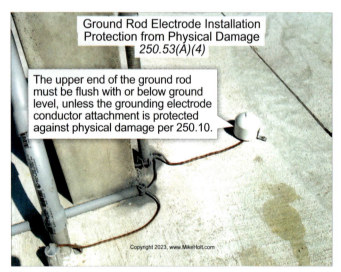

▶Figure 250–8

Author's Comment:

▸ When the grounding electrode attachment fitting is underground (below ground level), it must be listed for direct soil burial [250.70(A)].

(5) Plate Electrode. Plate electrodes must be installed no less than 30 in. below the surface of the earth.

250.64 Grounding Electrode Conductor Installation

Copper-clad aluminum has been added to 250.64(B), cable armor was added to the title of 250.64(E) to reflect the contents of the rule, and you are now prohibited from running a GEC through an enclosure vent.

Analysis

EDITED — To reflect the permission to use copper-clad aluminum in 250.64(A), copper-clad aluminum was added to 250.64(B)(1) and (2) to clarify that the same installation requirements apply to all permitted types of grounding electrode conductors.

EDITED — The term "cable armor" was added to the title of 250.64(E) reflect the requirements contained in the rule.

NEW — The new subdivision (G) was added to prohibit running a grounding electrode conductor through an equipment enclosure ventilation opening. This change was needed because routing multiple GECs through a ventilation opening could result in overheating. I guess it is time to get out the drill.

250.64 Grounding Electrode Conductor Installation

Grounding electrode conductors must be installed as specified in (A) through (G).

(A) Aluminum Conductors or Copper-Clad. Bare, covered, or insulated aluminum or copper-clad grounding electrode conductors must comply with the following:

(1) Bare or covered conductors without an extruded polymeric covering are not permitted to be installed where subject to corrosive conditions or to be installed in direct contact with concrete.

(2) Terminations must be made within listed enclosures identified for outdoor use within 18 in. of the bottom of the enclosure. If open-bottom enclosures are installed on a concrete pad, the concrete is not considered earth.

(3) Aluminum or copper-clad aluminum conductors external to buildings or equipment enclosures are not permitted to be terminated within 18 in. of the earth.

(B) Conductor Protection. If exposed, a grounding electrode conductor must be securely fastened to the surface on which it is carried.

(1) Not Exposed to Physical Damage. Grounding electrode conductors of copper, copper-clad aluminum, or aluminum sized 6 AWG and larger, can be installed exposed along the surface if securely fastened and not exposed to physical damage. ▶Figure 250-9

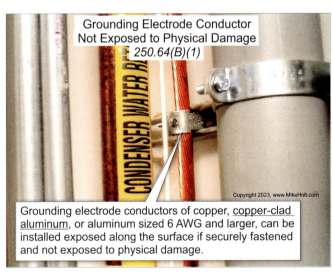

▶Figure 250-9

(2) Exposed to Physical Damage. Grounding electrode conductors of copper, copper-clad aluminum, or aluminum sized 6 AWG and larger, subject to physical damage, must be protected in rigid metal conduit (RMC), intermediate metal conduit (IMC), Schedule 80 rigid polyvinyl chloride conduit (PVC), reinforced thermosetting resin conduit Type XW (RTRC-XW), electrical metallic tubing (EMT), or cable armor. ▶Figure 250-10

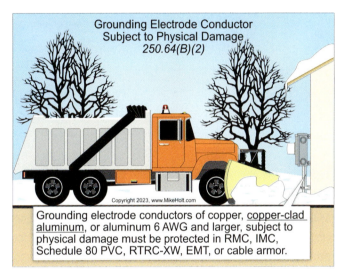

▶Figure 250-10

(3) 8 AWG and Smaller. Grounding electrode conductors 8 AWG and smaller must be installed in RMC, IMC, Schedule 80 PVC, RTRC-XW, EMT, or cable armor.

Author's Comment:

▸ While Table 250.66 permits the use of 8 AWG copper as the grounding electrode conductor for the phase conductor typically used for a 100A service, using a GEC smaller than 6 AWG is not common.

▸ Where grounding electrode conductors are installed in RMC, IMC, or EMT the metal raceways must be bonded at both ends per 250.64(E).

(4) In Contact with the Earth. Grounding electrode conductors and bonding jumpers in contact with the earth are not required to comply with the cover requirements of 300.5 but must be protected where subject to physical damage. ▶Figure 250-11

250.64 | Grounding and Bonding

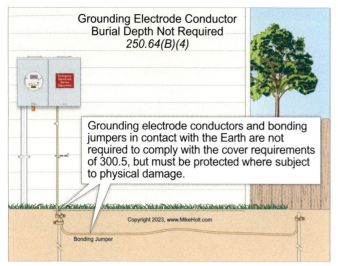

▶ Figure 250–11

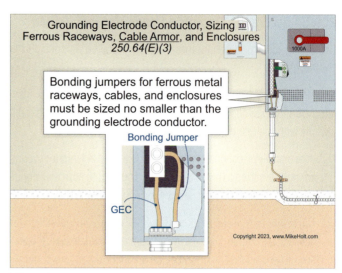

▶ Figure 250–13

(E) Ferrous Raceways, Cable Armor, and Enclosures Containing Grounding Electrode Conductors.

(1) General. Ferrous metal raceways, cables, and enclosures containing the grounding electrode conductor must have each end of the raceway, cable, or enclosure bonded to the grounding electrode conductor. ▶Figure 250–12

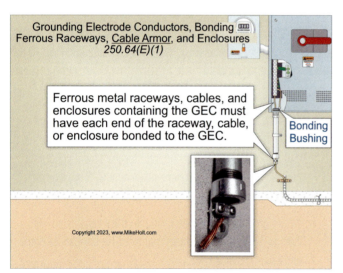

▶ Figure 250–12

(2) Methods. Bonding jumpers for ferrous metal raceways, cables, and enclosures must be in accordance with 250.92(B)(2) through (B)(4).

(3) Size. Bonding jumpers for ferrous metal raceways, cables, and enclosures must be sized no smaller than the grounding electrode conductor in the raceway, cable armor, or other enclosure. ▶Figure 250–13

Author's Comment:

▸ Nonferrous metal raceways, such as aluminum rigid metal conduit, enclosing the grounding electrode conductor are not required to meet the "bonding each end of the raceway to the grounding electrode conductor" provisions of this section.

▸ To save of time and effort, install the grounding electrode conductor in a nonmetallic raceway suitable for the application. Schedule 40 PVC can be used for exposed work [352.10(G)] but Schedule 80 PVC is required in areas subject to physical damage [250.64(B)(2)(3) and 352.10(K)]. ▶Figure 250–14

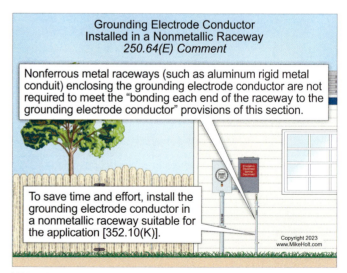

▶ Figure 250–14

Grounding and Bonding | 250.66

(G) Equipment with Ventilation Openings. Grounding electrode conductors are not permitted to be installed through equipment ventilation openings. ▶Figure 250–15

▶Figure 250–15

(A) Ground Rods. If a grounding electrode conductor or bonding jumper only connects to a ground rod [250.52(A)(5)], the grounding electrode conductor is not required to be larger than 6 AWG copper.
▶Figure 250–16

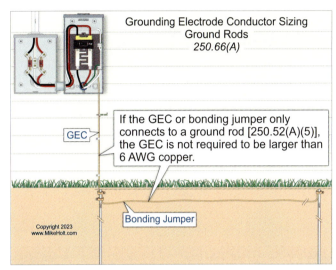

▶Figure 250–16

(B) Concrete-Encased Grounding Electrodes. If a grounding electrode conductor or bonding jumper only connects to a concrete-encased electrode [250.52(A)(3)], the grounding electrode conductor is not required to be larger than 4 AWG copper. ▶Figure 250–17

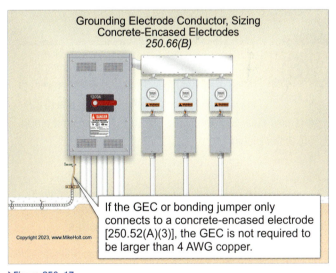

▶Figure 250–17

250.66 Sizing Grounding Electrode Conductors

The description of where this section applies was removed from the opening paragraph to make it easier to read.

Analysis

EDITED The application examples in the charging text for this section were removed since direct references to those rules are made where applicable. In addition, bonding jumpers were added to the charging text clarifying that both grounding electrode conductors and bonding jumpers are sized using this section.

250.66 Sizing Grounding Electrode Conductors

Except as permitted in (A) through (C), grounding electrode conductors and grounding electrode bonding jumpers must be sized in accordance with Table 250.66, based on the area of the largest phase conductor.

Table 250.66 Grounding Electrode Conductor

AWG or Area of Parallel Copper Conductors	Copper Grounding Electrode Conductor
2 AWG or Smaller	8 AWG
1 or 1/0 AWG	6 AWG
2/0 or 3/0 AWG	4 AWG
Over 3/0 through 350 kcmil	2 AWG
Over 350 through 600 kcmil	1/0 AWG
Over 600 through 1100 kcmil	2/0 AWG
Over 1100 kcmil	3/0 AWG

250.68 Grounding Electrode Conductor and Bonding Jumper Connection to Grounding Electrodes

The measurement rule for the GEC connection to water piping was clarified.

Analysis

CLARIFIED The measurement rule for the GEC connection being made within 5 ft of the point of entrance of water piping was clarified in (C)(1) and (C)(2). It is now clear that the linear distance is measured along the water piping.

250.68 Grounding Electrode Conductor and Bonding Jumper Connection to Grounding Electrodes

(C) Grounding Electrode Conductor Connections. Grounding electrode conductors and bonding jumpers are permitted to terminate at the following locations and to be used to extend the connection to an electrode(s):

(1) Metal Water Piping. Interior metal water piping that is electrically continuous with a metal underground water pipe electrode and is not more than 5 ft from the point of entrance to the building, as measured along the water piping, can be used to extend the connection to electrodes. Interior metal water piping more than 5 ft from the point of entrance to the building, as measured along the water piping, is not permitted to be used as a conductor to interconnect electrodes of the grounding electrode system. ▶Figure 250–18

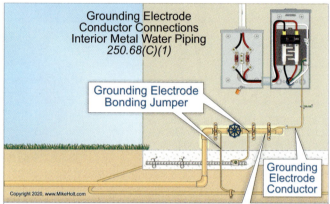

▶Figure 250–18

(2) Metal Structural Frame. The metal structural frame of a building can be used as a conductor to interconnect electrodes that are part of the grounding electrode system, or as a grounding electrode conductor where the hold-down bolts are connected to the concrete-encased electrode [250.52(A)(3)]. ▶Figure 250–19

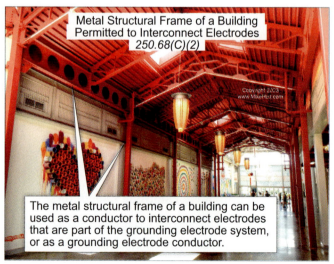

▶Figure 250–19

Grounding and Bonding | 250.70

The hold-down bolt connection to the concrete-encased electrode must be by welding, exothermic welding, steel tie wires, or other approved means. ▶Figure 250–20

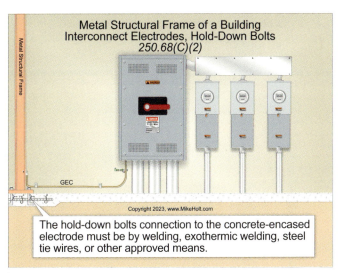
▶Figure 250–20

(3) Rebar from Concrete-Encased Electrode. A rebar-type concrete-encased electrode [250.52(A)(3)] with rebar extended to an accessible location above the concrete foundation or footing is permitted under the following conditions:

(a) Rebar extended to an accessible location to connect a grounding electrode conductor is permitted if the extension is connected to a rebar-type grounding electrode by steel tie wires or other effective means. ▶Figure 250–21

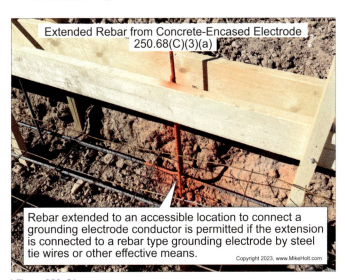
▶Figure 250–21

(b) The rebar extension from a concrete-encased electrode is not permitted to be in contact with the earth or subject to corrosion. ▶Figure 250–22

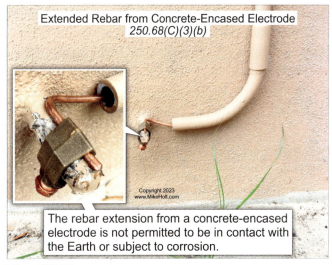
▶Figure 250–22

(c) The rebar extension is not permitted to be used as a conductor to interconnect the electrodes of grounding electrode systems.

250.70 Grounding Electrode Conductor Termination Fittings

This section was reorganized into two first level subdivisions and editorially revised for clarity. An Informational Note providing helpful information was also added.

Analysis

REORGANIZED This section was split up into (A), General Requirements, and (B), Indoor Communications Systems. Requirements for the use of listed sheet metal strap-type ground clamps were relocated from the list in (A) to subdivision (B).

NEW An Informational Note was added stating direct burial ground clamps are also suitable for concrete encasement. I guess we do not have to look this up in the UL guide anymore!

250.70 | Grounding and Bonding

250.70 Grounding Electrode Conductor Termination Fittings

(A) General.

Termination. The grounding electrode conductor must terminate to the grounding electrode by exothermic welding, listed lugs, listed pressure connectors, listed clamps, or other listed means. In addition, fittings terminating to a grounding electrode must be listed for the grounding electrode and the grounding electrode conductor. ▶Figure 250-23

▶Figure 250-23

Direct Burial or Concrete Encasement. When the termination to a grounding electrode is in the earth or encased in concrete, the termination fitting must be listed for direct soil burial or concrete encasement. ▶Figure 250-24

▶Figure 250-24

Only One Conductor. No more than one conductor can terminate on a single clamp or fitting unless the clamp or fitting is listed for multiple connections. ▶Figure 250-25

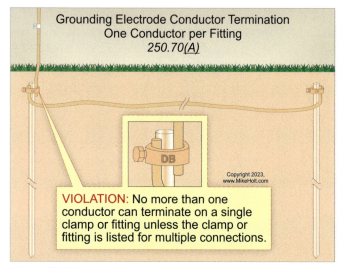

▶Figure 250-25

Note: Listed ground clamps identified for direct burial are also suitable for concrete encasement. ▶Figure 250-26

▶Figure 250-26

250.92 Bonding Metal Parts Containing Service Conductors

Threaded entries were added to the requirements in (B)(2) as an acceptable bonding connection.

Analysis

CLARIFIED In list item (B)(2), threaded entries were added as an acceptable bonding connection since some enclosures have threaded entries and not threaded hubs.

250.92 Bonding Metal Parts Containing Service Conductors

(A) Metal Raceways and Enclosures. The metal parts of equipment indicated below must be bonded together in accordance with 250.92(B). ▶Figure 250-27

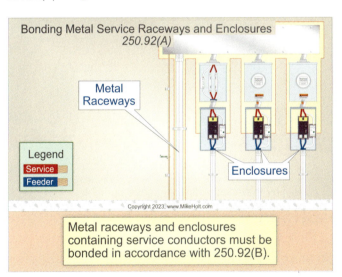

▶Figure 250-27

(1) Metal raceways containing service conductors.

(2) Metal enclosures containing service conductors.

(B) Methods of Bonding. Bonding jumpers are required around reducing washers or oversized ringed knockouts. ▶Figure 250-28

Standard locknuts are permitted to make a mechanical connection to the raceway(s), but they cannot serve as the bonding means required by this section. ▶Figure 250-29

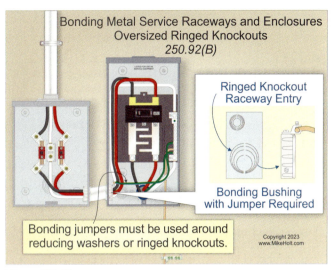

▶Figure 250-28

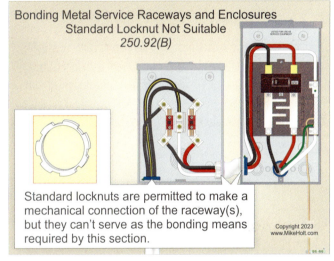

▶Figure 250-29

The bonding of metal enclosures and raceways must be ensured by one or more of the following methods:

(1) Service Neutral. Bonding metal parts to the service neutral conductor. ▶Figure 250-30

Author's Comment:

▸ A main bonding jumper is required to bond the service disconnect to the service neutral conductor [250.24(C) and 250.28].

250.92 | Grounding and Bonding

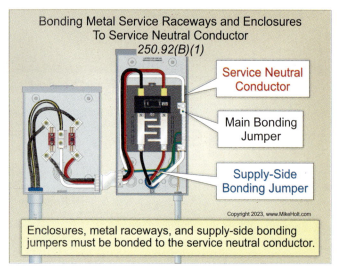

▶Figure 250–30

Author's Comment:

▸ At the service disconnect, the service neutral conductor provides the effective ground-fault current path to the power supply [250.24(D)]. A supply-side bonding jumper is therefore not required to be installed in PVC conduit containing service-entrance conductors [250.142(A)(1) and 352.60 Ex 2]. ▶Figure 250–31

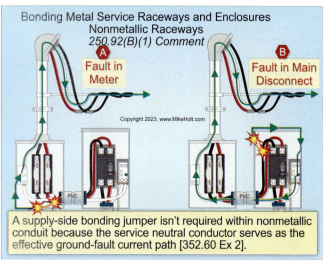

▶Figure 250–31

(2) Threaded Raceways. Connections made up wrenchtight using threaded couplings, threaded entries, or listed threaded hubs on enclosures. ▶Figure 250–32

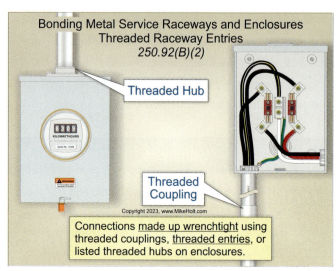

▶Figure 250–32

(3) Threadless Fittings. Terminating metal raceways to threadless fittings. ▶Figure 250–33

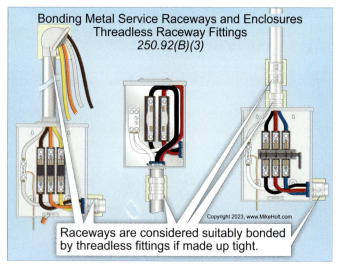

▶Figure 250–33

(4) Other Listed Fittings. Listed devices, such as bonding-type locknuts, bushings, wedges, or bushings with bonding jumpers to the service neutral conductor.

Author's Comment:

▸ A listed bonding wedge or bushing with a bonding jumper to the service neutral conductor is required when a metal raceway containing service conductors terminates to a ringed knockout. ▶Figure 250–34

Grounding and Bonding | 250.94

▶Figure 250–34

Author's Comment:

▸ A supply-side bonding jumper of the wire type used for this purpose must be sized in accordance with Table 250.102(C)(1), based on the size/area of the service phase conductors within the raceway [250.102(C)].

▸ A bonding-type locknut, bonding wedge, or bonding bushing with a bonding jumper can be used for a metal raceway that terminates to an enclosure without a ringed knockout.
▶Figure 250–35

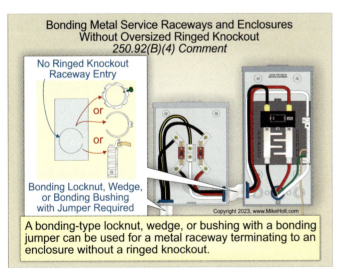

▶Figure 250–35

Author's Comment:

▸ A bonding locknut differs from a standard locknut in that it contains a bonding screw with a sharp point that drives into the metal enclosure to ensure a solid connection.

▸ Bonding one end of a service raceway to the service neutral provides the necessary low-impedance fault current path to the source required by this section. ▶Figure 250–36

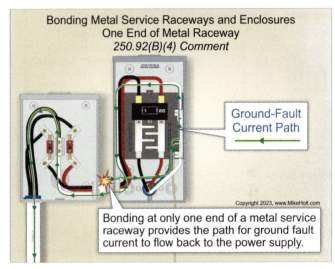

▶Figure 250–36

250.94 Bonding for Communications Systems

There were several editorial changes to provide clarification in this section.

Analysis

CLARIFIED   REORGANIZED

A variety of changes and reorganizations were made to this section making it much easier to read and understand. In addition, the rules in 250.94(A)(4)(a) and (b) now clearly require the IBT to be fastened to a "metal" enclosure or be electrically connected to the enclosure.

250.94 | Grounding and Bonding

250.94 Bonding Communications Systems

A bonding termination device must be provided for communications systems in accordance with (A) and (B). ▶Figure 250-37

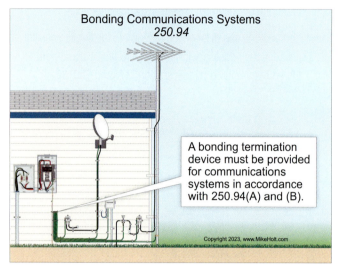
▶Figure 250-37

(A) Intersystem Bonding Termination Device. An intersystem bonding termination device must be installed at the service equipment, meter enclosures, or at the disconnect for a building supplied by a feeder or branch circuit and meet all the following requirements:

(1) Be accessible for connection and inspection. ▶Figure 250-38

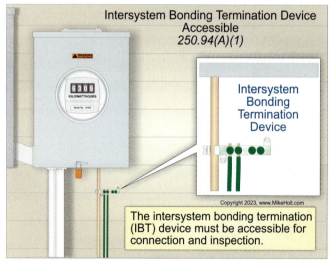
▶Figure 250-38

(2) Have a capacity for at least three intersystem bonding conductors.

(3) Be installed so it does not interfere with the opening of any enclosure.

(4) Be securely mounted as follows:

(a) To the metal service disconnect, the metal meter enclosure, the metal service raceway, or the metal raceway containing the grounding electrode conductor with a minimum 6 AWG copper conductor. ▶Figure 250-39

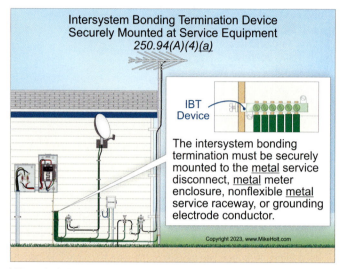
▶Figure 250-39

(b) To the metal disconnect supplied by a feeder or the metal raceway containing the grounding electrode conductor with a minimum 6 AWG copper conductor. ▶Figure 250-40

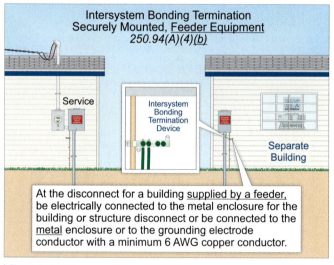
▶Figure 250-40

(5) Be listed as grounding and bonding equipment.

Ex: An intersystem bonding termination device is not required where communications systems are not likely to be used.

Grounding and Bonding | 250.102

Note: Communications systems within the scope of Chapter 8 (telephone, antennas, and CATV) must be bonded to the intersystem bonding termination device. ▶Figure 250–41

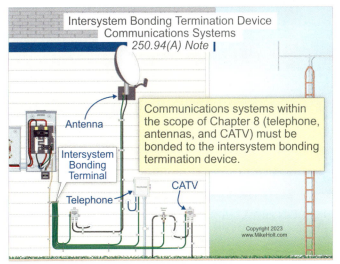

▶Figure 250–41

250.102 Neutral Conductor, Main Bonding Jumper, System Bonding Jumper, Supply-Side Bonding Jumper, Load-Side Bonding Jumper

The requirements of subdivision (C), including the Table, were clarified for ease of use without technical change.

Analysis

CLARIFIED The changes here are clarifications and a reorganization. One notable change to 250.102(C)(2)(2) clarifies how to size a single bonding jumper for two or more raceways. As has been done throughout this edition of the *Code,* unnecessary or redundant text was removed, and the remaining text was reorganized into lists that make the *NEC* much easier to read!

250.102 Neutral Conductor, Main Bonding Jumper, System Bonding Jumper, Supply-Side Bonding Jumper, Load-Side Bonding Jumper

(C) Supply-Side Bonding Jumper Sizing.

(1) Conductors in Single Raceway or Cable. Supply-side bonding jumpers must be sized in accordance with Table 250.102(C)(1), based on the size/area of the phase conductor within the raceway or cable. ▶Figure 250–42

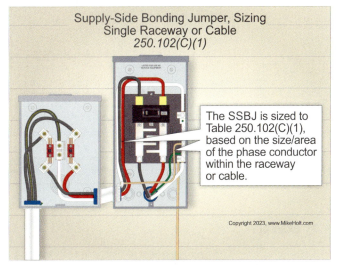

▶Figure 250–42

(2) Parallel Conductors in Two or More Raceways or Cables. If the phase conductors are connected in parallel in two or more raceways or cables, the supply-side bonding jumper must be sized in accordance with either of the following:

(1) An individual bonding jumper for each raceway or cable must be selected from Table 250.102(C)(1) based on the size/area of the largest phase conductor in each raceway or cable.

(2) A single bonding jumper for two or more raceways or cables must be sized in accordance with Table 250.102(C)(1) based on the sum of the circular mil areas of the largest phase conductors from each set connected in parallel in each raceway or cable.

Table 250.102(C)(1) Neutral Conductor, Main Bonding Jumper, System Bonding Jumper, and Supply-Side Bonding Jumper

Size of Largest Phase Conductor Per Raceway or Equivalent Area for Parallel Conductors (AWG/kcmil)		Size of Bonding Jumper or Neutral Conductor (AWG/kcmil)	
Copper	Aluminum or Copper-Clad Aluminum	Copper	Aluminum or Copper-Clad Aluminum
2 or smaller	1/0 or smaller	8	6
1 or 1/0	2/0 or 3/0	6	4
2/0 or 3/0	4/0 or 250	4	2
Over 3/0–350	Over 250–500	2	1/0
Over 350–600	Over 500–900	1/0	3/0
Over 600–1,100	Over 900–1,750	2/0	4/0
Over 1100	Over 1750	See Notes 1 and 2.	

Solution:

A 1/0 AWG supply-side bonding jumper is required for each raceway. [250.102(C)(2) and Table 250.102(C)(1)]. A single supply-side bonding jumper is permitted for multiple raceways based on the equivalent area of the supply-side phase conductors.

Answer: (d) 1/0 AWG

Note 1: The term "supply conductors" includes phase conductors that do not have overcurrent protection on their supply side and terminate at the service disconnect or the first disconnect of a separately derived system.

Note 2: See Chapter 9, Table 8 for the circular mil area of conductors 18 AWG through 4/0 AWG.

▶ Example

Question: What size copper supply-side bonding jumper is required for each of three metal raceways, if each raceway contains 400 kcmil copper service conductors in parallel? ▶Figure 250–43

(a) 4 AWG (b) 2 AWG (c) 1 AWG (d) 1/0 AWG

▶Figure 250–43

250.109 Metal Enclosures

This section was expanded to include plaster (mud) rings and extension rings as part of the equipment grounding path.

Analysis

EXPANDED The last *Code* cycle clarified that a metal enclosure or cover could be part of the effective ground-fault current path. In this cycle we discover that we can continue to do what we have done for decades because plaster (mud) rings and extension rings are now a recognized part of the effective ground-fault current path.

250.109 Metal Enclosures, Effective Ground-Fault Current Path

Metal enclosures can be used as part of the effective ground-fault current path. ▶Figure 250–44

Metal covers, metal plaster rings, and metal extension rings must be attached to metal enclosures to ensure an effective ground-fault current path or be connected with bonding jumpers or equipment grounding conductors to metal enclosures. ▶Figure 250–45

Grounding and Bonding | 250.140

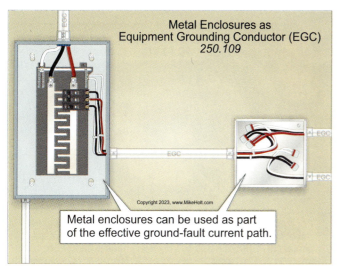

▶Figure 250–44

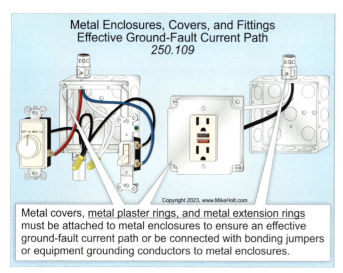

▶Figure 250–45

250.140 Frames of Ranges, Ovens, and Clothes Dryers

This rule was reorganized into parent text and two first level subdivisions, and the former Exception was expanded.

Analysis

REORGANIZED This section was reorganized with the former Exception becoming first level subdivision (B). Subdivision (A) covers the installation of a new circuit to supply a range or clothes dryer and requires the circuit to include an EGC. Subdivision (B) now contains the Exception permitting the circuit grounded conductor to function both as a grounded conductor and an EGC for existing circuits.

EXPANDED List item (5) to 250.140(B) was added to provide relief for existing circuits that were originally supplied by the service equipment but, because of a change (such as the installation of a generator and transfer switch), are now supplied from a feeder-supplied panel. It permits an existing circuit run using Type SE cable to continue to be used to supply a range or clothes dryer, provided the grounded conductor within the supply enclosure is field covered with listed insulating material to prevent the grounded conductor from having contact with any noncurrent-carrying metal parts.

250.140 Frames of Ranges, Ovens, and Clothes Dryers

The frames of electric ranges, wall-mounted ovens, counter-mounted cooking units, clothes dryers, and outlet boxes that are part of the circuit must be connected to the circuit equipment grounding conductor in accordance with 250.140(A) or (B).

(A) Equipment Grounding Conductor. The circuit supplying electric ranges, wall-mounted ovens, counter-mounted cooking units, and clothes dryers must include an equipment grounding conductor in accordance with 250.134 or 250.138. ▶Figure 250–46

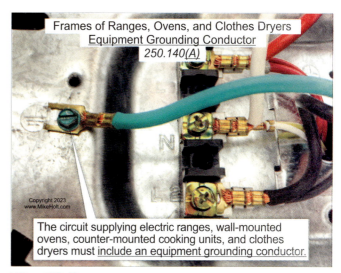

▶Figure 250–46

Changes to the National Electrical Code 2023 | MikeHolt.com | 137

250.148 | Grounding and Bonding

> **Caution**
>
> ⚡ **CAUTION:** Electric ranges and clothes dryers are shipped from the factory with a bonding strap that bonds the metal frame of the appliance to the neutral termination of the cord connection terminal block. The *Code* requires an insulated neutral for ranges and dryers using a 4-wire cord so the bonding strap must be removed from the appliance. If an existing 3-wire branch circuit is to supply a replacement appliance, the factory-installed bonding strap must remain in place [250.140(B)].
>
> ▶Figure 250–47

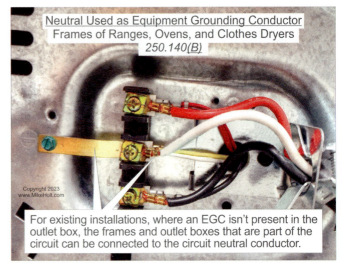

▶Figure 250–48

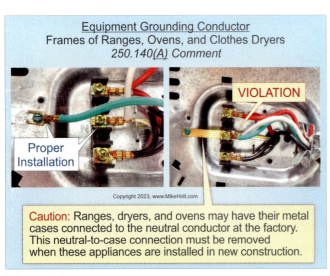

▶Figure 250–47

(B) Neutral Conductor. For existing installations, if an equipment grounding conductor is not present in the outlet box, the frames of electric ranges, wall-mounted ovens, counter-mounted cooking units, clothes dryers, and outlet boxes that are part of the circuit for these appliances may be connected to the circuit's neutral conductor.
▶Figure 250–48

250.148 Continuity of Equipment Grounding Conductors and Attachment in Boxes

The language in this section has been in process for a while. It was revised once again this cycle making it clear which EGCs must be connected to each other or to the box.

Analysis

CLARIFIED This rule has been in process for a while, and we may have a winner. The *Code* text now clearly specifies that all EGCs that are spliced or terminated in a box must be connected to each other or to the box, and that the terminations be made in accordance with 250.8. It is also clear that the bonding jumper or equipment grounding conductor connected to a box only must be sized using Table 250.122 based on the largest OCPD protecting circuit conductors in the box.

Grounding and Bonding | 250.148

250.148 Continuity and Attachment of Equipment Grounding Conductors in Boxes

If circuit conductors are spliced or terminate to equipment in the box, the equipment grounding conductor must comply with 250.148(A) through (D).

Ex: The circuit equipment grounding conductor for an isolated ground receptacle [250.146(D)] is not required to be connected to the other equipment grounding conductors or to the metal box. ▶Figure 250-49

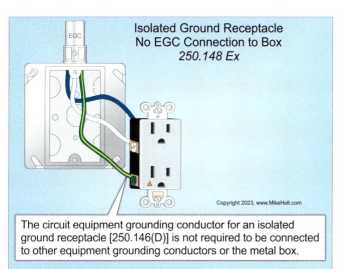

▶Figure 250-49

(A) Connections and Splices. Equipment grounding conductors that are spliced or terminated within the box must be connected together in accordance with 110.14(B) and 250.8. ▶Figure 250-50

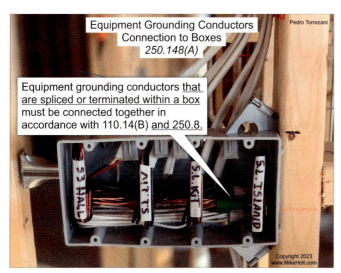

▶Figure 250-50

(B) Continuity of Equipment Grounding Conductors. Equipment grounding conductors must terminate in such a manner that the disconnection or removal of a receptacle, luminaire, or other device will not interrupt the electrical continuity of the equipment grounding conductor(s) providing an effective ground-fault current path. ▶Figure 250-51

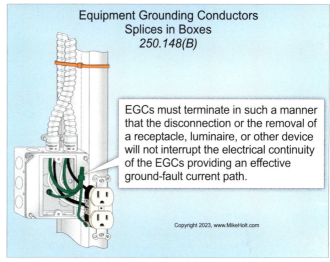

▶Figure 250-51

(C) Metal Boxes. Bonding jumpers or equipment grounding conductors for circuit conductors that are spliced or terminated on equipment within a metal box must be sized as shown Table 250.122 and have a connection to the metal box in accordance with 250.8. ▶Figure 250-52

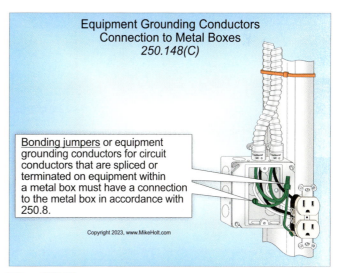

▶Figure 250-52

1st Printing — Changes to the National Electrical Code 2023 | MikeHolt.com | 139

250.148 | Grounding and Bonding

Author's Comment:

▸ Equipment grounding conductors are not permitted to terminate to a screw that secures a plaster ring, raised cover, or to drywall screws used to secure the box. ▶Figure 250-53

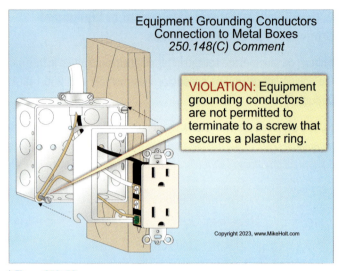

▶Figure 250-53

CHAPTER 3

WIRING METHODS AND MATERIALS

Introduction to Chapter 3—Wiring Methods and Materials

Chapter 3 focuses on wiring methods and materials, and provides some very specific installation requirements for conductors, cables, boxes, raceways, and fittings. This chapter includes detailed information about the installations and restrictions involved with wiring methods. Not fully understanding the information in this chapter may be the reason many people incorrectly apply these rules. Pay careful attention to every detail to be sure your installations comply with these requirements. Disregarding the rules for the wiring methods found in Chapter 3 can result in problems with power quality and can lead to fire, shock, and overall poor installations. The type of wiring method you will use depends on several factors such as job specifications, *Code* requirements, the environment, needs, the type of building construction, and the cost-effectiveness of the job just to name a few.

Chapter 3 begins with rules that are common to most wiring methods [Article 300]. It then covers conductors [Article 310], cabinets, cutout boxes, and meter socket enclosures [Article 312], and boxes and conduit bodies [Article 314]. The articles that follow become more specific and deal more in-depth with individual wiring methods such as specific types of cables [Articles 320 through 340] and various raceways [Articles 342 through 390]. The chapter winds up with Article 392 Cable Trays, which is a support system.

Notice as you read through the various wiring methods that the *Code* attempts to use similar section numbering for similar topics from one article to the next. It uses the same digits after the decimal point in the section numbers for the same topic. This makes it easier to locate the specific requirements of a particular article. For example, the rules for securing and supporting can be found in the section that ends with ".30" of each article.

Wiring Method Articles

▶ **Article 300—General Requirements for Wiring Methods and Materials.** Article 300 contains the general requirements for all wiring methods included in the *NEC*, except for signaling and communications systems (communications, antennas, and coaxial cable), which are covered in Chapters 7 and 8.

▶ **Article 310—Conductors for General Wiring.** This article contains the general requirements for conductors, such as insulation markings, ampacity ratings, and conductor use. There is also a section that addresses single-family dwelling service and feeder conductors exclusively. Article 310 does not apply to conductors that are part of flexible cords, fixture wires, or conductors that are an integral part of equipment [90.7 and 310.1].

▶ **Article 312—Cabinets and Meter Socket Enclosures.** Article 312 covers the installation and construction specifications for cabinets and meter socket enclosures.

▶ **Article 314—Outlet, Device, Pull, and Junction Boxes; Conduit Bodies; Fittings; and Handhole Enclosures.** Installation requirements for outlet boxes, pull and junction boxes, as well as conduit bodies and handhole enclosures are contained in this article.

...

Cable Articles

Articles 320 through 340 address specific types of cables. If you take the time to become familiar with the various types of cables, you will be able to:

- Understand what is available for doing the work.
- Recognize cable types having special *NEC* requirements.
- Avoid buying cable you cannot install due to *Code* requirements you cannot meet with that wiring method.

Here is a brief overview of those included in this material:

- **Article 320—Armored Cable (Type AC).** Armored cable is an assembly of insulated conductors, 14 AWG through 1 AWG, individually wrapped with waxed paper. The conductors are contained within a flexible metal (steel or aluminum) spiral sheath that interlocks at the edges. Armored cable looks like flexible metal conduit. Many electricians call this metal cable "BX®."

- **Article 330—Metal-Clad Cable (Type MC).** Metal-clad cable encloses insulated conductors in a metal sheath of corrugated, smooth copper or aluminum tubing, or spiral interlocked steel or aluminum. The physical characteristics of Type MC cable make it a versatile wiring method permitted in almost any location and for almost any application. The most used Type MC cable is the interlocking kind, which looks like armored cable or flexible metal conduit.

- **Article 334—Nonmetallic-Sheathed Cable (Type NM).** Nonmetallic-sheathed cable is commonly referred to by its trade name "Romex®." It encloses two, three, or four insulated conductors, 14 AWG through 2 AWG, within a nonmetallic outer jacket. Because this cable is manufactured in this manner, it contains a separate (usually bare) equipment grounding conductor. Nonmetallic-sheathed cable is commonly used for residential wiring applications but may sometimes be permitted for use in commercial occupancies.

Raceway Articles

Articles 342 through 390 address specific types of raceways. Refer to Article 100 for the definition of a raceway. If you take the time to become familiar with the various types of raceways, you will be able to:

- Understand what is available for doing the work.
- Recognize raceway types that have special *Code* requirements.
- Avoid buying a raceway you cannot install due to *NEC* requirements you cannot meet with that wiring method.

Here is a brief overview of each those included in this material:

- **Article 352—Rigid Polyvinyl Chloride Conduit (Type PVC).** Rigid polyvinyl chloride conduit is a nonmetallic raceway of circular cross section with integral or associated couplings, connectors, and fittings. It is listed for the installation of electrical conductors.

- **Article 356—Liquidtight Flexible Nonmetallic Conduit (Type LFNC).** Liquidtight flexible nonmetallic conduit (commonly referred to as "Carflex®") is a raceway of circular cross section with an outer liquidtight, nonmetallic, sunlight-resistant jacket over an inner flexible core, with associated couplings, connectors, and fittings.

- **Article 358—Electrical Metallic Tubing (EMT).** Electrical metallic tubing is a nonthreaded thinwall raceway of circular cross section designed for the physical protection and routing of conductors and cables. Compared to rigid metal conduit and intermediate metal conduit, electrical metallic tubing is relatively easy to bend, cut, and ream. EMT is not threaded, so all connectors and couplings are of the threadless type. It is available in a range of colors, such as red and blue.

▶ **Article 362—Electrical Nonmetallic Tubing (ENT).** Electrical nonmetallic tubing is a pliable, corrugated, circular raceway made of PVC. It resembles flexible tubing and is often referred to as "Smurf Pipe" or "Smurf Tube," because it was only available in blue when it was first available. The nickname is a reference to the children's cartoon characters "The Smurfs." It is now available in colors such as red and yellow.

▶ **Article 376—Metal Wireways.** A metal wireway is a sheet metal trough with hinged or removable covers making the electrical conductors and cables housed and protected inside accessible. Metal wireways must be installed as a complete and contiguous system.

Notes

ARTICLE 300 — GENERAL REQUIREMENTS FOR WIRING METHODS AND MATERIALS

Introduction to Article 300—General Requirements for Wiring Methods and Materials

Article 300 contains the general requirements for all wiring methods included in the *NEC*. However, it does not apply to twisted-pair cable and coaxial cable (which are covered in Chapters 7 and 8), unless Article 300 is specifically referenced.

This article is primarily concerned with how to install, route, splice, protect, and secure cables, conductors, and raceways. How well you understand and apply the requirements of Article 300 will usually be evident in the finished work. Many of its requirements will affect the appearance, longevity, and even the safety of the installation. Installing conductors takes critical thinking, for example installing the phase conductors in one raceway and the neutral conductors in another raceway will cause inductive heating effects. Pay close attention to the building construction to be aware of what to do when cables are installed through framing members or penetrate fire walls. After studying and learning the rules in this article, you will immediately realize that the burial depth requirements of 300.5 were possibly overlooked or ignored.

A good understanding of this article will start you on the path to correctly and safely installing the wiring methods included in Chapter 3. Be sure to carefully consider the accompanying illustrations and refer to the definitions in Article 100 as needed.

300.3 Conductors

The rule requiring all conductors of the circuit to be in the same raceway added language to include conduit bodies. In addition, the voltage ranges were expanded to include both 1000V ac and the newly added 1500V dc.

EXPANDED Subdivision (C) was expanded by allowing conductors carrying up to 1500V dc to occupy the same enclosure or raceway as conductors up to 1000V ac, if all conductor insulation is rated for the maximum circuit voltage present.

Analysis

CLARIFIED The rules in 300.3(B) require all conductors of the circuit, including any grounded or grounding conductors, to be in the same raceway. "Conduit bodies" were added to that list to address possible confusion in applying this rule.

300.3 Conductors

(B) Conductors Grouped Together. All conductors of a circuit, including the neutral and equipment grounding conductors, must be installed together in the same raceway, conduit body, cable, trench, cord, or cable tray except as permitted by (1) through (4). ▶Figure 300–1

300.3 | General Requirements for Wiring Methods and Materials

▶Figure 300–1

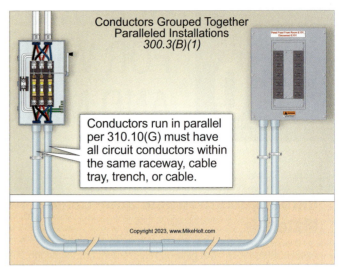

▶Figure 300–3

Author's Comment:

▶ The equipment grounding conductor must be grouped with the circuit conductors to provide a low impedance path during a short-circuit or ground-fault event. ▶Figure 300–2

Author's Comment:

▶ Grouping all phase, neutral, and equipment grounding and bonding conductors of the circuit helps minimize the inductive heating of the surrounding ferrous (iron) metal raceways and enclosures for alternating-current circuits. See 300.20(A). ▶Figure 300–4

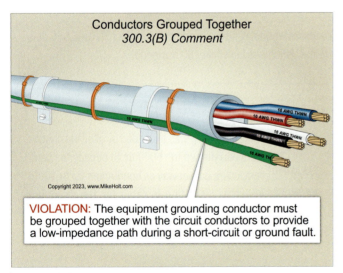

▶Figure 300–2

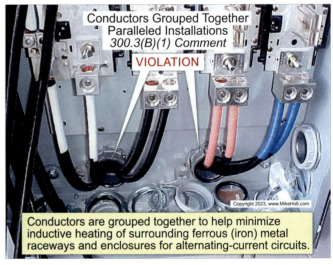

▶Figure 300–4

(1) Paralleled Installations. Conductors installed in parallel in accordance with 310.10(G) must have all circuit conductor sets grouped together within the same raceway, cable tray, trench, or cable. ▶Figure 300–3

Connections, taps, or extensions made from paralleled conductors must connect to all conductors of the paralleled set.

Ex: Isolated parallel phase and neutral conductors can be installed in individual underground nonmetallic raceways (Phase A in raceway 1, Phase B in raceway 2, and so forth) as permitted by 300.5(I) Ex 2 if the installation complies with 300.20(B). ▶Figure 300–5

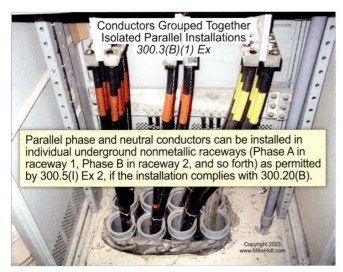
▶Figure 300–5

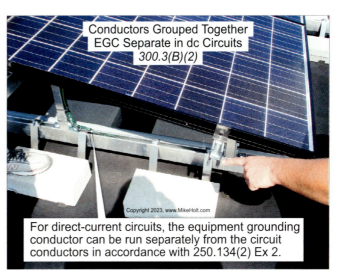
▶Figure 300–7

(2) Bonding Jumpers Outside the Raceway. Equipment bonding jumpers can be outside of a raceway if the bonding jumper is installed in accordance with 250.102(E)(2). ▶Figure 300–6

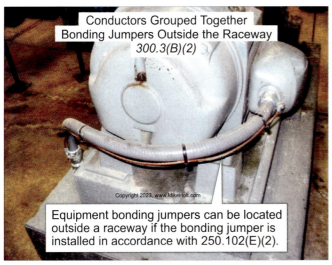
▶Figure 300–6

For direct-current circuits, the equipment grounding conductor can be run separately from the circuit conductors in accordance with 250.134(2) Ex 2. ▶Figure 300–7

(C) Mixing Conductors of Different Voltage Systems.

(1) Voltage Insulation Rating. Power conductors rated 1000V ac or 1500V dc or less can occupy the same raceway, cable, or enclosure if all conductors have an insulation voltage rating not less than the maximum circuit voltage. ▶Figure 300–8

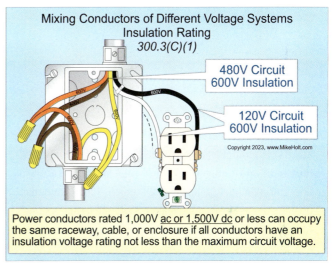
▶Figure 300–8

Author's Comment:

▸ The maximum circuit voltage in the raceway is what determines the minimum voltage rating for the insulation of the conductors, not the maximum insulation voltage of the conductors in the raceway. For example, a 120/240V circuit installed in a raceway with 600V insulated conductors must have all conductors with a minimum insulation voltage rating of 240V not 600V.

Note 1: Class 2 power-limited circuits must be separated from power circuits so the higher-voltage conductors do not accidentally energize the power-limited circuits [725.136(A)]. ▶Figure 300–9

300.4 | General Requirements for Wiring Methods and Materials

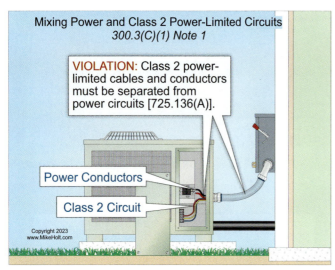
▶Figure 300–9

 CLARIFIED The requirements in (G) were clarified to indicate that where protective bushings are required, they must be installed before the conductors are pulled into the raceway. Who knew? Bummer...

300.4 Protection Against Physical Damage

Where subject to physical damage, conductors, raceways, and cables must be protected in accordance with (A) through (H).

(E) Wiring Under Metal-Corrugated Roof Decking. Cables, raceways, and boxes under metal-corrugated sheet roof decking are not permitted to be within 1½ in. of the roof decking, measured from the lowest surface of the roof decking to the top of the cable, raceway, or box.
▶Figure 300–10

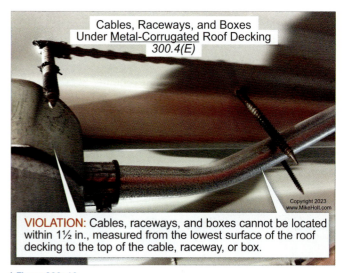
▶Figure 300–10

300.4 Protection Against Physical Damage

The phrase "nonmetallic conduit" was replaced with PVC and RTRC, protection requirements for bored holes in wood members and under corrugated roof decks were clarified and expanded, and the requirement for a protective bushing on raceways containing 4 AWG and larger conductors was clarified.

Analysis

 CLARIFIED The words "metal-corrugated" were added to the title in (E) clarifying the type of roof deck to which this section applies. The rule was correct, but the title did not reflect the rule's application.

 CLARIFIED Existing (E) Exception 1 now clearly tells us that RMC or IMC are not required to maintain the 1½ in. spacing when listed steel or malleable iron fittings and boxes are used.

 NEW The new (E) Exception 2 exempts metal-corrugated roof decks covered with at least 2 in. or more of concrete from the 1½ in. spacing requirement.

Author's Comment:

▸ A similar requirement applies to luminaires installed in or under roof decking [410.10(F)].

Note: Raceways or cables installed under metal roof decking might be penetrated by screws or other mechanical devices designed to "hold down" the waterproof membrane or roof insulating material.

Ex 1: Spacing from roof decking does not apply to rigid metal conduit and intermediate metal conduit with listed steel or malleable iron fittings and boxes.

Ex 2: The 1½ in. spacing is not required where metal-corrugated sheet roof decking is covered with a minimum of 2 in. of concrete, measured from the top of the corrugated roofing.

(G) Raceway Termination Fittings. Raceways containing insulated circuit conductors 4 AWG and larger that enter a cabinet, box, enclosure, or raceway must be protected prior to the installation of the conductors as follows:

(1) An identified raceway fitting providing a smoothly rounded insulating surface. ▶Figure 300-11

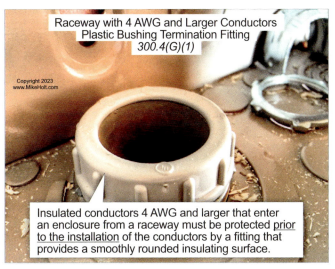

▶Figure 300-11

(2) A listed metal raceway fitting with smoothly rounded edges. ▶Figure 300-12

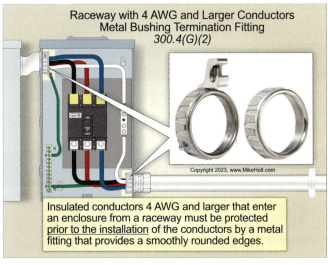

▶Figure 300-12

Conduit bushings constructed of metal can be used to secure a fitting or raceway.

Author's Comment:

▸ If IMC or RMC enters an enclosure without a connector, a bushing must be provided regardless of the conductor size [342.46 and 344.46].

(H) Structural Joints. A listed expansion/deflection fitting, or other means approved by the authority having jurisdiction, must be used where a raceway crosses a structural joint intended for expansion, contraction, or deflection.

300.5 Underground Installations

The voltages referenced in the rules were expanded to include "1500V dc" and the Table was expanded to include burial requirements for EMT.

Analysis

EXPANDED As with other Article 300 sections, the voltages to which these rules apply have been expanded by the addition of "1500V dc."

Column 3 of Table 300.5 was expanded to include EMT as a raceway that is permitted to be buried. A new Table Note 6 directs the user to 358.10, where 10(A)(1) permits EMT to be in contact with the earth, and where 10(B) addresses the need for additional corrosion protection as indicated by the UL Guide for EMT below grade level.

300.5 Underground Installations

(A) Minimum Cover Requirements. When cables or raceways are installed underground, they must have a minimum cover in accordance with Table 300.5(A). ▶Figure 300-13

Author's Comment:

▸ There are no cover requirements for raceways underneath a building. ▶Figure 300-14

300.6 | General Requirements for Wiring Methods and Materials

▶Figure 300–13

▶Figure 300–14

Table 300.5(A) Minimum Cover Requirements in Inches

Location	Column 1 Buried Cables	Column 2 RMC or IMC	Column 3 EMT or Nonmetallic Raceways
Under Building	0	0	0
Dwelling Unit	24/12*	6	18
Dwelling Unit Driveway	18/12*	6	18/12*
Under Roadway	24	24	24
Other Locations	24	6	18

Table 300.5(A) Minimum Cover Requirements in Inches
(continued)

*Residential branch circuits rated 120V or less with GFCI protection and maximum protection of 20A.

See the table in the NEC for full details.

Note 1 to Table 300.5: "Cover" is defined as the shortest distance from the top of the underground cable or raceway to the top surface of finished grade. ▶Figure 300–15

Note 6 to Table 300.5: Directly buried electrical metallic tubing (EMT) must comply with 358.10.

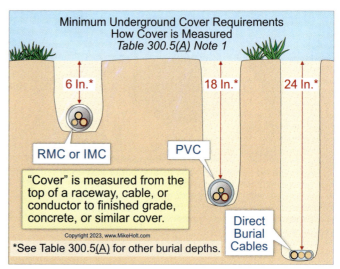

▶Figure 300–15

300.6 Protection Against Corrosion

The rules in this section were expanded to apply to all enclosures.

Analysis

EXPANDED The rules in this section were so specific that they left room to escape the requirements by working between the rules. With the addition of the word "enclosures," the rules now apply even to enclosure types that are not specifically named in the section.

General Requirements for Wiring Methods and Materials | 300.12

300.6 Protection Against Corrosion

Raceways, cable trays, cable armor, boxes, cable sheathing, cabinets, enclosures, elbows, couplings, fittings, supports, and support hardware must be suitable for the environment.

(A) Ferrous Metal Equipment. Ferrous metal raceways, enclosures, cables, cable trays, cabinets, enclosures, fittings, and support hardware must be protected against corrosion by a coating of approved corrosion-resistant material. ▶Figure 300–16

▶Figure 300–16

Author's Comment:

▸ According to UL "DYIX" Guide, supplementary corrosion protection is required when a ferrous metal raceway transitions from concrete encasement to the soil. ▶Figure 300–17

▶Figure 300–17

Where corrosion protection is required and IMC or RMC is threaded in the field, the threads must be coated with an approved electrically conductive, corrosion-resistant compound.

300.12 Mechanical Continuity— Raceways and Cables

Conduit bodies were added to this rule for consistency with other sections.

Analysis

EXPANDED Raceways and cables must be mechanically continuous between enclosures, boxes, cabinets, and newly added "conduit bodies." This addition was made to be consistent with the title of Section 300.15, which includes "conduit bodies."

300.12 Mechanical Continuity

Raceways and cable sheaths must be mechanically continuous between boxes, cabinets, conduit bodies, fittings, or other enclosures. ▶Figure 300–18 and ▶Figure 300–19

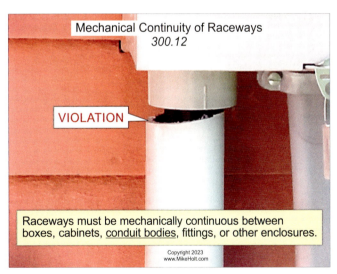

▶Figure 300–18

300.14 | General Requirements for Wiring Methods and Materials

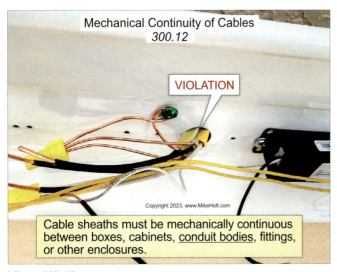
▶Figure 300–19

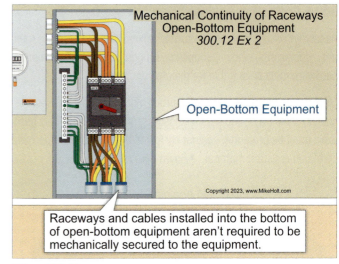
▶Figure 300–21

Ex 1: Short sections of raceways used to provide support or protection of cables from physical damage are not required to be mechanically continuous [250.86 Ex 2 and 300.10 Ex 1]. ▶Figure 300–20

Ex 2: Raceways and cables installed into the bottom of open-bottom equipment such as switchboards, motor control centers, and floor or pad-mounted transformers are not required to be mechanically secured to the equipment. ▶Figure 300–21

300.14 Length of Free Conductors at Outlets, Junctions, and Switch Points

New language clarifies that the required 6 in. of free conductor can be spliced!

Analysis

CLARIFIED This has been a point of contention for a long time, and now we have an answer—you can use spliced conductors to meet the requirement for 6 in. of free conductor in this rule. In the past, some AHJs read this rule to mean that conductors needed to be replaced if they were damaged or too short. Now it is clear that you can just splice them.

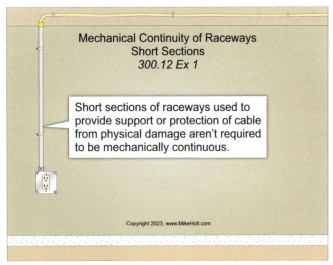
▶Figure 300–20

300.14 Conductor Length at Boxes

At least 6 in. of spliced or unspliced conductor, measured from the point in the box where the conductors enter the enclosure, must be provided for conductor splices or terminations. ▶Figure 300–22

General Requirements for Wiring Methods and Materials | 300.15

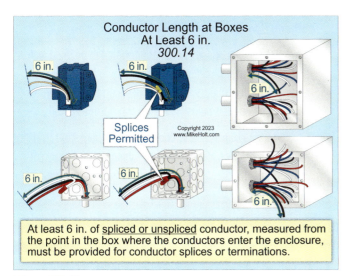
▸Figure 300–22

Boxes with openings less than 8 in. at any dimension must have at least 6 in. of conductor, measured from the point where the conductors enter the box, and at least 3 in. of conductor outside the box. ▸Figure 300–23

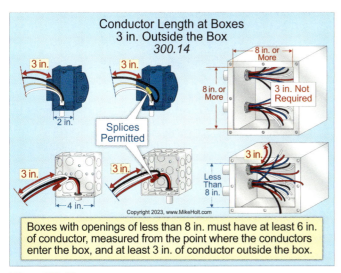
▸Figure 300–23

300.15 Boxes or Fittings

The language was revised to clarify that boxes are not required at wiring method transition points.

Analysis

CLARIFIED The word "conductor" was added throughout the charging text clarifying that a box is not required for a transition between two different wiring methods if there is no splice. Even though this was already covered in 300.15(F), it was not part of the charging statement.

300.15 Boxes or Fittings

A box or conduit body must be installed at each conductor splice point and conductor termination point, except as permitted by 300.15(A) through (L): ▸Figure 300–24 and ▸Figure 300–25

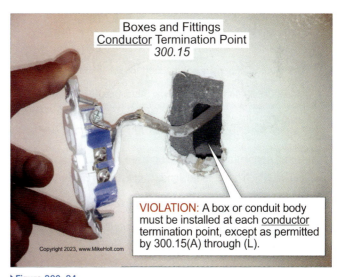
▸Figure 300–24

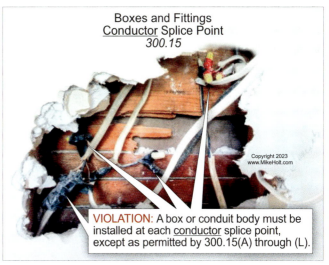
▸Figure 300–25

300.25 | General Requirements for Wiring Methods and Materials

Author's Comment:

▸ Boxes are not required for: ▸Figure 300–26
  ▸ Class 2 Power-Limited Circuits, 725.3
  ▸ Coaxial Cable, 800.3
  ▸ Optical Fiber Cable, 770.3

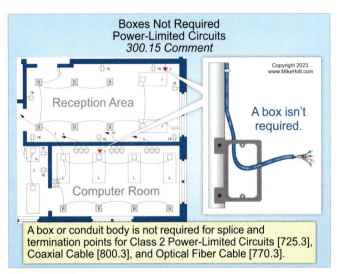

▸Figure 300–26

Fittings and connectors must only be used with the specific wiring methods for which they are designed and listed. ▸Figure 300–27

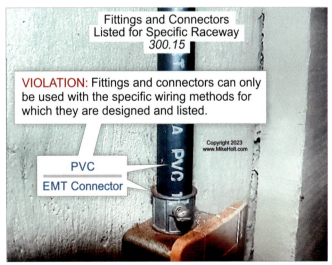

▸Figure 300–27

Author's Comment:

▸ Type NM cable connectors are not permitted to be used with Type AC cable, and electrical metallic tubing fittings are not permitted to be used with rigid metal conduit or intermediate metal conduit unless listed for the purpose.

▸ PVC conduit couplings and connectors are permitted to be installed with electrical nonmetallic tubing if the proper glue is used in accordance with the manufacturer's instructions [110.3(B)]. See 362.48.

(G) Underground Conductor and Cable Splices. A box is not required where a splice is made underground if the conductors and cables are spliced with a splicing device listed for direct burial. ▸Figure 300–28

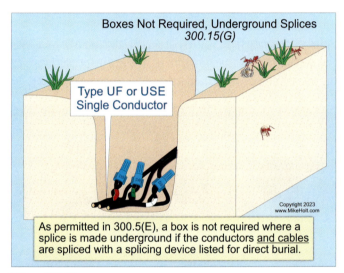

▸Figure 300–28

300.25 Exit Stair Towers

A revision to the rule and a new Exception permit stairwell exterior egress lighting to be powered from the stairwell circuit.

General Requirements for Wiring Methods and Materials | 300.25

Analysis

CLARIFIED The text in the main rule was revised to clarify that this requirement applies only to exit enclosures that "have a fire-resistance rating." Previously it applied to all exit enclosures required to be separate.

NEW The main rule requires wiring within a stair tower to only serve equipment within the stair tower. Stair towers often exit to the outside and require egress lighting outside those exits. This new Exception permits those lights to be powered from one of the circuits within the tower. This is a big win if you do multistory construction.

Where an exit stair tower is required to have a fire-resistance rating, only the wiring methods serving equipment permitted by the authority having jurisdiction in the exit stair tower are permitted to be installed within the exit stair tower.

▶Figure 300–29

300.25 Exit Stair Towers

Where an exit stair tower is required to have a fire-resistance rating, only the wiring methods serving equipment permitted by the authority having jurisdiction in the exit stair tower are permitted to be installed within the exit stair tower. ▶Figure 300–29

Ex: Egress lighting located outside exterior doorways from the exit stair tower can be supplied from a circuit located inside the exit stair tower.

Author's Comment:

▸ Fire-resistance rating is a defined term in the *International Building Code*. The fire rating rules for walls surrounding a stair tower are much more stringent and serve to "separate" it from the main building.

▸ Typically, only lighting and heat are necessary to serve a stair tower. If a stair tower landing is the only place for a sub-panel (for example) to be installed, it will require documented special permission from the authority having jurisdiction.

Note: For more information, refer to NFPA 101, *Life Safety Code*, 7.1.3.2.1(10)(b).

Notes

ARTICLE 310 CONDUCTORS FOR GENERAL WIRING

Introduction to Article 310—Conductors for General Wiring

This article contains the general requirements for conductors such as their insulation markings, ampacity ratings, and conditions of use. It does not apply to conductors that are part of flexible cords, fixture wires, or to those that are an integral part of equipment [90.7 and 300.1(B)].

310.10 Uses Permitted

Several editorial changes were made throughout this section for clarity and increased ease of use.

Analysis

EDITED Edits were made to the text in (G)(1) and (G)(3) for clarity.

Editorial changes were made to (G)(2) adding the term "supply-side bonding jumper" in recognition that supply-side bonding jumpers may be in parallel.

The title of (G)(4) was changed to include ampacity "correction" to match the content of the rule.

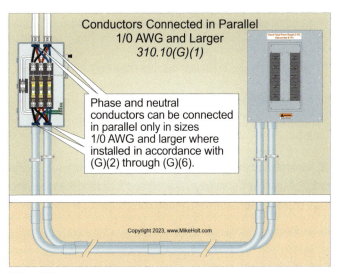
▶Figure 310–1

Authors Comment:

▸ When conductors are installed in parallel (electrically joined at both ends), the current flow will be evenly distributed between the individual parallel conductors.

(2) Conductor and Installation Characteristics. All parallel phase conductors, neutral conductors, equipment grounding conductors, and supply-side bonding jumpers must comply with the following:
▶Figure 310–2

310.10 Uses Permitted

Conductors described in Table 310.4(1) are permitted for use in any of the wiring methods covered in Chapter 3.

(G) Conductors Connected in Parallel.

(1) 1/0 AWG and Larger. Phase, neutral, and equipment grounding conductors are permitted to be connected in parallel (electrically joined at both ends). When paralleling phase and neutral conductors, they must be sized 1/0 AWG and larger. ▶Figure 310–1

310.10 | Conductors for General Wiring

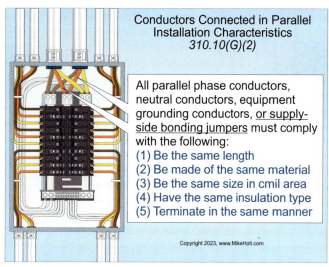
▶Figure 310-2

(1) Be the same length.

(2) Be of the same conductor material (copper, aluminum, or copper-clad aluminum).

(3) Be the same size in circular mil area (minimum 1/0 AWG).

(4) Have the same type of insulation.

(5) Terminate in the same manner (set screw versus compression fitting).

(3) Separate Raceways or Cables. The raceways or cables for parallel circuits must have the same number of conductors and the same electrical characteristics (metallic versus nonmetallic). ▶Figure 310-3

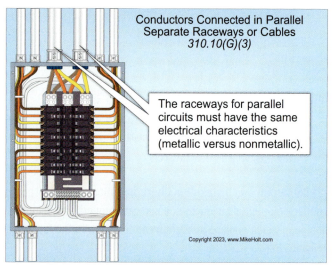
▶Figure 310-3

Author's Comment:

▸ Raceways or cables containing parallel conductors for Phase A, Phase B, Phase C, neutral, and equipment grounding conductor must have the phase, neutral, and equipment grounding conductors or supply-side bonding jumpers in each raceway [300.3(B)(1)]. ▶Figure 310-4

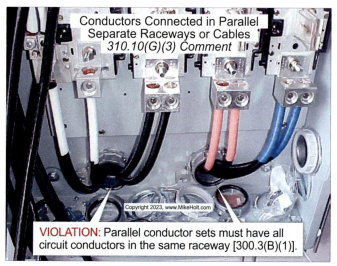
▶Figure 310-4

Conductors that comprise one paralleled set are not required to have the same physical characteristics as those of another paralleled set. ▶Figure 310-5

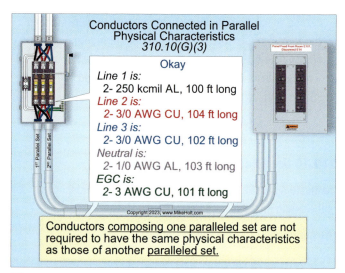
▶Figure 310-5

(4) Conductor Ampacity Correction or Adjustment. Conductors installed in parallel must have their ampacity corrected based on the ambient temperature in accordance with 310.15(B)(1)(1) and adjusted for conductor bundling in accordance with 310.15(C)(1).

(5) Equipment Grounding Conductors. Equipment grounding conductors must be sized in accordance with 250.122(F), but they are not required to be 1/0 AWG and larger. ▶Figure 310–6

(6) Bonding Jumpers. Supply-side bonding jumpers must be sized in accordance with 250.102(C)(1) and load-side bonding jumpers must be sized in accordance with 250.102(D), but they are not required to be 1/0 AWG and larger.

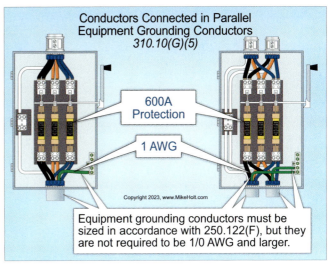

▶Figure 310–6

Notes

ARTICLE 312 — CABINETS, CUTOUT BOXES, AND METER SOCKET ENCLOSURES

Introduction to Article 312—Cabinets, Cutout Boxes, and Meter Enclosure

Notice that Article 408 covers switchboards, switchgear, and panelboards, with the primary emphasis on the interior (or "guts") while the cabinet used to enclose a panelboard is covered here in Article 312. Therefore, you will find that some important considerations such as wire-bending space at the terminals of panelboards are included in this article. A cutout box is a disconnect enclosure with externally operable type switches and circuit breakers (see 404.3 [wire bending space] and 404.4 [surface-mounted enclosures in wet locations]) must also comply with Article 312.

312.5 Cabinets, Cutout Boxes, and Meter Socket Enclosures

The text was revised to make it clear this section applies to both cable assemblies and insulated conductors that enter an enclosure.

Analysis

 CLARIFIED There are occasions where a cable or conductor directly enters an enclosure or cabinet. These rules are intended to protect those cables and conductors from abrasion when they do. The rule text recognized the hazard for individual conductors and this change clarifies that it is also intended to protect cables.

▶Figure 312–1

312.5 Enclosures

(C) Cable Termination. Cables must be secured to the cabinet, cutout box, or meter socket enclosures with fittings listed for the cable type. See 300.12 and 300.15. ▶Figure 312–1 and ▶Figure 312–2

312.8 | Cabinets, Cutout Boxes, and Meter Socket Enclosures

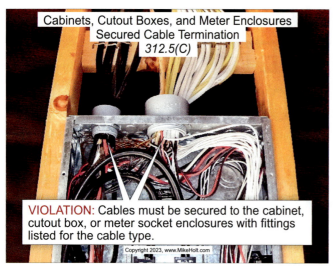
▶Figure 312-2

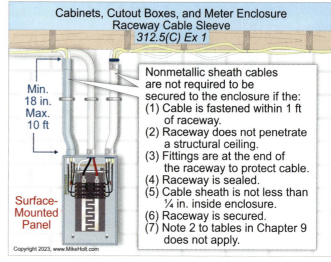
▶Figure 312-4

Author's Comment:

▸ Cable clamps or cable connectors are only suitable for a single cable unless that clamp or connector is identified for more than one cable. Some Type NM cable clamps are listed for two or more Type NM cables within a single fitting (UL Product iQ). ▶Figure 312-3

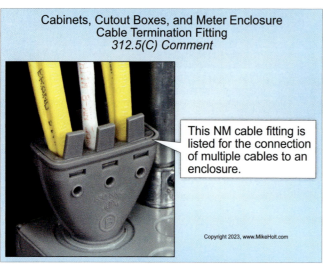
▶Figure 312-3

Ex: 1 Nonmetallic sheaths cables are not required to be secured to the cabinet, cutout box, and meter socket enclosure if the cables enter the top of a surface-mounted enclosure through a nonflexible raceway not less than 18 in. or more than 10 ft long, if all the following conditions are met: ▶Figure 312-4

(1) Each cable is fastened within 12 in. from the raceway.
(2) The raceway does not penetrate a structural ceiling.
(3) Fittings are provided on the raceway to protect the cables from abrasion.
(4) The raceway is sealed.
(5) Each cable sheath extends into the enclosure beyond the fitting not less than ¼ in.
(6) The raceway is properly secured.
(7) Where installed as conduit or tubing, Chapter 9, Table 1 Notes 5 and 9 apply. Note 2 to the tables in Chapter 9 does not apply to this condition.

312.8 Overcurrent Device Enclosures

A new list item adds bending space requirements. Editorial revisions were made to clarify that power management equipment can be field installed in a switch or overcurrent device enclosure.

Analysis

EXPANDED — A new list item requires adequate bending space per 314.28(A)(2) to be provided for feed-through, spliced, or tapped conductors 4 AWG or larger.

Cabinets, Cutout Boxes, and Meter Socket Enclosures | 312.10

 CLARIFIED Editorial revisions were made to (B) clarifying that power management equipment of either the field-installed or listed kit type (these are two different product types and standards) may be installed in a switch or overcurrent device enclosure.

312.8 Overcurrent Device Enclosures

Cabinets for panelboards are permitted to contain wiring as provided in 312.8 (A) and (B).

(A) Splices, Taps, and Feed-Through Conductors. The wiring space within cabinets for panelboards can be used for conductors feeding through, spliced, or tapped where all the following conditions are met:

(1) The area of all conductors at any cross section does not exceed 40 percent of the cross-sectional area of that space. ▶Figure 312–5

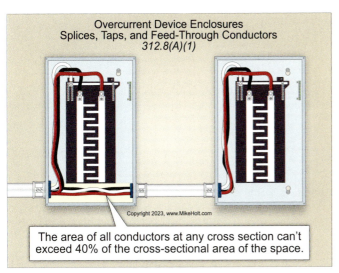

▶Figure 312–5

(2) The area of all conductors, splices, and taps installed at any cross section does not exceed 75 percent of the cross-sectional area of that space. ▶Figure 312–6

Author's Comment:

▸ The 40 and 75 percent requirements apply to all conductors, all splices, and all taps within the cross-sectional area, not just conductors, splice(s), or tap(s) being added.

(3) The bending space for conductors 4 AWG and larger complies with 314.28(A)(2).

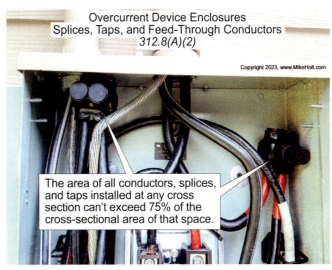

▶Figure 312–6

(4) Where conductors feed through the cabinet, a permanently affixed warning label sufficiently durable to withstand the environment involved, and complying with 110.21(B), must be applied on the cabinet to identify the location of the disconnect for the feed-through conductors. ▶Figure 312–7

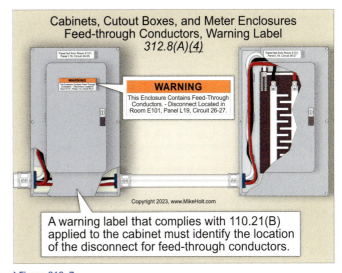

▶Figure 312–7

312.10 Screws or Other Fasteners

This new section addresses the hazards created by screws or fasteners that enter the wiring spaces of enclosures.

312.10 | Cabinets, Cutout Boxes, and Meter Socket Enclosures

Analysis

NEW

Factory provided enclosure screws are often too short or lost and replaced with longer screws that may have pointed ends. These replacement screws can damage installed conductors. This new section provides the requirements for those fasteners that enter the wiring spaces to have blunt ends and extend no more ¼ in. into the enclosure. An Exception will allow screws or fasteners to extend no more than ⁷⁄₁₆ in. into the enclosure if within ⅜ in. of the enclosure wall.

312.10 Screws or Other Fasteners

Screws or other fasteners installed in the field that enter wiring spaces must be as provided by or specified by the manufacturer or comply with the following:

(1) Screws must be machine type with blunt ends.

(2) Other fasteners must have blunt ends.

(3) Screws or other fasteners are not permitted to extend into the enclosure more than ¼ in. unless the end is protected with an approved means.

Ex to (3): Screws or other fasteners are permitted to extend into the enclosure not more than ⁷⁄₁₆ in. if within ⅜ in. of an enclosure wall.

ARTICLE 314 — BOXES, CONDUIT BODIES, AND HANDHOLE ENCLOSURES

Introduction to Article 314—Boxes, Conduit Bodies, and Handhole Enclosures

Article 314 contains the installation requirements for outlet and device boxes, pull and junction boxes, conduit bodies, and handhole enclosures. The conditions of use have a bearing on the type of material and equipment selected for the installation, for example in a wet location the boxes and fittings must be listed for wet locations to prevent moisture from entering the box.

The information contained in this article will help you size an outlet box using the proper cubic-inch capacity as well as calculating the minimum dimensions for pull boxes. There are limits on the amount of weight that can be supported by an outlet box, and rules on how to support a device or outlet box to various surfaces. Article 314 will help you understand these rules so your installation will be compliant with the *NEC*. As always, the clear illustrations will help you visualize the finished installation.

314.5 Screws or Other Fasteners

This new section provides requirements for field-installed screws or fasteners used in the boxes, fittings, and enclosures covered by this article.

Analysis

NEW

Like the requirements added in Article 312, these rules require fasteners that enter a box through a cover or a wall to be machine screws or other fasteners with blunt ends and have a limited extension into the box. An Exception permits longer screws if the end of the screw is protected by an approved means.

(1) Screws must be machine type with blunt ends.

(2) Other fasteners must have blunt ends.

(3) Screws attaching a cover must extend no more than ⅜ in.

(4) Screws or other fasteners, other than in (1), penetrating a cover must extend no more than ⁵⁄₁₆ in.

(5) Screws or other fasteners penetrating a wall of a box exceeding 100 cu in. must extend no more than ¼ in., or more than ⁷⁄₁₆ in. if within ⅜ in. of an adjacent box wall.

(6) Screws or other fasteners penetrating the wall of a box not exceeding 100 cu in. and not covered in 314.23(B)(1) must be made flush with the box interior.

(7) Screws or other fasteners penetrating the wall of a conduit body must be made flush with the conduit body interior.

Ex 1 to (3) through (6): A screw can be longer if the end of the screw is protected with an approved means.

314.5 Screws or Other Fasteners

Screws or other fasteners installed in the field that enter a wiring space must be as provided by the manufacturer, or specified by the manufacturer, or comply with the following:

314.17 Conductors and Cables Entering Boxes, Conduit Bodies, or Fittings

The phrase "and cables" was added in the title and to the parent language of (A) and (B) of this section to clarify that these rules apply to both conductors and cables.

Analysis

CLARIFIED The title in this rule did not identify that both conductors and cables were covered inside so "and cables" was added for clarity. Language was also changed to clarify that the protective tubing in (B)(1) and the cable sheath in (B)(2) must extend at least ¼ in. beyond the end of the cable clamp.

314.17 Conductors and Cables That Enter Boxes or Conduit Bodies

(B) Boxes. The installation of the conductors and cables in boxes must comply with the following:

(2) Cables Entering Through Cable Clamps. Where cable assemblies (Type NM or UF) are used, the sheath must extend not less than ¼ in. inside the box and beyond the end of any cable clamp. ▶Figure 314–1

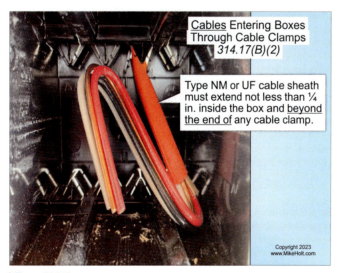

▶Figure 314–1

Author's Comment:

▸ Two Type NM cables can terminate in a single cable clamp if it is listed for this purpose.

314.23 Supports

This section now clarifies that a cord connected to a box with a hub must be made with a listed cord grip marked for use with a threaded hub.

Analysis

CLARIFIED Language was added to (H)(1) to clarify that where a cord is connected to a box with a hub, the cord-to-box connection must be made with a listed cord grip that is marked for use with a threaded hub.

314.23 Support of Boxes

(H) Pendant Boxes.

(1) Flexible Cord. Boxes containing a hub are permitted to use a listed cord grip attachment fitting marked for use with a threaded hub to support a box from a flexible cord [400.10(A)(1) and 400.14]. ▶Figure 314–2

▶Figure 314–2

Boxes, Conduit Bodies, and Handhole Enclosures | 314.25

314.25 Covers and Canopies

Conduit bodies were added to the types of enclosures covered in this section. In addition, connecting metal covers or plates to the EGC are now clearly required.

Analysis

EXPANDED New language in the parent text requires conduit bodies to be installed with a cover, lampholder, or device. The previous language did not address conduit bodies, only boxes.

CLARIFIED The requirement to connect a metal cover or plate to an EGC was not clear in subdivision (A). New language states metal covers or plates must be connected to the EGC in accordance with 250.110.

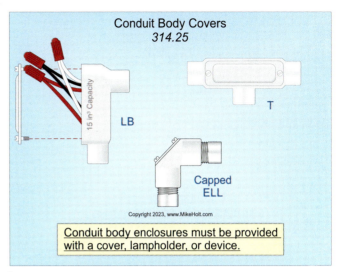
▶Figure 314-4

Screws used for attaching covers to the box must be machine screws that match the thread gage and size of the screw holes in the box.
▶Figure 314-5

314.25 Covers and Canopies

Each box must be provided with a cover, faceplate, lampholder or luminaire canopy, or similar device. ▶Figure 314-3

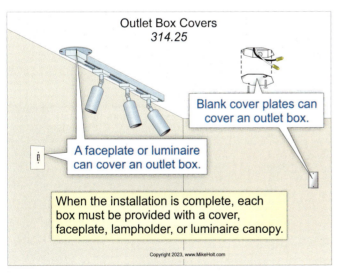
▶Figure 314-3

Conduit body enclosures must be provided with a cover, lampholder, or device. ▶Figure 314-4

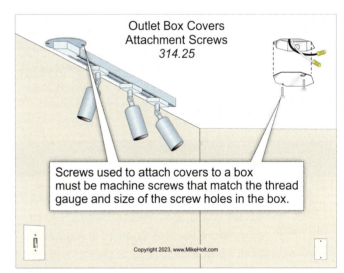
▶Figure 314-5

(A) Metal Covers. Where metal covers or plates are used, they must be connected to the circuit equipment grounding conductor in accordance with 250.110. ▶Figure 314-6

Author's Comment:

▶ Metal switch cover plates are connected to the circuit equipment grounding conductor in accordance with 404.9(B), and metal receptacle cover plates are connected to the circuit equipment grounding conductor in accordance with 406.6(B).

314.29 | Boxes, Conduit Bodies, and Handhole Enclosures

▶Figure 314-6

In Buildings and Other Structures. Boxes and conduit bodies must be installed so the wiring <u>and devices contained within</u> the boxes and conduit bodies are accessible. ▶Figure 314-7

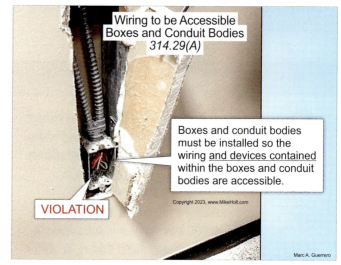

▶Figure 314-7

Author's Comment:

▸ According to the definition contained in Article 100, Accessible (as applied to wiring methods) means "Capable of being removed or exposed without damaging the building structure or finish or not permanently closed in or blocked by the building structure, other electrical equipment, other building systems piping, ducts, drains, or other mechanical systems, or the building finish." ▶Figure 314-8

▶Figure 314-8

314.29 Boxes, Conduit Bodies, and Handhole Enclosures to be Accessible

The required accessibility for wiring in boxes, conduit bodies, and handhole enclosures now extends to the devices they contain, and the Exception allows them to be covered.

Analysis

EXPANDED

Section 314.29 already required wiring in boxes, conduit bodies, and handhole enclosures to be accessible. It has been expanded to require any devices installed within them to be accessible as well.

A change to the Exception permits boxes and handhole enclosures to be covered where the location is effectively described and made available to those who access, maintain, or inspect the wiring.

314.29 Wiring to be Accessible

Boxes, conduit bodies, and handhole enclosures must be installed so that wiring <u>and devices contained within the boxes, conduit bodies, or handhole enclosures</u> can be rendered accessible in accordance with 314.29(A) and (B).

(B) Underground. Underground boxes and handhole enclosures must be installed so that the wiring <u>and devices contained within</u> the underground box or handhole enclosure are accessible without excavating sidewalks, paving, earth, or other substance used to establish the finished grade.
▶Figure 314–9

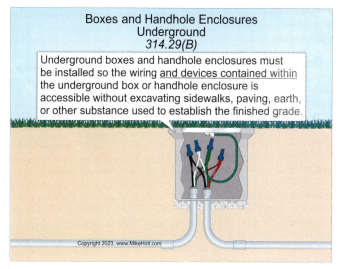

▶Figure 314–9

Notes

ARTICLE 320 — ARMORED CABLE (TYPE AC)

Introduction to Article 320—Armored Cable (Type AC)

Armored cable (Type AC) is an assembly of insulated conductors, 14 AWG through 1 AWG, individually wrapped in waxed paper (jute) and contained within a flexible spiral metal sheath. To the casual observer the outside appearance of armored cable is like flexible metal conduit and metal-clad cable (Type MC), however the metal outer armor has a bare solid 16 AWG aluminum bonding strip that is in intimate contact with all the metal spiral convolutions throughout its entire cable length and so the metal sheath qualifies as an equipment grounding conductor [250.118(A)(8)]. Type AC cable has been referred to as "BX®" cable over the years.

320.23 In Accessible Attics

The phrase "floor joists" was removed from the title and text of (A).

Analysis

EDITED The phrase "floor joists" was removed from this section and replaced with "framing members" to clarify that all framing surfaces in ceilings and floors are included no matter what they might be called. There was no technical change to the rule.

320.23 In Accessible Attics or Roof Spaces

(A) Cables Run Across the Top of Framing Members. Where run across the top of framing members, or across the face of rafters or studding within 7 ft of the floor or horizontal surface, Type AC cable must be protected throughout the entire attic by guard strips that are at least as high as the cable.

If this space is not accessible by permanently installed stairs or ladders, protection is required only within 6 ft of the nearest edge of the scuttle hole or attic entrance. ▶Figure 320–1

▶Figure 320–1

320.30 Securing and Supporting

A new sentence was added to say that AC cable fittings are permitted as a means of cable support.

320.30 | Armored Cable (Type AC)

Analysis

EXPANDED New language says that AC cable fittings are permitted as a means of cable support. This was previously located in (D), Unsupported Cables. The relocation to (A), General, makes it clear that the cable fitting can be the required support for any AC cable installation, not just for unsupported cables.

320.30 Securing and Supporting

(A) General. Type AC cable must be supported and secured by staples, cable ties listed and identified for securing and supporting, straps, hangers, similar fittings, or other approved means designed and installed so the cable is not damaged. ▶Figure 320–2

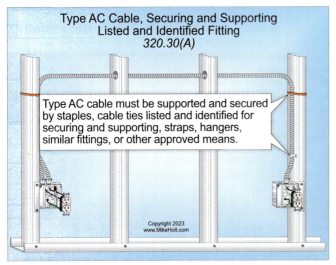
▶Figure 320–2

Type AC cable fittings are permitted as a means of cable support.

(B) Securing. Type AC cable must be secured within 12 in. of every outlet box, junction box, cabinet, or fitting and at intervals not exceeding 4½ ft. ▶Figure 320–3

(C) Supporting. Type AC cable must be supported at intervals not exceeding 4½ ft. Cables installed horizontally through wooden or metal framing members are considered supported and secured if such support does not exceed 4½-ft intervals. ▶Figure 320–4

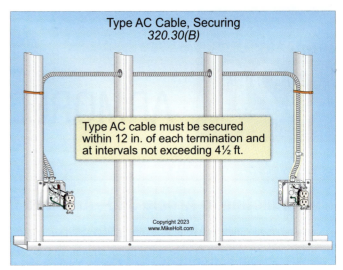
▶Figure 320–3

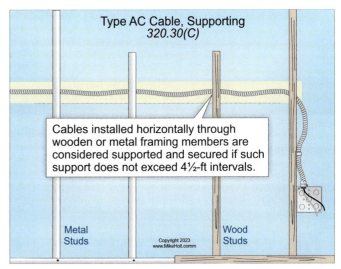
▶Figure 320–4

(D) Unsupported Cables. Type AC cable can be unsupported and unsecured where:

(1) Fished through concealed spaces

(2) Not more than 2 ft long at terminals where flexibility is necessary

(3) Not more than 6 ft long from the last point of cable support or Type AC cable fitting to the point of connection to a luminaire or electrical equipment within an accessible ceiling. ▶Figure 320–5

Armored Cable (Type AC) | 320.30

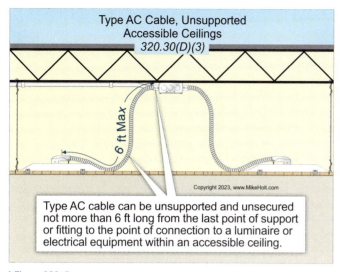
▶Figure 320–5

Notes

ARTICLE 330 — METAL-CLAD CABLE (TYPE MC)

Introduction to Article 330—Metal-Clad Cable (Type MC)

Metal-clad cable (Type MC) is probably the most often used metal-protected wiring method. Type MC cable encloses insulated conductors in a metal sheath of either corrugated or smooth copper or aluminum tubing, or in spiral interlocked steel or aluminum. The physical characteristics of Type MC cable make it a versatile wiring method that can be used in almost any location, and for almost any application. The most used Type MC cable is the interlocking kind, which looks like armored cable or flexible metal conduit. Traditional interlocked Type MC cable is not permitted to serve as an equipment grounding conductor so this cable must contain an equipment grounding conductor in accordance with 250.118(A)(1). Another type of Type MC cable is called interlocked Type MC^AP® cable. It contains a bare aluminum grounding/bonding conductor running just below the metal armor, which allows the sheath to serve as an equipment grounding conductor [250.118(A)(10)(b)].

Definitions. The following definition(s) contained in Article 100 are important as they relate to this article.

Metal-Clad Cable (Type MC). A factory assembly of one or more insulated circuit conductors, with or without optical fiber members, enclosed in an armor of interlocking metal tape, or a smooth or corrugated metallic sheath [Article 100]. ▶Figure 330–1

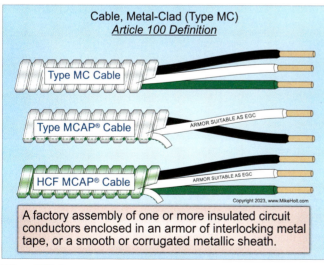

▶Figure 330–1

330.10 Uses Permitted

The word "damp" was added to list item (11).

Analysis

EXPANDED This will provide installation requirements for MC cable in damp locations to be the same as those in wet locations. PVC jacketed MC cable is rated for wet locations and corrosive environments. It is also 100 percent acceptable in a lesser restrictive damp location. Since UL 1569 is silent on these locations, the *NEC* makes it clear its use is permitted in damp locations.

330.10 Uses Permitted

(A) General Uses. Type MC cable can be used:

(1) For branch circuits, feeders, and services.

(2) For power, lighting, and power-limited circuits.

(3) For indoor or outdoor locations.

330.30 | Metal-Clad Cable (Type MC)

(4) Exposed or concealed.

(5) To be directly buried (if identified for the purpose).

(6) In a cable tray (if identified for the purpose).

(7) In a raceway.

(8) As aerial cable on a messenger.

(9) In hazardous (classified) locations as permitted in 501.10(B)(5), 502.10(B)(4), and 503.10(A)(1).

(10) Embedded in plaster in dry locations.

(11) In damp or wet locations, where a corrosion-resistant jacket is provided over the metallic sheath. ▶Figure 330–2

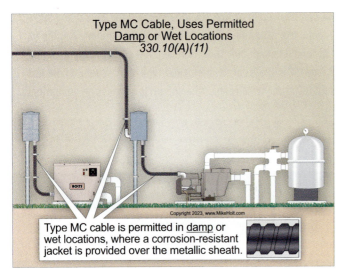

▶Figure 330–2

(B) Specific Uses.

(1) Cable Tray. Type MC cable can be installed in a cable tray in accordance with Article 392.

(2) Direct Buried. Direct-buried cables must be protected in accordance with 300.5.

(3) Installed as Service-Entrance Cable. Type MC cable is permitted to be used as service-entrance cable when installed in accordance with 230.43.

(4) Installed Outside Buildings. Type MC cable installed outside buildings must comply with 225.10, 396.10, and 396.12.

330.30 Securing and Supporting

A new sentence was added to say that MC cable fittings are permitted as a means of cable support.

Analysis

EXPANDED
New language says that MC cable fittings are permitted as a means of cable support. This was previously located in (D), Unsupported Cables. The relocation to (A), General, makes it clear that the cable fitting can be the required support for any MC cable installation and not just for unsupported cables.

330.30 Securing and Supporting

(A) General. Type MC cable must be supported and secured by staples, cable ties listed and identified for securing and supporting, straps, hangers, similar fittings, or other approved means designed and installed so the cable is not damaged. ▶Figure 330–3

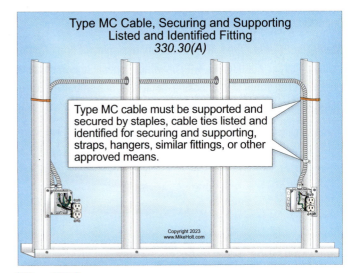

▶Figure 330–3

Type MC cable fittings are permitted as a means of cable support.

(B) Securing. Type MC cable with four or fewer conductors sized no larger than 10 AWG must be secured within 12 in. of every outlet box, junction box, cabinet, or fitting and at intervals not exceeding 6 ft.
▶Figure 330–4

Metal-Clad Cable (Type MC) | 330.30

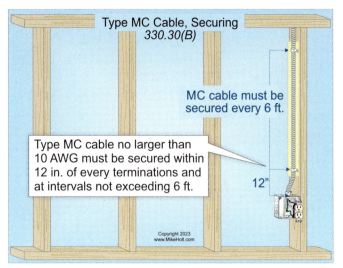
▶Figure 330-4

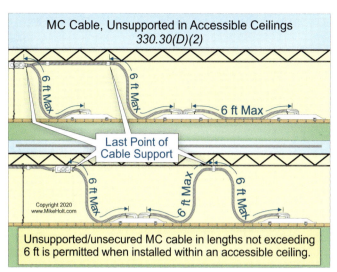
▶Figure 330-6

(C) Supporting. Type MC cable must be supported at intervals not exceeding 6 ft. Cables installed horizontally through wooden or metal framing members are considered secured and supported if such support does not exceed 6-ft intervals. ▶Figure 330-5

(3) Type MC cable can be unsupported and unsecured where not more than 3 ft from the last point where it is securely fastened to provide flexibility for equipment that requires movement after installation, or to connect equipment where flexibility is necessary to minimize the transmission of vibration from the equipment. ▶Figure 330-7

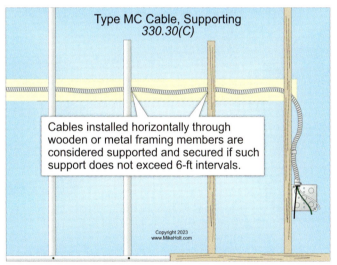
▶Figure 330-5

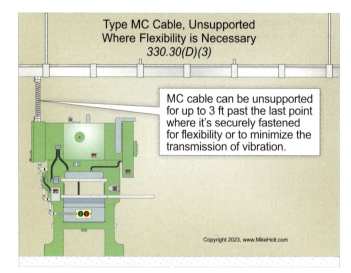
▶Figure 330-7

(D) Unsupported and Unsecured Cables.

(1) Type MC cable can be unsupported and unsecured where fished through concealed spaces in a finished building and support is impractical.

(2) Type MC cable can be unsupported and unsecured where not more than 6 ft long from the last point of cable support to the point of connection to a luminaire or electrical equipment within an accessible ceiling. ▶Figure 330-6

Changes to the National Electrical Code 2023 | MikeHolt.com | 177

Notes

ARTICLE 334 — NONMETALLIC-SHEATHED CABLE: TYPES NM AND NMC

Introduction to Article 334—Nonmetallic-Sheathed Cable: Types NM and NMC

Nonmetallic-sheathed cable (Type NM) provides very limited physical protection for the conductors inside, so the installation restrictions are stringent, and the use of Type NM cable is limited by building construction types. Its low cost and relative ease of installation makes it a common wiring method for residential branch circuits.

Definitions. The following definition(s) contained in Article 100 is(are) important as they relate to this article.

Nonmetallic-Sheathed Cable (Type NM). A wiring method that encloses two or more insulated conductors within a nonmetallic jacket [Article 100]. ▶Figure 334–1

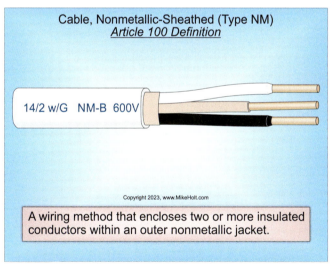

▶Figure 334–1

Author's Comment:

▸ It is the generally accepted practice in the electrical industry to call Type NM cable, "Romex®," which is a registered trademark of the Southwire Company.

334.10 Uses Permitted

List item (2) now permits the use of NM cable in detached garages associated with multifamily dwellings where the garages are of Types III, IV, and V construction.

Analysis

EXPANDED Detached garages associated with multifamily dwellings are often permitted to be of Types III, IV, or V construction and are like other locations where NM cable is permitted, so this change allows them to be wired in the same way.

334.10 Uses Permitted

Type NM cables can be used in:

(1) One-family and two-family dwellings and their garages and storage buildings. ▶Figure 334–2

(2) Type NM cable is permitted in multifamily dwellings <u>and their detached garages</u> in buildings of Types III, IV, and V construction. ▶Figure 334–3

(3) Other buildings of Types III, IV, and V construction where the cable must be concealed within walls, floors, or ceilings that provide a thermal barrier of material with at least a 15-minute finish rating, as identified in listings of fire-rated assemblies. ▶Figure 334–4

334.10 | Nonmetallic-Sheathed Cable: Types NM and NMC

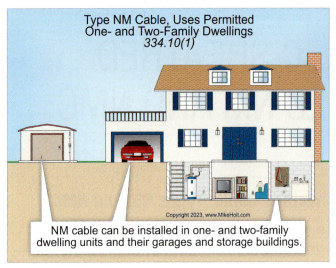
▶Figure 334–2

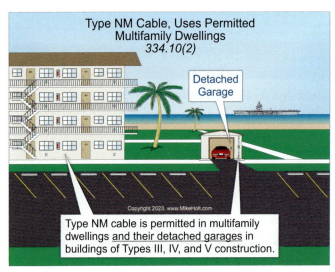
▶Figure 334–3

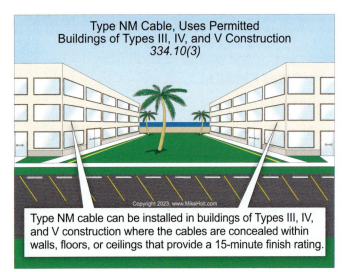
▶Figure 334–4

Note 2: See Annex E of the *NEC* for the determination of building types and the limits of the number of stories permitted for each type.

> **Author's Comment:**
> ▸ See the definition of "Concealed" in Article 100.

Note 1: For additional information on building code construction types, see NFPA 220, *Standard on Types of Building Construction*.

334.12 Uses Not Permitted

(A) Type NM. Type NM cable is not permitted:

(1) In any dwelling or structure not specifically permitted in 334.10(1), (2), (3), and (5).

(2) Exposed within a dropped or suspended ceiling in other than dwelling units. ▶Figure 334–5

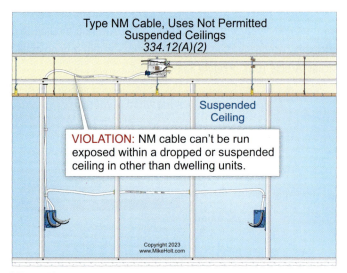
▶Figure 334–5

(3) As service-entrance cable.

(4) In commercial garages having hazardous (classified) locations, as defined in 511.3.

(5) In theaters and similar locations, except where permitted in 518.4(B).

(6) In motion picture studios.

(7) In storage battery rooms.

(8) In hoistways, or on elevators or escalators.

(9) Embedded in poured cement, concrete, or aggregate.

(10) In any hazardous (classified) location, except where permitted by other sections in this *Code*.

(B) Type NM. Type NM cable is not permitted to be used under the following conditions, or in the following locations:

(1) If exposed to corrosive fumes or vapors.

(2) If embedded in masonry, concrete, adobe, fill, or plaster.

(3) In a shallow chase in masonry, concrete, or adobe and covered with plaster, adobe, or similar finish.

(4) In wet or damp locations. ▶Figure 334-6

▶Figure 334-6

Author's Comment:

▶ Raceways above the vapor barrier in ground floor slabs are not located in a wet location because the concrete is not in direct contact with the Earth [Article 100].

334.15 Exposed Work

New language requires protection from abrasion at the entrance and exit of conduit or tubing used to provide protection for NM cable.

Analysis

EXPANDED New language in (B) and (C) requires NM cable to be protected from abrasion at the entrance and exit of conduit or tubing used to provide protection for the cable. Most installers do this anyway but this change will remove potential conflict from the enforcement side of things.

334.15 Exposed Work

Except as provided in 300.11(B), exposed Type NM cable can be installed as follows:

(A) Surface of the Building. Exposed Type NM cable must closely follow the surface of the building.

(B) Protected from Physical Damage. Nonmetallic-sheathed cable must be protected from physical damage by a raceway (Schedule 80 PVC, RMC, IMC, or EMT), guard strips, or other means approved by the authority having jurisdiction. ▶Figure 334-7

Where Type NM cable is installed in a raceway, a bushing or adapter that provides protection from abrasion at the point of cable entry is required. ▶Figure 334-8

(C) In Unfinished Basements and Crawl Spaces. If Type NM cable is installed at angles with joists in unfinished basements and crawl spaces, cables containing conductors not smaller than two 6 AWG, or three 8 AWG can be secured directly to the lower edges of the joists. Smaller cables must be installed through bored holes in joists or on running boards. ▶Figure 334-9

334.19 | Nonmetallic-Sheathed Cable: Types NM and NMC

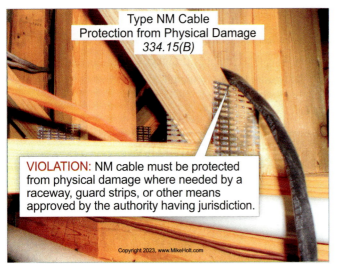
▶Figure 334–7

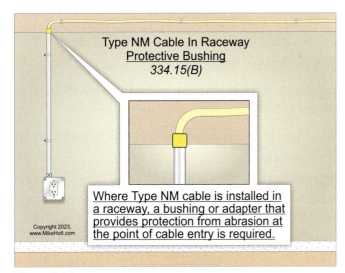
▶Figure 334–8

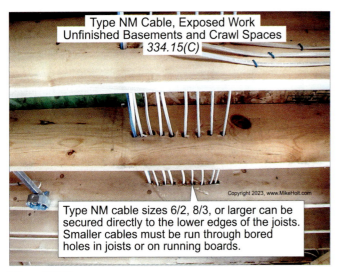
▶Figure 334–9

Type NM cable installed on a wall of an unfinished basement or crawl space subject to physical damage must be protected in accordance with 300.4 or be installed within a raceway with a nonmetallic bushing or adapter that provides protection from abrasion at the point where the cable enters the raceway. The cable must be secured within 12 in. of the point where it enters the raceway.

334.19 Cable Entries

A new requirement was added for the sheath of NM cable to extend at least ¼ in. past any cable clamp or cable entry.

Analysis

NEW This requirement is already in 314.17(B)(2) for boxes and was added here to cover all cable entries, regardless of the enclosure type. This ensures the conductor is protected from abrasion by the cable sheath until it is inside the enclosure.

334.19 Cable Entries

The sheath on nonmetallic-sheathed cable must extend no less than ¼ in. beyond any cable clamp or cable entry. ▶Figure 334–10

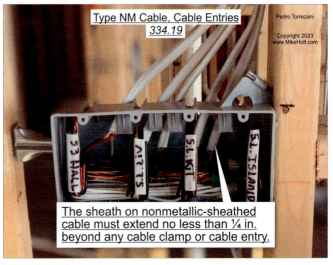
▶Figure 334–10

334.40 Boxes and Fittings

Splicing self-contained devices is now permitted in concealed locations for both existing and new buildings.

Analysis

EXPANDED These devices have been in use for years with no problem. As prefab construction gains popularity, permitting the use of these splicing devices in concealed locations for both existing and new buildings just makes sense. In the previous *Code*, they were only permitted to be installed in concealed locations for repairs in existing buildings.

334.40 Boxes and Fittings

(B) NM Cable Interconnector Devices. A listed for use without a box nonmetallic-sheathed cable interconnector device can be installed in both exposed and concealed installations. ▶Figure 334–11

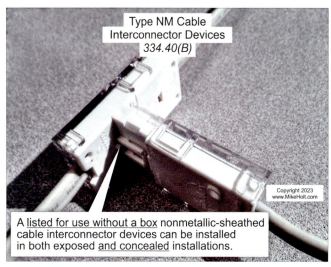

A listed for use without a box nonmetallic-sheathed cable interconnector devices can be installed in both exposed and concealed installations.

▶Figure 334–11

Notes

ARTICLE 352 — RIGID POLYVINYL CHLORIDE CONDUIT (PVC)

Introduction to Article 352—Rigid Polyvinyl Chloride Conduit (PVC)

Rigid polyvinyl chloride conduit (PVC) is a rigid nonmetallic conduit that provides many of the advantages of rigid metal conduit while allowing installation in wet or corrosive areas. It is an inexpensive raceway and easily installed, lightweight, easily cut and glued together, and relatively strong. However, rigid polyvinyl chloride (PVC) is brittle when cold and will sag when hot. This type of conduit is commonly used as an underground raceway because of its low cost, ease of installation, and resistance to corrosion and decay. There are two types of PVC, one is schedule 40 which is used in most applications and schedule 80 which is used were the conduit is subject to physical damage.

Definitions. The following definition(s) contained in Article 100 is(are) important as they relate to this article.

Rigid Polyvinyl Chloride Conduit (PVC). A rigid nonmetallic raceway of circular cross section with integral or associated couplings, listed for the installation of electrical conductors [Article 100]. ▶Figure 352–1

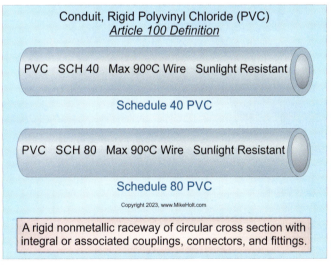

▶Figure 352–1

352.10 Uses Permitted

A new subdivision (B) permits PVC to be encased in concrete and subdivision (K), Physical Damage, was added.

Analysis

NEW — The new subdivision (B) permits PVC to be encased in concrete. We have done this for years, but the practice was not specifically permitted in the *Code*. The remaining subdivisions were reorganized to allow for the new subdivision (B).

NEW — The requirements in the new subdivision (K) installations that are subject to physical damage are more specific than what was previously in (F). Now PVC that is subject to physical damage must be Schedule 80 PVC and listed fittings must be used. A new Informational Note tells us that PVC fittings are suitable for use with both Schedule 40 and Schedule 80 PVC conduit.

352.10 | Rigid Polyvinyl Chloride Conduit (PVC)

352.10 Uses Permitted

PVC conduit is permitted in the following applications:

Note: In extreme cold, PVC conduit can become brittle and is more susceptible to physical damage.

(A) Concealed. PVC conduit can be concealed within walls, floors, or ceilings.

(B) Encased in Concrete. PVC conduit is permitted to be encased in concrete. ▶Figure 352-2

▶Figure 352-2

(C) Corrosive Influences. PVC conduit is permitted in areas subject to severe corrosion for which the material is specifically approved by the authority having jurisdiction.

(E) Wet Locations. PVC conduit is permitted in wet locations such as dairies, laundries, canneries, car washes, and other areas frequently washed. It is also permitted in outdoor locations. Support fittings such as straps, screws, and bolts must be made of corrosion-resistant materials or must be protected with a corrosion-resistant coating in accordance with 300.6(A).

(F) Dry and Damp Locations. PVC conduit is permitted in dry and damp locations except where limited in 352.12.

(G) Exposed. Schedule 40 PVC conduit is permitted to be installed in exposed locations where the raceway is not subject to physical damage. ▶Figure 352-3

Note: PVC Schedule 80 conduit is identified for use in areas subject to physical damage.

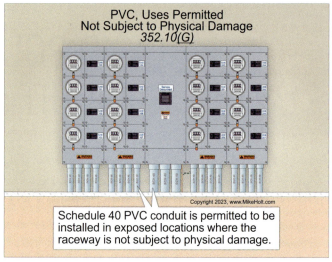

▶Figure 352-3

(H) Underground. PVC conduit is permitted to be installed underground and in concrete and must comply with the burial requirements of 300.5.

(K) Physical Damage. Where subject to physical damage, Schedule 80 PVC and associated fittings must be used. ▶Figure 352-4

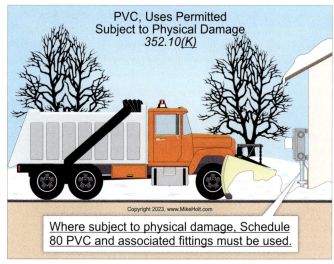

▶Figure 352-4

Note: All listed PVC conduit fittings are suitable for connection to both Schedule 40 and Schedule 80 PVC conduit.

Rigid Polyvinyl Chloride Conduit (PVC) | 352.44

352.44 Expansion Fittings

The previous text of this section became subdivision (A), Thermal Expansion and Contraction, and a new subdivision (B), Earth Movement, was added.

Author's Comment:

▸ When determining the number and setting of expansion fittings, you must read the manufacturer's documentation. For example, instructions for Carlon® expansion fittings for PVC conduit say that when it has sunlight exposure, 30°F must be added to the high ambient temperature.

Analysis

REORGANIZED   EXPANDED

The previous text of this section became subdivision (A), Thermal Expansion and Contraction, with no technical change. A new subdivision (B), Earth Movement, was added requiring expansion fittings be used to address earth movement including frost heave where runs of PVC emerge from the earth. This was already common practice in colder climates but is now clearly required.

352.44 Expansion Fittings

(A) Thermal Expansion and Contraction. If PVC conduit is installed in a straight run between securely mounted items such as boxes, cabinets, elbows, or other conduit terminations, expansion fittings must be provided if the expansion or contraction length change in accordance with Table 352.44(A) is expected to be ¼ in. or greater. ▸Figure 352–5

Table 352.44(A) Expansion Characteristics of PVC Rigid Nonmetallic Conduit Coefficient of Thermal Expansion			
Temperature Change (°C)	Length of Change of PVC Conduit (mm/m)	Temperature Change (°F)	Length Change of PVC Conduit (in./100 ft)
5	0.30	5	0.20
10	0.61	10	0.41
15	0.91	15	0.61
20	1.22	20	0.81
25	1.52	25	1.01
30	1.83	30	1.22
35	2.13	35	1.42
40	2.43	40	1.62
45	2.74	45	1.83
50	3.04	50	2.03
55	3.35	55	2.23
60	3.65	60	2.43
65	3.95	65	2.64
70	4.26	70	2.84
75	4.56	75	3.04
80	4.87	80	3.24
85	5.17	85	3.45
90	5.48	90	3.65
95	5.78	95	3.85
100	6.08	100	4.06

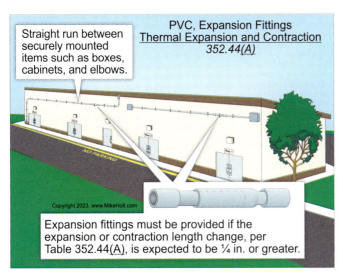

▸Figure 352–5

(B) Earth Movement. When necessary to compensate for earth settling or movement including frost heave, expansion fittings above ground must be installed.

Note: See 300.5(J).

Notes

ARTICLE 356 — LIQUIDTIGHT FLEXIBLE NONMETALLIC CONDUIT (LFNC)

Introduction to Article 356—Liquidtight Flexible Nonmetallic Conduit (LFNC)

Liquidtight flexible nonmetallic conduit (Type LFNC) is a listed raceway of circular cross section with an outer liquidtight, nonmetallic, sunlight-resistant jacket over an inner flexible core with associated couplings, connectors, and fittings. It is commonly referred to as "Carflex®."

Definitions. The following definition(s) contained in Article 100 is(are) important as they relate to this article.

Liquidtight Flexible Nonmetallic Conduit (LFNC). A raceway of circular cross section, with an outer liquidtight, nonmetallic, sunlight-resistant jacket over a flexible inner core, with associated couplings, connectors, and fittings, listed for the installation of electrical conductors [Article 100]. ▶Figure 356–1

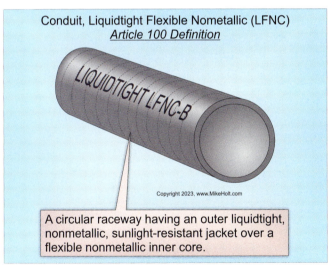

▶Figure 356–1

356.10 Uses Permitted

A new list item (8) permits LFNC to be installed in locations subject to severe corrosive influences.

Analysis

NEW The new list item (8) permits LFNC to be installed in locations subject to severe corrosive influences from chemicals. LFNC is specifically approved for use in these areas as covered by 300.6. This addition permits the specific approvals found in Article 680 for pool equipment.

EDITED The rule in former item (8) was relocated to (9) and states that conductors and cables with a higher temperature rating than LFNC are permitted to be used if they are not operated at a temperature that exceeds the rating of LFNC.

356.10 Uses Permitted

Listed LFNC is permitted, either exposed or concealed, at any of the following purposes and locations:

(1) If flexibility is required.

(2) If protection from liquids, vapors, machine oils, or solids is required.

(3) Outdoors, if listed and marked for this purpose.

356.10 | Liquidtight Flexible Nonmetallic Conduit (LFNC)

(4) Directly buried in the Earth if listed and marked for this purpose.
▶Figure 356–2

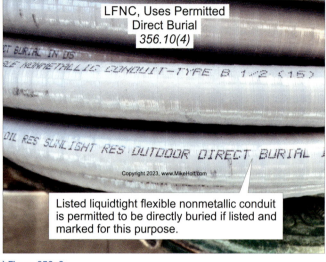

▶Figure 356–2

(5) Installed in lengths over 6 ft if secured in accordance with 356.30.

(6) LFNC-B (black color) as a listed manufactured prewired assembly.

(7) Encasement in concrete if listed for direct burial.

(8) In locations subject to severe corrosive influences as covered in 300.6, and where listed for exposure to specific chemicals.

(9) Conductors or cables rated at a temperature higher than the listed temperature rating of LFNC conduit are permitted to be installed in LFNC, provided the conductors or cables are not operated at a temperature higher than the listed temperature rating of the LFNC.

Note: Extreme cold can cause some types of nonmetallic conduits to become brittle and therefore more susceptible to damage from physical contact.

ARTICLE 358

ELECTRICAL METALLIC TUBING (EMT)

Introduction to Article 358—Electrical Metallic Tubing (EMT)

Electrical metallic tubing (EMT) is perhaps the most used raceway in commercial and industrial installations. It is a lightweight raceway that is relatively easy to bend, cut, and ream. Because EMT is not threaded, all connectors and couplings are of the threadless type (either set screw or compression) and provide for quick, easy, and inexpensive installations as compared to other metallic raceway systems—all of which make it very popular.

Definitions. The following definition(s) contained in Article 100 is(are) important as they relate to this article.

Electrical Metallic Tubing (EMT). An unthreaded thinwall circular metallic raceway used for the installation of electrical conductors. When joined together with listed fittings and enclosures as a complete system, it is a reliable wiring method providing both physical protection for conductors as well an effective ground-fault current path [Article 100]. ▶Figure 358–1

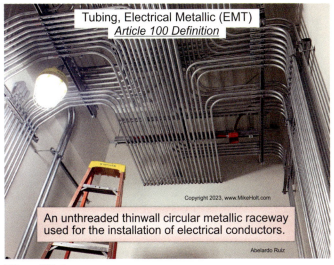

▶Figure 358–1

358.10 Uses Permitted

Two permitted uses for EMT were added.

Analysis

NEW

Two permitted uses for EMT were added in list item (1) and list item (4).

List item (1) was expanded to permit the use of EMT for direct burial applications when used with fittings listed and identified for direct burial.

New item (4) permits EMT to be used for manufactured wiring systems as permitted in 604.100(A)(2). That is going to be a real time saver for floor level connections!

358.10 Uses Permitted

(A) Exposed and Concealed. EMT is permitted to be used exposed and concealed for the following applications: ▶Figure 358–2

358.10 | Electrical Metallic Tubing (EMT)

▶Figure 358–2

(1) In concrete and in direct contact with the earth with fittings identified for direct burial. ▶Figure 358–3

▶Figure 358–3

(2) In dry, damp, or wet locations.

(3) In any hazardous (classified) location as permitted by other articles in this *Code*.

(B) Corrosive Environments.

(1) Galvanized Steel. Galvanized and stainless steel EMT, elbows, and fittings can be installed in concrete, in direct contact with the earth, or in areas subject to severe corrosive influences if protected by corrosion protection and approved as suitable for the condition.

> **Author's Comment:**
>
> ▸ According to UL "FJMX" Guide, supplementary corrosion protection is required when EMT and associated fittings are buried. In addition, supplementary corrosion protection is required at the point where EMT transitions from concrete encasement to the soil.

(D) Wet Locations. Support fittings such as screws, straps, and so on, installed in a wet location must be made of corrosion-resistant material.

Note: See 300.6 for protection against corrosion.

> **Author's Comment:**
>
> ▸ If installed in wet locations, fittings for EMT must be listed for use in wet locations and prevent moisture or water from entering or accumulating within the enclosure in accordance with 314.15 [358.42].

ARTICLE 362 ELECTRICAL NONMETALLIC TUBING (ENT)

Introduction to Article 362—Electrical Nonmetallic Tubing (ENT)

Electrical nonmetallic tubing is a pliable, corrugated, circular raceway. It resembles the flexible tubing you might see used at swimming pools. It is often referred to as "Smurf Pipe" or "Smurf Tube" (as a reference to the children's cartoon characters "The Smurfs") because it was only available in blue when it first came out. It can now be purchased in additional colors such as red and yellow.

Definitions. The following definition(s) contained in Article 100 is(are) important as they relate to this article.

Electrical Nonmetallic Tubing (ENT). A pliable corrugated raceway of circular cross section, with integral or associated couplings, connectors, and fittings that are listed for the installation of electrical conductors. It is composed of a material that is resistant to moisture and chemical atmospheres and is flame retardant [Article 100]. ▶Figure 362-1

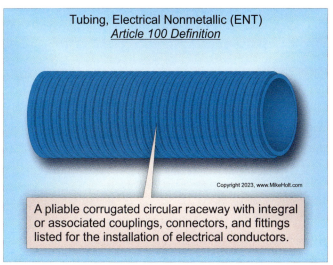

▶Figure 362-1

Electrical nonmetallic tubing can be bent by hand with reasonable force but without other assistance [Article 100].

362.10 Uses Permitted

Editorial changes were made in list item (2) and its Exception, and to list items (5) and (7). List item (6) was added to allow concrete encasement.

Analysis

EDITED Editorial changes were made in list item (2) and its Exception, and to list items (5) and (7) to simplify the language and provide clarity, but no technical changes were made.

One of the common uses for ENT is encasement in concrete. The new list item (6) clarifies that ENT can be encased in poured concrete floors, ceilings, walls, and slabs. The remaining list items were reorganized to allow for this new item.

362.10 Uses Permitted

Electrical nonmetallic tubing is permitted as follows:

(1) In buildings not exceeding three floors. ▶Figure 362-2

   a. Exposed, where not prohibited by 362.12.

   b. Concealed within walls, floors, and ceilings.

362.10 | Electrical Nonmetallic Tubing (ENT)

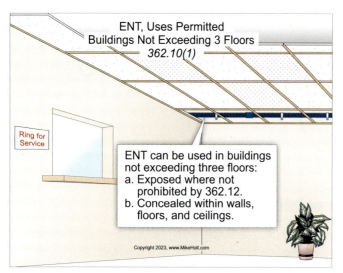
▶Figure 362–2

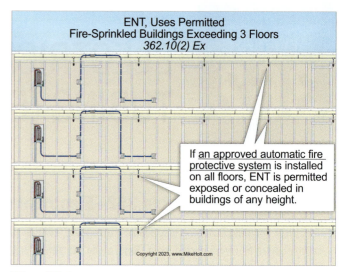
▶Figure 362–4

(2) In buildings exceeding three floors, where installed concealed within combustible or noncombustible walls, floors, or ceilings that provide a thermal barrier having a 15-minute finish rating, as identified in listings of fire-rated assemblies. ▶Figure 362–3

(3) In severe corrosive and chemical locations [300.6] when identified for this use.

(4) In dry and damp concealed locations if not prohibited by 362.12.

(5) Above a suspended ceiling if the suspended ceiling provides a thermal barrier having a 15-minute finish rating, as identified in listings of fire-rated assemblies. ▶Figure 362–5

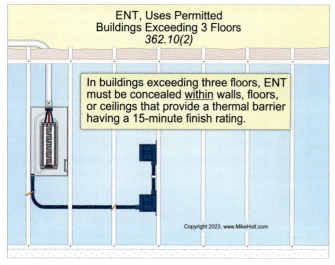
▶Figure 362–3

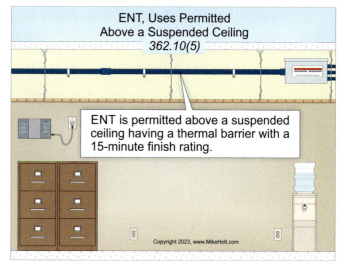
▶Figure 362–5

Ex to (2): If an approved automatic fire protective system is installed on all floors, electrical nonmetallic tubing is permitted exposed or concealed in buildings of any height. ▶Figure 362–4

Author's Comment:

▸ ENT is not permitted above a suspended ceiling used as a plenum space [300.22(C)].

Ex to (5): If an approved automatic fire protective system is installed on all floors, ENT is permitted above a suspended ceiling that does not have a 15-minute finish rated thermal barrier. ▶Figure 362–6

(6) Encased in poured concrete floors, ceilings, walls, and slabs.

(7) Embedded in a concrete slab provided fittings identified for the purpose are used.

Electrical Nonmetallic Tubing (ENT) | 362.10

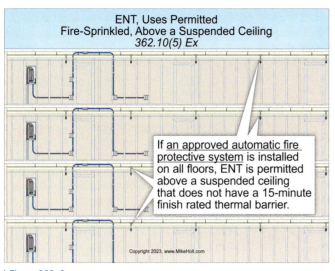
▶Figure 362-6

(8) In wet locations, or in a concrete slab on or below grade, with fittings that are listed for the purpose.

Notes

ARTICLE 376 — METAL WIREWAYS

Introduction to Article 376—Metal Wireways

Metal wireways are commonly used where access to conductors inside a raceway is required to make terminations, splices, or taps to several devices at a single location. High cost precludes their use for other than short distances, except in some commercial or industrial occupancies where the wiring is frequently revised.

They are often incorrectly called "troughs," "auxiliary gutters," "auxiliary wireways," or "gutters" in the field. Wireways and auxiliary gutters are similar in design but one of the main differences is in the application. A wireway is a raceway (Article 100) while an auxiliary gutter [Article 366] is a supplemental enclosure for wiring and is not considered a raceway.

Definitions. The following definition(s) contained in Article 100 is(are) important as they relate to this article.

Metal Wireway. A sheet metal trough with hinged or removable covers for housing and protecting electrical conductors and cable, and in which conductors are placed after the raceway has been installed [Article 100]. ▶Figure 376–1

A sheet metal trough with hinged or removable covers for housing and protecting electric wires and cable, and in which conductors are placed after the raceway has been installed.

▶Figure 376–1

376.60 Equipment Grounding Conductor

This new section permits a listed metal wireway to be used as an EGC.

Analysis

NEW — This new section permits listed metal wireways to be used as EGCs in accordance with 250.118(A)(13). Metal wireways are not required to be listed, so unlisted wireways will still require an EGC of the wire type.

376.60 Equipment Grounding Conductor

Listed metal wireways are permitted to serve as an equipment grounding conductor in accordance with 250.118(A)(13). ▶Figure 376–2

376.60 | Metal Wireways

▶ Figure 376-2

CHAPTER 4
EQUIPMENT FOR GENERAL USE

Introduction to Chapter 4—Equipment for General Use

With the first three chapters of the *NEC* behind you, this fourth one is necessary for building a solid foundation in general equipment installations. Some examples of general equipment include but are not limited to luminaires, heaters, motors, air-conditioning units, generators, and transformers. It helps you apply the first three chapters to installations involving general equipment. You need to understand the first four chapters of the *Code* to properly apply the requirements to Chapters 5, 6, and 7, and at times to Chapter 8.

Chapter 4 is arranged in the following manner although not all of these are covered in this material:

- **Article 400—Flexible Cords and Flexible Cables.** Article 400 covers the general requirements, applications, and construction specifications for flexible cords and flexible cables.

- **Article 402—Fixture Wires.** This article covers the general requirements and construction specifications for fixture wires.

- **Article 404—Switches.** The requirements of Article 404 apply to switches of all types. These include snap (toggle) switches, dimmer switches, fan switches, knife switches, circuit breakers, and automatic switches such as time clocks, timers, and switches and circuit breakers used for disconnects.

- **Article 406—Receptacles and Attachment Plugs (Caps).** This article covers the rating, type, and installation of receptacles and attachment plugs. It also covers flanged surface inlets.

- **Article 408—Switchboards and Panelboards.** Article 408 covers specific requirements for switchboards, panelboards, and distribution boards that supply lighting and power circuits.

Author's Comment:

▸ See Article 100 for the definitions of "Panelboard" and "Switchboard."

- **Article 410—Luminaires and Lamps.** This article contains the requirements for luminaires, lampholders, and lamps. Because of the many types and applications of luminaires, manufacturer's instructions are very important and helpful for proper installation.

- **Article 411—Low-Voltage Lighting.** Article 411 covers lighting systems, and their associated components, which operate at no more than 30V alternating current, or 60V direct current.

- **Article 422—Appliances.** This article covers electric appliances used in any occupancy.

...

Chapter 4 | Equipment for General Use

> **Author's Comment:**
>
> ▸ Dishwashers, water heaters, ovens, and cooktops, are all appliances per the Article 100 definition. It is a very broad term that covers utilization equipment that as a unit performs one or more functions.
>
> - **Article 424—Fixed Electric Space-Heating Equipment.** Article 424 covers fixed electric equipment used for space heating. For the purposes of this article, heating equipment includes heating cable, unit heaters, boilers, central systems, and other fixed electric space-heating equipment. Article 424 does not apply to process heating or room air-conditioning.
>
> - **Article 430—Motors, Motor Circuits, and Controllers.** This article contains the specific requirements for conductor sizing, overcurrent protection, control circuit conductors, motor controllers, and disconnects. The installation requirements for motor control centers are covered in Article 430, Part VIII. This Article has fourteen parts [XIV], the most in the *Code*.
>
> - **Article 440—Air-Conditioning Equipment.** Article 440 applies to electrically driven air-conditioning equipment with a motorized hermetic compressor. The requirements in this article are in addition to, or amend, the requirements in Article 430 and others.
>
> - **Article 445—Generators.** Article 445 contains the electrical installation requirements for both portable generators and stationary generators which are required to be listed [445.6]. Installation requirements such as where they can be located, nameplate markings, conductor ampacity, and disconnects are also covered.
>
> - **Article 450—Transformers.** This article covers the installation of transformers. Understanding the overcurrent protection Table 450.3(B) and the disconnect location is important to provide protection properly.
>
> - **Article 480—Storage Batteries.** Article 480 covers stationary installations of storage batteries.

ARTICLE 404 SWITCHES

Introduction to Article 404—Switches

The requirements of Article 404 address switches of all types including snap (toggle) switches, dimmer switches, fan switches, disconnect switches, circuit breakers, and automatic switches such as time clocks and timers.

404.1 Scope

New language tells us that Article 404 does not apply to battery-powered wireless control equipment.

Analysis

CLARIFIED A new sentence was added clarifying that Article 404 does not apply to wireless control equipment that is not connected to circuit conductors like a wireless remote control. Now if we can just figure out what a listed wall-mounted control device is we are going to be doing well.

A new Informational Note tells us to see 210.70 for a related requirement where battery-powered control devices are used to control a required lighting outlet.

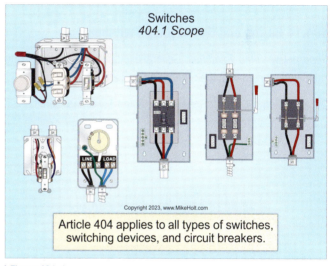

▶Figure 404–1

404.1 Scope

The requirements of Article 404 apply to all types of switches, switching devices, and circuit breakers. ▶Figure 404–1

This article does not cover wireless control equipment to which circuit conductors are not connected.

Note: See 210.70 for additional information related to branch circuits that include switches or listed wall-mounted control devices.

404.14 Rating and Use of Switches

A new subdivision (D) was added addressing push-in terminals, and 15A and 20A snap switches not marked CO/ALR can now be used with copper-clad aluminum.

404.14 | Switches

Analysis

NEW — The new (D)(1) clarifies that 15A and 20A snap switches not marked CO/ALR can be used with copper and copper-clad aluminum.

NEW — A new (D)(2) clarifies that snap switches marked CO/ALR can be used with copper, aluminum, and copper-clad aluminum as stated in the UL guide information.

NEW — The new (D)(3) restricts the use of push-in terminals to 14 AWG solid copper conductors unless the switch is listed and marked otherwise.

404.14 Rating and Use of Snap Switches

General-Use Snap Switches. General-use snap switches must be listed and marked with their ratings as indicated.

(A) Alternating-Current General-Use Snap Switches. General-use snap switches are permitted to control:

(4) Motor loads not exceeding 80 percent of the ampere rating of the switch at its rated voltage [430.109(C)(2)].

(5) Electronic ballasts, self-ballasted lamps, compact fluorescent lamps, and LED lamp loads with their associated drivers, not exceeding 20A and not exceeding the ampere rating of the switch at the voltage applied.

(C) CO/ALR Snap Switches. Aluminum conductors connected to snap switches rated 20A or less must be marked CO/ALR.

(D) Snap Switch Terminations. Snap switch terminations must be installed in accordance with the following:

(1) 15A and 20A snap switches not marked CO/ALR can only be used with copper and copper-clad aluminum conductors.

(2) Switch terminals marked CO/ALR can be used with aluminum, copper, and copper-clad aluminum conductors.

(F) Dimmer and Electronic Control Switches. General-use dimmer switches, timer switches, and occupancy sensors are only permitted to control connected loads, such as permanently installed incandescent luminaires, unless listed for the control of other loads.

Such switches must be marked by the manufacturer with their current and voltage ratings and used for loads not exceeding their ampere rating at the voltage applied.

ARTICLE 406
RECEPTACLES, ATTACHMENT PLUGS, AND FLANGED INLETS

Introduction to Article 406—Receptacles, Attachment Plugs, and Flanged Inlets

This article covers the rating, type, and installation of receptacles, attachment plugs, and flanged inlets. There are many types of receptacles such as self-grounding, isolated ground, tamper resistant, weather resistant, GFCIs and AFCIs, energy controlled, work surface and countertop assemblies, USBs, surge protectors, and so on. Examine the rules carefully and remember an outlet is not a receptacle.

406.3 Receptacle Rating and Type

The title of (C) was changed to clarify that this section covers receptacles marked CO/ALR and a new subdivision (D) is another change related to the use of copper-clad aluminum conductors.

Analysis

CLARIFIED — The title of (C) was changed to clarify that this section covers receptacles marked CO/ALR. This rule only applies to receptacles rated 20A or less.

NEW — Subdivision (D) was added to address the use of copper-clad aluminum conductors. Where a 15A or 20A receptacle is not marked CO/ALR, it can only be used with copper or copper-clad aluminum conductors. The CO/ALR marking permits the receptacle to be used with aluminum, copper, or copper-clad aluminum conductors. Where the receptacle has push-in terminals, it can only be installed on 14 AWG solid copper conductors.

406.3 Receptacle Rating and Type

(A) Receptacles. Receptacles must be listed and marked with the manufacturer's name or identification and voltage and ampere ratings.

(C) CO/ALR Receptacles. Aluminum conductors connected to receptacles rated 20A or less must be marked CO/ALR.

(D) Receptacle Terminations. Receptacle terminations must be in accordance with the following:

(1) Terminals for 15A and 20A receptacles not marked CO/ALR can only be used with copper and copper-clad aluminum conductors.

(2) Receptacle terminals marked CO/ALR can be used with aluminum, copper, and copper-clad aluminum conductors.

(E) Isolated Ground Receptacles. Receptacles with an isolated equipment grounding conductor connection must be identified by an orange triangle on the face of the receptacle. ▶Figure 406–1

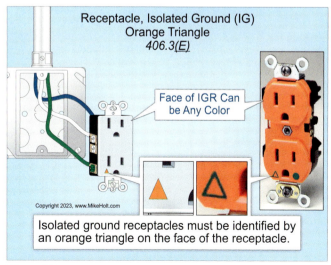

▶Figure 406–1

406.4 | Receptacles, Attachment Plugs, and Flanged Inlets

(1) Isolated ground receptacles must have the grounding contact of the receptacle connected to an insulated equipment grounding conductor installed with the circuit conductors in accordance with 250.146(D). ▶Figure 406-2

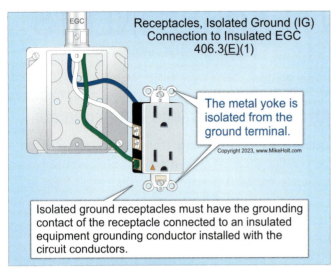

▶Figure 406-2

(F) Controlled Receptacle Marking. Nonlocking, 15A or 20A, 125V nonlocking-type receptacles that are automatically controlled to remove power for energy management or building automation must be permanently marked with the word "controlled" and have a visible power symbol on the receptacle after installation. ▶Figure 406-3

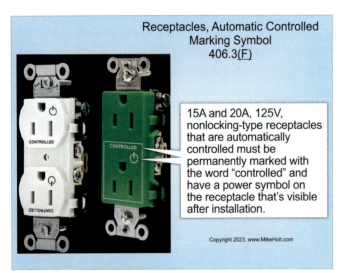

▶Figure 406-3

Author's Comment:

▸ ICC Energy Code C405.6 and ASHREA 90.1 section 8.4 requires "Automatic Receptacle Control" to reduce electrical power demands on commercial buildings from cord-and-plug-connected loads such as cell phone chargers, computer monitors, task lighting, and other equipment that consumes energy even in the off state.

406.4 General Installation Requirements

The titles of both (B) and (C) were changed to be specific as to the type of grounding conductor covered in the subdivision. In addition, a new last sentence was added to (D)(3) requiring a GFCI to be a listed device.

Analysis

CLARIFIED The titles of both (B) and (C) talked about "grounding" conductors. They were revised to clarify that these rules are about "equipment grounding" conductors.

EDITED Editorial changes in (C) added a reference to 250.146, and the language for cord connectors was revised to clarify that EGCs must be connected to the cord connector.

CLARIFIED A new last sentence in (D)(3) requires the GFCI to be a listed device. In addition, the new (D)(8) requires GFPE protection to be provided when receptacles are replaced that require such protection, such as marina shore power receptacles.

NEW A new (G) contains relocated requirements for floor receptacles and adds a requirement for GFCI protection in certain locations.

Receptacles, Attachment Plugs, and Flanged Inlets | 406.4

406.4 General Installation Requirements

(A) Grounding Type. Receptacles installed on 15A and 20A branch circuits must be of the grounding type, except as permitted for 2-wire receptacle replacements as permitted in 406.4(D)(2). ▶Figure 406–4

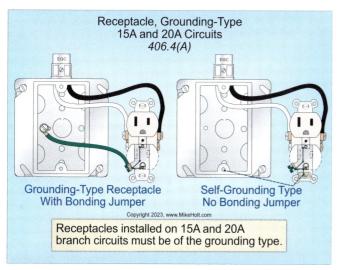

▶Figure 406–4

Grounding-type receptacles must be installed on circuits rated in accordance with Table 210.21(B)(1) for single receptacles and Table 210.21(B)(2) or Table 210.21(B)(3) for two or more receptacles.

Table 210.21(B)(3) Receptacle Ratings	
Circuit Rating	Receptacle Rating
15A	15A
20A	15A or 20A
30A	30A
40A	40A or 50A
50A	50A

(C) Methods of Connection to Equipment Grounding Conductor. The equipment grounding conductor contacts of receptacles must be connected to the equipment grounding conductor of the circuit supplying the receptacle in accordance with 250.146. ▶Figure 406–5

Cord connectors must be connected to the circuit equipment grounding conductor.

Note 1: For acceptable types of equipment grounding conductors see 250.118(A).

Note 2: See 250.130 for extensions of existing branch circuits.

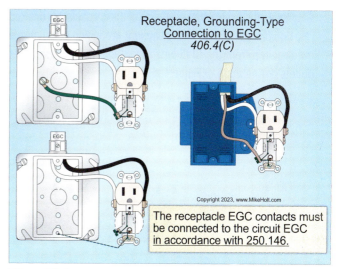

▶Figure 406–5

(D) Receptacle Replacement. If the receptacle to be replaced is in a location that requires AFCI- and/or GFCI-type receptacles, the replacement receptacle must be installed at a readily accessible location and comply with (D)(1) though (D)(8).

(1) Equipment Grounding Conductor in Outlet Box. If an equipment grounding conductor exists in an outlet box, replacement receptacles must be of the grounding type and the receptacle's grounding terminal must be connected to the circuit equipment grounding conductor in accordance with 406.11.

(2) No Equipment Grounding Conductor in Box. If an equipment grounding conductor does not exist in the outlet box, replacement receptacles can be a:

(a) Nongrounding-type receptacle. ▶Figure 406–6

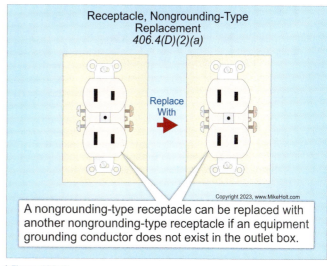

▶Figure 406–6

406.4 | Receptacles, Attachment Plugs, and Flanged Inlets

(b) GFCI-type receptacle if the receptacle or the cover plate is marked "No Equipment Ground." An equipment grounding conductor is not required from the GFCI-type receptacle to any receptacle outlets downstream. ▶Figure 406–7

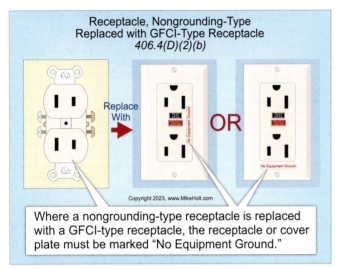

▶Figure 406–7

(c) Grounding-type receptacle where GFCI protected if the receptacle or the cover plate is marked "GFCI Protected" and "No Equipment Ground." An equipment grounding conductor is not required from the GFCI-protected grounding-type receptacle to any receptacle outlets downstream. ▶Figure 406–8

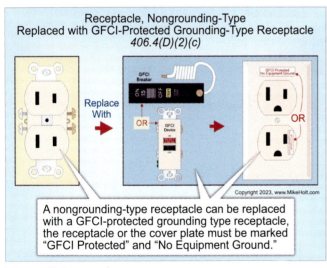

▶Figure 406–8

Author's Comment:

▸ GFCI protection functions properly on a 2-wire circuit without an equipment grounding conductor because the circuit's equipment grounding conductor serves no role in the operation of a GFCI device. See the Article 100 definition of "Ground-Fault Circuit Interrupter" in this material for more information. ▶Figure 406–9

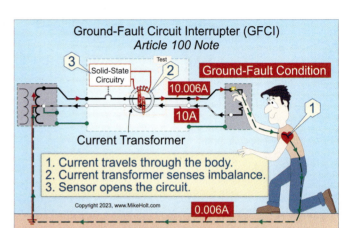

▶Figure 406–9

CAUTION: The permission to replace nongrounding-type receptacles with GFCI-protected grounding-type receptacles does not apply to new receptacle outlets extending from an existing outlet box that is not connected to an equipment grounding conductor. ▶Figure 406–10

Note 1: Some equipment or appliance manufacturers require the branch circuit to the equipment or appliance to include an equipment grounding conductor.

Note 2: See 250.114 for a list of cord-and-plug-connected equipment or appliances that require an equipment grounding conductor.

(3) GFCI Protection Required. When existing receptacles are replaced in locations where GFCI protection is required, the replacement receptacles must be GFCI protected.

Ex: Where the outlet box size will not permit the installation of a GFCI receptacle, a GFCI-protected grounding-type receptacle marked "GFCI Protected" and "No Equipment Ground" in accordance with 406.4(D) is permitted.

Receptacles, Attachment Plugs, and Flanged Inlets | **406.6**

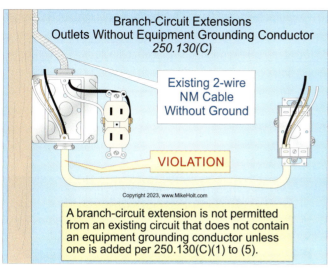
▶Figure 406–10

Author's Comment:

▸ See 210.8 for specific locations requiring GFCI protection.

▸ Where an *NEC* rule requires GFCI protection, it can be provided by a GFCI circuit breaker, GFCI receptacle, or downstream of a feed-through type GFCI receptacle.

(4) Arc-Fault Circuit Interrupters. When existing receptacles are replaced in locations where AFCI protection is required [210.12(B)], the replacement receptacle(s) must be one of the following:

(1) A listed AFCI receptacle.

(2) A receptacle protected by a listed AFCI receptacle.

(3) A receptacle protected by an AFCI circuit breaker.

(5) Tamper-Resistant Receptacles. When existing receptacles are replaced in locations where tamper resistance is required [406.12], the replacement receptacle(s) must be listed tamper resistant, except as follows:

(1) Where a nongrounding receptacle is replaced with another nongrounding receptacle.

(2) Where a receptacle, connected to aluminum conductors, is replaced with a CO/ALR receptacle.

(6) Weather-Resistant Receptacles. When existing receptacles are replaced in locations where weather resistance is required, replacement receptacles must be weather resistant in accordance with 406.9(A) and (B).

(7) Controlled Receptacles. Automatically controlled receptacles must be replaced with an equivalently controlled receptacle. If automatic control of the receptacle is no longer required, the replacement receptacle must not be marked in accordance with 406.3(F).

(8) Ground-Fault Protection of Equipment (GFPE). Receptacles must be provided with GFPE where replacements are made at receptacle outlets that are required to be GFPE protected.

(G) Protection of Floor Receptacles.

(1) Physical Protection. Physical protection of floor receptacles must allow floor-cleaning equipment to be operated without damaging the receptacles.

(2) GFCI Protected. All 125V, single-phase, 15A and 20A floor receptacles in food courts and waiting spaces of passenger transportation facilities must be GFCI protected.

406.6 Receptacle Faceplates

One of the coolest recent additions to the array of device faceplates is the integral night light and USB charger faceplate. Changes this cycle limit the maximum power they can use.

Analysis

CLARIFIED A recent addition to the world of receptacle faceplates includes those with nightlights and chargers that connect via spring clips to the receptacle screws. While this is more of a DIY product than an installation product, they have shown up on every shelf. To limit the risk of fire, the maximum load is limited to 1W, and they are limited to devices with brass or copper alloy receptacle terminal screws. An Exception will permit their use with receptacles having steel terminal screws if the faceplate device is listed and identified for use with steel screws. This Exception is effective January 1, 2026.

406.9 | Receptacles, Attachment Plugs, and Flanged Inlets

406.6 Receptacle Faceplates

Faceplates for receptacles must completely cover the outlet openings and press against the mounting surface. ▶Figure 406–11

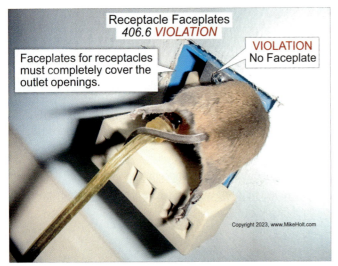
▶Figure 406–11

(B) Grounding. Metal faceplates for receptacles must be connected to the circuit equipment grounding conductor.

> **Author's Comment:**
> ▸ The *Code* does not specify how this is accomplished, but 517.13(B)(1)(4) for health care facilities permits the metal mounting screw(s) securing the faceplate to a metal outlet box or wiring device to be suitable for this purpose. ▶Figure 406–12

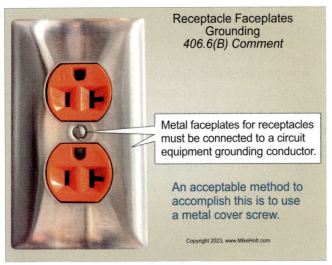
▶Figure 406–12

(D) Receptacle Faceplates with Integral Night Light/USB Charger. Listed receptacle faceplates with an integral night light, USB charger, or both, that rely solely on spring-tensioned contacts must be connected to only brass or copper alloy receptacle terminal screws.

406.9 Receptacles in Damp or Wet Locations

Hinged covers of outlet box hoods must now open at least 90° after installation, other than 15A and 20A receptacles are required to be weather resistant, and bathroom receptacle rules have become more complicated.

Analysis

EXPANDED New language was added to (A) and (B), requiring hinged covers of outlet box hoods be able to open at least 90° after installation, or to open fully if not designed to open 90°. This will ensure it will be easier to connect the attachment plug and reset a tripped GFCI.

Receptacles rated 30A or more are commonly installed and exposed to severe environmental influences as are 15A and 20A receptacles. Corrosion can cause overheating at the terminals of the receptacle. Because of that, new language in (B)(2) requires them to be of the weather-resistant type and improves electrical safety.

Revisions to (C), Bathtub and Shower Space, clarify that the horizontal zone from the top of the bathtub rim or shower stall threshold that prohibits receptacles includes the area below the zone. This closed a loophole inadvertently left after changes last cycle.

NEW The new Exception No. 1 permits the hydromassage bathtub receptacle to be within the tub or shower zone. It is typically installed in the equipment space under the tub.

Receptacles, Attachment Plugs, and Flanged Inlets | 406.9

CLARIFIED Exception No. 2 was revised to clarify that the bathroom sink receptacles required by 210.52(D) in a small dwelling unit bathroom can be located within the tub or shower zone as specified within the rule.

NEW Exception No. 4 was added to permit a single receptacle for an electronic toilet or electronic bidet seat to be in the tub or shower zone, but it must be on the opposite side of the toilet from the tub or shower.

406.9 Receptacles in Damp or Wet Locations

(A) Damp Locations. Receptacles installed in a damp location must be of the weather-resistant (WR) type and installed in an enclosure that is weatherproof when an attachment plug is not inserted (damp location rated), or when the attachment plug is inserted when the cover is closed (wet location rated). ▶Figure 406–13

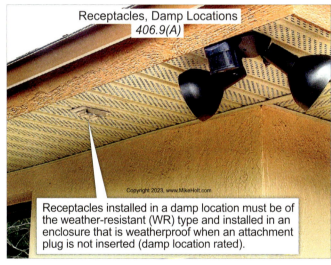
▶Figure 406–13

An example of a damp location is one where a receptacle is under roofed open porches, canopies, or marquees, and will not be subjected to a beating rain or water runoff.

Hinged covers of outlet box hoods must be able to open at least 90°, or fully open if the cover is not designed to open 90° from the closed to open position, after installation.

Author's Comment:

▸ The main difference between the cover for a 15A or 20A receptacle in a damp location [406.9(A)] and a wet location [406.9(B)] is whether it is weather resistant when the attachment plug is inserted. ▶Figure 406–14

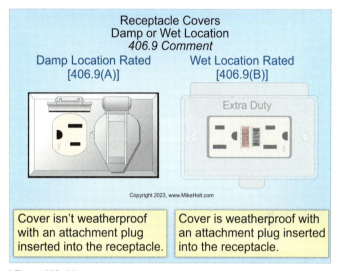
▶Figure 406–14

(B) Wet Locations.

(1) 15A and 20A Receptacles. 15A and 20A receptacles installed in a wet location must be within an enclosure that is weatherproof when an attachment plug is inserted using an outlet box hood identified as "extra duty." ▶Figure 406–15

▶Figure 406–15

406.9 | Receptacles, Attachment Plugs, and Flanged Inlets

Hinged covers of outlet box hoods must be able to open at least 90°, or fully open if the cover is not designed to open 90° from the closed to open position, after installation. ▶Figure 406-16

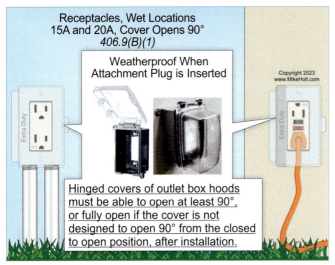

▶Figure 406-16

Nonlocking-type 15A and 20A receptacles in a wet location must be listed as the weather-resistant type. ▶Figure 406-17

▶Figure 406-17

Author's Comment:

▸ Exposed plastic surface material of weather-resistant receptacles must have UV resistance to ensure deterioration from sunlight either does not take place or is minimal. In testing, receptacles are subjected to temperatures cycling from very cold to very warm conditions, and then subjected to additional dielectric testing. The rapid transition from the cold to warm temperatures changes the relative humidity and moisture content on the device, and the dielectric test ensures this will not create a breakdown of the insulation properties.

▸ A wet location is an area subject to saturation with water and unprotected locations exposed to weather [Article 100].

(2) Other Receptacles. Receptacles rated 30A or more installed in a wet location must be listed as the weather-resistant type and comply with (a) or (b).

(a) Unattended While in Use. A receptacle where the load is not attended while in use must be in an enclosure that is weatherproof when an attachment plug is inserted.

(b) Attended While in Use. A receptacle that will only be used while someone is nearby, such as one used with portable tools, can use an enclosure that is weatherproof when the cover is closed.

(C) Bathtub and Shower Space. Receptacles are not permitted inside a tub or shower or within 3 ft horizontally from any outside edge of a bathtub or shower stall, including the space measured vertically from the floor to 8 ft vertically above the top of the bathtub rim or shower stall threshold. ▶Figure 406-18

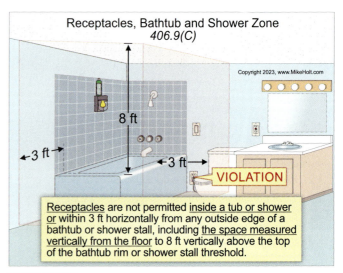

▶Figure 406-18

Ex 1: Receptacles for hydromassage bathtubs installed in accordance with 680.73 are permitted to be installed in the prohibited receptacle zone. ▶Figure 406-19

Receptacles, Attachment Plugs, and Flanged Inlets | **406.12**

▶Figure 406–19

▶Figure 406–21

Ex 2: In dwelling unit bathrooms with less than the required zone, the bathroom sink receptacle, required by 210.52(D), is permitted to be in the prohibited receptacle zone if on the furthest wall opposite the bathtub rim or shower stall threshold. ▶Figure 406–20

406.12 Tamper-Resistant Receptacles

These rules were expanded once again to include additional required locations.

Analysis

EXPANDED Tamper-resistant receptacles have been protecting curious minds for years now. This *Code* cycle, additional locations that require protection were added to the list.

CLARIFIED Exception No. 3 was clarified to say that a single receptacle for a single appliance, or a duplex receptacle for two appliances, not readily accessible and located within the space designated for the appliance(s) are exempt from this rule.

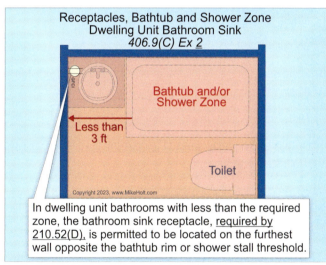
▶Figure 406–20

Ex 4: In dwelling unit bathrooms, a single receptacle for an electronic toilet or electronic bidet seat is permitted in the prohibited receptacle zone if the receptacle is not in the space between the toilet and the bathtub or shower. ▶Figure 406–21

406.12 Tamper-Resistant Receptacles

Nonlocking-type 15A and 20A receptacles in the following areas must be tamper resistant "TR":

406.12 | Receptacles, Attachment Plugs, and Flanged Inlets

Author's Comment:

▸ Inserting an object into one slot of a tamper-resistant receptacle does not open the internal shutter mechanism. Simultaneous pressure applied to the polarized slots is required to insert the plug. ▸Figure 406–22

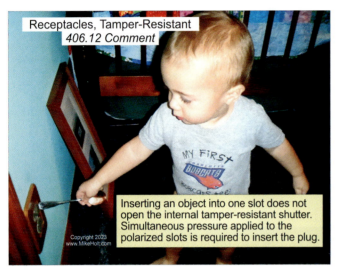

▸Figure 406–22

(1) In dwelling units, boathouses, mobile homes, and manufactured homes, including their attached and detached garages and accessory buildings, and common areas of multifamily dwellings.
▸Figure 406–23

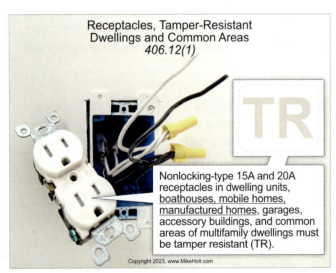

▸Figure 406–23

(2) In hotel and motel guest rooms and guest suites, and their common areas.

(3) In childcare facilities.

Author's Comment:

▸ A childcare facility is a building or portions of a building used for educational, supervision, or personal care services for five or more children seven years in age or less [Article 100].

(4) In preschools and education facilities.

Author's Comment:

▸ This applies to all educational facilities including high schools, colleges, vocational schools, universities, and so forth.

(5) Within clinics, medical and dental offices, outpatient facilities, and the following spaces:

   a. Business offices accessible to the general public
   b. Lobbies and waiting spaces
   c. Spaces of nursing homes and limited care facilities used exclusively as patient sleeping rooms

(6) Places of awaiting transportation, gymnasiums, skating rinks, fitness centers, and auditoriums.

(7) Dormitory units.

(8) Residential care/assisted living facilities, social and substance abuse rehabilitation facilities, and group homes.

(9) Foster care facilities, nursing homes, and psychiatric hospitals.

(10) Areas and common areas of agricultural buildings accessible to the general public.

Note 3: Areas of agricultural buildings frequently converted to hospitality areas include petting zoos, stables, and buildings used for recreation or educational purposes.

Ex to (1) through (10): Receptacles in the following locations are not required to be tamper resistant:

(1) Receptacles more than 5½ ft above the floor. ▸Figure 406–24
(2) Receptacles that are part of a luminaire or appliance.
(3) A receptacle within dedicated space for an appliance that in normal use is not easily moved.
(4) Nongrounding receptacles installed as permitted in 406.4(D)(2)(a).

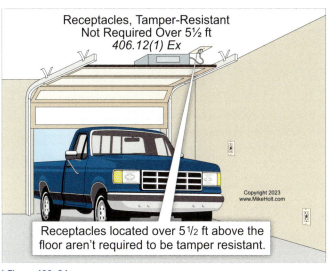
▶Figure 406-24

Notes

ARTICLE 408 SWITCHBOARDS, SWITCHGEAR, AND PANELBOARDS

Introduction to Article 408—Switchboards, Switchgear, and Panelboards

Article 408 covers the specific requirements for switchboards, switchgear, and panelboards that control power and lighting circuits. As you study this article, keep these key points in mind:

- Perhaps the most important objective of Article 408 is to ensure that the installation will prevent contact between current-carrying conductors and people or equipment.
- The circuit directory of a panelboard must clearly identify the purpose or use of each circuit that originates in the panelboard.
- You must understand the detailed grounding and overcurrent protection requirements for panelboards.

408.4 Circuit Directory and Descriptions of Circuit Source

The term "identification" in 408.4(A) was replaced with the term "description" in this section (and in the title) to avoid confusion with the defined term "identified." Additional language was added to subdivision (B) that requires the marking to include the physical location of the power source.

Analysis

CLARIFIED The term "identification" in 408.4(A) was replaced with the term "description" to avoid confusion with the defined term "identified." The rule was also reorganized into a list format for clarity. Two of the six list items are new requirements. Item (4) requires a degree of detail in the description that will make confusion between circuits unlikely, and (6) requires that symbols or abbreviations, if used, be clearly explained.

EXPANDED Subdivision (B) was reorganized into a list. In addition, new language requires the physical location of the power source to be marked on the panel in other than one- or two-family dwellings. This will make it easier to find and shut off the power in larger buildings.

408.4 Circuit Directory and Descriptions of Circuit Source

(A) Circuit Descriptions. Circuits and circuit modifications must be provided with a legible and permanent description on a circuit directory as follows:

(1) Switchboard. Located at each switch or circuit breaker in a switchboard.

(2) Panelboard. Be located on the face of, inside of, or in an approved location adjacent to the panel door in the case of a panelboard. ▶Figure 408–1

(3) Purpose of Circuit Description. The directory must identify the specific purpose or use of each circuit including spare positions for unused overcurrent protective devices. ▶Figure 408–2

408.9 | Switchboards, Switchgear, and Panelboards

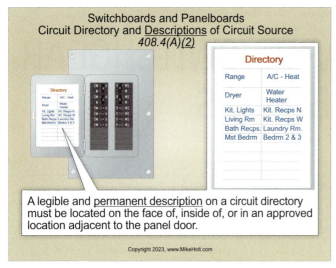
▶Figure 408–1

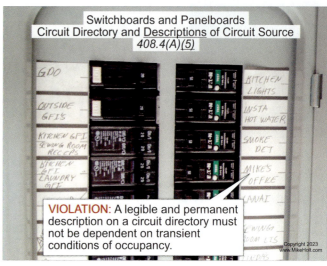
▶Figure 408–3

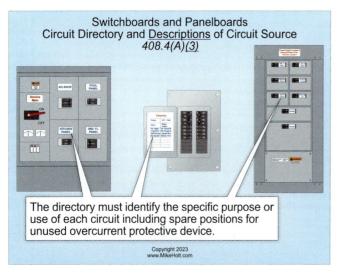
▶Figure 408–2

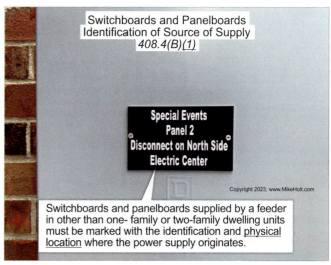
▶Figure 408–4

(4) Circuit Description Details. Described with a degree of detail and clarity that is unlikely to result in confusion between circuits.

(5) Transient Conditions. Not dependent on transient conditions of occupancy such as "Dad's Office." ▶Figure 408–3

(6) Abbreviations and Symbols. Clear in explaining abbreviations and symbols when used.

(B) Description of Source of Supply. Switchboards and panelboards supplied by a feeder, in other than one- family or two-family dwelling units must be marked as follows:

(1) With the identification and physical location where the power supply originates. ▶Figure 408–4

(2) With a permanent label that withstands the environment involved in accordance with 110.22(A).

(3) Using a method that is not handwritten.

408.9 Replacement Panelboards

This is a new section that provides guidance for installing new "guts" in an existing enclosure.

Switchboards, Switchgear, and Panelboards | 408.43

Analysis

NEW — This is a new section, but the information was previously found in the reconditioning rule. It permits the installation of a new panelboard in an existing enclosure and provides guidance for two installation options.

408.9 Replacement Panelboards

(B) Panelboards Not Listed for the Specific Enclosure.

10,000A and Greater. If the available fault current is greater than 10,000A, the completed work must be field labeled.

Authors Comment:

▸ In accordance with Article 100, "Field Labeled" is defined as "equipment or materials which have a label, symbol, or other identifying mark of a field evaluation body (FEB) indicating the equipment or materials were evaluated and found to comply with the requirements described in the accompanying field evaluation report."

Not Over 10,000A. If the available fault current is 10,000A or less, the replacement panelboard must be identified for the application. Any previously applied listing marks on the cabinet that pertain to the panelboard must be removed.

408.43 Panelboard Orientation

This rule was expanded to prohibit face-down installations of panelboards.

Analysis

EXPANDED — Last *Code* cycle, a new rule prohibited panelboards from being installed in the face-up position to address a common practice in laundry facilities. Changes this cycle also prohibit a face-down installation. I am not sure how often that is really done, but it is good to know that you cannot do it.

408.43 Panelboard Orientation

Panelboards are not permitted to be installed in the face-up or face-down position. ▸Figure 408–5

▸Figure 408–5

Notes

ARTICLE 410 — LUMINAIRES, LAMPHOLDERS, AND LAMPS

Introduction to Article 410—Luminaires, Lampholders, and Lamps

This article covers luminaires, lampholders, lamps, decorative lighting products, and lighting for temporary seasonal and holiday use. Even though Article 410 is highly detailed, it is broken down into 16 parts. The first five are sequential, and apply to all luminaires, lampholders, and lamps:

- Part I. General
- Part II. Locations
- Part III. Outlet Boxes and Covers
- Part IV. Supports
- Part V. Equipment Grounding Conductors

Author's Comment:

- Article 411 addresses "Low-Voltage Lighting" which are lighting systems and their associated components that operate at no more than 30V alternating current or 60V direct current.

410.10 Luminaires in Specific Locations

Ceiling fans with light kits are not permitted in the bathtub/shower zone, and changes to 410.10(F) prohibit luminaire installations within 1½ in. of a roof deck.

Analysis

CLARIFIED We have been fighting about fans in bathrooms for a long time. This cycle (D)(1) clarifies that ceiling fans with light kits are not permitted in the bathtub or shower zone. Without a light kit, this rule does not apply. Be sure to check out the new rule, 422.18(B), for details.

EXPANDED The rule in 410.10(F) previously prohibited the installation of luminaires within 1½ in. of a corrugated metal roof deck. It mirrored 300.4(E). Changes this *Code* cycle now modify the requirement for any luminaire under any roof decking that is subject to physical damage. The good news is this only applies where luminaires are subject to physical damage.

A new Exception to this rule says that metal roof decks covered by at least 2 in. of concrete are exempt.

410.10 Luminaires in Specific Locations

(A) Wet or Damp Locations. Luminaires installed in wet locations must be marked as suitable for wet locations. Luminaires installed in damp locations must be marked as suitable for wet locations or suitable for damp locations. ▶Figure 410–1 and ▶Figure 410–2

410.10 | Luminaires, Lampholders, and Lamps

▶Figure 410-1

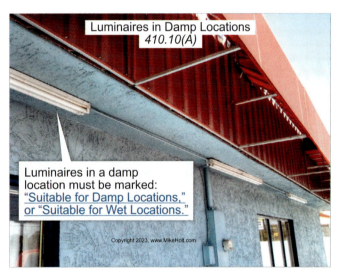

▶Figure 410-2

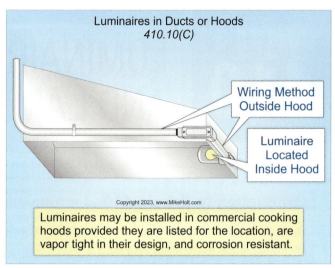

▶Figure 410-3

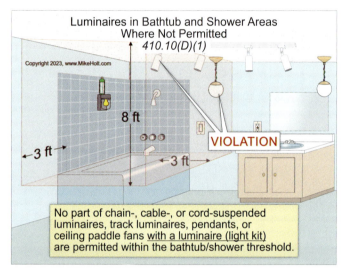

▶Figure 410-4

(B) Corrosive Locations. Luminaires installed in corrosive locations must be suitable for the location.

(C) In Ducts or Hoods. Luminaires may be installed in commercial cooking hoods provided they are listed for the location, are vapor tight in their design, and corrosion resistant. ▶Figure 410-3

(D) Bathtub and Shower Areas. A luminaire installed in a bathtub or shower area must meet all the following requirements:

(1) No part of chain-, cable-, or cord-suspended luminaires, track luminaires, pendants, or ceiling paddle fans with a luminaire (light kit) can be within 3 ft horizontally and 8 ft vertically of the top of the bathtub rim or shower stall threshold. This zone is all-encompassing and includes spaces over tubs or showers. ▶Figure 410-4

(2) Luminaires within 3 ft horizontally and 8 ft vertically of the top of the bathtub rim or shower stall threshold must be marked for damp locations or marked suitable for wet locations. Where subject to shower spray, the luminaires must be marked suitable for wet locations. ▶Figure 410-5

(E) Luminaires in Indoor Sports, Mixed-Use, and All-Purpose Facilities. Luminaires using a mercury vapor or metal halide lamp subject to physical damage and installed in playing and spectator seating areas of indoor sports, mixed-use, or all-purpose facilities must be of the type that has a glass or plastic lamp shield. Such luminaires can have an additional guard. ▶Figure 410-6

Luminaires, Lampholders, and Lamps | 410.71

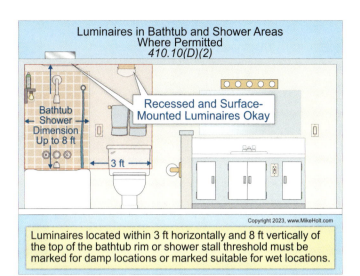
▶Figure 410-5

▶Figure 410-6

(F) Luminaires Installed Under Roof Decking. Luminaires installed under roof decking where subject to physical damage must be installed at least 1½ in. from the lowest surface of the roof decking, measured from the bottom of the decking to the top of the luminaire.

Ex: The 1½ in. spacing is not required where metal-corrugated sheet roof decking is covered with a minimum thickness 2 in. concrete slab, measured from the top of the corrugated roofing.

410.42 Luminaire(s) with Exposed Conductive Surfaces

This section was condensed into parent text and an Exception, and the title was changed to reflect the new content.

Analysis

CLARIFIED The word "parts" was replaced with "surfaces" throughout this rule to improve clarity. Now it is clear that exposed conductive surfaces must be connected to an EGC. An Exception was added with the existing language broken into list items that used to be part of the rule with no technical changes.

410.42 Luminaire(s) with Exposed Conductive Surfaces

Exposed conductive surfaces must be connected to an equipment grounding conductor.

Ex: Exposed conductive parts that comply with any of the following are not required to be connected to an equipment grounding conductor:

(1) Surfaces separated from all live parts by a listed system of double insulation.

(2) Surfaces on small, isolated parts, such as mounting screws, clips, and decorative bands on glass spaced at least 1½ in. from lamp terminals.

410.71 Disconnecting Means for Fluorescent or LED Luminaires that Utilize Double-Ended Lamps

This rule was relocated here from 410.130(G) since LEDs fall under the scope of Part VI of Article 410.

410.71 | Luminaires, Lampholders, and Lamps

Analysis

EXPANDED **RELOCATED**

Disconnecting LED lighting falls under Part VI of Article 410, not Part XII, so it was hard to find. Relocating these rules here matches the scope of Part VI and fits alongside other similar disconnect rules for fluorescent luminaires.

REORGANIZED

Exception No. 4 was reorganized into a list format for clarity. If all four conditions are met, the luminaire is not required to have a disconnecting means.

410.71 Disconnecting Means for Fluorescent or LED Luminaires that Utilize Double-Ended Lamps

(1) General. In indoor locations other than dwellings and associated accessory structures, fluorescent or LED luminaires that utilize double-ended lamps and contain a ballast(s) or LED driver(s) that can be serviced in place must have a disconnect either internal or external to each luminaire. ▶Figure 410-7

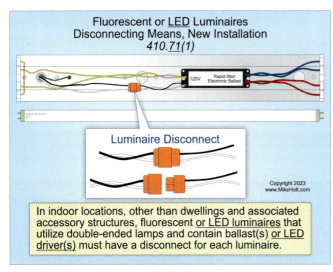
▶Figure 410-7

For existing installed luminaires without a disconnect when a fluorescent ballast or LED driver is added or replaced, a disconnect must be installed. The line-side terminals of the disconnect must be guarded.
▶Figure 410-8

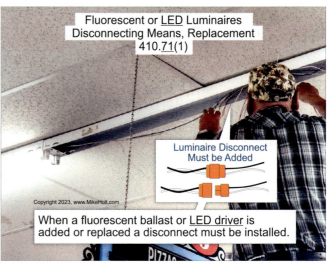
▶Figure 410-8

Ex 1: A disconnect is not required for luminaires installed in hazardous (classified) locations.

Ex 2: A disconnect is not required for luminaires that provide the emergency illumination required in 700.16.

Ex 3: For cord-and-plug-connected luminaires, an accessible separable connector or an accessible plug and receptacle is permitted to serve as the disconnect.

Ex 4: A disconnecting means is not required for every luminaire in a building area if all the following conditions apply:

(1) More than one luminaire is installed in the building area
(2) The luminaires are not connected to a multiwire branch circuit
(3) The design of the installation includes a disconnect
(4) The building area will not be left in total darkness should only one disconnect be opened

(2) Multiwire Branch Circuits. When connected to multiwire branch circuits, the disconnect must simultaneously break all the supply conductors to the ballast or driver, including the neutral conductor.

(3) Location. The disconnect must be accessible to qualified persons before servicing or maintaining the ballast or driver. Where the disconnect is external to the luminaire, it must be a single device, and it must be attached to the luminaire, or the luminaire must be within sight of the disconnect.

410.184 Ground-Fault Circuit-Interrupter (GFCI) Protection and Special Purpose Ground-Fault Circuit-Interrupter (SPGFCI) Protection

The title and text of this rule were revised to clarify that GFCI protection is required when horticultural lighting is connected using flexible cords connected with separable connectors or attachment plugs. In addition, a new Exception addresses SPGFCI protection for circuits over 150V to ground.

Analysis

CLARIFIED As the horticultural lighting industry grows, so do the hazards associated with the increasing number of installations. To address some of these hazards, it was clarified that GFCI protection is required where the horticultural lighting is connected with flexible cords using separable connectors or attachment plugs.

NEW A new Exception allows lighting equipment supplied by circuits over 150V to be protected with a listed special purpose ground-fault circuit interrupter which trips at 20 mA instead of 6 mA.

410.184 GFCI and Special Purpose GFCI Protection

Lighting equipment identified for horticultural use using flexible cord(s) with separable connector(s) or attachment plug(s) must be supplied by GFCI-protected lighting outlets.

Ex: Circuits exceeding 150V to ground must be protected by a listed special purpose ground-fault circuit interrupter.

Notes

ARTICLE 422 APPLIANCES

Introduction to Article 422—Appliances

Article 422 covers electric appliances that are fastened in place, permanently connected, or cord-and-plug-connected. The core content of this article is contained in Parts II and III. Part II provides installation requirements for branch circuits and overcurrent protection and Part III covers requirements for disconnects. Parts IV and V are primarily for manufacturers, but you should examine appliances for compliance before installing them.

422.5 GFCI Protection

The title of this section was shortened to use "GFCI," and drinking water fountains were added to the list of appliances requiring GFCI protection in (A).

Analysis

EDITED

Throughout the *Code* this cycle, the acronym "GFCI" as listed in Article 100, has replaced "ground-fault circuit-interrupter." That change is evident here in the section title, and some minor editorial changes were made for (A).

List item (2) was revised to include "drinking water fountains" to clear up confusion about what is required to be protected since the plumbing code uses this term as well as drinking water coolers for similar equipment.

▶Figure 422–1

422.5 GFCI Protection

(A) General. The following appliances rated 60A or less and for systems not exceeding 150V to ground must be GFCI protected.

(1) Automotive vacuum machines. ▶Figure 422–1

(2) Drinking water coolers, drinking water fountains, and bottle fill stations. ▶Figure 422–2

(3) Cord-and-plug-connected high-pressure spray washing machines.

(4) Tire inflation machines. ▶Figure 422–3

(5) Vending machines. ▶Figure 422–4

(6) Sump pumps. ▶Figure 422–5

(7) Dishwashers. ▶Figure 422–6

422.5 | Appliances

▶Figure 422-2

▶Figure 422-3

▶Figure 422-4

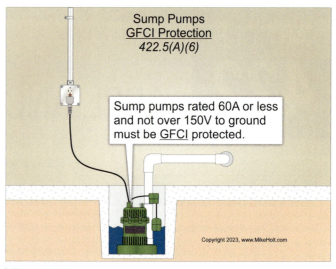

▶Figure 422-5

▶Figure 422-6

Note: See 210.8 which specifies requirements for GFCI protection for branch-circuit outlets where the location warrants such protection.

(B) Type and Location. The GFCI must be readily accessible and be:

(1) A GFCI circuit breaker,

(2) A GFCI faceless device or receptacle,

(3) A GFCI integral with the attachment plug,

(4) A GFCI within the supply cord not more than 12 in. from the attachment plug, or

(5) A factory installed GFCI within the appliance.

Appliances | **422.13**

422.13 Storage-Type Water Heaters

A couple minor editorial changes clarify what we are sizing and how the 125 percent applies.

Analysis

EDITED This rule is about sizing the branch-circuit conductors and OCPD for storage-type water heaters. The words "be sized not smaller" were replaced with the phrase "have an ampere rating of not less," and the word "ampere" was added after 125 percent.

422.13 Storage Water Heaters

The branch-circuit overcurrent protective device and conductors for storage-type water heaters with a capacity of 120 gallons or less must have an ampere rating of not less than 125 percent of the ampere rating of the water heater. ▶Figure 422–7

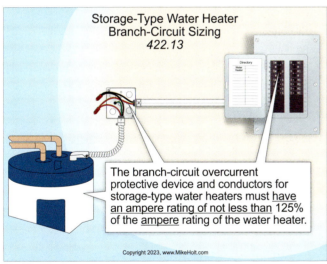
▶Figure 422–7

▶ Example

Question: What size conductor and overcurrent protection are required for a 4500W, 240V water heater? ▶Figure 422–8

(a) 20A/12 AWG
(b) 25A or 30A/10 AWG
(c) 40A/8 AWG
(d) 50A/6 AWG

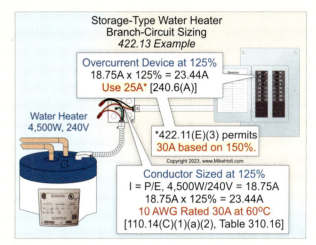
▶Figure 422–8

Solution:

Step 1: *Determine the branch-circuit rating [422.13].*

Circuit Current = 4500W/240V
Circuit Current = 18.75A

Circuit Rating = 18.75A × 125%
Circuit Rating = 23.44A

Circuit Conductor = 10 AWG rated 30A at 60°C [110.14)(C)(1)(a)(2) and Table 310.16]

Step 2: *Determine the overcurrent protection rating [422.13].*

Circuit Current = 4500W/240V
Circuit Current = 18.75A

Circuit Protection = 18.75A × 125%
Circuit Protection = 23.44A, use the next size up, 25A [240.6(A)]

Note: 422.11(E)(3) permits the overcurrent protective device to be sized up to 150 percent of the appliance rating.

Circuit Protection = 18.75A × 150%
Circuit Protection = 28.75A, use the next size up, 30A [240.6(A)]

Answer: *(b) 25A or 30A/10 AWG*

422.16 | Appliances

422.16 Flexible Cords

A new list item in (A)(3) contains information about flexible cords relocated from 422.43, and some other editorial changes were made to (B) for clarity.

Analysis

RELOCATED Sometimes it is hard to find all the requirements for a particular application. Moving the appliance flexible cord rules into a single section greatly improves usability. Another notable change is the removal of the 50W minimum for heater cords. Now, heater cords are required for electrically heated appliances that produce temperatures exceeding 250°F on surfaces with which the cord is likely to be in contact.

EDITED EXPANDED Editorial changes were made throughout (B) to address cord length and required protection where trash compactor cords pass through an opening into an adjacent compartment. These requirements are now similar to those for a dishwasher.

EXPANDED Subdivisions (B)(2)(4) and (5) have been expanded to permit the cord for a trash compactor or dishwasher to pass through a smoothed edge hole in the cabinet partition. This change acknowledges the common practice of sanding the edges of the opening to eliminate a sharp edge.

422.16 Flexible Cords

(A) General. Flexible cords are permitted for appliances when needed for:

(1) Facilitating frequent interchange or preventing the transmission of noise and vibration [400.10(A)(6) and 400.10(A)(7)].

(2) Facilitating the removal of appliances fastened in place where the fastening means and mechanical connections are specifically designed to permit ready removal [400.10(A)(8)].

Author's Comment:

▸ Flexible cords are not permitted for the connection of water heaters, furnaces, and other appliances fastened in place unless they are specifically identified to be used with a flexible cord.
▸Figure 422–9

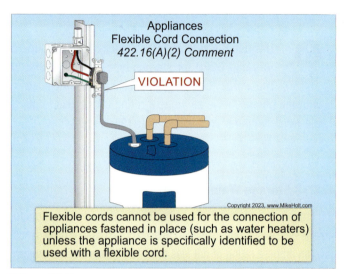
▸Figure 422–9

(3) All cord-and-plug-connected electrically heated appliances that produce temperatures exceeding 121°C (250°F) on surfaces with which the cord is likely to be in contact must be provided with one of the types of heater cords listed in Table 400.4.

(B) Specific Appliances.

(1) In-Sink Waste Disposal. A flexible cord is permitted for an in-sink waste disposal if: ▸Figure 422–10

▸Figure 422–10

(1) The flexible cord is at least 18 in. long and does not exceed 3 ft. in length.

(2) The receptacles are located so the flexible cord is protected from damage.

(3) The receptacle is accessible.

(4) The flexible cord has an equipment grounding conductor and is terminated with a grounding-type attachment plug.

Ex: A listed appliance distinctly marked to identify it as protected by a system of double insulation is not required to be terminated with a grounding-type attachment plug.

(2) Built-In Dishwashers and Trash Compactors. A flexible cord is permitted for a dishwasher or trash compactor if:

(1) For a trash compactor, the flexible cord cannot be less than 3 ft long or exceed 4 ft in length, measured from the rear plane of the appliance. ▶Figure 422–11

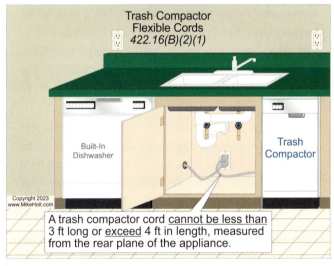
▶Figure 422–11

(2) For a dishwasher, the length of the flexible cord cannot be less than 3 ft long or exceed 6 ft 6 in. in length, measured from the face of the attachment plug to the rear plane of the appliance. ▶Figure 422–12

(3) The receptacles are located so the flexible cord is protected from damage.

(4) The receptacle for a trash compactor must be in the space occupied by the trash compactor or be in the space adjacent to the trash compactor. If a flexible cord passes through an opening, the cord must be protected against damage by a bushing, grommet, smoothed edged, or other approved means.

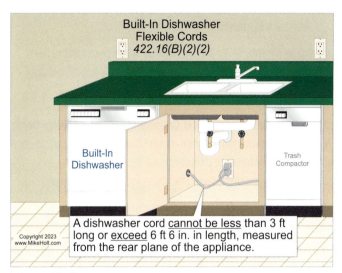
▶Figure 422–12

(5) The receptacle for the dishwasher is in the space adjacent to the dishwasher. If the flexible cord passes through an opening, it must be protected against damage by a bushing, grommet, smoothed edged, or other approved means. ▶Figure 422–13

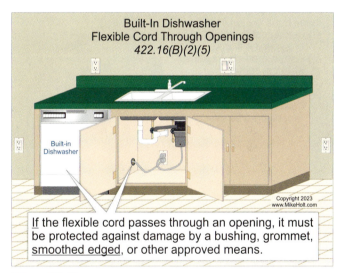
▶Figure 422–13

(6) The receptacle is accessible.

(7) The flexible cord has an equipment grounding conductor and is terminated with a grounding-type attachment plug.

Ex: A listed appliance distinctly marked to identify it as protected by a system of double insulation is not required to be terminated with a grounding-type attachment plug.

422.18 | Appliances

> **Author's Comment:**
> ▸ The receptacle for the dishwasher is not permitted to be of the GFCI Type, because it is not in a readily accessible spot as required by 210.8.

(3) Wall-Mounted Ovens and Counter-Mounted Cooking Units. Wall-mounted ovens and counter-mounted cooking units can be cord-and-plug-connected with a flexible cord identified as suitable for the purpose in the instructions of the appliance's manufacturer.

(4) Range Hoods and Microwave Oven/Range Hood Combinations. Range hoods and over-the-range microwave ovens with integral range hoods are permitted to be cord-and-plug-connected with a flexible cord identified as suitable for use on range hoods in the instructions of the appliance's manufacturer where all the following conditions are met: ▸Figure 422–14

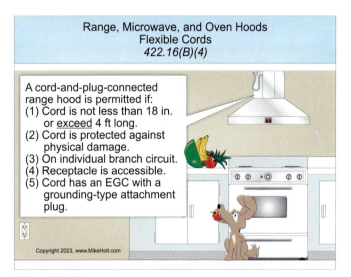

▸Figure 422–14

(1) The length of the cord is not less than 18 in. long and does not exceed 4 ft in length.

(2) Receptacles are located to protect against physical damage to the flexible cord.

(3) The receptacle is supplied by an individual branch circuit.

(4) The receptacle is accessible.

(5) The flexible cord has an equipment grounding conductor and is terminated with a grounding-type attachment plug.

Ex: A listed appliance distinctly marked to identify it as protected by a system of double insulation is not required to be terminated with a grounding-type attachment plug.

422.18 Ceiling-Suspended (Paddle) Fans

Revisions to the rules clarify that fan boxes must be identified for fan support. In addition, the terms "weight supporting ceiling receptacle" (WSCR) and "weight supporting attachment fitting" (WSAF) make an appearance along with a rule addressing the installation of paddle fans in tub and shower areas.

Analysis

EDITED There was a minor reorganization here and the rule in (1) was revised to use the phrase "fan support" where applicable. This alerts us to the fact that a fan box is to be identified for "fan support." While this adds clarity, there is no technical change.

The phrase "locking support and mounting receptacle, and a compatible factory installed attachment fitting designed for support" in list item (2) was replaced with the more descriptive terms "weight supporting ceiling receptacle" (WSCR) and "weight supporting attachment fitting" (WSAF). These newly defined terms are found in Article 100.

EXPANDED A new subdivision (B) prohibits any metal part of a ceiling-suspended paddle fan from being in a zone 3 ft horizontally and 8 ft vertically from the top of a bathtub rim or shower stall threshold. This requirement was previously in 410.10(D)(1), but that section only applies to paddle fans with a light kit, so it was added here as well. The good news is that most fans have nonmetallic blades so you still may be able to fit a fan in that bathroom!

422.18 Support of Ceiling-Suspended (Paddle) Fans

(B) Location. Metallic parts of ceiling fans in bathrooms and shower spaces are not permitted to be located within a zone measured 3 ft horizontally and 8 ft vertically from the top of the bathtub rim or shower stall threshold. ▸Figure 422–15

Appliances | 422.33

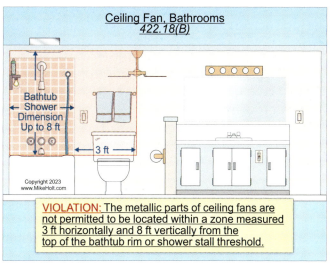

▶Figure 422–15

422.33 Disconnection of Cord-and-Plug-Connected or Attachment Fitting-Connected Appliances

The rule in (B) clarifies that a cord-and-plug connection for a range is considered accessible by the removal of the drawer at the front of the range.

Analysis

CLARIFIED This clarification of the previous text confirms that a cord-and-plug connection that is made accessible by the removal of a drawer meets the intent of 422.33(A).

422.33 Disconnection of Cord-and-Plug-Connected or Attachment Fitting-Connected Appliances

(A) Attachment Plug or Attachment Fitting. A cord-and-plug connection can serve as the appliance disconnect. ▶Figure 422–16

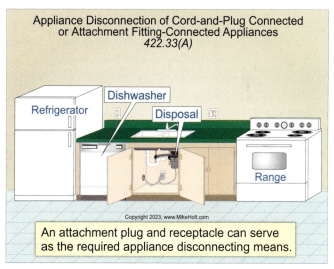

▶Figure 422–16

Changes to the National Electrical Code 2023 | MikeHolt.com

Notes

ARTICLE 424 — FIXED ELECTRIC SPACE-HEATING EQUIPMENT

Introduction to Article 424—Fixed Electric Space-Heating Equipment

Many people are surprised to see how many pages there are in Article 424. This is a nine-part article on fixed electric space heaters. Why is there so much text for what seems to be a simple application? The answer is that this article covers a variety of applications—heaters come in various configurations for various uses. Not all these parts are for the electrician in the field—the requirements in Part IV are for manufacturers.

Fixed space heaters (wall-mounted, ceiling-mounted, or free-standing) are common in many utility buildings and other small structures, as well as in some larger structures. When used to heat floors, space-heating cables address the thermal layering problem typical of forced-air systems—so it is likely you will encounter them. Duct heaters are very common in large office and educational buildings since they provide a distributed heating scheme. Locating the heater in the ductwork, but close to the occupied space, eliminates the waste of transporting heated air through sheet metal routed in unheated spaces, so it is likely you will encounter those as well.

424.4 Branch Circuits

The title and text of (B) were revised to clarify that this subdivision is about the sizing of the branch-circuit "conductors."

Analysis

CLARIFIED The word "conductor" was added to the title clarifying that this subdivision is about sizing branch-circuit conductors and not the overcurrent protection which is found in 424.22. The rule text was also revised to clarify that the branch-circuit conductor ampacity cannot be less than 125 percent of the fixed electric space-heating and any associated motor loads.

424.4 Branch Circuits

(B) Branch-Circuit Conductor Sizing. The branch-circuit conductor ampacity for fixed electric space-heating equipment and associated motors must be sized at not less than 125 percent of the heating equipment and its associated motor loads. ▶Figure 424–1

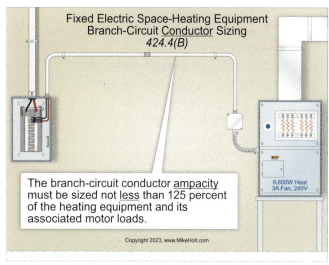
▶Figure 424–1

▶ Example

Question: What size NM cable is required for a 9600W, 240V fixed electric space heater with a 3A, 240V blower motor? ▶Figure 424–2

(a) 10 AWG   (b) 8 AWG   (c) 6 AWG   (d) 6 AWG

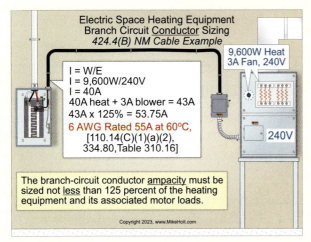

▶Figure 424–2

Solution:

Step 1: Determine the total load.

I = Watts/Volts

I = 9600W/240V

I = 40A

Total Amperes = 40A (heat) + 3A (blower)
Total Amperes = 43A

Step 2: Size the conductors at 125 percent of the total current load [424.4(B)].

Conductor = 43A × 125%
Conductor = 53.75A, use 6 AWG rated 55A at 60°C
[110.14(C)(1)(a)(2), 334.80, and Table 310.16]

Answer: (d) 6 AWG

ARTICLE 430 MOTORS

Introduction to Article 430—Motors

Article 430 contains the specific rules for conductor sizing, overcurrent protection, control circuit conductors, controllers, and disconnects for electric motors.

This is one of the longest articles in the *NEC*. It is also one of the most complex, but motors are complex equipment. They take electrical energy to perform mechanical work, but what makes motor applications complex is the fact that they are inductive loads with a high-current demand at start-up that is typically six (or more) times the running current. This makes overcurrent protection for motor applications necessarily different from the overcurrent protection employed for other types of equipment.

430.1 Scope

This section is unusual in that is has a pictorial directory of the parts of the article along with the associated references in its scope. As complex as this article is, this tool is invaluable.

Analysis

EDITED The mini table of contents located in this section was moved into Informational Note No. 1. This clarifies that it is not *Code* text, but it is a great directory of information to help the reader locate the applicable parts of Article 430.

NEW Additional Informational Notes 2 and 3 were added to direct the *Code* user to rules in other articles that may apply to a motor installation. Informational Note No. 4 was added to help us identify what part of Article 430 applies to adjustable-speed drive systems.

430.1 Scope

Article 430 covers motor branch-circuit and feeder conductors and their protection, motor overload protection, motor control circuits, motor controllers, and adjustable-speed drives. ▶Figure 430–1

▶Figure 430–1

Author's Comment:

▸ This article is divided into several parts, the most important being: ▶Figure 430–2

430.6 | Motors

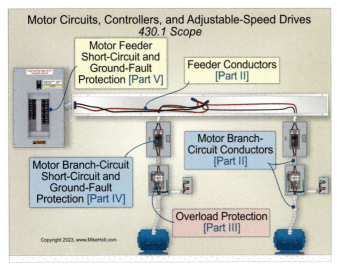
▶Figure 430–2

- General—Part I
- Conductor Sizing—Part II
- Overload Protection—Part III
- Branch-Circuit Short-Circuit and Ground-Fault Protection—Part IV
- Feeder Short-Circuit and Ground-Fault Protection—Part V
- Motor Control Circuits—Part VI
- Motor Controllers—Part VII
- Motor Control Centers—Part VIII
- Disconnecting Means—Part IX
- Adjustable-Speed Drives—Part X
- Full-Load Current Tables—Part XIV

Note 1: See Note Figure 430.1 in the *NEC* for the arrangement of this article.

Note 3: The requirements related to air-conditioning and refrigerating equipment with hermetic refrigerant motor-compressors are contained in Article 440, not Article 430.

Note 4: See the Part X requirements for motors utilizing adjustable-speed drive systems.

430.6 Conductor Ampacity and Motor Rating Determination

Editorial and organizational changes were made throughout this section for clarity and usability.

Analysis

CLARIFIED   REORGANIZED

The rules in (A)(1) were reorganized into three list items for clarity. There was no technical change, but the requirements for low-speed, high-torque, or multispeed motors were moved into (A)(2).

NEW These changes are mostly a reorganization of material, however, the addition of canned pumps in (A)(2) and large motors in (A)(3) is new information. The current draw of canned motor pumps and large motors often do not match the motor current tables. This just lines up the *Code* with what was already being done in the field.

430.6 Motor Table FLC versus Motor Nameplate Current Rating

(A) General Requirements. Motor current ratings used for the application of this article are determined by (A)(1) and (A)(2). ▶Figure 430–3

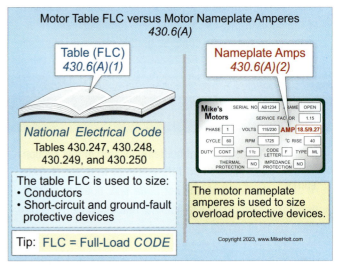
▶Figure 430–3

(1) Table Full-Load Current (FLC). The motor full-load current ratings contained in Tables 430.248 and 430.250 must be used, instead of the actual current rating marked on the motor nameplate to determine the following: ▶Figure 430–4

(1) Ampacity of conductors [430.22 and 430.24]

(2) Current rating for disconnect (switches) [430.110]

Motors | **430.31**

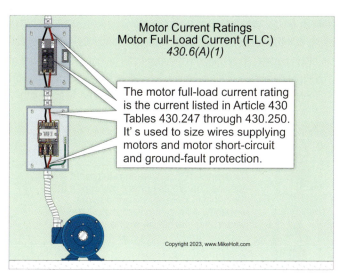
▶Figure 430–4

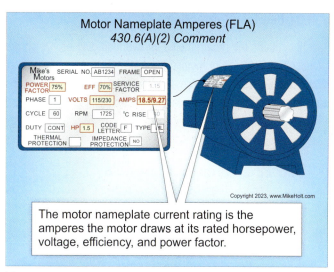
▶Figure 430–5

(3) Current rating of the short-circuit and ground-fault protective device [430.52 and 430.62]

Author's Comment:

▸ The motor full-load amperes (FLA) identified on the motor nameplate [430.6(A)(2)] is not permitted to be used to determine the conductor ampacity or the motor short-circuit and ground-fault overcurrent protective device, except for other than continuous-duty motor applications as covered in 430.22(E).

(2) Motor Nameplate Current Rating (FLA). The motor nameplate full-load amperes (FLA) must be used to determine the following:

(1) Overload protective devices [430.31]

(2) Ampacity of conductors for other than continuous-duty motors [430.22(E)]

Author's Comment:

▸ The motor nameplate current rating is identified as full-load amperes (FLA). The FLA rating is the current in amperes the motor draws while producing its rated horsepower load at its rated voltage, based on its rated efficiency and power factor.
▶Figure 430–5

▸ The actual current drawn by the motor depends on the load on the motor and the actual operating voltage at the motor terminals. If the load increases, the current also increases, or if the motor operates at a voltage below its nameplate rating, the operating current will increase.

Caution

⚡ **CAUTION:** In accordance with the NEMA MG1-standard, to prevent damage to motor windings from excessive heat (caused by excessive current), never load a motor above its horsepower rating and be sure the applied voltage is within 10 percent of the motor's voltage rating.

430.31 General

This section was reduced from three paragraphs and reorganized into parent text and two subdivisions with no technical changes.

Analysis

REORGANIZED At first glance there appears to be new text here, but it is just an excellent job of reorganizing the material into subdivisions, which is a much friendlier format.

430.31 Overload Protection

Part III contains the requirements for overload devices, which are intended to protect motors, motor control equipment, and motor branch-circuit conductors against excessive heating due to motor overloads and failure to start, but not against short circuits or ground faults.

Author's Comment:

▸ Overload devices can be: ▶Figure 430–6

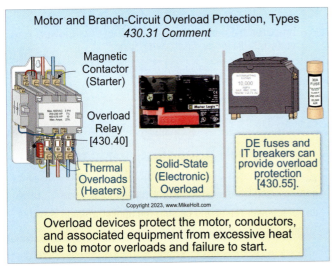

▶Figure 430–6

- *Thermal Overloads*. Thermal overloads (heaters) in an overload relay of a motor contactor (starter). These heater units are selected using a chart or size given by the manufacturer.

- *Solid-State (Electronic) Overloads.* Solid-state overload devices have an adjustment dial that can be used to set the trip level. They are installed in an overload relay of a motor contactor (starter).

- *Inverse Time Circuit Breaker and Dual-Element Fuses.* Inverse time circuit breakers and dual-element fuses are permitted to serve as both motor overload protection and the motor short-circuit ground-fault protection if the requirements of 430.32 are met [430.55].

- *Fuses*. Fuses can be used for overload protection when sized in accordance with 430.32(A) [430.36].

Note 2: An overload occurs when equipment operates above its current rating or if the current exceeds a conductor's ampacity. If an overload condition persists long enough, the result can be equipment failure or a fire from damaging or dangerous overheating. A fault, such as a short circuit or ground fault, is not an overload [Article 100]. ▶Figure 430–7

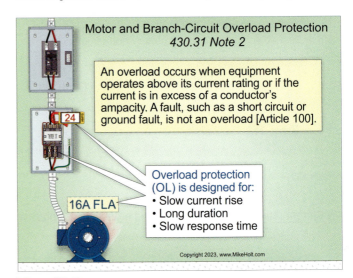

▶Figure 430–7

(A) Power Loss Hazard. Overload protection is not required where it might introduce additional or increased hazards due to power loss, as in the case of fire pumps [695.6(C)].

Note: See 695.4 for overcurrent protective device sizing for fire pump supply conductors.

430.83 Ratings

A new subdivision (F) was added regarding short-circuit ratings of motor controllers.

Analysis

NEW — Subdivision (F) was added and requires motor controllers to have short-circuit ratings adequate for the available fault current. This rule serves as a reminder since it is sometimes overlooked on motor control equipment.

430.83 Motor Controller Horsepower Rating

(A) General. The controller for a motor must have one of the following ratings:

(1) Horsepower Rating. For other than circuit breakers and molded case switches, the motor controller must have a horsepower rating of not less than the motor. ▶Figure 430-8

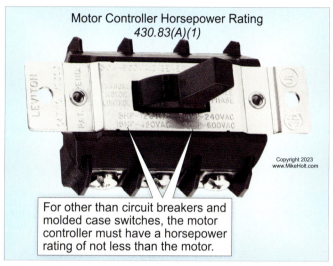

▶Figure 430-8

(2) Circuit Breakers. A circuit breaker can serve as a motor controller.

Author's Comment:
▸ Circuit breakers are not required to be horsepower rated.

(3) Molded Case Switch. A molded case switch, rated in amperes, can serve as a motor controller.

Author's Comment:
▸ A molded case switch is not required to be horsepower rated.

(C) Stationary Motors of Two Horsepower or Less. For stationary motors rated at 2 hp or less and 300V or less, the motor controller can be:

(2) General-Use Snap Switch. The motor controller can be a general-use snap switch for motors rated 2 hp or less where the motor FLC is not more than 80 percent of the ampere rating of the switch. ▶Figure 430-9

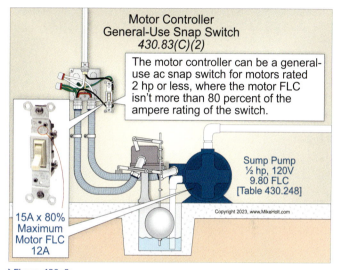

▶Figure 430-9

(F) Short-Circuit Current Rating. A motor controller cannot be installed where the available fault current exceeds the motor controller's short-circuit current rating.

Note: The short-circuit current rating might be marked on the device or specified in the motor controller's technical manual or instruction sheet.

Notes

ARTICLE 440 — AIR-CONDITIONING AND REFRIGERATING EQUIPMENT

Introduction to Article 440—Air-Conditioning and Refrigerating Equipment

This article applies to electrically driven air-conditioning equipment. Each air-conditioning equipment manufacturer has the motor for a given hermetic refrigerant motor-compressors, air-conditioning unit built to its own specifications. For each motor, the manufacturer has worked out all the details and identifies the minimum conductor ampacity, maximum overcurrent protective device rating, and other information such as running load amperes on the nameplate.

440.8 Single Machine and Location

This section was expanded to prohibit air-conditioning and refrigeration equipment from being installed in a bathtub or shower zone.

Analysis

EXPANDED Mini-split installations are becoming more common in bathrooms, and because of a lack of space they are being installed near the tub or shower. This could create a big hazard, so these rules were revised to prohibit air-conditioning and refrigeration equipment from being installed in a bathtub or shower zone.

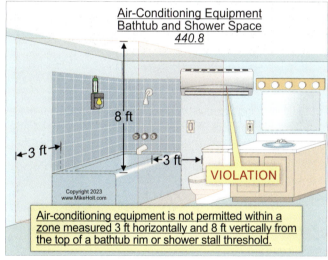

▶Figure 440–1

440.8 Bathtub and Shower Space

Air-conditioning equipment cannot be installed within a zone measured 3 ft horizontally and 8 ft vertically from the top of a bathtub rim or shower stall threshold. ▶Figure 440–1

440.11 General

This rule was revised to require disconnecting means with doors that expose live parts to be lockable or require tools to open them when installed in areas readily accessible to unqualified persons.

440.14 | Air-Conditioning and Refrigerating Equipment

Analysis

EXPANDED — Disconnects in dwelling units are often accessible to homeowners and children. To prevent a hazard from energized parts that can be exposed when the disconnect door is opened, disconnects readily accessible to unqualified persons must be capable of being locked or require a tool to open them.

440.11 General

If the air-conditioning disconnecting means is readily accessible to unqualified persons, the disconnect enclosure or hinged door that exposes energized parts when opened must require a tool to open or be capable of being locked. ▶Figure 440–2

▶Figure 440–2

440.14 Location

A revision to this rule points us to Article 110 for working space requirements at an air-conditioning disconnect.

Analysis

EXPANDED — How much clearance is required for an air-conditioning disconnect? A new last sentence points to 110.26(A) making it easier for the user to understand where to find the specifics. That was easy!

440.14 Location

A disconnect for air-conditioning equipment must be within sight from, and readily accessible from the air-conditioning equipment. It must also meet the required working space requirements of 110.26(A). ▶Figure 440–3

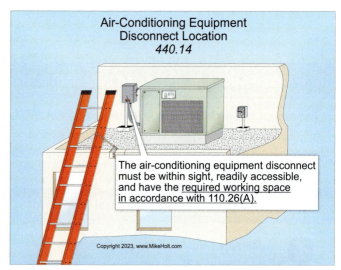

▶Figure 440–3

Author's Comment:

▸ According to Article 100, "Within Sight" means it is visible and not more than 50 ft from the location of the equipment.

▸ The air-conditioning equipment disconnect is required to be readily accessible from the air-conditioning equipment. This means the disconnect must be accessible without having to climb over/under or remove obstacles.

The disconnect can be mounted on or within the equipment but is not permitted to be on panels designed to allow access to internal wiring, or where it obscures the equipment nameplate. ▶Figure 440–4

Air-Conditioning and Refrigerating Equipment | 440.22

▶Figure 440–4

440.22 Short-Circuit and Ground-Fault Protective Device Size

(A) Individual Motor Compressor. The branch-circuit short-circuit and ground-fault protective device must be capable of carrying the starting current of the motor. The rating or setting must not exceed 175 percent of the rated load current.

Ex 1: If the values for branch-circuit short-circuit and ground-fault protection in accordance with 440.22(A) do not correspond to the standard sizes or ratings of fuses, nonadjustable circuit breakers, thermal protective devices, or available settings of adjustable circuit breakers, a higher size, rating, or available setting that does not exceed the next higher standard ampere rating is permitted.

Ex 2: If the values for branch-circuit short-circuit and ground-fault protection in accordance with 440.22(A) or the rating modified by Ex 1 is not sufficient for the starting current of the motor, the rating or setting is permitted to be increased up to 225 percent of the motor rated-load current or branch-circuit selection current, whichever is greater.

(B) Rating or Setting for Equipment. The equipment branch-circuit short-circuit and ground-fault protective device must be capable of carrying the starting current of the equipment. Where the equipment incorporates more than one hermetic refrigerant motor-compressor or a hermetic refrigerant motor-compressor and other motors, the equipment branch-circuit short-circuit and ground-fault protection must comply with 440.22(B)(1).

(1) Motor-Compressor Largest Load. Where a hermetic refrigerant motor-compressor is the largest load connected to the circuit, the rating or setting of the branch-circuit short-circuit and ground-fault protective device is not permitted to exceed the value specified in 440.22(A) for the largest refrigerant motor-compressor plus the sum of the nameplate current ratings of the other motor loads.

440.22 Application and Selection

This section was reorganized into a rule and two Exceptions instead of a long sentence.

Analysis

REORGANIZED   EXPANDED

This rule states that the protective device must have a rating not exceeding 175 percent of the rated load current. However, there was no provision to use the next larger standard size device. Exception No. 1 now permits using the next size up rule. Exception No. 2 was just a relocation that permits the protective device to exceed the load by 175 percent but not more than 225 percent to permit the unit to start.

440.22 | Air-Conditioning and Refrigerating Equipment

▶ Motor-Compressors and Other Motors Example

Question: What size branch-circuit short-circuit ground-fault protective device is required for a 17.60A refrigerant motor-compressor with a 1.20A fan? ▶Figure 440–5

(a) 35A   (b) 40A   (c) 45A   (d) 50A

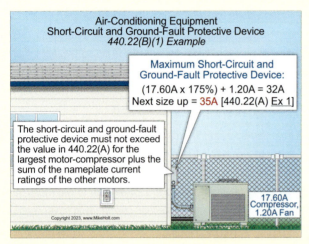

▶Figure 440–5

Solution:

Maximum Branch-Circuit Short-Circuit Ground-Fault Protective Device = (17.60A × 175%) + 1.20A

Maximum Branch-Circuit Short-Circuit Ground-Fault Protective Device = 30.8A + 1.20A

Maximum Branch-Circuit Short-Circuit Ground-Fault Protective Device = 32A, use the next size up [440.22(A) Ex 1]

Maximum Branch-Circuit Short-Circuit Ground-Fault Protective Device = 35A

Answer: (a) 35A

ARTICLE 445 GENERATORS

Introduction to Article 445—Generators

This article contains the electrical installation and other requirements for generators. These rules include such things as where generators can be installed, nameplate markings, conductor ampacity, transference of power, and disconnect requirements.

445.11 Marking

This section was edited for clarity and a new requirement for the nameplate to be accessible was added.

Analysis

EDITED The first three list items have additional wording for clarity but no technical change. We might finally be able to read the manufacturer's nameplate without contorting in all directions as the rule now requires it to be accessible.

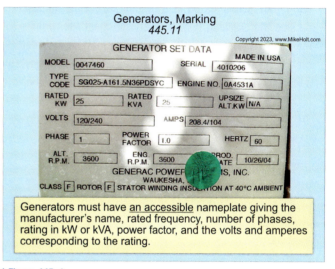

Generators must have an accessible nameplate giving the manufacturer's name, rated frequency, number of phases, rating in kW or kVA, power factor, and the volts and amperes corresponding to the rating.

▶Figure 445–1

445.11 Marking

Generators must have an accessible nameplate giving the manufacturer's name, the rated frequency, number of phases, rating in kilowatts or kilovolt-amperes, power factor, and the volts and amperes corresponding to the rating. ▶Figure 445–1

Markings by the manufacture must indicate whether the neutral is bonded to the frame or not. If the bonding is modified in the field from bonded to unbonded (floating neutral) additional marking is required. See 702.7(C).

445.19 Emergency Shutdown of Prime Mover

These rules were relocated here from 445.18 and only relate to the emergency shutdown requirements that apply to the prime mover.

445.19 | Generators

Analysis

RELOCATED

Subdivision (A) was relocated here from 445.18(B) without change. It requires the generator to have provisions to shut down the prime mover.

Subdivision (B) was relocated here from 445.18(C) and requires generators with a rating greater than 15 kW to have a remote emergency stop switch to shut down the prime mover for other than one- and two-family dwellings. In addition, new text permits the remote emergency stop to be mounted on the exterior of the generator enclosure, and that it be labeled "Generator Emergency Shutdown."

Subdivision (C) was relocated here from 445.18(D) and requires the emergency shutdown device for one- and two-family dwellings be in a readily accessible location outside the dwelling unit. It must also meet the requirements of (A)(1) and (A)(2). This switch may be mounted on the exterior of the generator enclosure and must have a label marking stating "Generator Emergency Shutdown."

445.19 Emergency Shutdown of Prime Mover

(C) Emergency Shutdown in One- and Two-Family Dwelling Units. The generator prime mover remote emergency stop switch mounted on the exterior of the generator enclosure must be labeled "Generator Emergency Shutdown," and the label must meet the requirements of 110.21(B). ▶Figure 445–2

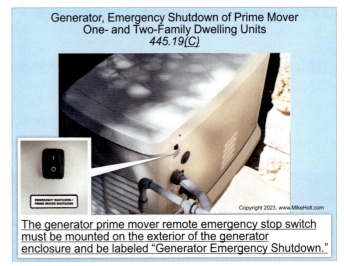

▶Figure 445–2

Author's Comment:

▸ This rule aligns with similar emergency shutdown dwelling unit requirements for services to be outside and in a readily accessible location in accordance with 230.85.

ARTICLE 450

TRANSFORMERS AND TRANSFORMER VAULTS (INCLUDING SECONDARY TIES)

Introduction to Article 450—Transformers and Transformer Vaults (Including Secondary Ties)

This article covers transformers supplying power and lighting loads. For the purposes of Article 450 only, a transformer is an individual power transformer, single- or poly-phase, identified by a single nameplate—unless otherwise indicated.

A major concern with transformers is preventing overheating. The *Code* does not completely address this issue. Article 90 explains that the *NEC* is not a design manual, and it assumes that anyone using the *Code* has a certain level of expertise. Proper transformer selection is an important part of preventing them from overheating. The *NEC* assumes you have already selected a transformer suitable for the load characteristics. For the *Code* to tell you how to do that would push it into the realm of a design manual. Article 450 then takes you to the next logical step—providing overcurrent protection and the proper connections. But this article does not stop there because 450.9 provides ventilation requirements, and 450.13 contains accessibility requirements.

Part I contains the general requirements such as guarding, marking, and accessibility, Part II contains those for different types of transformers, and Part III covers transformer vaults.

450.1 Scope

The previous exceptions in the text were converted to rules and the references to complete articles were removed to comply with the requirements of the *NEC* Style Manual.

Analysis

REORGANIZED Although it looks like a lot happened here it was really a rework of the existing rules. This section previously had an odd start in that it stated all the things it did not cover as Exceptions. The Exceptions have now been relocated into the scope text as list items (1) through (8). There were no technical changes with this reorganization.

450.1 Scope

Article 450 covers the installation requirements of all transformers other than the following: ▶Figure 450–1

▶Figure 450–1

450.10 | Transformers and transformer vaults (including secondary ties)

1. Current transformers
2. Transformers that constitute a component part of another apparatus
3. Transformers that are an integral part of an X-ray, high-frequency, or electrostatic-coating apparatus
4. Transformers for Class 2 and Class 3 circuits
5. Transformers for signs
6. Transformers for electric-discharge lighting
7. Transformers for power-limited fire alarm circuits
8. Transformers used for research, development, or testing

450.10 Grounding and Bonding

The word "Bonding" was added to the title of the section as the rule address both grounding and bonding.

Analysis

EDITED
The *NEC* Style Manual requires the title of a section reflect the section's content, so the word "Bonding" was added to the title.

450.10 Grounding and Bonding

(A) Dry-Type Transformer Enclosures. A terminal bar for equipment grounding conductors, system bonding jumpers, supply-side bonding jumpers, and grounding electrode conductors must be installed and bonded inside the transformer enclosure. ▶Figure 450–2

▶Figure 450–2

The terminal bar must be bonded to the transformer enclosure in accordance with 250.12 and not installed on or over any vented portions.

ARTICLE 480 STATIONARY STANDBY BATTERIES

Introduction to Article 480—Stationary Standby Batteries

The stationary battery is the heart of any uninterruptible power supply. Article 480 addresses stationary batteries for commercial and industrial grade power supplies rather than the small, "point of use" uninterruptible power supply (UPS) boxes.

Stationary batteries are also used for emergency power systems. Regardless of the application, if stationary batteries are used, this article applies.

Lead-acid stationary batteries fall into two general categories—flooded and valve regulated (VRLA). These differ markedly in such ways as maintainability, total cost of ownership, and scalability. The *NEC* does not address these differences since they are engineering issues rather than fire safety or electrical safety matters [90.2].

The *Code* does not address such design issues as optimum tier height, distance between tiers, determination of charging voltage, or string configuration. Nor does it address battery testing, monitoring, or maintenance. All of these involve highly specialized areas of knowledge and are required for optimizing operational efficiency. Standards other than the *NEC* address these topics.

What the *Code* does address in Article 480 are issues relating to preventing electrocution and the ignition of gases that all stationary batteries (even "sealed" ones) emit.

Article 480 Stationary Standby Batteries

The title of the article was changed from "Storage Batteries" to "Stationary Standby Batteries."

Analysis

EDITED The article title was edited to reflect the type of batteries to which this article applies. The changes in the article are intended to clarify that it does not apply to batteries used as an energy storage system. The term "stationary standby batteries" was added in several *Code* sections.

480.4 Battery and Cell Terminations

Editorial revisions clarify when antioxidants must be used.

Analysis

CLARIFIED This rule says that where mating dissimilar metals, an antioxidant must be used where recommended by the manufacturer's installation and instruction manual. Previously it just said, "where recommended by the battery manufacturer."

480.10 | Stationary Standby Batteries

480.4 Battery and Cell Terminations

(A) Dissimilar Metals. Where connections between dissimilar metals occur, antioxidant material must be used where recommended by the battery manufacturer's installation instruction manual. ▶Figure 480–1

▶Figure 480–1

(D) Accessibility. The terminals of all cells or multicell units must be readily accessible for readings, inspections, and cleaning where required by the equipment design. One side of transparent battery containers must be readily accessible for inspection of the internal components.

480.10 Battery Locations

Personnel doors in battery rooms must now open 90° in addition to having listed panic or fire exit hardware.

Analysis

EXPANDED — The doors providing entrance to and egress from rooms designated as battery rooms must open at least 90° in the direction of egress.

480.10 Battery Locations

Battery locations must conform with the following:

(E) Egress. Personnel doors intended for entrance to, and egress from, rooms designated as battery rooms must open 90° in the direction of egress and be equipped with listed panic or listed fire exit hardware.

CHAPTER 5
SPECIAL OCCUPANCIES

Introduction to Chapter 5—Special Occupancies

Chapter 5, which covers special occupancies, is the first of four *NEC* chapters that deal with special occupancies. What exactly is a "Special Occupancy"? It is a location where a facility, or its use, creates specific conditions that require additional measures to ensure the "practical safeguarding of people and property," which is the purpose of the *NEC* as put forth in Article 90.

Many people struggle to understand the requirements for special occupancies (especially hazardous (classified) locations), mostly because of the narrowness of application. If you study the illustrations and explanations here, you will better understand them.

- **Article 500—Hazardous (Classified) Locations.** Article 500 contains the general requirements applicable to all hazardous (classified) locations. A hazardous (classified) location is an area where the possibility of fire or explosion exists due to the presence of flammable or combustible liquid-produced vapors, flammable gases, combustible dusts, or easily ignitible fibers/flyings.

- **Article 501—Class I Hazardous (Classified) Locations.** A Class I hazardous (classified) location is an area where flammable or combustible liquid-produced vapors or flammable gases may present the hazard of a fire or explosion.

- **Article 502—Class II Hazardous (Classified) Locations.** A Class II hazardous (classified) location is an area where the possibility of fire or explosion may exist due to the presence of combustible dust.

- **Article 511—Commercial Garages, Repair and Storage.** These occupancies include locations used for service and repair operations in connection with self-propelled vehicles including passenger automobiles, buses, trucks, and tractors in which flammable liquids or flammable gases are used for fuel or power.

- **Article 514—Motor Fuel Dispensing Facilities.** Article 514 covers gasoline dispensing and service stations where gasoline or other volatile liquids are transferred to the fuel tanks of self-propelled vehicles. Wiring and equipment in the area of service and repair rooms of service stations must comply with the installation requirements in Article 511.

- **Article 517—Health Care Facilities.** This article applies to electrical wiring in human health care facilities such as hospitals, nursing homes, limited care facilities, clinics, medical and dental offices, and ambulatory care—whether permanent or movable. It does not apply to animal veterinary facilities.

- **Article 518—Assembly Occupancies.** Article 518 covers buildings or portions of buildings specifically designed or intended for the assembly of 100 or more persons.

...

Chapter 5 | Special Occupancies

- **Article 547—Agricultural Buildings.** Article 547 covers agricultural buildings or those parts of buildings or adjacent areas where excessive dust or dust with water may accumulate, or where a corrosive atmosphere exists.

- **Article 555—Marinas, Boatyards, and Commercial and Noncommercial Docking Facilities.** This article covers the installation of wiring and equipment in the areas that comprise fixed or floating piers, wharves, docks, and other areas in marinas, boatyards, boat basins, boathouses, and similar locations used (or intended to be used) for the repair, berthing, launching, storing, or fueling of small craft and the mooring of floating buildings.

- **Article 590—Temporary Installations.** Article 590 covers temporary power and lighting for construction, remodeling, maintenance, repair, demolitions, and decorative lighting.

ARTICLE 500 — HAZARDOUS (CLASSIFIED) LOCATIONS, CLASSES I, II, AND III, DIVISIONS 1 AND 2

Introduction to Article 500—Hazardous (Classified) Locations, Classes I, II, and III, Divisions 1 and 2

A hazardous (classified) location is an area where the possibility of fire or explosion can be created by the presence of flammable or combustible vapors, or flammable gasses, combustible dusts, or easily ignitible fibers/flyings. Electric arcs, sparks, and/or heated surfaces can serve as a source of ignition in such environments.

Article 500 provides the foundation for applying Article 501 (Class I Locations), Article 502 (Class II Locations), and Article 503 (Class III Locations). This article also provides a foundation for using Articles 510 through 516.

Before you apply any of the articles just mentioned you must understand and use Article 500, which is fairly long and detailed. You will notice when studying this article that there are many Informational Notes which you should review. Although these notes are not *NEC* requirements [90.5(C)], they contain information that helps *Code* users better understand the related *NEC* rules.

A Fire Triangle (fuel, oxygen, and energy source) helps illustrate the concept of how combustion occurs. ▶Figure 500–1

- *Fuel.* Flammable gases or vapors, combustible dusts, and easily ignitible fibers/flyings.
- *Oxygen.* Air and oxidizing atmospheres.
- *Ignition Source (Heat).* Electric arcs or sparks, heat-producing equipment such as luminaires and motors, failure of transformers, coils, or solenoids, as well as sparks caused by metal tools dropping on metal surfaces.

Many of the illustrations contained in Chapter 5 of this material and video use two shades of red to identify a division location (darker red for Division 1 and lighter red to identify Division 2). In some cases, these color schemes are used as a background color to help you tell if the illustration applies to Division 1, Division 2, or both (split color background).

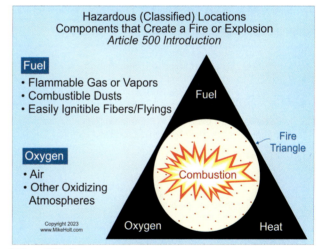

▶Figure 500–1

500.1 | Hazardous (Classified) Locations, Classes I, II, and III, Divisions 1 and 2

500.1 Scope

This scope statement was revised and some of the Informational Notes were relocated into the rule.

Analysis

EXPANDED Two new sentences were added to the scope telling us that Article 500 does not cover the area classification for the zone system and that the unique hazards associated with explosives, pyrotechnics, and blasting agents are not within the scope of this article.

500.1 Scope—Articles 500 Through 503

(A) Installations Covered. Article 500 covers area classification and general requirements for electrical and electronic equipment and wiring where fire or explosion hazards might exist due to flammable gases, flammable liquid-produced vapors, combustible liquid-produced vapors, combustible dusts, combustible fibers/flyings, or ignitible fibers/flyings. Specific requirements are in: ▶Figure 500-2

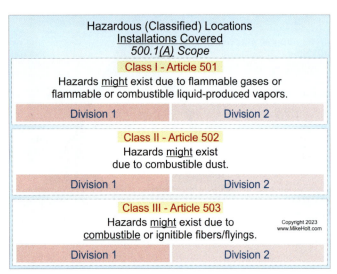

▶Figure 500-2

(1) Article 501. Class I—Flammable Gases or Flammable or Combustible Liquid-Produced Vapors

(2) Article 502. Class II—Combustible Dust

(3) Article 503. Class III—Combustible or Ignitible Fibers/Flyings

Author's Comment:

▸ Article 500 provides information related to the classifications [500.5], material groups [500.6], protection techniques [500.7], and equipment types [500.8] that are unique and required for Class I, Class II, and Class III locations. Articles 501, 502, and 503 cover the specific wiring requirements in hazardous (classified) areas.

Articles containing installation requirements for hazardous (classified) locations in special occupancies include:

▸ Article 511. Commercial Garages, Repair and Storage
▸ Article 513. Aircraft Hangars
▸ Article 514. Motor Fuel Dispensing Facilities
▸ Article 515. Bulk Storage Plants
▸ Article 516. Spray Application, Dipping, and Coating Processes
▸ Article 517. Health Care Facilities

500.4 Documentation

Revisions clarify that documentation on an area classification drawing is required for areas that require classification and areas deemed unclassified.

Analysis

CLARIFIED Revisions this cycle clarify that area classification documentation must be available for both classified and adjacent unclassified areas. This is an important rule since the area classification specifies the installation methods required by Articles 501, 502, and 503. An area classification drawing is required along with other associated proper documentation. Language was also added requiring the documentation to be made available to the AHJ.

500.4 Documentation

Areas designated as hazardous (classified) locations or determined to be unclassified must be documented on an area classification drawing and other associated documentation. The documentation must be available to the authority having jurisdiction (AHJ) and those who are authorized to design, install, inspect, maintain, or operate the electrical equipment.

> **Author's Comment:**
>
> ▸ Proper documentation of hazardous (classified) locations assists the designer, installer, and authority having jurisdiction in ensuring adherence to the stringent requirements contained in Articles 501 through 517 of the *Code*. The required classification drawings must indicate the hazardous location (classified) location area classification(s) and the boundaries between classified and unclassified areas, material group properties such as auto ignition temperatures, and equipment construction suitability.
>
> ▸ Articles 511 through 517, provide established details on the areas that are classified for those occupancies. Additional determination of classified areas is not required for those areas that are classified by those articles. Determining the classification of a specific hazardous (classified) location area is the responsibility of those who understand the dangers of the products being used such as the fire marshal, plant facility engineer, or insurance underwriter. It is not the responsibility of the electrical designer, electrical contractor, or electrical inspector. Before performing any wiring in or near a hazardous (classified) location, contact the plant facility and design engineer to ensure that proper installation methods and materials are used. Be sure to review 500.4(B) for additional standards that might need to be consulted.

500.5 Classifications of Locations

This rule, like many others this cycle, was reorganized into a list format.

Analysis

REORGANIZED Reorganization was a large part of the changes in the *NEC* this cycle. In this section, both (A) and (B) were broken up into second level subdivisions. The notes were also revised for clarity but without any technical change.

CLARIFIED EXPANDED Several changes were made in (D) clarifying that a Class III location is where ignitible "quantities" of fibers/flyings are present. The word "quantities" was added because the hazard only exists if there is a sufficient quantity of these materials to support combustion.

NEW A new Informational Note tells us that combustible fibers/flyings include flat platelet-shaped particulates such as metal flakes and fibrous board.

EXPANDED Changes similar to those in (D)(1) were made in (D)(2), including three new list items and revisions to the parent text to indicate what a Class III, Division 2 area is.

500.5 Classifications of Hazardous (Classified) Locations

(D) Identification of a Class III Location. A Class III location is a location meeting the requirements of 500.5(D)(1)(a) and (D)(2)(b).

(1) Class III, Division 1 Location. A Class III, Division 1 location includes the following:

(a) Combustible Fibers/Flyings. Locations where nonmetal combustible fibers/flyings are in the air under normal operating conditions in quantities sufficient to produce explosive mixtures or where mechanical failure or abnormal operation of machinery or equipment might cause combustible fibers/flyings to be produced and might also provide a source of ignition through simultaneous failure of electrical equipment, through operation of protective devices, or from other causes are classified as Class III, Division 1. Locations where metal combustible fibers/flyings are present must be classified as Class II, Division 1, Group E.

Note 1: Such locations usually include some parts of rayon, cotton, and other textile mills or clothing manufacturing plants as well as facilities that create sawdust and combustible fibers/flyings by pulverizing or cutting wood.

Note 2: Combustible fibers/flyings include flat platelet-shaped particulates, such as metal flakes, and fibrous board such as particle board.

(b) Ignitible Fibers/Flyings. Locations where ignitible fibers/flyings are handled, manufactured, or used are classified as Class III, Division 1.

Note 1: Such locations usually include some parts of rayon, cotton, and other textile mills or clothing manufacturing plants as well as facilities that create sawdust and ignitible fibers/flyings by pulverizing or cutting wood.

Note 2: Ignitible fibers/flyings can include rayon, cotton (including cotton linters and cotton waste), sisal or henequen, istle, jute, hemp, tow, cocoa fiber, oakum, baled waste kapok, Spanish Moss, excelsior, and other materials of similar nature.

(2) Class III, Division 2 Location. A Class III, Division 2 location includes the following:

(a) Combustible Fibers/Flyings. Locations where nonmetal combustible fibers/flyings might be present in the air in quantities sufficient to produce explosive mixtures due to abnormal operations or where accumulations of nonmetal combustible fibers/flyings accumulations are present but are insufficient to interfere with the normal operation of electrical equipment or other apparatus but could, as a result of infrequent malfunctioning of handling or processing equipment, become suspended in the air are classified as Class III, Division 2.

A combustible fiber/flying can produce an explosive mixture when suspended in air. See the Article 100 definition of "Fibers/Flyings, Combustible."

(b) Ignitible Fibers/Flyings. Locations where ignitible fibers/flyings are stored or handled, other than in the process of manufacture, are classified as Class III, Division 2.

Author's Comment:
- Ignitible fibers/flyings are not likely to form an explosive mixture when suspended in air but could produce an ignitible layer fire hazard. See the Article 100 definition of "Fibers/Flyings, Ignitible."

ARTICLE 501 CLASS I LOCATIONS

Introduction to Article 501—Class I Locations

If sufficient flammable or combustible gases, vapors, or liquids are (or might be) present to produce an explosive or ignitible mixture, you have a Class I location. Examples of such locations include some fuel storage areas, certain solvent storage areas, grain processing facilities (where hexane is used), plastic extrusion areas where oil removal is part of the process, refineries, and paint storage areas. Article 500 contained a general background on hazardous (classified) locations, described the differences between Class I, II, and III locations, and the differences between Division 1 and Division 2. Article 501 contains the Class I, Division 1 and Division 2 installation requirements, including wiring methods, seals, and specific equipment requirements.

501.1 Scope

The scope statement was edited to match the scope more closely in Article 500.

Analysis

EDITED This section clarifies that the hazards this article protects against are the vapors from flammable or combustible liquids. Replacing the phrase "flammable liquids" with "flammable liquid-produced vapors or combustible liquid-produced vapors" helps clarify what this article is about and aligns it with the language used in the scope of Article 500.

▶Figure 501–1

501.1 Scope

This article covers the electrical equipment and wiring for Class I, Division 1 and Division 2 locations where flammable gases, flammable liquid-produced vapors, or combustible liquid-produced vapors are, or might be, present in the air in quantities sufficient to produce explosive or ignitible mixtures. ▶Figure 501–1

501.10 Wiring Methods

There were many changes throughout this section that made the rules easier to read and understand. A few of the more notable changes are listed in the analysis below.

501.10 | Class I Locations

Analysis

CLARIFIED Language was added to (A)(1)(1) clarifying that threaded RMC and IMC with supplemental corrosion protection coatings are permitted to be used in a Class I, Division 1 location.

EDITED The Exception that followed list item (A)(1) was relocated into rule (A)(1)(2). There was no technical change in the language, and it still permits the use of PVC, RTRC, and HDPE conduits in Class I, Division 1 locations under specific conditions.

EDITED Some editorial changes were made to (A)(2) to correlate with the "if flexibility is necessary" language found in 250.118(5) and (6).

CLARIFIED The language in (A)(3) was revised to clarify that boxes and fittings used in Class I, Division 1 locations must be identified for such use. The previous language required them to only be approved.

CLARIFIED Language was added to (B)(1)(1) clarifying that threaded RMC and IMC with supplemental corrosion protection coatings are permitted to be used in a Class I, Division 2 location.

CLARIFIED EXPANDED List item (B)(2), covering flexible connections, was clarified to say that "If flexibility is necessary..." Also, (B)(2)(2) and (B)(2)(4) were revised to require that if flexible connections are made with FMC or LFMC, they must be bonded in accordance with 501.30(B), which requires the use of a wire-type equipment bonding jumper.

501.10 Wiring Methods

(A) Class I, Division 1.

(1) General. Only the following wiring methods are permitted within a Class I, Division 1 location.

(1) Threaded rigid metal conduit (RMC) or threaded intermediate metal conduit (IMC), including RMC or IMC conduits with supplemental corrosion protection coatings. ▶Figure 501–2

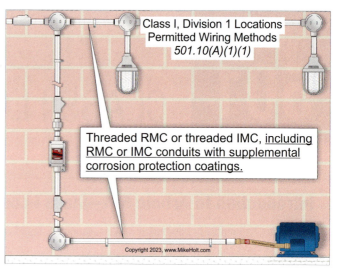
▶Figure 501–2

Author's Comment:

▸ According to the UL "DYIX" Guide, supplementary corrosion protection is required when ferrous metal raceways are buried in soils having a resistivity of less than 2000Ω, and at the point where the ferrous metal raceway transitions from concrete encasement to the soil. ▶Figure 501–3

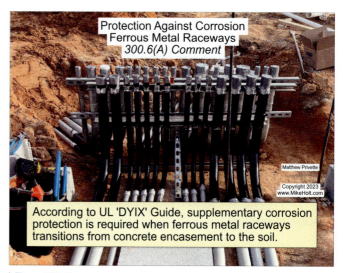
▶Figure 501–3

(2) PVC conduit, RTRC conduit, or HDPE conduit, where encased in a concrete envelope a minimum of 2 in. thick and provided with not less than 24 in. of cover measured from the top of the conduit to grade. RMC or IMC conduit must be used for the last 24 in. of the underground run to emergence or to the point of connection to the aboveground raceway. An equipment grounding conductor must be included in the raceway.

(2) Class 1, Division 1 Flexible Connections. If flexibility is necessary to minimize the transmission of vibration from equipment during operation or to allow for movement after installation during maintenance, the following wiring methods are permitted: ▶Figure 501–4

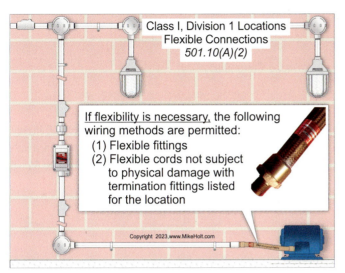

▶Figure 501–4

(1) Flexible fittings listed for the location.

(2) Flexible cords in accordance with 501.140, where the cable is not subject to physical damage and terminates with fittings listed for the location.

(3) Boxes and Fittings. Boxes and fittings must be identified for Class I, Division 1 locations. ▶Figure 501–5

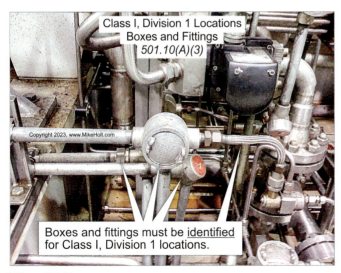

▶Figure 501–5

(B) Class I, Division 2.

(1) General. All wiring methods included in Class 1, Division 1 locations [501.10(A)] and the following wiring methods are permitted within a Class I, Division 2 location.

(1) Rigid and intermediate metal conduit with listed threaded or threadless fittings, including RMC or IMC conduits with supplemental corrosion protection coatings. ▶Figure 501–6

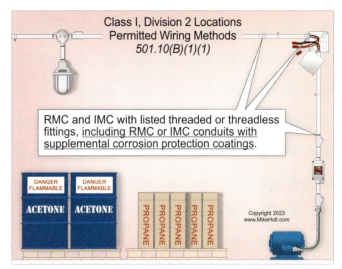

▶Figure 501–6

(2) Enclosed gasketed busways and wireways.

(3) Types PLTC and PLTC-ER cable used for Class 2 power-limited circuits. Type PLTC-ER cable must include an equipment grounding conductor in addition to any drain wire that might be present.

(5) Types MC, MV, TC, or TC-ER cable terminated with listed fittings, including installation in cable tray systems. Type TC-ER cable must include an equipment grounding conductor in addition to any drain wire that might be present.

(6) Where metallic conduit does not provide the corrosion resistance needed for the environment, any of the following wiring methods are permitted:

   a. Listed reinforced thermosetting resin conduit (RTRC), factory elbows, and associated fittings, all marked with the suffix "-XW,"

   b. PVC-coated rigid metal conduit (RMC), factory elbows, and associated fittings, or

   c. PVC-coated intermediate metal conduit (IMC), factory elbows, and associated fittings.

501.15 | Class I Locations

(7) Optical fiber cables can be installed in cable trays or raceways [501.10(B)] and must be sealed in accordance with 501.15. ▶Figure 501-7

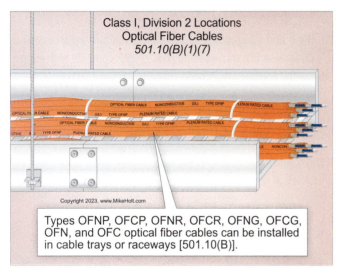

▶Figure 501-7

(2) Class 1, Division 2 Flexible Connections. If flexibility is necessary to minimize the transmission of vibration from equipment during operation or to allow for movement after installation during maintenance, the following wiring methods are permitted: ▶Figure 501-8

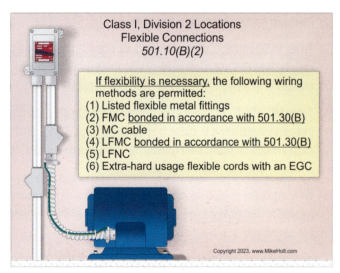

▶Figure 501-8

(1) Listed flexible metal fittings.

(2) Flexible metal conduit with listed fittings and bonded in accordance with 501.30(B).

(3) Interlocked Type MC cable with listed fittings.

(4) Liquidtight flexible metal conduit with listed fittings and bonded in accordance with 501.30(B).

(5) Liquidtight flexible nonmetallic conduit with listed fittings.

(6) Flexible cords listed for extra-hard usage containing an equipment grounding conductor and terminated with listed fittings.

Author's Comment:

▸ If flexible cords are used, they must comply with 501.140.

(4) Boxes and Fittings. General-purpose enclosures and fittings in Class 1, Division 2 locations are permitted unless the enclosure contains make-and-break contacts [501.115(B)(1)]. ▶Figure 501-9

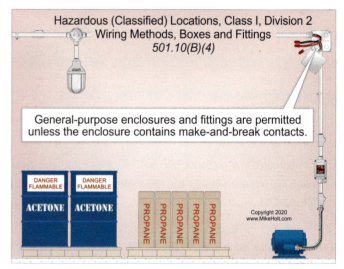

▶Figure 501-9

501.15 Sealing and Drainage

The boundary seal rules from 501.10(B)(1) were relocated to this section and the wiring methods permitted to cross the Class I Division 2 boundary were expanded. Some corrections were made to language adopted in the 2020 *NEC* and the Exception permitting cables to pass through a Division 2 location without a seal was revised.

Analysis

RELOCATED The rule in (A)(4) requiring the Division 1 wiring method to extend to the boundary seal located in the Division 2 area was relocated here from 501.10(B)(1) with no technical change. This is a more appropriate section for this rule.

EXPANDED The part of the rule in (B)(2) specifying permitted wiring methods was revised to include RMC and IMC, PVC coated RMC or IMC, and nonmetallic raceways where metal conduit will not provide sufficient corrosion resistance.

EXPANDED The 2020 *Code* expanded the wiring methods permitted to be installed in Class I, Division 1 areas to include Type TC-ER-HL and Type P cable for some uses. A sealing requirement was not added at that time and was corrected this cycle in (D)(1).

CLARIFIED Exceptions in both (D)(2) and (E)(1) allowing shielded cables and twisted-pair cables to pass through a classified area without removing the jacket, separating conductors, and installing a seal, was revised to clarify how it was to be done. This is a big relief for Datacom techs.

501.15 Conduit and Cable Seals

Seals for conduit and cable systems must comply with 501.15(A) through (F).

Note 1: Conduit and cable seals must be installed to: ▶Figure 501–10

- Minimize the passage of gases and vapors from one portion of electrical equipment to another through the conduit or cable.
- Prevent the passage of flames from one portion of electrical equipment to another through the conduit or cable.
- Contain internal explosions within the explosionproof enclosure.

(A) Conduit Seal—Class I, Division 1. In Class I, Division 1 locations, conduit seals must be as follows:

(1) Entering Enclosures. A conduit seal is required in each conduit that enters an explosionproof enclosure if either (1) or (2) apply:

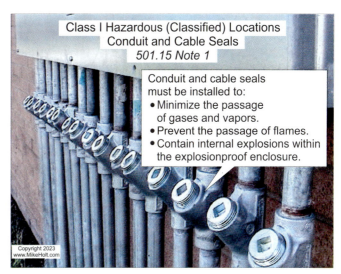
▶Figure 501–10

(1) If the explosionproof enclosure contains make-and-break contacts. ▶Figure 501–11

▶Figure 501–11

Ex: A conduit seal is not required if the make-and-break contacts are:

(1) Within a hermetically sealed chamber. ▶Figure 501–12

(2) Immersed in oil in accordance with 501.115(B)(1)(2).

(3) Contained within an enclosure that is marked "Leads Factory Sealed," "Factory Sealed," "Seal not Required," or the equivalent.

(2) If a trade size 2 or larger conduit enters an explosionproof enclosure containing splices, terminals, or taps. ▶Figure 501–13

501.15 | Class I Locations

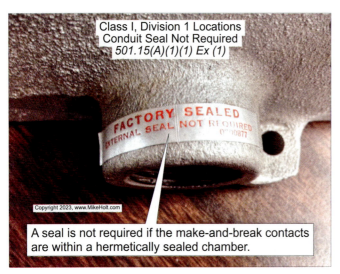
▶Figure 501-12

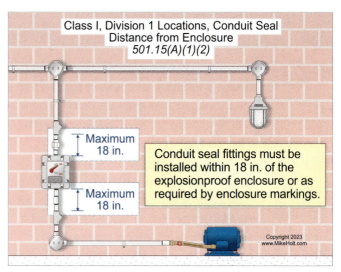
▶Figure 501-14

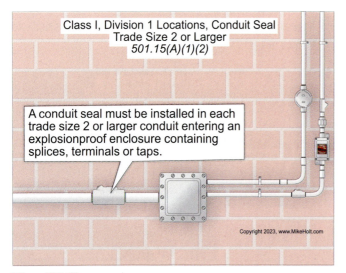
▶Figure 501-13

▶Figure 501-15

Author's Comment

▸ If a trade size 2 or larger conduit enters an explosionproof enclosure without make-and-break contacts and the conductors pass through without a splice, terminal, or tap a conduit seal is not required.

The conduit seal fitting must be installed within 18 in. of the explosionproof enclosure or as required by the enclosure markings. ▶Figure 501-14

Only threaded couplings or explosionproof fittings such as unions, reducers, elbows, and capped elbows are permitted between the conduit seal and the explosionproof enclosure. ▶Figure 501-15

(2) Pressurized Enclosures. A conduit seal fitting must be installed in each conduit that is not pressurized where the conduit enters a pressurized enclosure. The conduit seal fitting must be installed within 18 in. of the pressurized enclosure.

(3) Between Explosionproof Enclosures. A single conduit seal fitting is permitted between two explosionproof enclosures containing make-and-break contacts if the conduit seal fitting is not more than 18 in. from either of the explosionproof enclosures. ▶Figure 501-16

(4) Class I, Division 1 Boundary Seal. A conduit seal fitting must be installed in each conduit that leaves a Class I, Division 1 location within 10 ft of the Class I, Division 1 location on either side of the boundary. ▶Figure 501-17

Class I Locations | 501.15

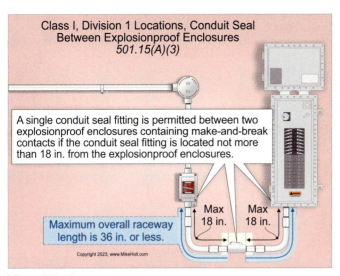
▶Figure 501-16

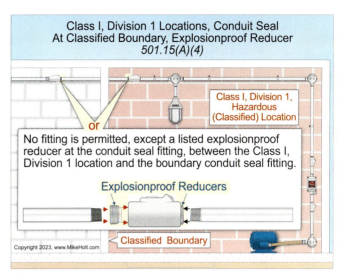
▶Figure 501-18

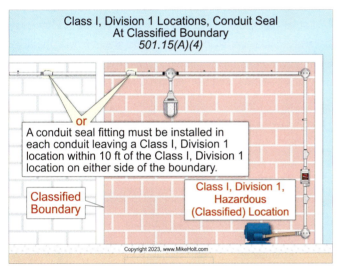
▶Figure 501-17

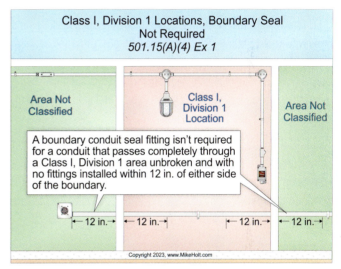
▶Figure 501-19

There must be no fitting, except for a listed explosionproof reducer installed at the conduit seal fitting, between the point at which the conduit leaves the Class I, Division 1 location and the boundary conduit seal fitting. ▶Figure 501-18

Where the Class 1 Division 1 boundary seal is on a Division 2 area, the Class 1 Division 1 wiring method must extend into the Division 2 area boundary seal.

Ex 1: A conduit boundary seal fitting is not required for a conduit that passes completely through a Class I, Division 1 area unbroken and with no fittings installed within 12 in. of either side of the boundary. ▶Figure 501-19

Ex 2: If the conduit boundary is below grade, the conduit seal can be above grade. There must be no fitting, except for a listed explosionproof reducer installed at the conduit seal fitting, between the conduit seal fitting and the point at which the conduit emerges from below grade. ▶Figure 501-20

Author's Comment:

▸ The wiring method between the conduit seal fitting and the Class I, Division 1 boundary must be rigid metal conduit or intermediate metal conduit [501.10(A)(1)(1)].

(D) Cable Seal—Class I, Division 1. In Class I, Division 1 locations, seal fittings must be as follows:

501.15 | Class I Locations

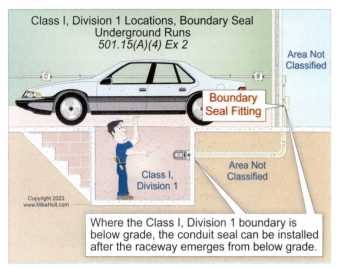
▶Figure 501–20

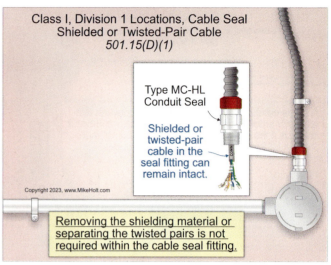
▶Figure 501–22

(1) Cable Termination Fittings. Cables must be sealed at all terminations with sealing fittings in accordance with 501.15(C) and installed within 18 in. of the enclosure or as required by the enclosure marking. Only threaded couplings or explosionproof fittings such as unions, reducers, elbows, and capped elbows can be installed between the cable seal fitting and the enclosure.

Type MC-HL cable is inherently gas/vaportight by the construction of the cable. Type TC-ER-HL cable and Type IM cable must be sealed with listed termination fittings that permit the sealing compound to surround each individual insulated conductor to minimize the passage of gases or vapors. ▶Figure 501–21

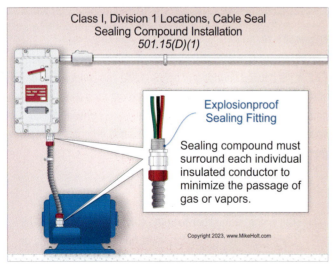
▶Figure 501–21

For shielded cables and twisted-pair cables, removing the shielding material or separating the twisted pairs is not required within the cable seal fitting. ▶Figure 501–22

(2) Cables Capable of Transmitting Gases or Vapors in a Raceway. Raceways containing cables must be sealed after removing the jacket and any other coverings so the sealing compound will surround each individual insulated conductor or optical fiber tube in a manner that minimizes the passage of gases and vapors.

Ex: Removing the outer sheathing of multiconductor cables or separating the twisted pairs is not required, provided the cable core is sealed within the conduit seal fitting. ▶Figure 501–23

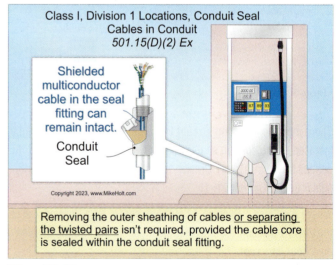
▶Figure 501–23

(3) Cables Not Capable of Transmitting Gases or Vapors in a Raceway. Each multiconductor cable installed within a raceway is considered to be a single conductor if the cable is incapable of transmitting gases or vapors through the cable core.

501.30 Grounding and Bonding

The title of this section was shortened, there were several editorial changes driven by the effort to make these rules comply with the *NEC* Style Manual, and some clarifications and technical revisions identify how things should be bonded and grounded.

Analysis

EDITED — The title of this section was revised to be simply "Grounding and Bonding" since the article only covers installations in Class I, Division 1 and 2 locations.

EDITED — The requirement to comply with Article 250 in the parent text was replaced with a requirement to comply with 501.30(A) and (B).

NEW — Subdivision (A) now requires systems and equipment to be grounded in accordance with Part I and Part VI of Article 250.

REORGANIZED   EXPANDED — The rules in (B) were reorganized into two subdivisions. The previous (A) became list item (B)(1)(a) where cable trays were added to the list of things to bond, and a new requirement was added to bond metal struts, angles, or channels used for support or physical protection in accordance with 250.102. There was no technical change.

NEW — Revisions in (2)(b) act as an Exception to (a) specifying the conditions where you are not required to install the wire type equipment bonding jumper.

501.30 Grounding and Bonding

Because of the explosive conditions associated with electrical installations in hazardous (classified) locations [500.5], electrical continuity of metal parts of equipment and raceways must be ensured, regardless of the voltage of the circuit, in accordance with 501.30(A) and (B).

(B) Bonding. Bonding must comply with 501.30(B)(1) and (B)(2).

(1) Specific Bonding Means. Bonding in a Class 1 hazardous (classified) location must comply with the following:

(a) Locknuts are not suitable in hazardous (classified) locations. Bonding jumpers with identified fittings or bonding locknuts must be used for all metal conduit terminations to fittings, boxes, cable trays, and enclosures between Class I locations and service equipment or separately derived systems. ▶Figure 501-24

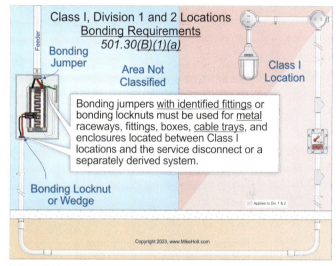
▶Figure 501-24

Author's Comment:

▸ Regardless of the circuit voltage, the electrical continuity of metal parts of equipment and raceways in hazardous (classified) locations must be ensured by using bonding-type locknuts, wedges, or bushings with bonding jumpers [250.92(B)(4)], whether equipment grounding conductors of the wire type are installed in the raceway [250.100] or not. Threaded couplings and hubs made up wrenchtight provide a suitable low-impedance fault current path [250.92(B)(2)]. Locknuts alone are not sufficient to serve this purpose.

▸ A separate equipment grounding conductor of the wire type is not required if a metal raceway is used for equipment grounding [250.100]. ▶Figure 501-25

(2) Flexible Metal Conduit and Liquidtight Flexible Metal Conduit.

(a) Where flexible metal conduit and liquidtight flexible metal conduit is installed as permitted by 501.10(B)(2)(a), an equipment bonding jumper of the wire type must be installed in accordance with 250.102. ▶Figure 501-26

501.135 | Class I Locations

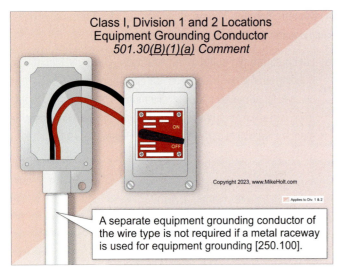
▶Figure 501–25

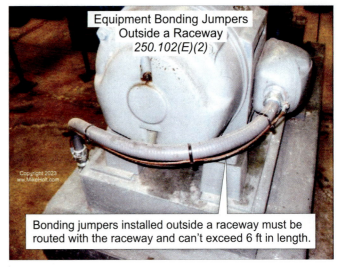
▶Figure 501–27

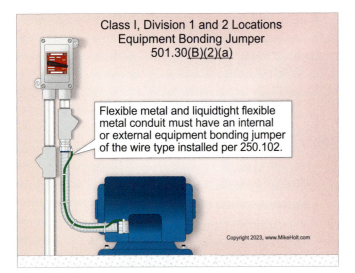
▶Figure 501–26

Author's Comment:

▸ Load-side bonding jumpers are sized in accordance with Table 250.122 based on the rating of the overcurrent protective device [250.102(D)]. Where installed outside a raceway, the length of bonding jumpers is not permitted to exceed 6 ft and they must be routed with the raceway [250.102(E)(2)].
▶Figure 501–27

501.135 Utilization Equipment

Luminaires were added to the list of equipment included in this rule.

Analysis

NEW Luminaires are utilization equipment but were not previously listed in this section. While they are covered in 501.130 they were added to (B) to clarify that luminaires installed in Class I, Division 2 locations must meet the requirements found in 501.130.

501.135 Utilization Equipment

(A) Class I, Division 1. Utilization equipment such as heaters, motors, switches, circuit breakers, fuses, and luminaires in Class I, Division 1 locations must be identified for use in Class I, Division 1 locations.

(B) Class I, Division 2. Utilization equipment such as heaters, motors, switches, circuit breakers, fuses, and luminaires in Class I, Division 2 locations must be identified for use in Class I, Division 2 locations.

Class I Locations | **501.145**

501.145 Receptacles and Attachment Plugs, Class I, Division 1 and Division 2

The scope of this article was expanded to require receptacles and attachment plugs to be listed.

Analysis

EXPANDED Parent text was added to require receptacles and attachment plugs to be listed for the location, except as permitted by 501.105(B)(6).

501.145 Receptacles

Receptacles must be listed for the hazardous (classified) location.
▶Figure 501–28

Author's Comment:

▸ Receptacles listed for Class I locations can be any of the following types:

   ▸ *Interlocked Switch Receptacle.* This receptacle contains a built-in rotary switch interlocked with the attachment plug. The switch must be off before the attachment plug can be inserted or removed.
   ▸ *Manual Interlocked Receptacle.* The attachment plug is inserted into the receptacle and then rotated to operate the receptacle's switching contacts.
   ▸ *Delayed Action Receptacle.* This receptacle requires an attachment plug and receptacle constructed so that an electrical arc will be confined within the explosionproof chamber of the receptacle.

▶Figure 501–28

Notes

ARTICLE 502 CLASS II LOCATIONS

Introduction to Article 502—Class II Locations

If an area has combustible dust present, it is considered a Class II location. Examples of such locations include flour mills, grain silos, coal bins, wood pulp storage areas, and munitions plants.

Article 502 follows a logical arrangement similar to that of Article 501 and provides guidance in selecting equipment and wiring methods for Class II locations, including distinctions between Class II, Division 1 and Class II, Division 2 requirements.

502.10 Wiring Methods

As we have seen in other areas of Chapter 5, revisions were made to allow the use of coated RMC and IMC. The bonding requirements for LFMC were clarified as well.

Analysis

EXPANDED Revisions to (A)(1)(1) clarify that the use of RMC and IMC with supplemental corrosion protection coatings are permitted in these locations, and (A)(2)(2) clarifies that LFMC must be bonded in accordance with 502.30(B).

NEW New parent text was added to (B) to clarify that the wiring methods for Class II, Division 2 locations must be in accordance with 502.10(B)(1) through (4).

CLARIFIED The rules in (B)(1)(2) now clarify that RMC and IMC with supplemental corrosion protection coatings (PCV coated conduit) are permitted, and (B)(1)(3) clarifies that the use of listed compression-type connectors and couplings are required for EMT in Class II, Division 2 locations.

EXPANDED The rule in (B)(1)(7) now clearly permits the use of other raceways like Schedule 80 PVC and RTRC in restricted industrial establishments.

502.10 Wiring Methods

(A) Class II, Division 1.

(1) General. The following wiring methods can be installed in a Class II, Division 1 location: ▶Figure 502-1

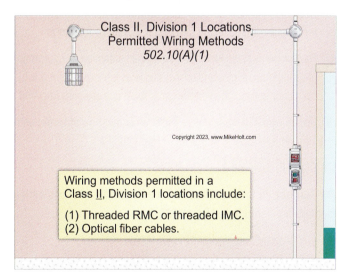

▶Figure 502-1

502.10 | Class II Locations

(1) Threaded rigid metal conduit (RMC) or threaded intermediate metal conduit (IMC).

(4) Optical fiber cable can be installed in RMC or IMC conduits [502.10(A)(1)(1)] and must be sealed in accordance with 502.15.

(2) Flexible Connections. If flexible connections are necessary, any of the following wiring methods are permitted in a Class II, Division 1 location: ▶Figure 502–2

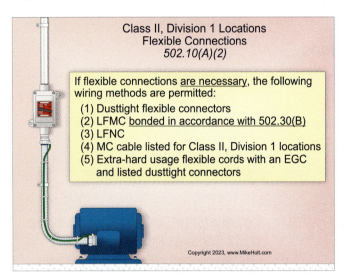

▶Figure 502–2

(1) Dusttight flexible connectors.

(2) Liquidtight flexible metal conduit (LFMC) with listed fittings and bonded in accordance with 502.30(B).

(3) Liquidtight flexible nonmetallic conduit (LFNC) with listed fittings.

(4) Interlocked armor Type MC cable with an impervious jacket and termination fittings listed for Class II, Division 1 locations.

(5) Flexible cords listed for extra-hard usage containing an equipment grounding conductor and terminated with listed dusttight flexible cord connectors. The flexible cords must comply with 502.140.

(3) Boxes and Fittings. Boxes and fittings must be provided with threaded entries and be dusttight. ▶Figure 502–3

(B) Class II, Division 2.

(1) General. In Class II, Division 2 locations, the following wiring methods are permitted: ▶Figure 502–4

(1) Any of the wiring methods in 502.10(A).

(2) Rigid metal conduit (RMC) and intermediate metal conduit (IMC) with listed threaded or threadless fittings, including RMC or IMC conduits with supplemental corrosion protection coatings.

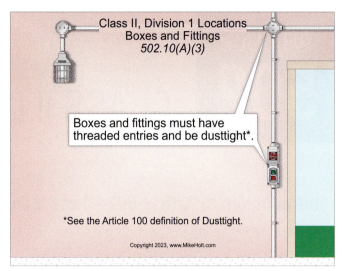

▶Figure 502–3

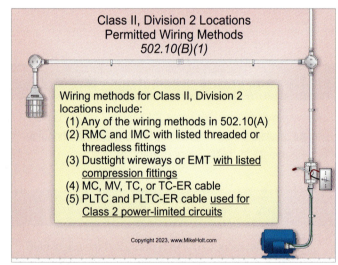

▶Figure 502–4

(3) Dusttight wireways or electrical metallic tubing (EMT) with listed compression-type connectors or couplings.

(4) Types MC, MV, TC, or TC-ER cable terminated with listed fittings, including installation in cable tray systems. Type TC-ER cable must include an equipment grounding conductor in addition to any drain wire that might be present.

(5) Types PLTC and PLTC-ER cable used for Class 2 power-limited circuits, including installation in cable tray systems. The cable must be terminated with listed fittings. Type PLTC-ER cable must include an equipment grounding conductor in addition to any drain wire that might be present.

(8) Optical fiber cables can be installed in cable trays or RMC or IMC conduits [502.10(B)(1) and (2)] and must be sealed in accordance with 502.15.

Class II Locations | 502.15

(2) Flexible Connections. If flexibility is necessary, wiring methods complying with 502.10(A)(2) are permitted in a Class II, Division 2 location.

(4) Boxes and Fittings. Boxes and fittings in Class II, Division 2 areas must be dusttight. ▶Figure 502-5

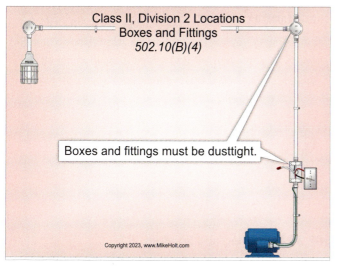

▶Figure 502-5

Author's Comment:

▶ A standard weatherproof box with a cover and gasket meets this requirement.

502.15 Sealing

An Informational Note about electrical sealing putty was relocated into the rule.

Analysis

NEW In the 2020 *Code* an Informational Note advised that "electrical sealing putty" is a method of sealing. This was seen as a recommendation so the text was relocated into a new list item, (5), clarifying that it can be used for sealing.

502.15 Sealing

In Class II, Division 1 and 2 locations, combustible dust must be prevented from entering the required dust-ignitionproof enclosure from a raceway by any of the following methods:

(1) A permanent and effective seal.

(2) A horizontal raceway not less than 10 ft long. ▶Figure 502-6

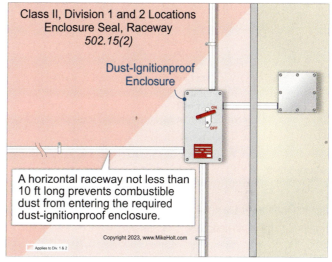

▶Figure 502-6

(3) A vertical raceway that extends downward for not less than 5 ft from the dust-ignitionproof enclosure.

(4) A raceway installed in a manner equivalent to (2) or (3) that extends only horizontally and downward from the dust-ignitionproof enclosure.

(5) Electrical sealing putty. ▶Figure 502-7

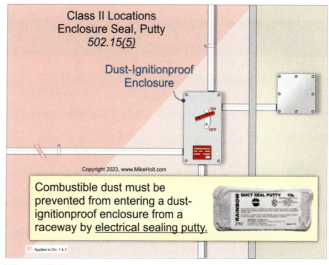

▶Figure 502-7

502.30 | Class II Locations

A conduit seal is not required between a dust-ignitionproof enclosure and an enclosure in an unclassified location. ▶Figure 502–8

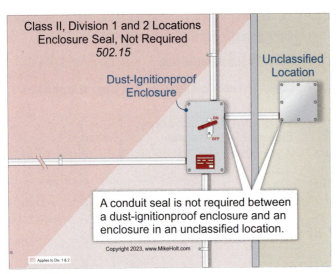
▶Figure 502–8

Sealing fittings for Class II locations must be accessible and are not required to be explosionproof.

502.30 Grounding and Bonding

The title of this section was shortened, there were several editorial changes driven by the effort to make these rules comply with the *NEC* Style Manual, and some clarifications and technical revisions identify how things should be bonded and grounded.

Analysis

EDITED — The title of this section was revised to simply "Grounding and Bonding" since the article only covers installations in Class I, Division 1 and 2 locations.

EDITED — The requirement to comply with Article 250 in the parent text was replaced with a requirement to comply with 502.30(A) and (B).

NEW — Subdivision (A) now requires systems and equipment to be grounded in accordance with Part I and Part VI of Article 250.

REORGANIZED   EXPANDED — The rules in (B) were reorganized into two subdivisions. The previous (A) became list item (B)(1)(a) where cable trays were added to the list of things to bond, and a new requirement was added to bond metal struts, angles, or channels used for support or physical protection in accordance with 250.102.

NEW — Revisions in (2)(b) act as an Exception to (a) specifying the conditions where you are not required to install the wire type equipment bonding jumper.

502.30 Grounding and Bonding

Because of the explosive conditions associated with electrical installations in hazardous (classified) locations [500.5], electrical continuity of the metal parts of equipment and raceways must be ensured regardless of the voltage of the circuit.

(B) Bonding.

(1) Specific Bonding Means.

(a) Locknuts are not suitable for bonding purposes in hazardous (classified) locations so bonding jumpers with identified fittings or other approved means of bonding must be used. Such means of bonding apply to all metal raceways, fittings, boxes, cable trays, and enclosures, and other parts of raceway systems between Class II locations and service disconnects or the grounding point of a separately derived system. ▶Figure 502–9

Author's Comment:

▸ A separate equipment grounding conductor of the wire type is not required if a metal raceway is used for equipment grounding [250.100]. ▶Figure 502–10

▸ The special bonding requirements for Class II locations are the same as those for 501.30(A) Class 1 locations [250.94(B)(4)]. Threaded couplings and hubs made up wrenchtight provide a suitable low-impedance fault current path [250.92(B)(2)].

Class II Locations | 502.30

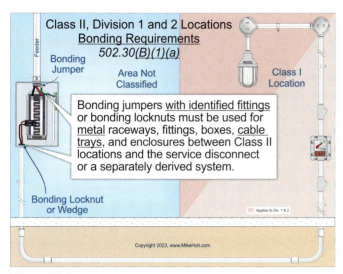
▶Figure 502-9

Author's Comment:

▶ Load-side bonding jumpers must be sized in accordance with 250.122 based on the rating of the overcurrent protective device [250.102(D)]. Where the bonding jumper is installed outside a raceway, the length of the bonding jumpers is not permitted to exceed 6 ft and they must be routed with the raceway [250.102(E)(2)]. ▶Figure 502-12

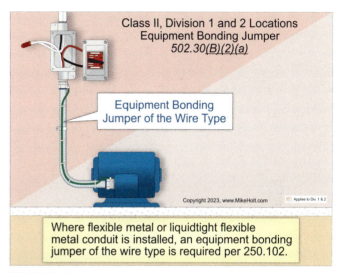
▶Figure 502-11

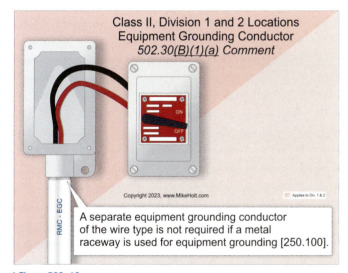
▶Figure 502-10

(2) Flexible Metal Conduit and Liquidtight Flexible Metal Conduit.

(a) Type LFMC. Where flexible metal or liquidtight flexible metal conduit is installed as permitted by 502.10(A)(2), an equipment bonding jumper of the wire type must be installed in accordance with 250.102.
▶Figure 502-11

▶Figure 502-12

Notes

ARTICLE 511

COMMERCIAL GARAGES, REPAIR AND STORAGE

Introduction to Article 511—Commercial Garages, Repair and Storage

Article 511 covers locations used for the service and repair of vehicles that use volatile flammable liquids or flammable gases for fuel.

First, it is essential to understand whether the facility is a major or minor repair garage. Pay careful attention to these definitions as you study this article. The next factor that makes a difference in the classification of a location is the presence or absence of a below-floor pit. Finally, mechanical ventilation is critical and can change the classification of a location. Read this material carefully, review the illustrations, and you will find that the Article 511 requirements are not very difficult.

511.3 Area Classification

Clarifications were made to the ventilation rules in (E), so they are easier to understand.

Analysis

CLARIFIED This rule previously allowed an adjacent area to be unclassified where ventilated at four or more air changes per hour if it was "effectively cut off by walls or partitions." To clarify the intent of the rule, it was revised to read "separated by an unpierced wall, roof, or other solid partition." This provides clarity and aligns the text here with that in 514.3(B)(1).

511.3 Classification of Hazardous Areas

General. Where flammable liquids or gaseous fuels are stored, handled, or transferred, electrical wiring and electrical utilization equipment must be designed in accordance with the requirements for Class I, Division 1 or 2 hazardous (classified) locations.

(E) Modifications to Classification.

(1) Classification of Adjacent Areas. Areas adjacent to classified locations are not classified if mechanically ventilated at a rate of four or more air changes per hour, designed with positive air pressure, or when separated by an unpierced wall, roof, or other solid partition.
▶Figure 511-1

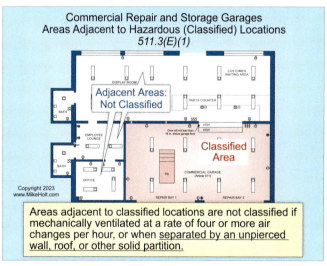
▶Figure 511-1

(2) Alcohol-Based Windshield Washer Fluid. Areas used for the storage, handling, or dispensing into motor vehicles of alcohol-based windshield washer fluid in repair garages are unclassified unless otherwise classified by a provision of 511.3.

511.7 | Commercial Garages, Repair and Storage

511.7 Wiring and Equipment Installed Above Hazardous (Classified) Locations

The term "Class I" was replaced by "Hazardous (Classified)." This section went through quite a transformation as it was reorganized into a list format with additional requirements for listed fittings and EGCs added to the mix.

Analysis

EDITED The term "Class I" was replaced by "Hazardous (Classified)" in five locations, including the title of this section, as the zone classification system no longer uses the "Class I" designation.

REORGANIZED This section was reorganized from a long paragraph into nine list items for usability and requirements were added to most of the wiring methods.

EXPANDED The rule in (A)(1) permits the use of RMC, IMC, and EMT. Additional language specifies that RMC and IMC must be used with listed threaded or threadless fittings, and EMT must be used with listed fittings.

- List item (2) previously specified rigid nonmetallic conduit, but the reference has been incorrect since the 2008 *Code* when the title of Article 352 was changed to Rigid Polyvinyl Chloride Conduit and RTRC was given its own article [Article 355.]
- List Item (3) permits FMC, LFMC, and LFNC conduit and requires listed fittings.
- Item (4) covers AC, MC, TC, and TC-ER cables. Type TC-ER cable must have an EGC and be terminated using listed fittings.

511.7 Wiring and Equipment Above Hazardous (Classified) Locations

(A) Wiring in Spaces Above Hazardous (Classified) Locations.

(1) Fixed Wiring. Fixed wiring above hazardous (classified) locations is permitted by one or more of the following wiring methods: ▶Figure 511–2

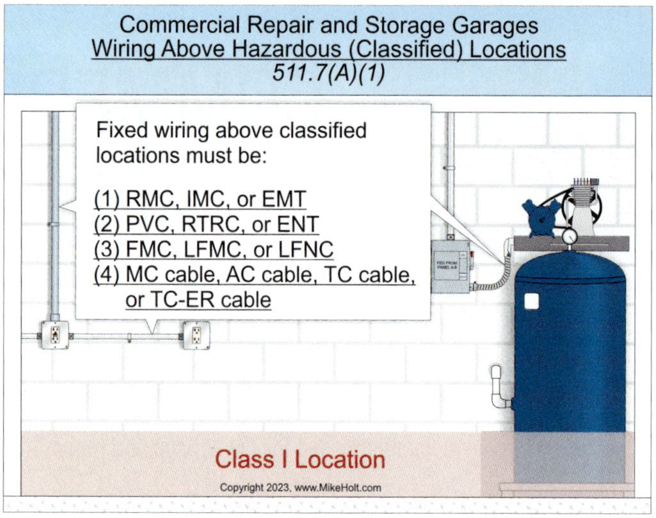

▶Figure 511–2

(1) Rigid metal conduit (RMC) and intermediate metal conduit (IMC) with threaded or threadless fittings, or electrical metallic conduit (EMT) with listed fittings.

(2) Rigid polyvinyl chloride conduit (PVC), reinforced thermosetting resin conduit (RTRC), or electrical nonmetallic tubing (ENT) with listed fittings.

(3) Flexible metal conduit (FMC), liquidtight flexible metal conduit (LFMC), or liquidtight flexible nonmetallic conduit (LFNC) with listed fittings.

(4) Types MC cable, AC cable, TC cable, or TC-ER cable with listed fittings, including installation in cable trays. Type TC-ER cable must include an equipment grounding conductor in addition to any drain wire.

(2) Pendant (Drop-Cords). For pendants, flexible cord suitable for the type of service and listed for hard usage must be used.

(B) Equipment Above Hazardous (Classified) Locations.

(1) Fixed Electrical Equipment. Fixed electrical equipment must be above the level of any defined hazardous (classified) location or be identified for the location.

(a) Arcing Equipment. Equipment with make-and-break contacts installed less than 12 ft above the floor level must be of the totally enclosed type or constructed to prevent sparks or hot metal particles from escaping.

(b) Fixed Lighting. Luminaires over travel lanes or where exposed to physical damage must be at least 12 ft above the floor level, unless the luminaires are of the totally enclosed type or constructed to prevent sparks or hot metal particles from escaping. ▶Figure 511–3

Commercial Garages, Repair and Storage | **511.8**

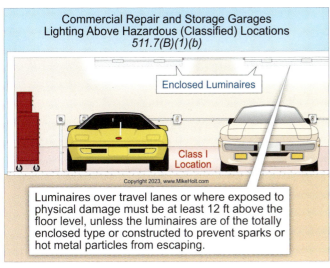
▶Figure 511–3

511.8 Underground Wiring Below Hazardous (Classified) Locations

Underground wiring below a commercial garage must be one of the following wiring methods:

(1) Threaded rigid metal conduit (RMC) or threaded intermediate metal conduit (IMC) with listed threaded fittings.

(2) PVC conduit, RTRC conduit, or HDPE conduit can be installed below a commercial garage if buried under not less than 2 ft of cover. Threaded rigid metal conduit or threaded intermediate metal conduit must be used when the raceway has less than 2 ft of cover.
▶Figure 511–4

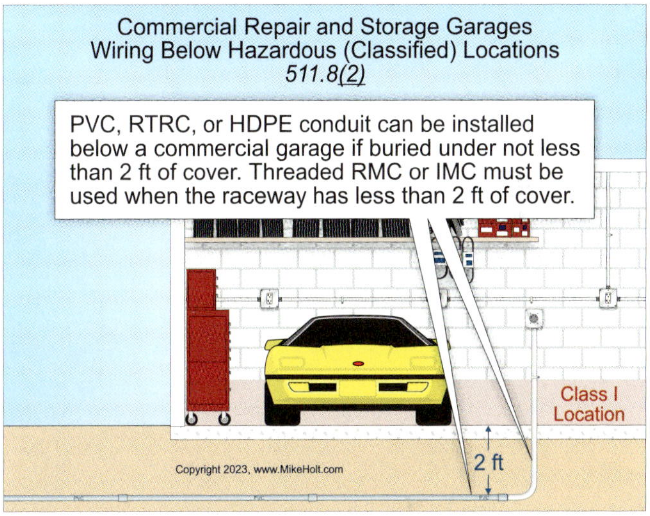

▶Figure 511–4

511.8 Underground Wiring Hazardous (Classified) Locations

The term "Class I" was replaced by "Hazardous (Classified)." This section was reorganized into a list format and the Exception was relocated into the rule.

Analysis

EDITED — The term "Class I" was replaced by "Hazardous (Classified)" in the title of this section as the zone classification system no longer uses the "Class I" designation.

EXPANDED — The new list item (1) clarifies that IMC must be threaded, and both RMC and IMC must be used with listed threaded fittings.

REORGANIZED — This section previously had parent text and an Exception allowing the use of PVC and RTRC. The Exception was relocated into list item (2).

Changes to the National Electrical Code 2023 | MikeHolt.com

Notes

ARTICLE 514 MOTOR FUEL DISPENSING FACILITIES

Introduction to Article 514—Motor Fuel Dispensing Facilities

The portion of a facility where fuel is stored and dispensed into the fuel tanks of motor vehicles and marine craft, or into approved containers, must comply with Article 514.

What is most striking is the large table that makes up about half of this article. It does not provide any electrical requirements, list any electrical specifications, or address any electrical equipment. What it does tell you is how to classify a motor fuel dispensing area. The rest of this article contains specific provisions and refers to other articles that must be applied.

Author's Comment:

▸ Diesel fuel is not a flammable liquid. Therefore, areas associated with diesel dispensing equipment and associated wiring are not required to comply with the hazardous (classified) location requirements of Article 514 [514.3(A)]. However, the other requirements in this article still apply.

514.7 Wiring and Equipment Above Hazardous (Classified) Locations

The term "Class I" was replaced by "Hazardous (Classified)." If these changes seem vaguely familiar, it is because this is a parallel version of the reorganization and revisions that happened in 511.7.

Analysis

EDITED The term "Class I" was replaced by "Hazardous (Classified)" in two locations, including the title of this section, as the zone classification system no longer uses the "Class I" designation.

REORGANIZED This section was reorganized from a long paragraph into nine list items for usability and requirements were added to most of the wiring methods.

EXPANDED The rule in (1) permits the use of RMC, IMC, and EMT. Additional language specifies that RMC and IMC must be used with listed threaded or threadless fittings, and EMT must be used with listed fittings.

▸ List item (2) previously specified rigid nonmetallic conduit, but the reference has been incorrect since the 2008 *Code* when the title of Article 352 was changed to Rigid Polyvinyl Conduit and RTRC was given its own article. These raceways (PVC and RTRC-XW) are specified for aboveground use.

▸ List Item (3) permits FMC, LFMC, and LFNC conduit and requires listed fittings.

▸ Item (4) covers AC, MC, TC, and TC-ER cables. Type TC-ER cable must have an EGC and be terminated using listed fittings.

514.7 Wiring and Equipment Above Hazardous (Classified) Locations

Fixed wiring above a hazardous (classified) location is permitted by one or more of the following: ▶Figure 514–1

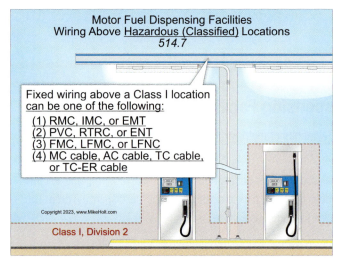

▶Figure 514–1

(1) Rigid metal conduit (RMC) and intermediate metal conduit (IMC) with threaded or threadless fittings, or electrical metallic conduit (EMT) with fittings.

(2) Rigid polyvinyl chloride conduit (PVC), reinforced thermosetting resin conduit (RTRC), or electrical nonmetallic tubing (ENT) with listed fittings.

(3) Flexible metal conduit (FMC), liquidtight flexible metal conduit (LFMC), or liquidtight flexible nonmetallic conduit (LFNC) with listed fittings.

(4) Types MC cable, AC cable, TC cable, or TC-ER cable with listed fittings, including installation in cable trays. Type TC-ER cable must include an equipment grounding conductor in addition to any drain wire.

ARTICLE 517 HEALTH CARE FACILITIES

Introduction to Article 517—Health Care Facilities

Health care facilities differ from other types of buildings in many important ways. Article 517 is primarily concerned with those parts of health care facilities where human patients are examined and treated. Whether those facilities are permanent or movable, they still fall under the scope of this article. However, the Article 517 wiring and protection requirements do not apply to business offices or waiting rooms, nor do they apply to animal veterinary facilities.

Definitions. Terms contained in Article 100 that are important for the application of Article 517 include:

Health Care Facilities. Buildings, portions of buildings, or mobile enclosures in which medical, dental, psychiatric, nursing, obstetrical, or surgical care is provided for humans.

Note: Examples of health care facilities include, but are not limited to, hospitals, nursing homes, limited care facilities, supervisory care facilities, clinics, medical and dental offices, and ambulatory care facilities.

Limited Care Facility. A building or an area of a building used for the housing, on a 24-hour basis, of four or more persons who are incapable of self-preservation because of age, physical limitations due to accident or illness, or limitations such as intellectual disability, developmental disability, mental illness, or chemical dependency.

Patient Bed Location. The location of an inpatient sleeping bed.

Patient Care Space Category. Any space of a health care facility where patients are intended to be examined or treated (Article 517). ▶Figure 517-1

Note 2: Business offices, corridors, lounges, day rooms, dining rooms, or similar areas are not classified as patient care spaces.

Patient Care Vicinity. A space extending 6 ft beyond the patient bed, chair, table, treadmill, or other device that supports the patient during examination and treatment and extending vertically to 7 ft 6 in. above the floor (Article 517). ▶Figure 517-2

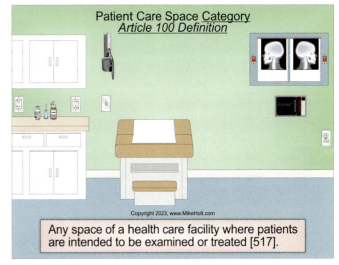

▶Figure 517-1

517.1 | Health Care Facilities

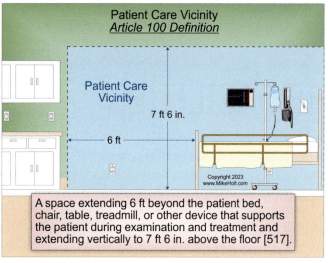
▶Figure 517–2

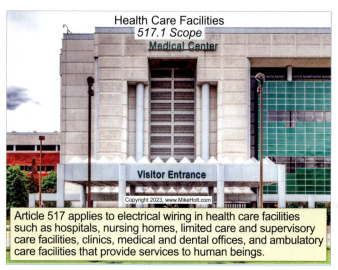
▶Figure 517–3

517.1 Scope

Text was relocated from an Informational Note in 517.11 that had information related to the scope of this article.

Analysis

EXPANDED — The scope of article 517 was revised to incorporate the language and Informational Note previously found in 517.11 of the 2020 *NEC*.

517.1 Scope

This article applies to electrical wiring in health care facilities such as hospitals, nursing homes, limited care and supervisory care facilities, clinics, medical and dental offices, and ambulatory care facilities that provide services to human beings. ▶Figure 517–3

Author's Comment:
- This article does not apply to animal veterinary facilities.
- Areas of health care facilities not used for the treatment of patients (such as business offices and waiting rooms) are not required to comply with the provisions contained in Article 517.

The requirements contained in Article 517 specify the installation criteria and wiring methods that minimize electrical hazards by adequate low-potential differences only between exposed conductive surfaces that are likely to become energized and those that could be contacted by a patient.

Note 1: In a health care facility, it is difficult to prevent the occurrence of a conductive or capacitive path from the patient's body to some grounded object, because that path might be established accidentally or through instrumentation directly connected to the patient. Other electrically conductive surfaces that might make an additional contact with the patient, or instruments that might be connected to the patient, become possible sources of electric currents that can traverse the patient's body.

517.10 Applicability

A clarification in 517.10(B) says that a pharmacy area is not considered a health care facility.

Analysis

EXPANDED — This section lists the areas not covered by this article. New text in (B)(3)(e) clarifies that pharmacy areas that are not contiguous to health care facilities are not covered. This is a big area of conflict in some parts of the country and will provide much needed clarification.

517.10 Applicability

(A) Applicability. Part II applies to patient care spaces.

(B) Not Covered. The requirements contained in Part II of Article 517 do not apply to:

(1) Business offices, corridors, waiting rooms, or similar areas in clinics, medical and dental offices, and outpatient facilities.

(2) Spaces of nursing homes and limited care facilities used exclusively for patient sleeping rooms as determined by the health care facility's governing body.

(3) Areas used exclusively for:

   a. Intramuscular injections (immunizations)

   b. Psychiatry and psychotherapy

   c. Alternative medicine

   d. Optometry

   e. Pharmacy services not contiguous to health care facilities

---

517.13 Equipment Grounding Conductor for Receptacles and Fixed Electrical Equipment in Patient Care Spaces

Editorial revisions were made throughout this section and it was clarified that metal faceplates can be bonded with the mounting screws.

Analysis

EDITED There were quite a few editorial revisions to this section but no real technical changes. One notable edit was the relocation of Exception No. 2 from (B)(1) to the parent text since it applies to the entire rule, not just to (B).

CLARIFIED The previous rule (B)(1)(4) for metal faceplates was confusing since (B)(1) required the insulated bonding or grounding conductor to connect directly to the equipment, but (B)(1)(4) allowed mounting screws to provide the required bonding for metal faceplates. This language was relocated into a new Exception No. 2 so now the rule makes sense.

517.13 Equipment Grounding Conductor for Receptacles and Fixed Electrical Equipment in Patient Care Spaces

Wiring, including homeruns, serving patient care spaces must comply with the requirements of 517.13(A) and (B):

Ex: Circuits for luminaires more than 7½ ft above the floor and switches outside the patient care vicinity must be installed in a 517.13(A) wiring method. An insulated copper equipment grounding conductor of the wire type is not required within the wiring method. ▶Figure 517–4

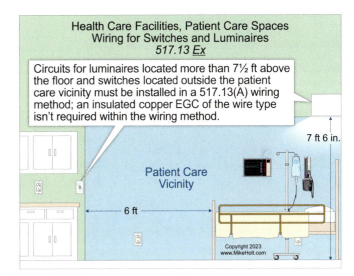
▶Figure 517–4

(A) Wiring Methods. Branch-circuit conductors, including homeruns, serving patient care spaces must be provided with an effective ground-fault current path installed in a metal raceway or metal cable having a metal sheath that qualifies as an equipment grounding conductor in accordance with 250.118. ▶Figure 517–5

Author's Comment:

▸ The metal sheath of traditional Type MC interlocked cable does not qualify as an equipment grounding conductor [250.118(A)(10)(a)], therefore this wiring method is not permitted to be used for circuits in patient care spaces. ▶Figure 517–6

517.13 | Health Care Facilities

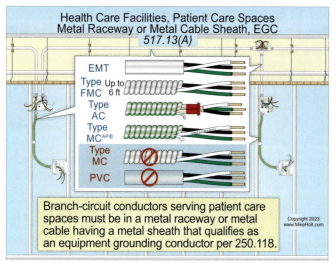

▶Figure 517-5

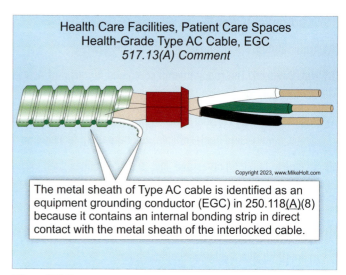

▶Figure 517-7

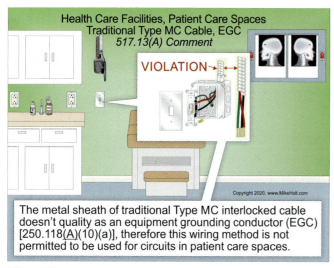

▶Figure 517-6

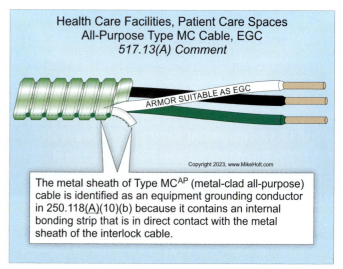

▶Figure 517-8

- The metal sheath of Type AC cable is identified as an equipment grounding conductor in 250.118(A)(8) because it contains an internal bonding strip that is in direct contact with the metal sheath of the interlock cable. ▶Figure 517-7

- The metal sheath of Type MC^AP (metal-clad all-purpose) cable is identified as an equipment grounding conductor in 250.118(A)(10)(b) because it contains an internal bonding strip that is in direct contact with the metal sheath of the interlock cable. ▶Figure 517-8

(B) Insulated Equipment Grounding Conductors.

(1) General. An insulated copper equipment grounding conductor with green insulation along its entire length, installed within a suitable wiring method as required in 517.13(A), must be connected to the following:

(1) Grounding terminals of receptacles, other than isolated ground receptacles, must be directly connected to a green insulated copper equipment grounding conductor. ▶Figure 517-9

(2) Metal boxes and enclosures containing circuit conductors must be directly connected to a green insulated copper equipment grounding conductor. ▶Figure 517-10

(3) Metal parts of fixed electrical equipment operating at over 100V must be directly connected to an insulated copper equipment grounding conductor. ▶Figure 517-11

Ex 2: Metal faceplates must be connected to the effective ground-fault current path by means of a metal mounting screw(s) securing the faceplate to a metal yoke or strap of a receptacle, or to a metal outlet box. ▶Figure 517-12

Health Care Facilities | 517.13

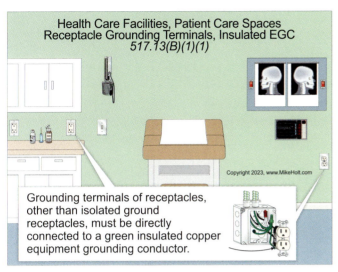
▶Figure 517-9

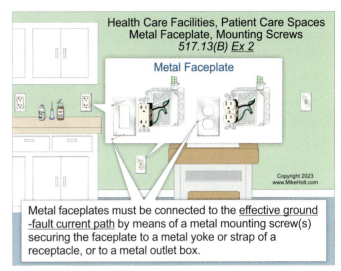
▶Figure 517-12

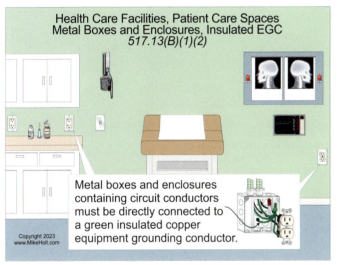
▶Figure 517-10

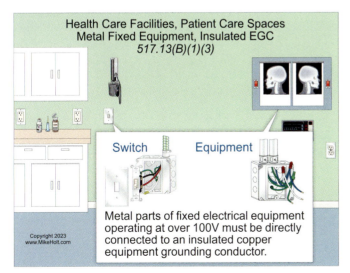
▶Figure 517-11

Author's Comment:

▸ Patient care spaces, as designated by the facility administrator, include patient rooms as well as examining rooms, therapy areas, treatment rooms, and some patient corridors. They do not include business offices, corridors, lounges, day rooms, dining rooms, or similar areas not classified as patient care spaces [Article 100].

▸ Often referred to as redundancy, equipment grounding requirements in patient care spaces are based on the concept of two different types of equipment grounding conductors so if there is an installation error, the effective ground-fault current paths are not lost. One effective ground-fault current path is "mechanical" (the wiring method) and the other is of the "wire type." Section 517.13(A) requires the wiring method to be a metal raceway or metal cable that qualifies as an equipment grounding conductor in accordance with 250.118(A)(8) and (10)(b), and 517.13(B) requires an insulated copper equipment grounding conductor of the wire type in accordance with 250.118(A)(1).

(2) Sizing. Equipment grounding conductors and equipment bonding jumpers must be sized in accordance with 250.122. ▶Figure 517-13

517.13 | Health Care Facilities

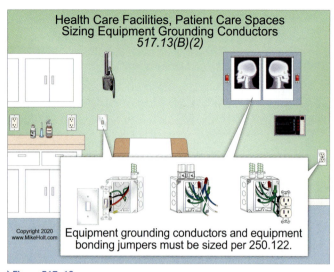
▶Figure 517-13

ARTICLE 518 ASSEMBLY OCCUPANCIES

Introduction to Article 518—Assembly Occupancies

More commonly referred to as "Places of Assembly," these are buildings or portions of buildings specifically designed or intended for the assembly of 100 or more people and fall under the requirements of Article 518. This article goes out of its way to eliminate any confusion about the types of occupancies to which it is intended to apply. See 518.2 for a list of occupancies.

518.2 General Classification

Casinos were added to the list of places of assembly in (A).

Analysis

EXPANDED
Sometimes things are just overlooked, and this was one of those cases. A new list item added casinos and gaming facilities, and since the list is in alphabetical order, it was inserted as list item (5).

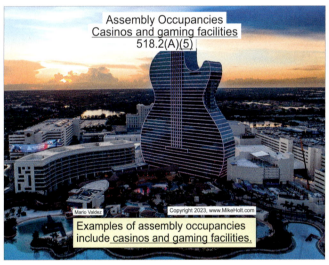
▶Figure 518-1

518.2 General Classifications

(A) Examples. Assembly occupancies include, but are not limited to:

(1) Armories
(2) Assembly halls
(3) Auditoriums
(4) Bowling lanes
(5) Casinos and gaming facilities ▶Figure 518-1
(6) Club rooms
(7) Conference rooms
(8) Courtrooms
(9) Dance halls
(10) Dining facilities
(11) Exhibition halls
(12) Gymnasiums
(13) Mortuary chapels
(14) Multipurpose rooms
(15) Museums
(16) Places awaiting transportation
(17) Places of religious worship
(18) Pool rooms
(19) Restaurants
(20) Skating rinks

518.2 | Assembly Occupancies

(B) Multiple Occupancies. The requirements contained in Article 518 only apply to that portion(s) of any building specifically designed or intended for the assembly of 100 or more persons. ▶Figure 518–2

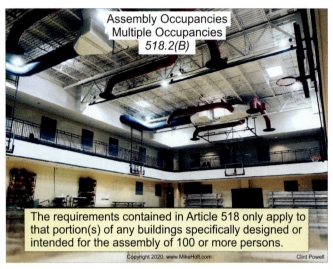

▶Figure 518–2

ARTICLE 547 AGRICULTURAL BUILDINGS

Introduction to Article 547—Agricultural Buildings

Three factors (dust, moisture, and an overall corrosive environment) have a tremendous influence on the lifespan of agricultural equipment.

Dust gets into mechanisms and causes premature wear. Add electricity to the mix, and dust adds two additional dangers—fire and explosion. Dust from hay, grain, and fertilizer is highly flammable. Litter materials, such as straw, are also highly flammable.

Another factor to consider in agricultural buildings is moisture which causes corrosion. Water is present for many reasons, including wash down.

Excrement from farm animals may cause corrosive vapors that eat at mechanical equipment and wiring methods and can cause electrical equipment to fail. For these reasons, Article 547 includes requirements for dealing with dust, moisture, and corrosion.

This article also has other rules. For example, you must install equipotential planes in all concrete floor confinement areas of livestock buildings containing metallic equipment accessible to animals and likely to become energized.

Livestock animals have a low tolerance to small voltage differences, which can cause loss of milk production and (at times) livestock fatality. As a result, the *NEC* contains specific requirements for an equipotential plane in buildings that house livestock.

Definitions. The following definition(s) contained in Article 100 is(are) important as they relate to this article.

Equipotential Plane (as applied to agricultural buildings). An area where conductive elements are embedded in or placed under concrete, bonded to all metal structures and nonelectrical equipment that could become energized, and connected to the electrical system to minimize voltage differences within the plane. ▶Figure 547–1

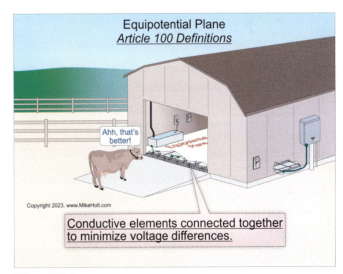

▶Figure 547–1

547.20 Wiring Methods

Permitted wiring methods for agricultural spaces was relocated here from 547.5 and editorially revised.

Analysis

REORGANIZED This section was previously 547.5(A). It was reorganized into a list format and relocated here with minor editorial changes.

547.20 Wiring Methods

(A) Wiring Methods. Wiring methods in agricultural buildings are limited to the following:

(1) Type UF cable

(2) Type NMC cable

(3) Type SE copper cable

(4) Jacketed Type MC cable

(5) Raceways suitable for the locations identified in 547.1(A) and (B)

547.25 Flexible Connections

This new section is reorganized text that was relocated here from 547.5(D) with no technical change.

Analysis

RELOCATED This rule was relocated to this new section from 547.5(D) as part of the reorganization of this article. The text was reorganized into a list format but there was no technical change.

547.25 Flexible Connections

Where necessary for flexible connections, the following wiring methods are permitted:

(1) Dusttight flexible connectors

(2) Liquidtight flexible metal conduit

(3) Liquidtight flexible nonmetallic conduit

(4) Flexible cord listed for hard usage terminated with listed dusttight cord connectors

547.26 Physical Protection

This new section was relocated here from 547.5(E) and some requirements were added.

Analysis

RELOCATED NEW This rule was relocated here from 547.5(E). Previously, wiring and equipment that was subject to physical damage had to be protected.

New requirements prohibit the use of nonmetallic cables concealed within walls or ceilings of buildings that are connected to livestock confinement areas.

A new Informational Note explains that rodents and other pests are prevalent in these areas and often chew up the nonmetallic cable causing damage.

547.26 Physical Protection

Electrical wiring and equipment must be protected where subject to physical damage. Nonmetallic cables are not permitted to be concealed within walls and above ceilings of buildings which are contiguous with, or physically adjoined to, livestock confinement areas.

Note: Rodents often damage nonmetallic cable and conductor insulation within the walls and ceilings of livestock containment areas.

Agricultural Buildings | **547.44**

547.44 Equipotential Planes and Bonding of Equipotential Planes

This new section was relocated here from 547.10, and the point where the equipotential plane must be connected was clarified.

Analysis

RELOCATED These requirements were relocated from 547.10 with several editorial changes. A technical change in (B) clarifies that the permitted points of connection for the equipotential planes are the grounding electrode system or the equipment grounding terminal in any panelboard associated with the equipotential plane.

547.44 Equipotential Planes

(A) Where Required. Equipotential planes must be installed as follows:

(1) Indoor Concrete Confinement Areas. An equipotential plane must be installed in indoor livestock confinement areas where metal equipment is accessible to livestock. ▶Figure 547–2

▶Figure 547–2

(2) Outdoor Concrete Confinement Areas. An equipotential plane must be installed in outdoor livestock confinement areas where metal equipment is accessible to livestock. ▶Figure 547–3

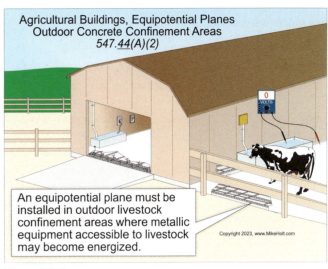
▶Figure 547–3

(B) Bonding. The equipotential plane must be bonded to the grounding electrode system or an equipment grounding terminal in any panelboard of the building's electrical grounding system associated with the equipotential plane by using a solid copper bonding conductor not smaller than 8 AWG. ▶Figure 547–4

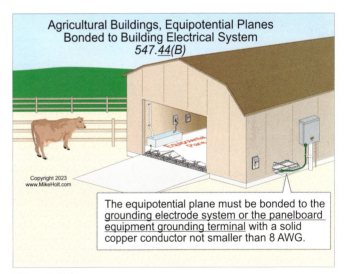
▶Figure 547–4

Note 1: ASABE Standard EP473.2, *Equipotential Planes in Animal Containment Areas*, provides the recommendation of a voltage gradient ramp at the entrances of agricultural buildings.

Note 2: See the American Society of Agricultural and Biological Engineers (ASABE) EP342.2, *Safety for Electrically Heated Livestock Waterers*.

547.44 | Agricultural Buildings

Author's Comment:

- The bonding requirements contained in Article 547 are unique because of the sensitivity of livestock to small voltage differences, especially in wet or damp concrete animal confinement areas.

- In most instances the voltage difference between metal parts and the Earth will be too low to present a shock hazard to people. However, livestock might detect the voltage difference if they come into contact with metal parts. Although voltage differences may not be life threatening to the livestock, it has been reported that as little as 0.50V RMS can adversely affect milk production.

ARTICLE 555
MARINAS, BOATYARDS, FLOATING BUILDINGS, AND COMMERCIAL AND NONCOMMERCIAL DOCKING FACILITIES

Introduction to Article 555—Marinas, Boatyards, Floating Buildings, and Commercial and Noncommercial Docking Facilities

Water levels are not constant. Ocean tides rise and fall, while lakes and rivers vary in depth in response to rain. To provide power to a marina or docking facility, you must allow for these variations in water level between the point of use and the electric power source. Article 555 addresses this issue.

This article begins with the concept of the electrical datum plane. You might think of it as the border of a "demilitarized zone" for electrical equipment. Or you can think of it as a line that marks the beginning of a "no man's land" where you simply do not place electrical equipment. Once you determine where this plane is, do not place transformers, connections, or receptacles below that line.

Because of recent electric shock drowning (ESD) incidents, installations supplying shore power in marinas and boatyards have increased electrical safety with the use of ground-fault protection (GFPE), leakage devices, and warning signs to raise awareness of possible hazardous voltage and currents present in the water of marinas and docking facilities.

555.4 Location of Service Equipment

There were two changes to the location requirements for service equipment.

555.15 Replacement of Equipment

A new section was added on how to deal with equipment that is replaced at docking facilities.

Analysis

EXPANDED Two changes as to the location of the service equipment in this section require the service equipment to be no closer than 5 ft horizontally from the water, and at least 12 in. above the electrical datum plane.

Analysis

NEW This new section requires that where electrical equipment is modified or replaced at a docking facility, those repairs, modifications, or replacements must comply with the provisions of this *Code*. The circuit that supplies the equipment must then be inspected. If existing equipment is damaged, it must be identified, documented, and repaired by a qualified person to the minimum requirements of the edition of this *Code* to which it was originally installed.

555.4 Location of Service Equipment

The service equipment for a floating dock or marina must be on land no closer than 5 ft horizontally from the water. Service equipment must be located no less than 12 in. above the electrical datum plane.

555.15 Replacement of Equipment

Modifications and Replaced Equipment. Modification or replacement of electrical enclosures, devices, or wiring on a docking facility must comply with the provisions of this *Code* and the installation requires an inspection of the entire circuit.

Existing Equipment. Existing equipment that has been damaged must be identified, documented, and repaired by a qualified person to the minimum requirements of the edition of this *Code* to which it was originally installed.

Author's Comment:

▸ According to Article 100, the definition of qualified persons is "a person with skills and knowledge related to the construction and operation of electrical equipment and installations. This person must have received safety training to recognize and avoid the hazards involved with electrical systems." ▸Figure 555-1

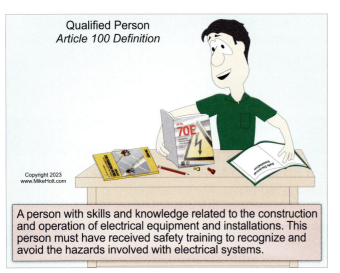

▸Figure 555-1

Note: NFPA 303, *Fire Protection Standard for Marinas and Boatyards*, is a resource for guiding the electrical inspection of a marina.

555.30 Electrical Equipment and Connections

The title of this section was revised to reflect its contents and terminology used in the rules was revised for clarity.

Analysis

REORGANIZED The title of this section was revised to indicate it covers both electrical equipment and electrical connections. Subdivisions (A) and (B) were combined into (A) without technical change, and (C) became (B). Other editorial revisions replaced the term "piers" with "structures" clarifying that this rule applies to all fixed and floating structures.

555.30 Electrical Equipment and Connections

(A) New Installation. Electrical equipment and connections (splices and terminations) not intended for operation while submerged must be located at least 12 in. above the deck of a fixed or floating structure, but not below the electrical datum plane. ▸Figure 555-2 and ▸Figure 555-3

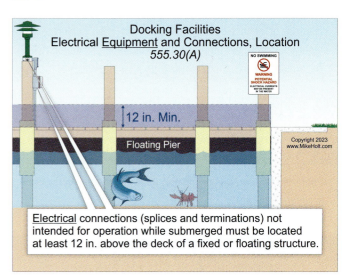

▸Figure 555-2

Author's Comment:

▸ According to Article 100, an "Electrical Datum Plane" is defined as "the vertical distance above the high water level where electrical equipment can be installed, and electrical connections can be made." ▸Figure 555-4

(B) Replacements. Where equipment is replaced, electrical connections (splices and terminations) must be located at least 12 in. above the deck of a fixed or floating structure. ▸Figure 555-5

Marinas, Boatyards, Floating Buildings, and Commercial and Noncommercial Docking Facilities | 555.34

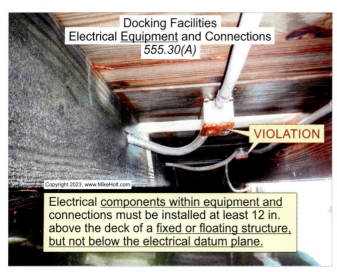
▶Figure 555–3

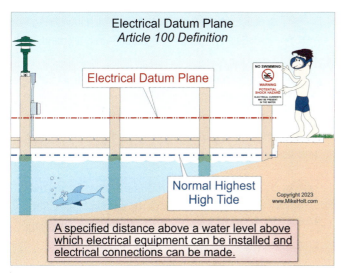
▶Figure 555–4

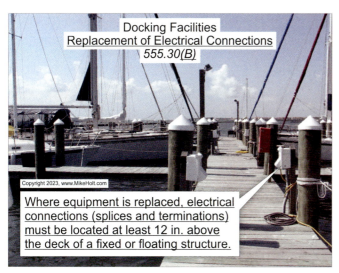
▶Figure 555–5

Author's Comment:

▸ Sealed wire connector systems are limited to use with Types USE, RHW, XHHW, RW90 EP, RW90, XLPE, or TWU conductors, size 30 AWG through 2000 kcmil copper or aluminum per the UL Guide Information Sheet for "Sealed Wire Connector Systems (ZMWQ)."

555.34 Wiring Methods and Installation

A few changes were made in this section to compensate for the harsh environment in marinas.

Analysis

EXPANDED Revisions to (A)(1) now permit the use of any Chapter 3 wiring method identified for wet locations that has a wire-type insulated equipment grounding conductor.

CLARIFIED Revisions to (A)(2) require cords and portable power cables to be of the extra-hard usage type and listed for use in the environment in which they are installed.

Revisions in (B)(4) add IMC as a permitted wiring method to protect wiring up to 8 ft above docks, decks of piers, and landing stages.

555.34 Wiring Methods and Installation

(A) Wiring Methods.

(1) General. Any Chapter 3 wiring method identified for wet locations containing a wire-type insulated equipment grounding conductor is permitted.

(2) Portable Power Cables. Sunlight resistant, extra-hard usage cord and extra-hard usage portable power cables listed for use in the environment within which they are installed, are permitted as follows:

(1) As permanent wiring on the underside of piers (floating or fixed).

(2) Where flexibility is necessary as on piers composed of floating sections.

555.35 | Marinas, Boatyards, Floating Buildings, and Commercial and Noncommercial Docking Facilities

(B) Installation.

(2) Outdoor Branch Circuits and Feeders. Overhead branch-circuit and feeder wiring in locations of the boatyard other than those described in 555.34(B)(1) must be not less than 18 ft above grade. Multiple feeders and branch circuits are permitted for marina installations in accordance with only Part I of Article 225.

(3) Portable Power Cables.

(a) Portable power cables permitted by 555.13(A)(2) must be:

(1) Properly supported.

(2) Located on the underside of the pier.

(3) Securely fastened by nonmetallic clips to structural members other than the deck planking.

(4) Not be subject to physical damage.

(5) Protected against chafing by a permanently installed, oversized sleeve of nonmetallic material when cables pass through structural members.

(b) Where portable power cables are used, there must be a junction box of corrosion-resistant construction with permanently installed terminal blocks on each pier section to which the feeders are connected. A listed marina power outlet employing terminal blocks/bars is permitted in lieu of a junction box. Metal junction boxes and covers, and metal screws and parts that are exposed externally to the boxes, must be of corrosion-resistant materials or protected by material resistant to corrosion.

(4) Protection. Rigid metal conduit, intermediate metal conduit, reinforced thermosetting resin conduit (RTRC) listed for aboveground use, or rigid polyvinyl chloride (PVC) conduit suitable for the location must be used to protect wiring to a point at least 8 ft above the docks, decks of piers, and landing stages.

555.35 Ground-Fault Protection of Equipment (GFPE) and Ground-Fault Circuit Interrupter

This section was reorganized and rules from other *Code* sections for GFCI protection were relocated to this one. Most of these rules had no technical change but do have new section numbers.

Analysis

EXPANDED Revisions to (A) allow the protection setting of listed GFPEs to be rated at not more than 100 mA (instead of 30 mA) for feeders installed on docking facilities or wharfs.

Revisions to (B) now allow the protection setting of listed GFPEs for other than shore power outlets to be rated at not more than 100 mA (instead of 30 mA) on a docking facility.

The revisions in (B)(2) expand the requirements from just receptacles to outlets supplied by branch circuits not exceeding 150V to ground and 60A, single-phase, or 100A or less, three-phase. These branch circuits must now have GFCI protection.

NEW A new Exception to (B) excludes most low-voltage circuits from the GFCI protection requirement.

NEW The new rule in (C) was relocated here from 555.9 and requires GFCI protection for outlets supplying boat hoists and permits "other than shore power receptacles" that are GFCI protected to supply power to a boat hoist.

RELOCATED Revisions to (D) require a leakage current measurement device to be available where there are more than three receptacles supplying shore power to boats.

555.35 Ground-Fault Protection of Equipment (GFPE) and Ground-Fault Circuit-Interrupter (GFCI) Protection

Ground-fault protection for docking facilities must be provided in accordance with the following:

(A) Feeder Conductors with GFPE. Feeder conductors installed on docking facilities must be provided with GFPEs set to open at currents not exceeding 100 mA.

Coordination with the feeder GFPE overcurrent protective device is permitted.

Ex to (B): Transformer secondary conductors of a separately derived system that do not exceed 10 ft, and are installed in a raceway, are permitted to be installed without ground-fault protection. This exception also applies to the supply terminals of the equipment supplied by the transformer secondary conductors.

(B) Branch Circuits.

(1) Shore Power Receptacles, GFPE Protection. Receptacles providing shore power installed in accordance with 555.33(A) must have individual GFPE protection set to open at currents not exceeding 30 mA. ▶Figure 555–6

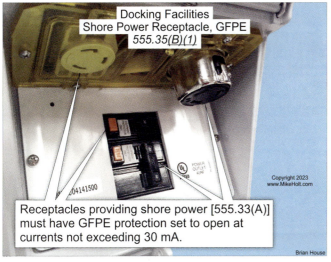
▶Figure 555–6

Author's Comment:

▸ In accordance with the research study by the American Boat and Yacht Council Foundation, Inc., 30 mA represents an acceptable threshold level for GFPE protection to prevent most electrical shock drowning incidents while remaining practical enough to minimize nuisance tripping.

▸ If shore power receptacles are replaced, they are required to have GFPE protection [406.4(D)(8).

(2) Outlets Other than Shore Power, GFCI Protection. GFCI protection is required for outlets rated 60A and less, single-phase, and 100A and less, three-phase for electrical systems not exceeding 150V to ground. ▶Figure 555–7

Ex: Circuits not requiring grounding, not exceeding the low-voltage contact limit, and supplied by listed transformers or power supplies complying with 680.23(A)(2) can be installed without GFCI protection.

(C) Boat Hoist. Boat hoist outlets on docking facilities must be GFCI protected where the circuit voltage does not exceed 240V. ▶Figure 555–8

▶Figure 555–7

▶Figure 555–8

(D) Leakage Current Measurement Device. Where more than three receptacles supply shore power to boats, a leakage current measurement device for use in marina applications must be available and be used to determine leakage current from each boat that will utilize shore power.

Note 1: Leakage current measurements will provide the capability to determine when an individual boat has defective wiring or other problems contributing to hazardous voltage and current. The use of this test device will allow the facility operator to identify a boat that is creating an electrical hazard. In some cases, a single boat could cause an upstream GFPE device protecting a feeder to trip even though multiple boats are supplied from the same feeder. The use of this test device will help the facility operator prevent a particular boat from contributing to hazardous voltage and current in the marina area.

555.36 | Marinas, Boatyards, Floating Buildings, and Commercial and Noncommercial Docking Facilities

Note 2: An annual test of each boat with the leakage current measurement device is a prudent step toward determining if a boat has defective wiring that could be contributing hazardous voltage and current. Where the leakage current measurement device reveals that a boat is contributing hazardous voltage and current, repairs should be made to the boat before it is permitted to utilize shore power.

Ex: Where the shore power equipment includes a leakage indicator and leakage alarm, a separate leakage test device is not required.

555.36 Shore Power Receptacle Disconnecting Means

A new subdivision adds a requirement for an emergency electrical disconnect.

Analysis

NEW The new subdivision (C) requires an externally operable emergency disconnect, clearly marked "Emergency Shutoff" that can de-energize all power at each marina power outlet or enclosure that provides shore power to boats. An emergency disconnect within sight of the marina power outlet will provide bystanders with the ability to shut off power if a swimmer comes into contact with an energized metal boat, dock, or ladder. As this rule is implemented in marinas, it will help to eliminate Electric Shock Drownings (ESDs).

555.36 Shore Power Receptacle Disconnecting Means

A disconnect is required for shore power receptacles.

(A) Type of Disconnecting Means. A circuit breaker or switch must identify the receptacle which it controls. ▶Figure 555–9

(B) Location. The shore power receptacle disconnect must be readily accessible and not more than 30 in. from the receptacle it controls.
▶Figure 555–10

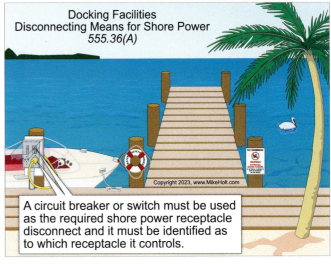

▶Figure 555–9

▶Figure 555–10

Author's Comment:

▸ This shore power receptacle disconnect is intended to eliminate the hazard of someone engaging or disengaging the boat's shore power attachment plug with wet, slippery hands and possibly contacting energized blades.

(C) Emergency Electrical Disconnect. Each marina power outlet or enclosure that provides shore power to boats must have a listed emergency shutoff device or disconnect that is marked "Emergency Shutoff" in accordance with 110.22(A). ▶Figure 555–11

Marinas, Boatyards, Floating Buildings, and Commercial and Noncommercial Docking Facilities | 555.37

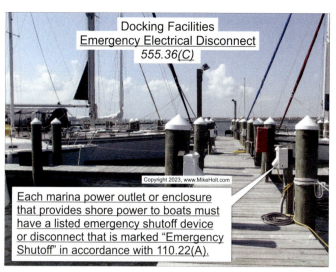

▶Figure 555–11

The emergency shutoff device or disconnect must be within sight of the marina power outlet, readily accessible, externally operable, and manually resettable. The emergency shutoff device or disconnect must de-energize the power supply to all circuits supplied by the marina power outlet(s). A circuit breaker handle is not permitted to be used for this purpose.

Authors Comment:

▶ An emergency disconnect within sight of the marina power outlet will provide bystanders with the ability to shut off power if a swimmer comes into contact with an energized metal boat, dock, or ladder and in cases where it appears that electric shock drowning (ESD) is occurring.

555.37 Equipment Grounding Conductor

This section was reorganized and editorially revised with no technical changes.

Analysis

EDITED Subdivisions (B) and (C) were combined into one section (B) and the rules describing how the EGC is to be identified were deleted since they are found 250.119. The remaining subdivisions were re-lettered.

 CLARIFIED Subdivision (C) clarifies that an EGC of the wire type must extend from the service equipment to a remote panelboard or other distribution equipment. This recognizes that not all remote equipment installations are panelboards.

 CLARIFIED A change to subdivision (D) is similar to that in (C). The insulated equipment grounding conductor for branch circuits must be terminated at a grounding terminal in a remote panelboard, other distribution equipment, or in the main service equipment.

555.37 Equipment Grounding Conductor

(A) Equipment to be Connected to the Equipment Grounding Conductor. The following items in a marina, boatyard, or docking facility must be connected to an equipment grounding conductor run with the circuit conductors:

(1) Metal boxes, metal cabinets, and all other metal enclosures.

(2) Metal frames of utilization equipment.

(3) Grounding terminals of grounding-type receptacles.

(B) Type of Equipment Grounding Conductor. An insulated copper, aluminum, or copper-clad aluminum equipment grounding conductor, sized in accordance with 250.122 but no smaller than 12 AWG, must be provided for all circuits in a marina, boatyard, or docking facility.
▶Figure 555–12

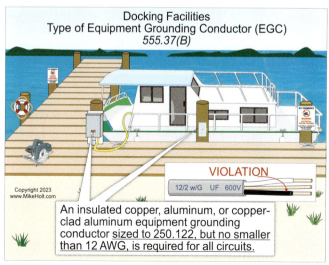

▶Figure 555–12

555.38 | Marinas, Boatyards, Floating Buildings, and Commercial and Noncommercial Docking Facilities

(C) Feeder Equipment Grounding Conductor. A feeder to a panelboard or other distribution equipment must have an insulated copper, aluminum, or copper-clad aluminum equipment grounding conductor [555.37(B)] run from the service to the remote panelboard or distribution equipment.

(D) Branch-Circuit Equipment Grounding Conductor. The required branch-circuit insulated copper, aluminum, or copper-clad aluminum equipment grounding conductor [555.37(B)] must terminate at a grounding terminal in a panelboard, distribution equipment, or service equipment.

555.38 Luminaires

A new subdivision addresses the requirements for luminaire installations and retrofits.

Analysis

NEW — A new rule (A) requires luminaires and retrofit kits installed in marinas to be listed and identified for the use in their intended environment and installed to prevent damage from watercraft or entanglement with sea life.

NEW — Subdivision (B) requires luminaires that are installed below the highest tide level, and likely to be periodically submersed, to be identified as submersible, operate below the low-voltage contact limit, and be supplied by a transformer or power supply in accordance with 680.23(A)(2).

555.38 Luminaires

(A) General. All luminaires and retrofit kits must be listed and identified for use in their intended environment. Luminaires and their supply connections must be secured to structural elements of the marina to limit damage from watercraft and prevent entanglement of, and interaction with, sea life.

(B) Underwater Luminaires. Luminaires installed below the highest high tide level or electrical datum plane and likely to be periodically submersed must be limited to the following:

(1) Identified as submersible

(2) Operate below the low-voltage contact limit as defined in Article 100

(3) Supplied by an isolating transformer or power supply in accordance with 680.23(A)(2)

CHAPTER 6 SPECIAL EQUIPMENT

Introduction to Chapter 6—Special Equipment

The first four chapters of the *Code* are sequential and form a foundation for each of the subsequent four. Chapter 6, which covers special equipment, is the second of the four *NEC* chapters that deal with special topics. Chapters 5 and 7 focus on special occupancies and special conditions respectively, while Chapter 8 covers communications systems.

What exactly is "Special Equipment"? It is equipment that, by the nature of its use, construction, or by its unique nature creates a need for additional measures to ensure the "safeguarding of people and property" mission of the *NEC*, as stated in Article 90. The *Code* groups the articles in this chapter logically, as you might expect. Note that not all these articles will be included in this material.

- **Article 600—Electric Signs.** This article covers the installation of conductors and equipment for electric signs as defined in Article 100. They include all products and installations that utilize neon tubing, such as signs, decorative elements, skeleton tubing, or art forms.

- **Article 604—Manufactured Wiring Systems.** Article 604 covers field-installed manufactured wiring systems used for branch circuits in accessible areas. The components of a listed manufactured wiring system can be assembled at the jobsite.

- **Article 620—Elevators, Escalators, and Moving Walks.** This article covers electrical equipment and wiring used in connection with elevators, dumbwaiters, escalators, moving walks, wheelchair lifts, and stairway chair lifts.

- **Article 625—Electric Vehicle Power Transfer System.** An electrically powered vehicle needs a dedicated charging circuit and that is where Article 625 comes in. It provides the requirements for the electrical equipment needed to charge automotive-type electric and hybrid vehicles including cars, bikes, and buses.

- **Article 630—Electric Welders.** Electric welding equipment does its job either by creating an electric arc between two surfaces or by heating a rod that melts from overcurrent. Either way results in a hefty momentary current draw. Welding machines come in many shapes and sizes. This article covers electric arc welding and resistance welding apparatus, and other similar welding equipment connected to an electric supply system.

- **Article 640—Audio Signal Amplification and Reproduction Equipment.** Article 640 covers equipment and wiring for audio signal generation, recording, processing, amplification and reproduction, distribution of sound, public address, speech input systems, temporary audio system installations, and electronic musical instruments such as electric organs, electric guitars, and electronic drums/percussion.

. . .

Chapter 6 | Special Equipment

- **Article 645—Information Technology Equipment.** This article applies to equipment, power-supply wiring, equipment interconnecting wiring, and grounding of information technology equipment and systems including terminal units in an information technology equipment room.

- **Article 680—Swimming Pools, Spas, Hot Tubs, Fountains, and Similar Installations.** Article 680 covers the installation of bonding and grounding devices for these installations, and the electric wiring and equipment that supply swimming, wading, therapeutic and decorative pools, fountains, hot tubs, spas, and hydromassage bathtubs.

- **Article 690—Solar Photovoltaic (PV) Systems.** This article focuses on reducing the electrical hazards that may arise from installing and operating a solar PV system, to the point where it can be considered safe for property and people. The requirements of the *NEC* Chapters 1 through 4 apply to these installations, except as specifically modified here.

- **Article 691—Large-Scale Solar Photovoltaic (PV) Electric Supply Stations.** Article 691 covers large-scale PV electric supply stations with a generating capacity of 5,000 kW or more and not under exclusive utility control.

- **Article 695—Fire Pumps.** This article covers the electric power sources and interconnecting circuits for electric motor-driven fire pumps. It also covers switching and control equipment dedicated to fire pump drivers. Article 695 does not apply to sprinkler system pumps in one- and two-family dwellings or to pressure maintenance (jockey) pumps.

ARTICLE 600 — ELECTRIC SIGNS AND OUTLINE LIGHTING

Introduction to Article 600—Electric Signs and Outline Lighting

One of the first things you will notice when entering a strip mall is that there is a sign for every store. Every commercial occupancy needs a form of identification, and the standard method is the electric sign. Therefore, 600.5 requires a sign outlet for the entrance of each tenant location. Section 600.6 requires a disconnect within sight of a sign unless it can be locked in the open position.

Author's Comment:

▸ Article 100 defines an electric sign as any "fixed, stationary, or portable self-contained, electrically illuminated utilization equipment with words or symbols designed to convey information or attract attention."

600.5 Branch Circuits

The text excluding non-public doors from the rules in (A) was converted to an Exception and a new Exception was added permitting associated loads to be on the sign circuit. It is now clear that when electrical enclosures are integral to signs, they can be used as junction boxes in (D).

Analysis

REORGANIZED **EXPANDED**

The previous allowance excluding non-public doors from the rules in (A) were converted into a new Exception and a second Exception now permits the required branch circuit to also supply other associated loads.

600.5 Branch Circuits

(A) Required Sign Outlet. Each commercial building or occupancy accessible to pedestrians must have a sign outlet at the entrance of each tenant space. The outlet must be supplied by a branch circuit rated at least 20A that serves no other loads. ▸Figure 600–1

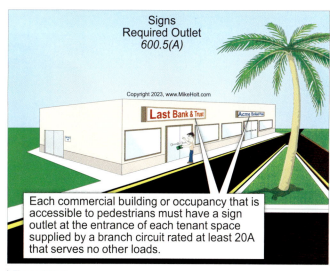
▸Figure 600–1

Ex 1: A sign outlet is not required at entrances intended to be used only by service personnel or employees. ▸Figure 600–2

Ex 2: The required sign branch circuit can supply loads directly related to the control of the sign such as electronic or electromechanical controllers.

(B) Disconnect Marking. A disconnect for a sign or controller must be marked to identity the sign or controller it controls.

600.6 | Electric Signs and Outline Lighting

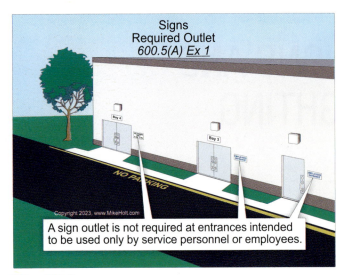

▶Figure 600-2

Ex: *An external disconnect that is mounted on the sign body, sign enclosure, sign pole, or controller is not required to identify the sign it controls.*

(C) Branch-Circuit Rating. Branch circuits that supply signs are considered a continuous load for circuit sizing. ▶Figure 600-3

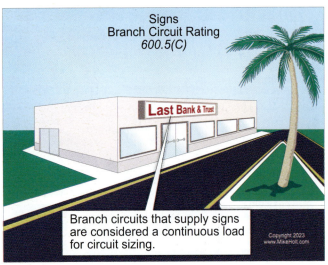

▶Figure 600-3

(D) Wiring Methods. Wiring methods used to supply signs must comply with 600.5(D)(1), (D)(2), and (D)(3).

(1) Supply. The wiring method used to supply signs must terminate within a sign, a suitable box, a conduit body, or panelboard.

(2) Enclosures as Pull Boxes.

(a) Listed and labeled sign enclosures are permitted as pull or junction boxes for conductors supplying:

(1) Other adjacent signs

(3) Floodlights that are part of a sign

(b) The sign enclosures in 600.5(D)(2)(a) can contain both branch-circuit and secondary conductors.

(c) Listed and labeled neon transformer enclosures are permitted to contain voltages over 1000V, provided the sign disconnect de-energizes all current-carrying conductors in these enclosures.

(3) Metal or Nonmetallic Poles. Metal or nonmetallic poles used to support signs are permitted to enclose supply conductors.

600.6 Disconnects

Editorial revisions to the sign disconnect rules make an impossible rule possible.

Analysis

REORGANIZED   EXPANDED

Revisions to this rule clearly identify list items (1), (2), and (3) as permitted locations for the sign disconnect, and list item (4) as a mandatory rule if the sign disconnect is located remotely. The previous language made all four rules mandatory, compliance with which would be impossible.

600.6 Disconnecting Means

The circuit conductors to a sign must be controlled by an externally operable switch or circuit breaker that will open all phase conductors. ▶Figure 600-4

Note: The location of the disconnect is intended to allow service or maintenance personnel and first responders complete and local control of the disconnect.

(A) Disconnect Location. The sign disconnect must be accessible and located in accordance with 600.6(A)(1), (A)(2), or (A)(3). If the sign disconnect is remote from the sign, it must comply with 600.6(A)(4).

(1) At the Point of Entry to a Sign. The sign disconnect must be located where the conductors enter the sign enclosure, sign body, or pole.
▶Figure 600-5

Electric Signs and Outline Lighting | 600.6

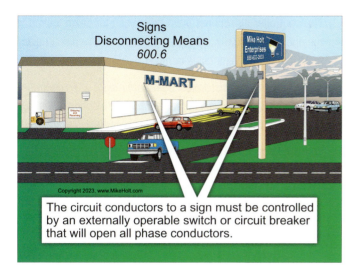
▶Figure 600–4

▶Figure 600–5

Ex 1: A sign disconnect is not required to be at the point the conductors enter a sign enclosure or sign body for conductors that pass through a sign where not accessible and enclosed in a Chapter 3 raceway or metal-jacketed cable.

Ex 2: A sign disconnect is not required to be at the point the conductors enter a sign enclosure or sign body for a feeder that supplies a panelboard within the sign under the following conditions: The feeder conductors must be enclosed where not accessible in a Chapter 3 raceway or metal-jacketed cable, a permanent field-applied danger label that is visible during servicing must be applied to the raceway or metal-clad cable at or near the point of the feeder circuit conductors' entry into the sign enclosure or sign body, and the danger label reads:

**DANGER. THIS RACEWAY CONTAINS
ENERGIZED CONDUCTORS**

The danger label must identify the location of the sign disconnect and the sign disconnect must be capable of being locked in the open position with provisions for locking to remain in place whether the lock is installed or not [110.25].

(2) Within Sight of the Sign. The sign disconnect must be within sight of the sign it controls. ▶Figure 600–6

▶Figure 600–6

If the sign disconnect is not within sight of the sign, the disconnect must be capable of being locked in the open position with provisions for locking to remain in place whether the lock is installed or not [110.25]. A permanent field-applied label that identifies the location of the sign disconnect must be on the sign where it will be visible during servicing. ▶Figure 600–7

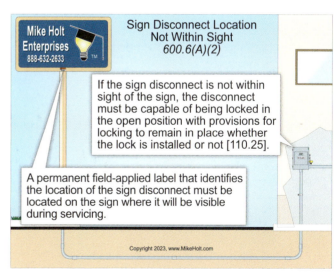
▶Figure 600–7

1st Printing | Changes to the National Electrical Code 2023 | MikeHolt.com | 305

600.6 | Electric Signs and Outline Lighting

Author's Comment:

▸ According to Article 100, "Within Sight" means that it is visible and not more than 50 ft from the location of the equipment.

(3) Controller Disconnect as Sign Disconnect. Signs operated by controllers external to the sign must have a disconnect for the sign controller in accordance with the following:

(1) The controller disconnect must be within sight of or within the controller enclosure.

(2) The controller disconnect must disconnect the sign and the controller from all phase conductors. ▸Figure 600-8

(3) The controller disconnect must be capable of being locked in the open position with provisions for locking to remain in place whether the lock is installed or not [110.25].

Ex: Where the controller disconnect is not within sight of the controller, a permanent field-applied label that identifies the location of the sign disconnect must be on the sign where it can be visible during servicing.

(4) Remote Location. The disconnect, if remote from the sign, sign body, or pole, must be mounted at an accessible location available to first responders and service personnel. ▸Figure 600-9

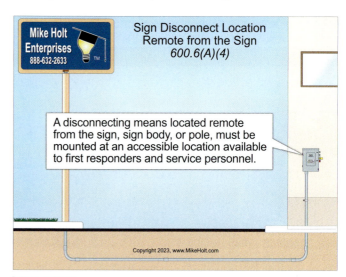

▸Figure 600-9

The location of the disconnect must be marked with a label at the sign location and marked as the disconnect for the sign.

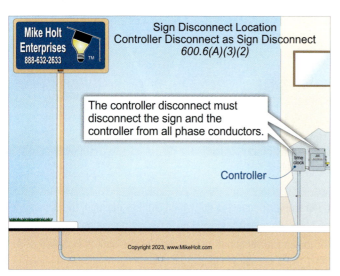

▸Figure 600-8

ARTICLE 620 — ELEVATORS, DUMBWAITERS, ESCALATORS, MOVING WALKS, PLATFORM LIFTS, AND STAIRWAY CHAIRLIFTS

Introduction to Article 620—Elevators, Dumbwaiters, Escalators, Moving Walks, Platform Lifts, and Stairway Chairlifts

Except for dumbwaiters, the equipment covered by Article 620 moves people. Thus, a major concept in this article is that of keeping people separated from electrical power. That is why, for example, 620.3 requires live parts to be enclosed. This article consists of 10 parts:

- Part I. General. This part provides the scope of the article, definitions, and voltage limitations.
- Part II. Conductors. The single-line diagram of Figure 620.13 in the *NEC* illustrates how the requirements of Part II work together.
- Part III. Wiring. This addresses wiring methods and branch-circuit requirements for different equipment.
- Part IV. Installation of Conductors. Part IV covers conductor fill, supports, and related items.
- Part V. Traveling Cables. Installation, suspension, location, and protection of cables that move with the motion of the elevator or lift are all covered.
- Part VI. Disconnecting Means and Control. The requirements vary with the application.
- Part VII. Overcurrent Protection. While most of this part refers to Article 430, it does include additional requirements such as providing selective coordination.
- Part VIII. Machine and Control Rooms and Spaces. The primary goal here is the prevention of unauthorized access.
- Part IX. Equipment Grounding Conductor. While most of this part refers to Article 250, it includes additional requirements as well. For example, 15A and 20A, 125V receptacles in certain locations must be GFCI protected.
- Part X. Emergency and Standby Systems. This deals with regenerative power and with the need for a disconnecting means that can disconnect an elevator from both the normal power system and the emergency or standby system.

620.6 Ground-Fault Circuit-Interrupter Protection for Personnel

Receptacles located in truss interiors now require GFCI protection, and a nice reorganization of the content into three subdivisions makes this much easier to read.

Analysis

These rules were reorganized into three subdivisions and the titles were revised to indicate which areas require different types of GFCI protection. The only technical changes were in (B) where "truss interiors," which are the supports between the landings of escalators, were added to the areas requiring a GFCI-protected receptacle, and in (C) which eliminates the single GFCI-receptacle requirement.

620.22 | Elevators, Dumbwaiters, Escalators, Moving Walks, Platform Lifts, and Stairway Chairlifts

620.6 GFCI Protection for Receptacles

(A) Pits, Hoistways, and Elevator Cars. Receptacles rated 15A and 20A, 125V in pits, hoistways, and elevator cars must be of the GFCI type. ▶Figure 620-1

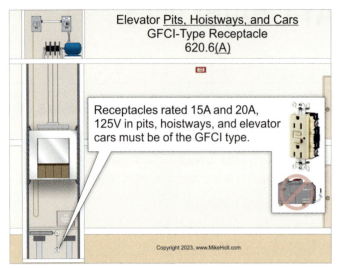

▶Figure 620-1

Author's Comment:

▸ A worker in an elevator pit area should not have to climb out of the pit to reset the GFCI protection, therefore this rule prohibits the use of a GFCI breaker or GFCI faceless device and requires the receptacle to be of the GFCI type.

(B) Machine Rooms, Control Spaces, Machinery Spaces, Control Rooms, and Truss Interiors. Receptacles rated 15A and 20A, 125V in machine rooms, control spaces, machinery spaces, control rooms, and truss interiors must be GFCI protected. ▶Figure 620-2

Author's Comment:

▸ In elevator machine rooms or spaces, accessibility to reset the GFCI is not as restricted as in pit areas, therefore receptacles in these spaces can be GFCI protected by either a GFCI breaker, GFCI receptacle, or GFCI faceless device.

(C) Sump Pumps. A permanently installed sump pump that is hard wired [422.5(A)(6)] or supplied by a receptacle must be GFCI protected.
▶Figure 620-3

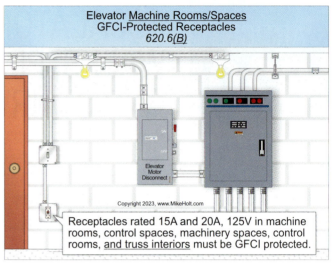

▶Figure 620-2

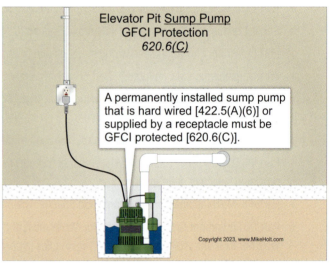

▶Figure 620-3

620.22 Branch Circuits for Car Lighting, Receptacle(s), Ventilation, Heating, and Air-Conditioning

The permitted locations of the branch-circuit OCPD in (B) for air-conditioning and heating were clarified.

Elevators, Dumbwaiters, Escalators, Moving Walks, Platform Lifts, and Stairway Chairlifts | 620.22

Analysis

CLARIFIED Continuing the revisions to car lighting and receptacle requirements in (A) last cycle, the branch-circuit OCPD can now be located outside the hoistway in a location accessible only to qualified persons. This change was also made in 620.25(B) for the location of the OCPD for other branch circuits that are not specified in 620.22, 620.23, and 620.24.

620.22 Branch Circuits for Elevator Car(s)

(A) Car Light, Receptacles, Auxiliary Lighting, and Ventilation. A separate branch circuit must supply the elevator car lights. This branch circuit is permitted to supply receptacles, alarm devices, emergency responder radio coverage, elevator car ventilation purification systems, monitoring devices not part of the control system, an auxiliary lighting power source, elevator car emergency signaling, communications devices including their associated charging circuits, and ventilation on each elevator car or inside the operation controller.

Where there is no machine room, control room, machinery space, or control space outside the hoistway, the overcurrent protective device must be outside the hoistway and accessible to qualified persons only.

(B) Air-Conditioning and Heating Source. Air-conditioning and heating units must be supplied by a separate branch circuit for each elevator car.

The overcurrent protective device protecting the branch circuit must be in the elevator machine room, control room, machinery space, or control space. If there is no machine room, control room, machinery space, or control space outside the hoistway, the overcurrent protective device must be outside the hoistway and accessible only to qualified persons.

Author's Comment:

▸ While the air-conditioning and heating must be served by an individual circuit for each elevator car, the branch circuit for the elevator car lights is permitted to serve more than one elevator car. Branch-circuit overcurrent protective devices for elevator cars must be in the elevator machine room.

Notes

ARTICLE 625 — ELECTRIC VEHICLE POWER TRANSFER SYSTEM

Introduction to Article 625—Electric Vehicle Power Transfer System

Electric vehicles have been around for a long time. Anyone who has worked in a factory or warehouse, or visited a big box store, has probably encountered an electric lift truck. And, of course, we are all familiar with golf carts. These and other off-road vehicles have charging requirements that are easily accommodated by small charging systems.

But today, a new challenge has emerged and is becoming increasingly common. That challenge is the electrically powered passenger vehicle, bus, truck, and motorcycle. Such vehicles, especially an electric car or bus, can weigh considerably more than a golf cart and just moving one takes a proportionately larger motor. In fact, many designs use multiple drive motors.

Those motors are powered by batteries. Adding to the battery sizing requirement are other demands. For example, these vehicles:

- Must be able to travel at highway speeds over distances roughly comparable to those traveled by their internal combustion engine counterparts.
- Have powered accessories that you typically will not find on a golf cart, such as air-conditioning, electric windows, stereo systems, windshield wipers, security systems, and window defrosters.
- Are expected to start in summer heat and in brutal winter cold.

The battery system for an electrically powered passenger vehicle is therefore considerably larger than that for a golf cart or other typical off-road electric vehicle. Consequently, the charging system must have the capability of delivering far more power than the one needed for a typical off-road electric vehicle.

An electrically powered passenger vehicle needs a dedicated charging circuit. Article 625 defines the requirements for the installation of the electrical equipment needed to charge automotive-type electric and hybrid vehicles including cars, motorcycles, and buses.

625.6 Listed

A clarification to this rule limits the equipment required to be listed by this article.

Analysis

CLARIFIED This rule was clarified to better indicate what equipment is required to be listed. Previously all equipment covered by the scope of Article 625 had to be listed. It is now clear that electric vehicle power transfer equipment for the purposes of power export, or bidirectional current flow must be listed.

625.40 | Electric Vehicle Power Transfer System

625.6 Listed

Electric vehicle power transfer system equipment for the purposes of charging, power export, or bidirectional current flow must be listed.
▶Figure 625–1

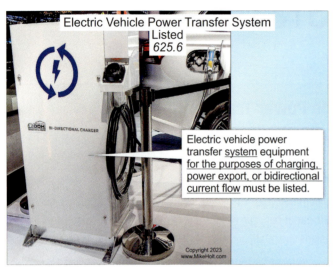
▶Figure 625–1

625.40 Electric Vehicle Branch Circuit

Multiple units of EVSE can finally share a circuit. It is about time!

Analysis

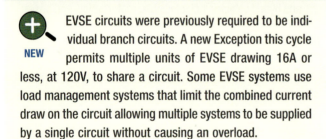 **NEW** EVSE circuits were previously required to be individual branch circuits. A new Exception this cycle permits multiple units of EVSE drawing 16A or less, at 120V, to share a circuit. Some EVSE systems use load management systems that limit the combined current draw on the circuit allowing multiple systems to be supplied by a single circuit without causing an overload.

625.40 Electric Vehicle Branch Circuit

Electric vehicle supply equipment rated greater than 16A or greater than 120V must be supplied by an individual branch circuit.

Ex: A single branch circuit is permitted to supply more than one electric vehicle supply equipment when the loads are managed by an energy management system in accordance with 625.42(A) or (B).

625.43 Disconnecting Means

EVSE and WPTE are now permitted to have remotely located disconnects!

Analysis

 EXPANDED This rule was expanded to permit the required disconnect to be remote from the EVSE. The term "equipment" was replaced with "EVSE" and "WPTE" [Article 100] to clarify what equipment requires a disconnect. If the disconnect is remote, a plaque is required specifying the location of the disconnecting means.

625.43 Disconnecting Means

Electric vehicle supply equipment (EVSE) or wireless power transfer equipment (WPTE) rated more than 60A must have a disconnect installed in a readily accessible location.

If the disconnect for the electric vehicle and wireless equipment is remote from the electric vehicle supply equipment or wireless power transfer equipment, a plaque must be placed on the equipment denoting the location of the disconnect.

The remote disconnect must be capable of being locked in the open position with provisions for locking to remain in place whether the lock is installed or not in accordance with 110.25.

625.49 Island Mode

This new section provides the requirements for EVPE and bidirectional EVSE to be part of an interconnected power system operating in island mode.

625.49 Island Mode

Electric vehicle power export equipment (EVPE) and bidirectional electric vehicle supply equipment (EVSE) that incorporate a power export function are permitted to be a part of an interconnected power system operating in island mode.

Analysis

NEW
We were all waiting for the day when we could use our electric car to provide power to our homes during an outage. Well, this new section permits EVPE and bidirectional EVSE that have a power export function to be part of an interconnected power system operating in island mode. Yes!

Notes

ARTICLE 630 ELECTRIC WELDERS

Introduction to Article 630—Electric Welders

Electric welding equipment does its job either by creating an electric arc between two surfaces or by heating a rod that melts from overcurrent. Either way results in a hefty momentary current draw. Welding machines come in many shapes and sizes. On the smaller end of the scale are portable welding units used for manual welding, such as in a fabrication shop. At the larger end are robotic welding machines the size of a house used for making everything from automobile bodies to refrigerator panels. All of these must comply with Article 630.

The primary concern of this article is adequately sizing the conductors and circuit protection to handle this type of load. Fortunately for the design engineer and the field electrician, Article 630 requires certain information to be provided on the nameplate of the equipment. This article explains how to use that information to properly size conductors and circuit protection.

630.8 Ground-Fault Circuit-interrupter Protection for Personnel

GFCI protection makes yet another appearance in the workplace and is now required for receptacles used for hand tools and portable lighting.

Analysis

NEW This is a new section that requires all 125V, single-phase, 15A and 20A receptacles for hand tools or portable lighting equipment in areas where welders are operated to be GFCI protected. This rule does not require GFCI protection for the receptacle that supplies the welder, however requirements in 210.8 may.

630.8 Receptacle, GFCI Protection

GFCI protection is required for all 15A and 20A, 125V receptacles used for electrical hand tools or portable lighting equipment installed in work areas where welders are operated. ▶Figure 630–1

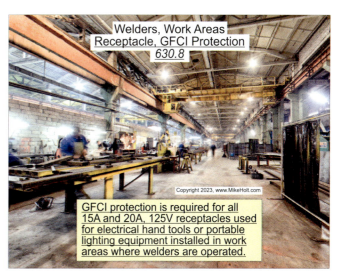

▶Figure 630–1

Notes

ARTICLE 680
SWIMMING POOLS, FOUNTAINS, AND SIMILAR INSTALLATIONS

Introduction to Article 680—Swimming Pools, Fountains, and Similar Installations

The requirements contained in Article 680 apply to the installation of electrical wiring and equipment for swimming pools, spas, hot tubs, fountains, and hydromassage bathtubs. The overriding concern of this article is to keep people and electricity separated.

This article is divided into eight parts. The various parts apply to certain types of installations, so be careful to determine which parts of this article apply to what and where. For instance, Part I and Part II apply to hot tubs installed outdoors, except as modified in Part IV. In contrast, hydromassage bathtubs are only covered by Part VII. Read the details of Article 680 carefully so you will be able to provide a safe installation.

680.5 Ground-Fault Circuit-Interrupter (GFCI) and Special Purpose Ground-Fault Circuit-Interrupter (SPGFCI) Protection

The section title and rules were expanded to include the use of SPGFCIs, and the section was split into three parts.

Analysis

EXPANDED This section was revised and expanded to include special purpose ground-fault circuit interrupters and now has three subdivisions. Subdivision (A) covers the general requirements, (B) covers GFCI for applications up to 150V to ground, and (C) covers SPGFCIs for applications over 150V to ground.

NEW A new Informational Note in (B) reminds us that high-leg delta systems and corner-grounded delta systems can have a voltage over 150V to ground which exceed the limits for Class A GFCIs. An Exception exempts listed equipment with ratings not exceeding the low-voltage contact limit from GFCI-protection requirements.

NEW The new subdivision (C) addresses SPGFCI protection for circuits over 150V to ground. The intent is to protect pool equipment in commercial installations that have higher voltages. A new Informational Note references UL 943C which tells us the threshold ground-fault trip current is not to exceed 20 mA.

680.5 GFCI and SPGFCI Protection

(A) General. The GFCI and SPGFCI requirements in this article are in addition to the requirements in 210.8.

(B) GFCI Protection. Where ground-fault protection is required in this article for branch circuits rated 150V or less to ground and 60A or less, a GFCI device must be used.

(C) SPGFCI. Where ground-fault protection is required in this article for branch circuits rated over 150V to ground, an SPGFCI device must be used.

680.7 | Swimming Pools, Fountains, and Similar Installations

Author's Comment:

▸ A GFCI protective device is intended to protect humans against maximum let-go levels (muscle contraction) for circuits rated not over 150V to ground, with a trip-open value of 6 mA. An SPGFCI protective device is intended to protect humans against ventricular fibrillation (electrocution) for circuits above 150V to ground, with a trip-open value of 20 mA.

680.7 Grounding and Bonding

These rules were reorganized, the title was updated to reflect the content of the section, and now it is clear that an EGC in a corrosive environment must be insulated.

Analysis

REORGANIZED This section title and text were revised because it applies to both grounding and bonding. It now has three subdivisions that organize requirements previously spread throughout this article. The new subdivision (A) requires the copper EGC to be insulated in a corrosive environment or wet location.

680.7 Grounding and Bonding

(A) Insulated Equipment Grounding Conductor. Feeders and branch circuits located in a corrosive environment or wet location must contain an insulated copper equipment grounding conductor sized in accordance with Table 250.122, but not smaller than 12 AWG.
▸Figure 680–1

(B) Cord-and-Plug Connections. Flexible cords must contain an equipment grounding conductor that is an insulated copper conductor sized in accordance with Table 250.122, but not smaller than 12 AWG. The flexible cord must terminate in a grounding-type attachment plug having a fixed grounding contact member.

(C) Terminals. Field-installed terminals in damp or wet locations, and corrosive environments must be listed for direct burial use.
▸Figure 680–2

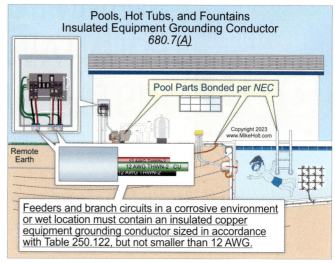

▸Figure 680–1

▸Figure 680–2

680.10 Electric Water Heaters and Heat Pumps

A revision to the title and text now includes heat pumps in the scope of this section.

Analysis

EXPANDED Previously this rule applied to electric pool water heaters but has been expanded to include heat pumps. Changes in the energy code have made electric-only pool heat almost obsolete and heat pumps have taken their place. The rules were reorganized into two subdivisions to accommodate the new rules for heat pumps.

680.10 Electric Water Heaters and Heat Pumps

(A) Water Heaters. Branch-circuit conductors and overcurrent protective devices for pool, spa, and hot tub water heaters must be sized at no less than 125 percent of the equipment nameplate current rating.
▶Figure 680–3

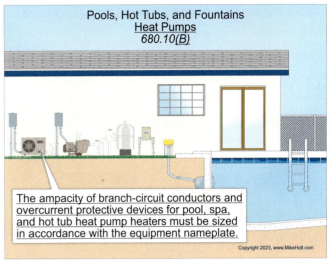
▶Figure 680–4

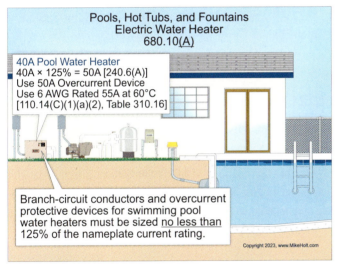
▶Figure 680–3

(B) Heat Pumps. The ampacity of branch-circuit conductors and overcurrent protective devices for pool, spa, and hot tub heat pump heaters must be sized in accordance with the equipment nameplate.
▶Figure 680–4

680.14 Corrosive Environment

The title was revised to reflect the contents of the rule. The requirement for the wiring methods to be listed was removed.

Analysis

EXPANDED This rule is about the environment and not what is in in the environment, so the title was changed to reflect that fact. In the last cycle, wiring methods used in a corrosive environment were required to be listed. Since there are no products meeting this requirement, it was replaced with "suitable for use." This cycle we also see LFNC added to the permitted wiring methods list as it was previously overlooked.

NEW A new (B) adds that equipment listed for pool or spa use is permitted, and other equipment can be installed in identified corrosion-resistant enclosures.

680.14 Wiring Methods and Equipment in Corrosive Environment

(A) Wiring Methods. Wiring methods suitable for use in corrosive environments must be rigid metal conduit, intermediate metal conduit, rigid polyvinyl chloride conduit, reinforced thermosetting resin conduit, or liquidtight flexible nonmetallic conduit. ▶Figure 680-5

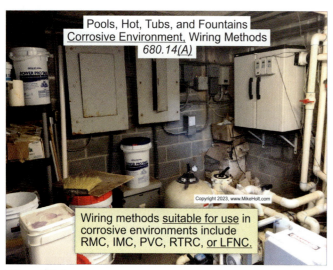

▶Figure 680-5

(B) Equipment. Equipment in a corrosive pool environment must be suitable for the use or be installed in identified corrosion-resistant enclosures.

Equipment listed for use in pools and spas are considered suitable for use in a corrosive pool environment. ▶Figure 680-6

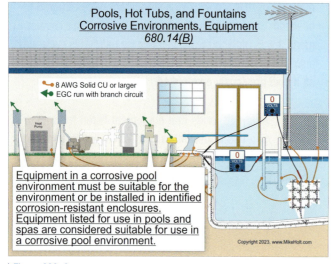

▶Figure 680-6

680.21 Pool Pump Motors

The title of (C) was revised to reflect the need for GFCI protection, and SPGFCI requirements were added.

Analysis

EXPANDED The addition of SPGFCIs to the 2023 *NEC* has allowed ground-fault protection of a wider array of equipment to be required. Revisions to the title and rule in this section expand the requirement for ground-fault protection to include all pool pump motors using either GFCIs or SPGFCIs depending on the application.

CLARIFIED To follow along with changes in (C) the rule in (D) now says that a pool pump motor that is replaced or repaired must be GFCI or SPGFCI protected.

680.21 Pool Pump Motors

(A) Wiring Methods. The wiring to a pool pump motor must comply with 680.21(A)(1) or (A)(2).

(1) Flexible Connections. If flexible connections are necessary for pool pump motors, liquidtight flexible metal conduit, liquidtight flexible nonmetallic conduit, and Type MC cable suitable for the use are permitted. ▶Figure 680-7

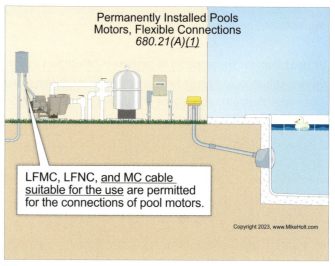

▶Figure 680-7

Swimming Pools, Fountains, and Similar Installations | **680.22**

(C) GFCI and SPGFCI Protection. GFCI protection is required for pool pump motor outlets rated 150V or less to ground. SPGFCI protection is required for pool pump motor outlets rated above 150V to ground. ▶Figure 680-8

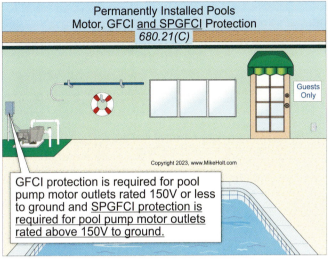

▶Figure 680-8

(D) Pool Pump Motor Replacement. Where a pool pump motor is replaced or repaired, the replacement or repaired pump motor must be provided with GFCI or SPGFCI protection in accordance with 680.5(B) or (C). ▶Figure 680-9

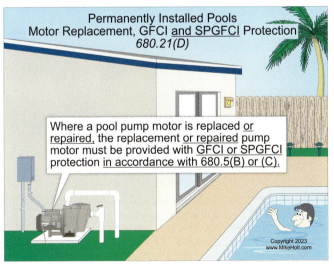

▶Figure 680-9

680.22 Receptacles, Luminaires, and Switches

All receptacles up to 60A within 20 ft of a pool wall are now required to be ground-fault protected, and the specific equipment listed in (A)(4) now requires SPGFCI protection if operating at over 150V to ground.

Analysis

EXPANDED The requirements for GFCI protection of receptacles in (A)(4) were expanded this cycle to include all receptacles rated 60A or less within 20 ft a pool wall. This previously only applied to 15A and 20A, 125V receptacles.

EXPANDED This section required GFCI protection for specific equipment installed in the area between 5 ft and 10 ft horizontally from the inside walls of a pool. New language in (B)(4) expands the required protection by adding an SPGFCI requirement that will allow equipment operating above 150V to ground to also be protected.

680.22 Receptacles, Luminaires, and Switches

(A) Receptacles.

(1) Required Receptacle. At least one 15A or 20A, 125V receptacle installed on a general-purpose branch circuit must be not less than 6 ft and not more than 20 ft from the inside wall of a permanently installed pool. This receptacle must be not more than 6½ ft above the floor, platform, or grade level serving the pool. ▶Figure 680-10

(2) Circulation System Receptacle. Receptacles for permanently installed pool motors, or other loads directly related to the circulation system, must be at least 6 ft from the inside walls of the pool and have GFCI protection. ▶Figure 680-11

(3) Other Receptacles. Receptacles for loads not directly related to the circulation system must be not less than 6 ft from the inside walls of a permanently installed pool. ▶Figure 680-12

680.22 | Swimming Pools, Fountains, and Similar Installations

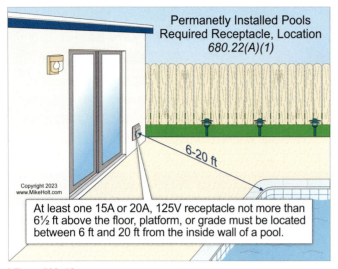
▶Figure 680–10

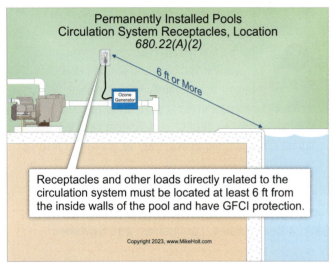
▶Figure 680–11

▶Figure 680–12

(4) GFCI and SPGFCI Protection. Receptacles rated 125V through 250V, 60A or less and 150V or less to ground within 20 ft of the inside wall of a pool must have GFCI protection. Receptacles rated above 150V to ground within 20 ft of the inside wall of a pool must have special purpose GFCI protection. ▶Figure 680–13

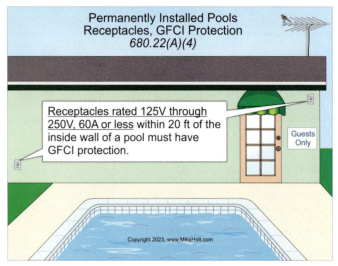
▶Figure 680–13

(5) How to Measure. When measuring receptacle distances from the pool water, the measurement is the shortest path a supply cord would follow without piercing a floor, wall, or ceiling. ▶Figure 680–14

▶Figure 680–14

(B) Luminaires and Ceiling Fans.

(1) New Outdoor Installations. Luminaires and lighting outlets installed not less than 5 ft horizontally from the inside walls of a permanently installed pool must be not less than 12 ft above the maximum water level. ▶Figure 680–15

Swimming Pools, Fountains, and Similar Installations | 680.22

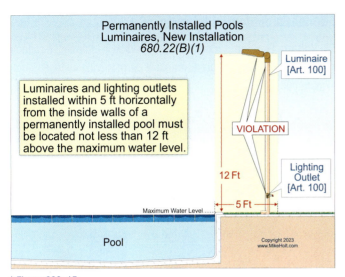
▶Figure 680-15

(3) Existing Installations. Existing lighting outlets within 5 ft horizontally from the inside walls of a permanently installed pool must not be less than 5 ft above the surface of the maximum water level, be rigidly attached to the existing structure, and be GFCI protected.
▶Figure 680-16

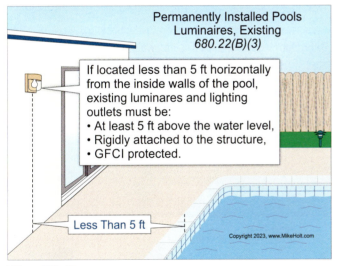
▶Figure 680-16

(4) GFCI and SPGFCI Protection. All luminaires, lighting outlets, and ceiling fans between 5 ft and 10 ft horizontally from the inside walls of a permanently installed pool, and not less than 5 ft above the maximum water, level must have GFCI protection in accordance with 680.5(B) or SPGFCI protection in accordance with 680.5(C).

(6) Low-Voltage Luminaires. Low-voltage lighting systems not exceeding low-voltage contact limits with a transformer or power supply that is listed, labeled, and identified for swimming pools or underwater luminaires can be installed without any distance limits to the water [680.23(A)(2)]. ▶Figure 680-17

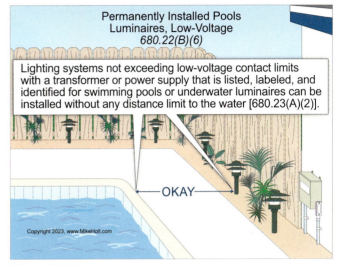
▶Figure 680-17

All other low-voltage lighting must not be installed within 10 ft from the edge of the water in accordance with 411.5(B).

(7) Low-Voltage Gas-Fired Luminaires, Fireplaces, Fire Pits, and Similar Equipment. Listed gas-fired luminaires, fireplaces, fire pits, and similar equipment using low-voltage ignitors supplied by listed transformers or power supplies that comply with 680.23(A)(2) and do not exceed the low-voltage contact limit can be less than 5 ft from the inside walls of the pool.

(8) Measurements. In determining the dimensions in this section addressing luminaires, the distance to be measured must be the shortest path an imaginary cord connected to the luminaire will follow without piercing a floor, wall, ceiling, doorway with a hinged or sliding door, window opening, or other effective permanent barrier.

680.26 Equipotential Bonding

There were a variety of editorial changes and clarifications in this section having to do with when equipotential bonding is required, how to measure the depth of the perimeter bond ring, when a pool shell is exempt from bonding, and when to bond metal parts close to a pool.

Analysis

CLARIFIED This is a small change that has a big meaning. It was not clear in (A) what to do with a pool that had no associated electrical equipment. New language clarifies that equipotential bonding is required for all pools, with or without associated electrical equipment.

CLARIFIED Revisions to (B) clarify that nonconductive pool shells are exempt from equipotential bonding requirements. But you are still required to bond the water in accordance with 680.26(C).

CLARIFIED Another clarification in (B)(2)(b)(5) answers a question we have all wondered about for a while. How do you measure the depth of the perimeter bonding ring? It is now clear that it must be no more than 6 in. below the finished grade of a paved surface, and between 4 in. and 6 in. below the finished grade of an unpaved surface. The same change is in (c)(4) for copper grids.

EDITED The rule in (B)(5) previously listed metal fittings not required to be bonded. It was converted to an Exception with three list items. There were no technical changes.

EXPANDED REORGANIZED A reorganized (B)(6) now has three list items. A new item (3) requires metal parts of any other electrical equipment within 5 ft horizontally from the inside wall of a pool, or 12 ft vertically from the maximum water level, to be bonded unless separated by a permanent barrier.

REORGANIZED There were no technical changes to (B)(7) but it was reorganized into a list containing former Exceptions 2 and 3.

680.26 Equipotential Bonding

(A) Voltage Gradients. Equipotential bonding is intended to reduce voltage gradients in the area around a permanently installed pool. ▶Figure 680–18

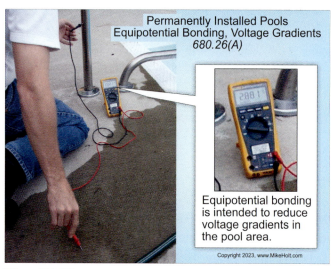
▶Figure 680–18

Equipotential bonding must be installed for pools with or without associated electrical equipment related to the pool.

(B) Equipotential Bonding. The parts of a permanently installed pool listed in (B)(1) through (B)(7) must be bonded together with a solid insulated or bare copper conductor not smaller than 8 AWG using a listed pressure connector, terminal bar, or other listed means in accordance with 250.8(A) [and 680.7]. ▶Figure 680–19

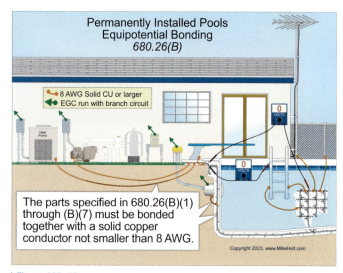
▶Figure 680–19

Equipotential bonding is not required to extend (or be attached) to any panelboard, service disconnect, or grounding electrode.

(1) Conductive Pool Shells. Cast-in-place concrete, pneumatically applied or sprayed concrete, and concrete block with painted or plastered coatings must be bonded. Reconstructed conductive pool shells must be bonded.

(a) Structural Reinforcing Steel. Unencapsulated structural reinforcing steel rebar can be bonded together by steel tie wires.
▶Figure 680-20

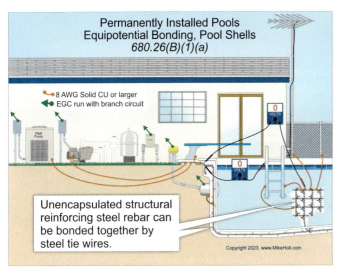

▶Figure 680-20

(b) Copper Conductor Grid. Where structural reinforcing steel is encapsulated in a nonconductive compound, a copper conductor grid must be installed as follows: ▶Figure 680-21

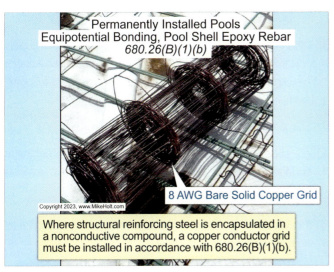

▶Figure 680-21

Author's Comment:

▶ Encapsulated structural reinforcing steel is used to prevent rebar corrosion and (if used) will make the pool shell insulated, therefore a conductive copper grid is required to bond the pool shell.

(1) Be constructed of a minimum of 8 AWG bare solid copper conductors bonded to each other at all points of crossing in accordance with 250.8 [and 680.7], or other approved means.

(2) Conform to the contour of the pool.

(3) Be arranged in a 12-in. by 12-in. network of conductors in a uniformly spaced perpendicular grid pattern with a tolerance of 4 in.

(4) Be secured within or under the pool no more than 6 in. from the outer contour of the pool shell.

(2) Perimeter Surfaces. Equipotential perimeter bonding must extend a minimum of 3 ft horizontally from the inside walls of a pool where not separated by a building or permanent wall 5 ft in height.
▶Figure 680-22

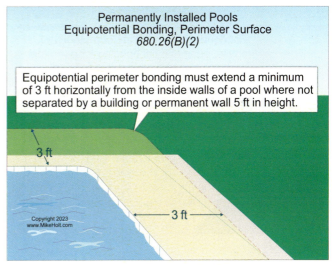

▶Figure 680-22

Perimeter surfaces less than 3 ft separated by a permanent wall or building 5 ft or more in height require equipotential bonding only on the pool side of the wall or building. ▶Figure 680-23

680.26 | Swimming Pools, Fountains, and Similar Installations

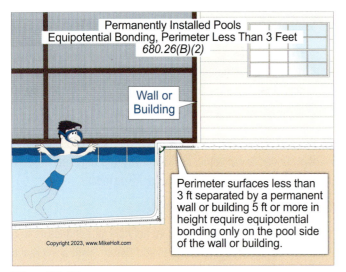
▶Figure 680-23

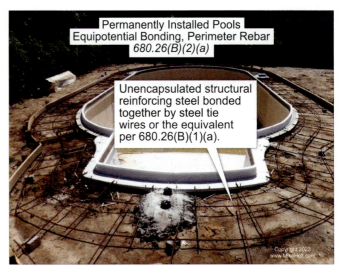
▶Figure 680-25

For conductive pool shells, equipotential bonding for perimeter surfaces must be attached to the concrete pool reinforcing steel rebar or copper conductor grid at a minimum of four points uniformly spaced around the perimeter of the pool and be one of the following: ▶Figure 680-24

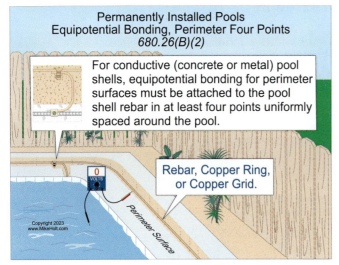
▶Figure 680-24

(a) Structural Reinforcing Steel Rebar. Unencapsulated structural reinforcing steel bonded together by steel tie wires or the equivalent in accordance with 680.26(B)(1)(a). ▶Figure 680-25

> **Author's Comment:**
>
> ▸ The *NEC* does not provide any guidance on the installation requirements for structural reinforcing steel when used as a perimeter surface equipotential bonding method. ▶Figure 680-26

▶Figure 680-26

(b) Copper Ring. Where structural reinforcing steel is not available or is encapsulated in a nonconductive compound, a copper conductor can be used for equipotential perimeter bonding where the following requirements are met: ▶Figure 680-27

(1) The copper ring is constructed of 8 AWG bare solid copper or larger.

(2) The copper ring conductor follows the contour of the perimeter surface.

(3) Only listed splicing devices or exothermic welding are used.

(4) The copper ring conductor is placed between 18 in. and 24 in. from the inside walls of the pool.

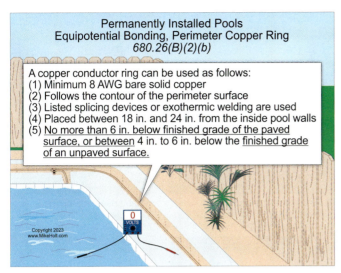
▶Figure 680-27

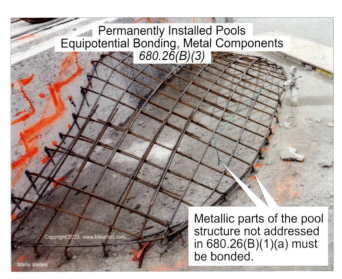
▶Figure 680-28

(5) The copper ring conductor is secured within a paved surface (concrete), no more than 6 in. below finished grade of the paved surface (pavers or concrete), or between 4 in. and 6 in. below the finished grade of an unpaved surface (dirt).

(c) Copper Grid. Where structural reinforcing steel is not available or is encapsulated in a nonconductive compound as an alternate method to a copper ring, a copper grid can be used for perimeter bonding where all the following requirements are met:

(1) The copper grid is constructed of 8 AWG solid bare copper and arranged in a 12-in. by 12-in. network of conductors in a uniformly spaced perpendicular grid pattern with a tolerance of 4 in. in accordance with 680.26(B)(1)(b)(3).

(2) The copper grid follows the contour of the perimeter surface extending 3 ft horizontally beyond the inside walls of the pool.

(3) Only listed splicing devices or exothermic welding are used.

(4) The copper grid is secured within a paved surface (concrete), no more than 6 in. below finished grade of the paved surface (pavers or concrete), or between 4 in. and 6 in. below the finished grade of an unpaved surface (dirt).

(3) Metallic Components of Pool Structure. Metallic components of the pool structure, not addressed in 680.26(B)(1)(a) must be bonded. ▶Figure 680-28

(4) Metal Forming Shells. All metal forming shells must be bonded.
▶Figure 680-29

Ex: Listed low-voltage lighting with nonmetallic forming shells are not required to be bonded.

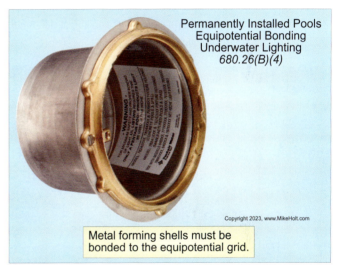
▶Figure 680-29

(5) Metal Pool Fittings. Metal fittings attached to the pool structure (such as ladders and handrails) must be bonded. ▶Figure 680-30

Ex: The following are not required to be bonded:

(1) Isolated parts not over 4 in. in any dimension and not penetrating the pool structure more than1 in.

(2) Metallic pool cover anchors in a concrete or masonry deck, 1 in. or less in any dimension and 2 in. or less in length.

(3) Metallic pool cover anchors in a wood or composite deck, 2 in. or less in any dimension and 2 in. or less in length.

(6) Electrical Pool Equipment. Metal parts of the following electrical equipment must be bonded.

(1) Electrically powered pool cover(s)

680.32 | Swimming Pools, Fountains, and Similar Installations

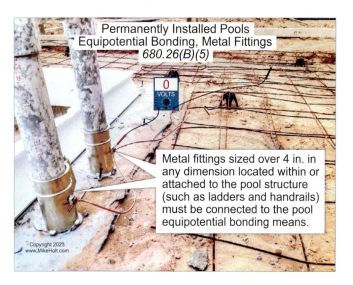

▶Figure 680–30

▶Figure 680–32

(2) Pool water circulation, treatment, heating, cooling, or dehumidification equipment ▶Figure 680–31

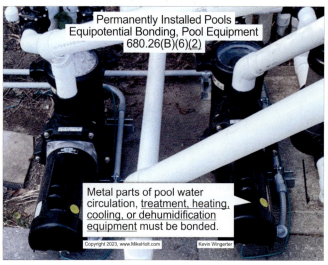

▶Figure 680–31

▶Figure 680–33

(3) Other electrical equipment within 5 ft horizontally and 12 ft vertically from the inside walls of the pool, unless separated from the pool by a permanent barrier

(7) Fixed Metal Parts. Fixed metal parts of metal awnings, metal fences, metal doors, and metal window frames within 5 ft horizontally and 12 ft vertically from the inside walls of the pool must be bonded. ▶Figure 680–32

Ex: Those separated from the pool by a permanent barrier that prevents contact by a person are not required to be bonded. ▶Figure 680–33

680.32 Ground-Fault Circuit-Interrupter (GFCI) and Special Purpose Ground-Fault Circuit-Interrupter (SPGFCI) Protection

Another set of revisions driven by the new SPGFCI requirements expand the application of rules in this section.

Swimming Pools, Fountains, and Similar Installations | 680.43

Analysis

 EXPANDED As we have seen in other sections of Article 680, the requirement to provide ground-fault protection is being expanded with the addition of SPGFCI requirements.

Analysis

 EXPANDED The required ground-fault protection of receptacles was expanded from those rated 125V, 30A or less to all receptacles rated 60A or less due to the addition of SPGFCIs this cycle. The protection must be in accordance with 680.5(B) or (C) as applicable.

680.32 GFCI or SPGFCI Protection

Receptacles rated 125V through 250V, 60A or less within 20 ft from the inside walls of a storable pool must have GFCI protection in accordance with 680.5(B) or SPGFCI protection in accordance with 680.5(C). ▶Figure 680-34

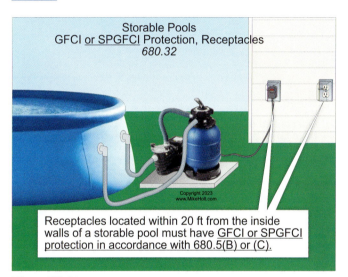

▶Figure 680-34

680.43 Indoor Installations

Electrical installations for an indoor hot tub must comply with Parts I and II of Article 680 except as modified by this section.

Indoor installations of spas or hot tubs can be connected by any of the wiring methods contained in Chapter 3.

Ex 2: The equipotential bonding requirements for perimeter surfaces contained in 680.26(B)(2) do not apply to a listed self-contained hot tub installed above an indoor finished floor.

(A) Receptacles. At least one 15A or 20A, 125V receptacle on a general-purpose branch circuit must be not less than 6 ft and not more than 10 ft from the inside wall of a hot tub. ▶Figure 680-35

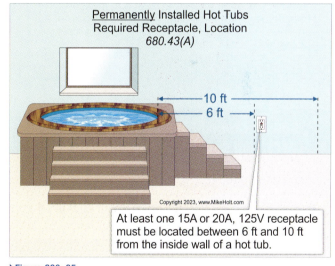

▶Figure 680-35

680.43 Indoor Installations

Following a theme throughout this article, the addition of SPGFCIs in (A)(2) expands the ground-fault protection requirements for hot tubs.

(1) Location. Receptacles must be not less than 6 ft measured horizontally from the inside walls of the hot tub.

(2) GFCI and SPGFCI Protection. Receptacles rated 125V through 250V, rated 60A or less within 10 ft of the inside walls of a hot tub must have GFCI protection in accordance with 680.5(B) or SPGFCI protection in accordance with 680.5(C).

(3) Protection, Hot Tub Supply Receptacle. Receptacles that provide power for hot tub equipment must be GFCI protected.

(4) Measurements. In determining the dimensions in this section, the distance to be measured is the shortest path a cord of an appliance connected to the receptacle will follow without piercing a floor, wall, ceiling, doorway with a hinged or sliding door, window opening, or other type of permanent barrier.

(C) Switches. Switches must be at least 5 ft, measured horizontally, from the inside wall of the indoor hot tub. ▶Figure 680-36

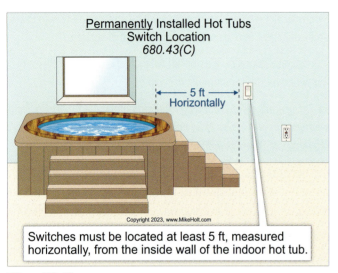

▶Figure 680-36

680.44 Ground-Fault Circuit-Interrupter (GFCI) and Special Purpose Ground-Fault Circuit-Interrupter (SPGFCI) Protection

Another section and another change driven by SPGFCIs.

Analysis

EXPANDED EDITED

The original parent text has become subdivision (A) and, due to the addition of SPGFCIs this cycle, hot tub assemblies must now be ground-fault protected in accordance with 680.5(B) or (C) as applicable.

680.44 GFCI or SPGFCI Protection

(A) General. Outlets that supply spa and hot tub assemblies must have GFCI protection in accordance with 680.5(B) or SPGFCI protection in accordance with 680.5(C). ▶Figure 680-37

(B) Listed Units. If so marked, a listed self-contained hot tub or a listed packaged equipment assembly that includes integral GFCI protection for all electrical parts, does not require additional GFCI protection. ▶Figure 680-38

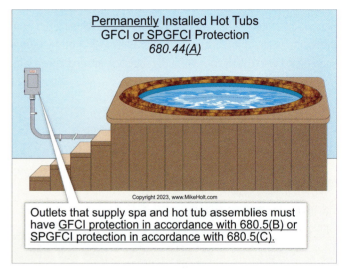

▶Figure 680-37

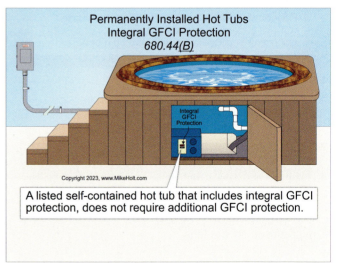

▶Figure 680-38

Swimming Pools, Fountains, and Similar Installations | **680.54**

680.50 General

A reorganization of this section into a list format makes it easier to read and new requirements for the location of electrical equipment were added in (B).

Analysis

EXPANDED   REORGANIZED

This section was reorganized like much of the rest of the article into a list format. A new subdivision (B) was added requiring electrical equipment operating above the low-voltage contact limit to be at least 5 ft horizontally from the inside wall of a fountain unless separated by a permanent barrier. This change mirrors those seen for hot tubs.

680.50 General

The general installation requirements contained in Part I apply to fountains and splash pads intended for recreational use, in addition to those requirements contained in Part V. Part II of Article 680 applies to fountains that have water common to pools.

> **Author's Comment:**
> ▸ According to Article 100, a "Fountain" is defined as an ornamental structure or recreational water feature from which one or more jets or streams of water are discharged into the air. They include splash pads, ornamental pools, display pools, and reflection pools.

(A) Additional Requirements.

(1) Fountains that have water common to a pool must comply with Part II of Article 680.

(2) Splash pads must have equipotential bonding in accordance with 680.26.

(B) Equipment Exceeding the Low-Voltage Contact Limit. Equipment with ratings exceeding the low-voltage contact limit must be at least 5 ft horizontally from the inside walls of a fountain, unless separated from the fountain by a solid fence, wall, or other permanent barrier.

680.54 Connection to an Equipment Grounding Conductor

A revision to (B) establishes the minimum size of the bonding conductor for fountains. The new section (C) identifies the portion of a splash pad required to have equipotential bonding.

Analysis

EXPANDED

New language in (B) specifies that where a bonding conductor is required for a fountain, it must be an 8 AWG solid copper conductor.

NEW

A new subdivision (C) attempts to define what the shell of a splash pad is for bonding purposes. After you read this rule, you may find it difficult to understand where the bonding begins. I suspect we will see some revisions to this in the next cycle.

680.54 Connection to an Equipment Grounding Conductor

(A) Connection to Equipment Grounding Conductor. The following must be connected to the circuit equipment grounding conductor:

(1) Electrical equipment within the fountain or within 5 ft of the inside wall of the fountain.

(2) Electrical equipment associated with the recirculating system of the fountain.

(3) Panelboards that supply electrical equipment associated with the fountain.

(B) Bonding, General. The following parts must be bonded together with a minimum 8 AWG solid copper conductor and connected to an equipment grounding conductor for a branch circuit supplying fountain equipment:

(1) Metal piping systems associated with the fountain.

(2) Metal fittings within or attached to the fountain.

(3) Metal parts of electrical equipment associated with the fountain water-circulating system.

680.58 | Swimming Pools, Fountains, and Similar Installations

(4) Metal raceways within 5 ft of the inside wall or perimeter of the fountain and not separated from it by a permanent barrier.

(5) Metal surfaces within 5 ft of the inside wall or perimeter of the fountain and not separated from it by a permanent barrier.

(6) Electrical equipment within 5 ft from the fountain's inside wall or perimeter.

(C) Equipotential Bonding of Splash Pad. The shell of splash pads for equipotential bonding is comprised of the area where pedestrians walk bounded by the footer of the splash pad that rises to an exposed surface and its collection basin area.

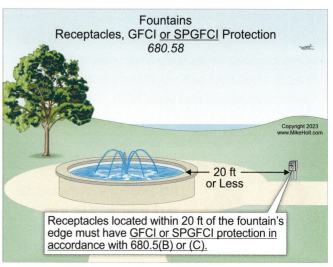
▶Figure 680–39

680.58 GFCI or SPGFCI Protection of Receptacles

This is a small change with a large impact as all receptacles around fountains must now have ground-fault protection.

Analysis

EXPANDED As in many other rules, the addition of SPGFCIs has expanded ground-fault protection requirements. Now all receptacles located within 20 ft from a fountain edge, rated 60A or less, must be protected in accordance with 680.5(B) or (C) as applicable.

680.58 GFCI or SPGFCI Protection of Receptacles

All receptacles rated 125V through 250V, 60A or less within 20 ft of the fountain's edge must have GFCI protection in accordance with 680.5(B) or SPGFCI protection in accordance with 680.5(C). ▶Figure 680–39

680.59 Ground-Fault Protection for Permanently Installed Nonsubmersible Pumps

All nonsubmersible pump motors must now be ground-fault protected.

Analysis

EXPANDED There are no voltage or current limitations here so all outlets suppling permanently installed nonsubmersible fountain pumps must have ground-fault protection in accordance with 680.5(B) or (C) as applicable.

A new Exception exempts listed low-voltage motors not requiring grounding and with a rating not exceeding the low-voltage contact limit.

680.59 Ground-Fault Protection for Permanently Installed Nonsubmersible Pumps

Outlets supplying permanently installed nonsubmersible pump motors must have GFCI protection in accordance with 680.5(B) or SPGFCI protection in accordance with 680.5(C).

680.74 Bonding

A new Exception exempts small devices from equipotential bonding requirements.

Analysis

NEW A new Exception 3 to (A) exempts small conductive surfaces of electrical equipment (like the yoke of switches and receptacles) that are not likely to become energized from the requirements of this rule.

680.74 Equipotential Bonding

(A) General. The following parts must be bonded together.

(1) Metal fittings within, or attached to, the hydromassage bathtub structure that are in contact with the circulating water.

(2) Metal parts of electrical equipment associated with the hydromassage bathtub water circulating system, including pump and blower motors.

(3) Metal-sheathed cables, metal raceways, and metal piping within 5 ft of the inside walls of the hydromassage bathtub and not separated from its area by a permanent barrier.

(4) Exposed metal surfaces within 5 ft of the inside walls of the hydromassage bathtub and not separated from it by a permanent barrier.

(5) Metal parts of electrical devices not associated with the hydromassage bathtub within 5 ft from the hydromassage bathtub.

Ex 1: Small conductive surfaces not likely to become energized such as air and water jets, supply valve assemblies, drain fittings not connected to metallic piping, towel bars, mirror frames, and similar nonelectrical equipment not connected to metal framing are not required to be bonded.

Ex 2: Double-insulated motors and blowers are not required to be bonded.

Ex 3: Small conductive surfaces of electrical equipment not likely to become energized, such as the mounting strap or yoke of a listed light switch or receptacle, are not required to be bonded.

(B) Bonding Conductor. Metal parts required to be bonded by 680.74(A) must be bonded together using an insulated or bare solid copper conductor not smaller than 8 AWG. Bonding jumpers are not required to be extended or attached to any remote panelboard, service disconnect, or any electrode.

A bonding jumper long enough to terminate on a replacement nondouble-insulated pump or blower motor must be provided, and it must terminate to the equipment grounding conductor of the branch circuit of the motor when a double-insulated circulating pump or blower motor is used.

Notes

ARTICLE 690 — SOLAR PHOTOVOLTAIC (PV) SYSTEMS

Introduction to Article 690—Solar Photovoltaic (PV) Systems

You have seen, or maybe own, devices powered by photovoltaic cells such as night lights, car coolers, and toys. These generally consist of a small solar module powering a small device running on a few volts and a fraction of an ampere. A solar PV system that powers a building or interconnects with an electric utility operates on the same principals but on a much larger scale.

Solar PV systems that provide electrical power to an electrical system are complex. There are many issues that require expert knowledge in electrical, structural, and architectural issues.

The purpose of the *NEC* is to safeguard persons and property from the hazards arising from the use of electricity [90.2(C)]. Article 690 is focused on the electrical hazards that may arise from installing and operating a PV system. It consists of eight parts.

The general *Code* requirements of Chapters 1 through 4 also apply to these installations, except as specifically modified by this article [90.3].

690.4 General Requirements

Revisions to (B) require field labeling, the defined term "electronic power converters" replaces outdated terminology, and floating solar arrays must be identified for the purpose.

Analysis

CLARIFIED The rule in (B) requires equipment to be listed or evaluated for the application and have a field label applied. The list was expanded to include "PV hazard control equipment" and "PV hazard control systems," and the terms "inverters" and "dc-to-dc converters" were replaced with the Article 100 term "electronic power converters."

NEW PV systems are now commonly being installed floating on bodies of water, and this practice is addressed in the new (G). Floating solar PV equipment must now be identified as suitable for the purpose and use wiring methods that allow for movement.

690.4 General Requirements

(A) PV Systems. A PV system is permitted to supply electric power to buildings or structures.

(B) Listed or FEB Labeled Equipment. Components of the PV system including electronic power converters, inverters, PV modules, ac modules, ac module systems, dc combiners, dc-to-dc converters, PV rapid shutdown equipment, PV hazard control equipment, PV hazard control systems, dc circuit controllers, and charge controllers must be listed or be evaluated for the application and have a field evaluation body (FEB) label applied. ▶Figure 690-1

Author's Comment:

▶ "Listing" means the equipment is included in a list published by a testing laboratory acceptable to the authority having jurisdiction [Article 100].

▶ "Field Labeled" means the equipment or materials which have a label, symbol, or other identifying mark of a field evaluation body (FEB) indicates the equipment or material was evaluated and found to comply with the requirements described in the field body evaluation report [Article 100].

690.7 | Solar Photovoltaic (PV) Systems

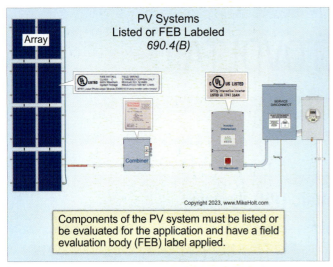
▶Figure 690–1

(C) Qualified Persons. The installation of PV systems must be performed by a qualified person.

> **Author's Comment:**
>
> ▶ A qualified person has the knowledge related to the construction and operation of PV equipment and installations, along with safety training to recognize and avoid hazards to persons and property [Article 100]. ▶Figure 690–2

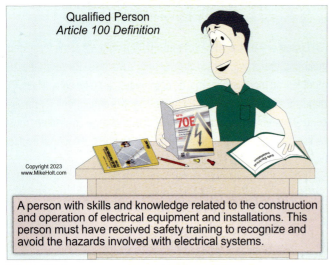
▶Figure 690–2

> **Author's Comment:**
>
> ▶ NFPA 70E, *Standard for Electrical Safety in the Workplace*, provides information on the safety training requirements expected of a "qualified person."

▶ Examples of this safety training include training in the use of special precautionary techniques, personal protective equipment (PPE), insulating and shielding materials, and in the use of insulated tools and test equipment when working on or near exposed conductors or circuit parts that can become energized.

▶ In many parts of the United States, electricians, electrical contractors, electrical inspectors, and electrical engineers must complete an *NEC* review course each year as a requirement to maintain licensing. This, in and of itself, does not make one qualified to deal with the specific hazards involved with PV systems.

(D) Multiple PV Systems. Multiple PV systems are permitted on or in a building. Where PV systems are remotely located from each other, a directory must be provided at each PV disconnect in accordance with 705.10.

(E) Where Not Permitted. No part of a PV system is permitted to be installed within a bathroom.

(F) Electronic Power Converters Not Readily Accessible. Electronic power converters (inverters and dc-to-dc converters) are not required to be readily accessible.

(G) PV Equipment Floating on Bodies of Water. PV equipment floating on or attached to structures floating on bodies of water must be identified as being suitable for the purpose and have wiring methods that allow for expected movement of the equipment.

Note: PV equipment in these installations is often subject to increased levels of humidity, corrosion, and mechanical and structural stresses. Expected movement of floating PV arrays is often included in the structural design.

690.7 Maximum PV System Direct-Current Circuit Voltage

There were no technical changes here, but the Code-Making Panel did a nice job reorganizing everything.

Analysis

 REORGANIZED The parent text in this section was reorganized into a list format with some minor revisions. There is no technical change.

 EDITED Revisions to (A) replaced the term "PV Output Circuit" with the newly defined term "PV String Circuit," but there was no technical change in the requirements.

690.7 Maximum PV System Direct-Current Circuit Voltage

The maximum voltage of a circuit value is used when selecting conductors, cables, equipment, determining working space, and other applications where circuit voltage ratings are used. The maximum voltage of a PV system dc circuit is defined as the highest voltage between any two conductors of a circuit.

(1) Commercial and Industrial Buildings—Maximum 1000V. For commercial and industrial buildings, the maximum PV system dc circuit voltage cannot exceed 1000V. ▶Figure 690-3

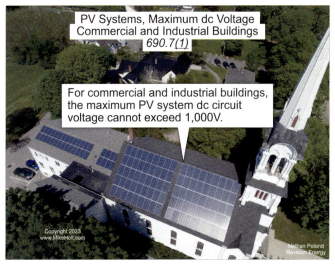
▶Figure 690-3

(2) One- and Two-Family Dwellings—Maximum 600V. For one- and two-family dwelling units, the maximum PV system dc circuit voltage cannot exceed 600V. ▶Figure 690-4

(3) 1000V PV Systems. See 690.31(G) for requirements and limitations.

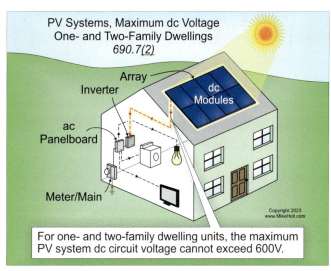
▶Figure 690-4

(A) Calculating PV System Direct-Current Source Circuit Voltage. The maximum calculated PV system dc source circuit voltage is determined by one of the following:

(1) Manufacturer's Instructions. The maximum PV system dc source circuit voltage is equal to the sum of the series-connected dc module open-circuit voltage (Voc) in a PV string circuit as corrected for the lowest expected ambient temperature using the manufacturer's voltage temperature coefficient correction. ▶Figure 690-5

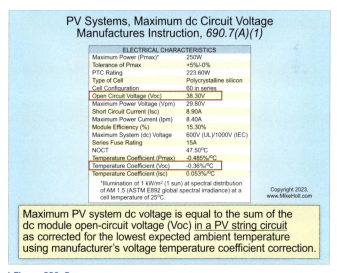
▶Figure 690-5

Author's Comment:

▶ A PV module's dc voltage has an inverse relationship with temperature which means that at lower ambient temperatures, the module's dc output voltage increases and at higher ambient temperatures, the modules' dc voltage output decreases.

690.12 | Solar Photovoltaic (PV) Systems

690.12 Rapid Shutdown of PV Systems on Buildings

A new Exception 2 exempts detached nonenclosed structures from rapid shutdown requirements, some editorial revisions clarify the application of these rules, and rapid shutdown marking requirements were relocated to this section.

Analysis

 NEW This new Exception 2 allows a PV system installed on detached nonenclosed structures to be exempt from the rapid shutdown requirements of this section. One reason for requiring a rapid shutdown is to protect fire fighters when roof operations are required, and these structures are unlikely to need such services.

 NEW New language in (B) permits listed equipment and systems, such as microinverters, to meet the rapid shutdown requirements for control conductors located within and outside of the array boundary.

 CLARIFIED List items (1) and (2) were revised for clarity without technical change and list item (3) was deleted.

 RELOCATED A new subdivision (D) was relocated here from 690.56(C) as this is where the marking requirements belong. There were some other editorial revisions but no technical changes.

690.12 Rapid Shutdown Device

PV system conductors on or in a building must be controlled by a rapid shutdown device to reduce shock hazards for firefighters in accordance with 690.12(A) through (D). ▶Figure 690-6

Ex 1: A rapid shutdown system is not required for ground-mounted PV system conductors that enter buildings whose sole purpose is to house PV system equipment.

Ex 2: PV equipment and circuits installed on nonenclosed detached structures including, but not limited to, parking shade structures, carports, solar trellises, and similar structures are not required to have a rapid shutdown system [690.12].

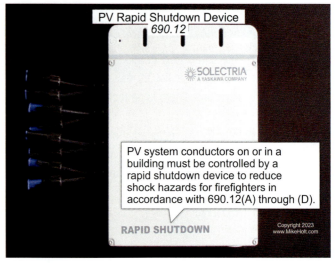

▶Figure 690-6

(A) Controlled Conductors. PV system conductors controlled by the rapid shutdown system include:

(1) PV system dc circuit conductors.

(2) Inverter output ac circuits originating from inverters within the array boundary.

Note: The ac output conductors from PV systems will be either de-energized after shutdown initiation or remain energized if supplied by a utility service. To prevent PV systems with ac output conductors from remaining energized, they must be controlled by the rapid shutdown system after shutdown initiation.

Ex: PV system circuits originating within or from arrays not attached to buildings that terminate on the exterior of buildings, and PV system circuits installed in accordance with 230.6, are not considered controlled conductors for rapid shutdown [690.12].

(B) Controlled Limits. Where rapid shutdown is required, the array boundary is defined as the area 1 ft outside the perimeter of the PV array.

Equipment and systems are permitted to meet the requirements of both inside and outside the array as defined by the manufacturer's instructions included with the listing.

(1) Outside the Array Boundary. PV system circuit conductors outside the PV array boundary or more than 3 ft from the point of entry inside a building must be limited to 30V within 30 seconds of rapid shutdown initiation.

(2) Inside the Array Boundary. The PV system rapid shutdown must comply with one of the following:

Solar Photovoltaic (PV) Systems | **690.12**

(1) The PV system must provide shock hazard control for firefighters by using a PV hazard control system installed in accordance with the manufacturer's instructions. Where a PV hazard control system requires initiation to transition to a controlled state, the rapid shutdown initiation device [690.12(C)] must perform this initiation.

Note: A listed or field-labeled PV hazard control system is comprised of either an individual piece of equipment that fulfills the necessary functions, or multiple pieces of equipment coordinated to perform the functions as described in the manufacturer's instructions to reduce the risk of electric shock hazard for firefighters.

(2) The PV system must provide shock hazard control for firefighters by limiting the voltage inside equipment or between any two conductors of a circuit, or any conductor and ground inside the array boundary to not more than 80V within 30 seconds of rapid shutdown initiation.

(C) Initiation Device. A rapid shutdown initiation device is required to initiate the rapid shutdown function of the PV system. When the rapid shutdown initiation device is placed in the "off" position, this indicates that the rapid shutdown function has been initiated.

For one- and two-family dwellings, the rapid shutdown initiation device must be outside the building at a readily accessible outdoor location.

For a single PV system, the rapid shutdown initiation must occur by the operation of any single initiation device that must be at least one of the following types:

(1) The service disconnect. ▶Figure 690-7

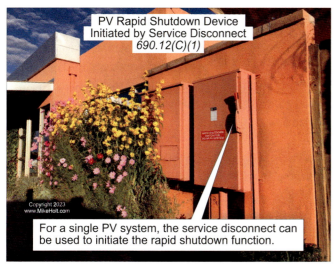
▶Figure 690-7

(2) The PV system disconnect. ▶Figure 690-8

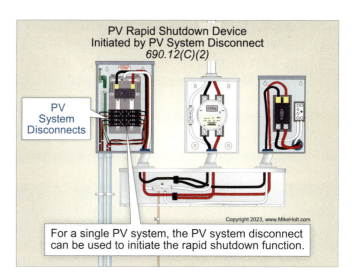
▶Figure 690-8

(3) A readily accessible switch that plainly indicates whether it is in the "off" or "on" position.

Where multiple PV systems are on a single service, the rapid shutdown initiation device(s) for the multiple PV systems must consist of not more than six switches or six sets of circuit breakers, or a combination of not more than six switches and sets of circuit breakers.

(D) Labels. A building with a rapid shutdown system must have a permanent label indicating the location of all rapid shutdown initiation devices. The label for the rapid shutdown initiation device must be located near the service equipment or at an approved readily visible location. The rapid shutdown initiation device label must include a diagram of the building with a roof and the following words:
▶Figure 690-9

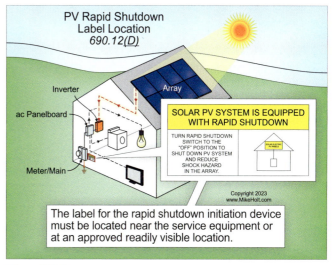
▶Figure 690-9

690.15 | Solar Photovoltaic (PV) Systems

SOLAR PV SYSTEM IS EQUIPPED WITH RAPID SHUTDOWN. TURN RAPID SHUTDOWN SWITCH TO THE "OFF" POSITION TO SHUT DOWN PV SYSTEM AND REDUCE SHOCK HAZARD IN THE ARRAY.

The title "SOLAR PV SYSTEM IS EQUIPPED WITH RAPID SHUTDOWN" must have capitalized characters with a minimum height of ⅜ in. All text must be legible and contrast with the background. ▶Figure 690–10

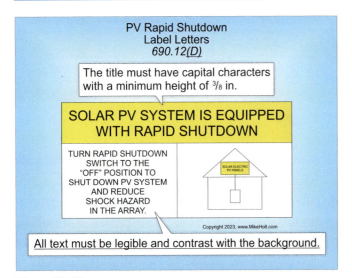

▶Figure 690–10

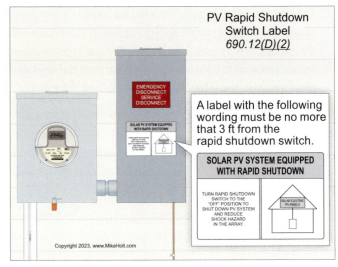

▶Figure 690–11

Note: See 690.12(D) in the *NEC* for an example.

(1) Buildings with More Than One Rapid Shutdown Type. A building having more than one rapid shutdown system, or a building without a rapid shutdown system, must have a label with a detailed plan view diagram of the roof showing each PV system with a dotted line around areas that remain energized after the rapid shutdown has been initiated.

(2) Rapid Shutdown Switch Label. A rapid shutdown switch must have a label that includes the following wording on or no more than 3 ft from the switch: ▶Figure 690–11

"RAPID SHUTDOWN SWITCH FOR SOLAR PV SYSTEM"

The rapid shutdown label must be reflective with all letters capitalized and have a minimum height of ⅜ in. in white on a red background.

690.15 PV Equipment Disconnect or Isolating Device

Revisions to (A) clarify disconnecting means requirements, when you can use an isolating device as part of listed equipment, and generally reorganized (C) and (D).

Analysis

   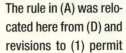
RELOCATED   EXPANDED   CLARIFIED

The rule in (A) was relocated here from (D) and revisions to (1) permit an equipment disconnecting means in accordance with 690.15(C) instead of only where the current is greater than 30A.

 A new list item (A)(2) permits the use of an isolating device as part of listed equipment if an interlock **NEW** prevents it from being opened under load.

 Subdivision (C) was reorganized into four list items without any technical changes. List **REORGANIZED** items, rather than long paragraphs, improve the *Code's* usability.

Solar Photovoltaic (PV) Systems | **690.15**

EXPANDED REORGANIZED Like subdivision (C), the rules in (D) were reorganized into list items and the title was changed to include "Control." References to 10 ft are removed and replaced with "readily accessible for whom access is required."

690.15 PV Equipment Disconnect or Isolating Device

A disconnect or isolating device must be provided for ac PV modules, fuses, dc-to-dc converters, inverters, and charge controllers. ▶Figure 690-12

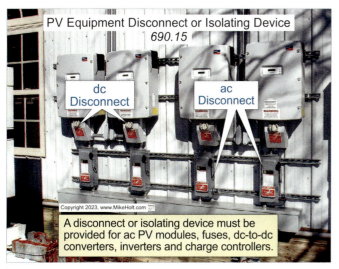

▶Figure 690-12

Author's Comment:

▸ The purpose of the PV disconnect is to ensure the safe and convenient replacement or maintenance of PV equipment without exposing qualified persons to energized conductors.

(A) Disconnecting Means. Where disconnects are required to isolate equipment, the disconnect must be one of the following types:

(1) Over 30A Circuits. A disconnect in accordance with 690.15(C).

(2) Isolating Device. An isolating device as part of listed equipment where an interlock or similar means prevents the opening of the isolating device under load.

(3) Not over 30A Circuits. An isolating device in accordance with 690.15(B).

(B) Isolating Device. An isolating device is not required to have an interrupting rating and, where not rated for interrupting the circuit current, it must be marked "Do Not Disconnect Under Load" or "Not for Current Interrupting." Isolating devices must be one of the following types:

(1) A mating connector meeting the requirements of 690.33 if listed and identified for use with specific equipment. ▶Figure 690-13

▶Figure 690-13

(2) A finger-safe fuse holder. ▶Figure 690-14

▶Figure 690-14

(3) An isolating device that requires a tool to place it in the open (off) position.

(4) An isolating device listed for the intended application.

690.31 | Solar Photovoltaic (PV) Systems

(C) Equipment Disconnecting Means. A PV equipment disconnect must comply with all the following:

(1) The PV equipment disconnect must have an ampere rating sufficient for the maximum circuit current, available fault current, and the voltage at the terminals of the disconnect. ▶Figure 690–15

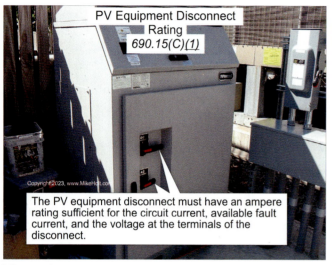

▶Figure 690–15

(2) The PV equipment disconnect must simultaneously disconnect all current-carrying circuit conductors to which it is connected.

(3) The PV equipment disconnect must be externally operable without exposing the operator to contact with energized parts and indicate whether it is in the open (off) or closed (on) position. ▶Figure 690–16

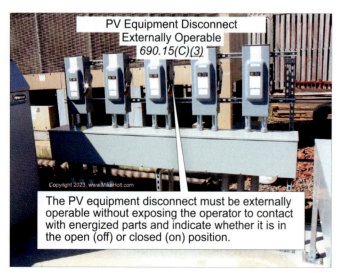

▶Figure 690–16

(4) The equipment disconnect must be of the same type as required in 690.13(E).

An equipment disconnect, other than those complying with 690.33, must be marked in accordance with the warning in 690.13(B) if the line and load terminals can be energized in the open position.

Author's Comment:

▸ According to 690.13(B), each PV system disconnect must indicate if it is in the open (off) or closed (on) position and the disconnect must be permanently marked "PV SYSTEM DISCONNECT" or equivalent. Where the line and load terminals of the PV system disconnect may be energized when the disconnect is in the open (off) position, the disconnect must be marked with the following words or equivalent: WARNING—ELECTRIC SHOCK HAZARD. TERMINALS ON THE LINE AND LOAD SIDES MAY BE ENERGIZED IN THE OPEN POSITION.

▸ The warning markings on the disconnect must be permanently affixed and have sufficient durability to withstand the environment involved [110.21(B)].

Note: A common installation practice is to terminate circuit conductors on the line side of a disconnect which will de-energize load-side terminals, blades, and fuses when the disconnect is in the open position.

(D) Location and Control. Isolating devices or equipment disconnects must comply with any of the following:

(1) Located within the PV equipment

(2) Located within sight and readily accessible from the PV equipment

(3) Lockable in accordance with 110.25

(4) Remote-controls with one of the following:

    a. The disconnect and their controls are within the same equipment.

    b. The disconnect is lockable in accordance with 110.25, and the location of the controls are marked on the disconnect.

690.31 Wiring Methods

This section was massively reorganized. Clarifications were made and requirements were added for single-conductor cables and systems operating over 1000V.

Solar Photovoltaic (PV) Systems | 690.31

Analysis

 CLARIFIED A new title for (A)(2) clarifies the conditions to which it applies and expands coverage to all PV dc circuits.

  REORGANIZED EXPANDED This entire section was reorganized to add new subdivisions and titles. In addition, it was editorially revised for usability.

 NEW As part of the reorganization, one new item was added to (C)(1)(2) for single-conductor cables requiring conductors larger than 8 AWG to be secured at intervals not to exceed 54 in.

 EXPANDED Additional new language in (C)(2) addresses the ampacity adjustment and installation of single-conductor PV wire smaller than 1/0 AWG in cable tray.

 REORGANIZED The former list item (D)(1) in this subdivision was deleted and replaced with the parent text. The reference to the use of MC cable as an EGC was changed from 250.118(10) to 250.118(A)(10)(b) or (10)(c) which prohibits the use of certain types of MC cable.

 NEW The new subdivision (G) specifies the permitted wiring methods for PV systems with dc circuits exceeding 1000V and prohibits their use on or in one- and two-family dwelling units, within buildings that contain habitable rooms, or less than 10 ft above grade.

690.31 Wiring Methods

(A) Wiring Systems.

(1) Serviceability. Where wiring devices with integral enclosures are used, a sufficient length of cable must be provided to facilitate replacement.

(2) Where Readily Accessible. PV system dc circuit conductors operating at over 30V that are readily accessible to unqualified persons must be guarded, or installed within a raceway in multiconductor jacketed cable, or Type MC cable. ▶Figure 690–17 and ▶Figure 690–18

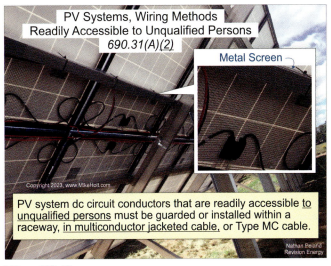
▶Figure 690–17

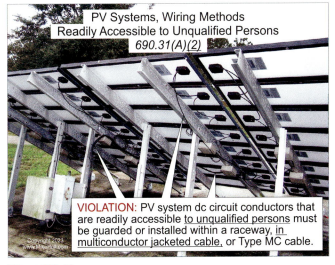
▶Figure 690–18

(3) Conductor Ampacity. PV circuit conductors with insulation rated at 105°C and 125°C must have their ampacities determined by Table 690.31(A)(3)(1) and corrected by Table 690.31(A)(3)(2).

690.31 | Solar Photovoltaic (PV) Systems

Table 690.31(A)(3)(1) Correction Factors

Ambient Temperature (°C)	Temperature Rating of Conductor 105°C (221°F)	Temperature Rating of Conductor 125°C (257°F)	Ambient Temperature (°F)
31–35	0.97	0.97	87–95
36–40	0.93	0.95	96–104
41–45	0.89	0.92	105–113
46–50	0.86	0.89	114–122
51–55	0.82	0.86	123–131
56–60	0.77	0.83	132–140
61–65	0.73	0.79	141–149
66–70	0.68	0.76	150–158
71–75	0.63	0.73	159–167
76–80	0.58	0.69	168–176
81–85	0.52	0.65	177–185
86–90	0.45	0.61	186–194
91–95	0.37	0.56	195–203
96–100	0.26	0.51	204–212
101–105	–	0.46	213–221
106–110	–	0.4	222–230
111–115	–	0.32	231–239
116–120	–	0.23	240–248

Table 690.31(A)(3)(2) Conductor Ampacity, Not More Than Three Current-Carrying Conductors in Raceway, Cable, or Earth, with Ambient Temperature of 30°C (86°F)

Wire Size AWG	PVC, CPE, XLPE 105°C	XLPE, EPDM 125°C
18	15	16
16	19	20
14	29	31
12	36	39
10	46	50
8	64	69
6	81	87
4	109	118
3	129	139
2	143	154
1	168	181
1/0	193	208
2/0	229	247
3/0	263	284
4/0	301	325

(4) Special Equipment. Wiring systems specifically listed for PV systems are permitted.

Note: See 110.14(C) for conductor temperature limitations due to termination provisions.

(B) Identification and Grouping.

(1) Mixing Conductors of Different Systems.

PV System Direct-Current Circuit Conductors. PV system dc circuit conductors are permitted to be installed in the same enclosure, cable, or raceway with other PV system dc circuit conductors, unless prohibited by equipment listing.

PV System Alternating-Current Circuit Conductors. PV system dc circuit conductors are not permitted to be installed in the same enclosure, cable, or raceway with inverter ac output circuit conductors or other conductors unless separated by a barrier or partition. ▶Figure 690–19

Ex: Where all conductors or cables have an insulation rating equal to at least the maximum circuit voltage applied to any conductor within the same wiring method, the following are permitted:

(1) Multiconductor jacketed cables containing power-limited circuits within the wiring enclosure, cable, or raceway as PV system dc circuits where all circuits serve the PV system.

(2) Inverter output ac circuits can occupy a junction box, pull box, or wireway with PV system dc circuits that are identified and grouped in accordance with 690.31(B)(2) and (B)(3).

Solar Photovoltaic (PV) Systems | **690.31**

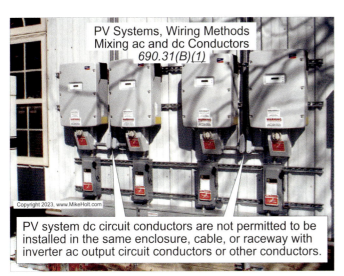
▶Figure 690-19

(3) PV system dc circuits within multiconductor jacketed cable, Type MC cable, or listed wiring harnesses identified for the application can be installed in the same enclosure, cable, or raceway with non-PV system circuits. All conductors, harnesses, or assemblies must have an insulation rating equal to at least the maximum circuit dc voltage applied to any conductor within the enclosure, cable, or raceway.

(2) Polarity Identification of Direct-Current Conductors. PV system dc circuit conductors must have all termination, connection, and splice points permanently identified for polarity by color coding, marking tape, tagging, or other approved means in accordance with 690.31(B)(2)(a) and (B)(2)(b). ▶Figure 690-20

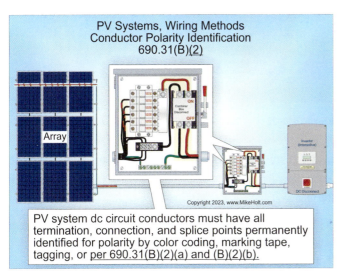
▶Figure 690-20

(a) Where color coding for polarity identification is not provided, conductors must be identified by an approved permanent marking means such as labeling, sleeving, or shrink-tubing that is suitable for the conductor size, and

(b) Must be identified by an approved marking that includes the positive sign (+) or the word "POSITIVE" or "POS" for the positive conductor and the negative sign (−) or the word "NEGATIVE" or "NEG" for the negative conductor. Polarity marking must be durable and be of a color other than green, white, gray, or red.

(3) Grouping of Direct-Current Conductors. Where PV system dc and ac circuit conductors are in the same enclosure, junction box, pull box or wireway, the PV system dc and ac circuit conductors must be grouped separately by using cable ties or similar means at least once and at intervals not to exceed 6 ft.

Ex: Grouping is not required if the dc circuit enters from a cable or raceway unique to the circuit that makes the grouping obvious.

(C) Cables. Type PV wire, Type PV cable, and Type DG cable must be listed.

(1) Exposed Conductors. Conductors for PV systems must comply with 690.31(C)(1)(a) through (C)(1)(c).

(a) Conductor Types. Conductors within the PV array that are exposed outdoors must be one of the following types: ▶Figure 690-21

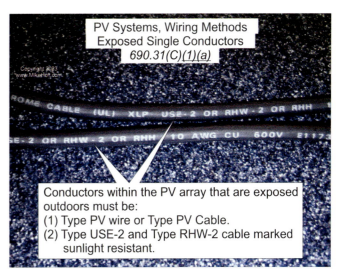
▶Figure 690-21

(1) Type PV wire or Type PV cable.

(2) Type USE-2 and Type RHW-2 cable marked sunlight resistant.

(b) Cables 8 AWG and Smaller. Exposed cables 8 AWG or smaller must be supported and secured at intervals not to exceed 24 in. by cable ties, straps, hangers, or similar fittings listed and identified for securement and support in outdoor locations.

690.31 | Solar Photovoltaic (PV) Systems

(c) Cables Larger than 8 AWG. Exposed cables larger than 8 AWG must be supported and secured at intervals not to exceed 54 in. by cable ties, straps, hangers, or similar fittings listed and identified for securement and support in outdoor locations.

(2) Cable Tray. Single-conductor Type PV wire, Type PV cable, or Type DG cable can be installed in cable trays in outdoor locations, provided the cables are supported at intervals not exceeding 12 in. and secured at intervals not exceeding 54 in.

Where installed in uncovered cable trays, the ampacity of single-conductor PV wire smaller than 1/0 AWG and the adjustment factors for 1/0 AWG single-conductor cables in 392.80(A)(2) can be used.

Where single-conductor PV wire smaller than 1/0 AWG is installed in ladder ventilated trough cable trays, the following apply:

(1) All single conductors must be installed in a single layer.

(2) Conductors that are bound together to comprise each circuit pair can be installed in other than a single layer.

(3) The sum of the diameters of all single-conductor cables must not exceed the cable tray width.

(3) Multiconductor Jacketed Cable. Where a multiconductor jacketed cable is part of a listed PV assembly, the cable must be installed in accordance with the manufacturer's instructions.

Multiconductor jacketed cable that is not part of a listed assembly or not covered in this *Code* must be installed in accordance with the product listing instructions. Multiconductor jacketed cable must be:

(1) In Raceways. Multiconductor jacketed cable on or in buildings must be installed in a raceway, except for rooftop installations.

(2) Not Within a Raceway. Where multiconductor jacketed cable is not installed within a raceway, the cable must:

    a. Be marked "Sunlight Resistant" in exposed outdoor locations.

    b. Be protected or guarded where subject to physical damage.

    c. Closely follow the surface of support structures.

    d. Be secured at intervals not exceeding 6 ft.

    e. Be secured within 24 in. of mating connectors or entering enclosures.

    f. Be marked "Direct Burial" where buried in the earth.

(4) Flexible Cords and Cables for Tracking PV Arrays. Flexible cords connected to moving parts of tracking PV arrays must be installed in accordance with Article 400, be identified as hard-service cord or portable power cable, be suitable for extra-hard usage, and be listed for outdoor use, water resistant, and sunlight resistant.

Stranded copper Type PV wire used for moving parts of tracking PV arrays must have a minimum number of strands as specified in Table 690.31(C)(4).

Table 690.31(C)(4) Minimum PV Wire Strands for Moving Parts of Tracking PV Arrays

PV Wire AWG	Minimum Strands
18	17
16–10	19
8–4	49
2	130
1 AWG–1000 MCM	259

(5) Flexible, Fine-Stranded Cables. Flexible, fine-stranded cables must terminate on terminals, lugs, devices, or connectors identified for the use of finely stranded conductors in accordance with 110.14.
▶Figure 690–22

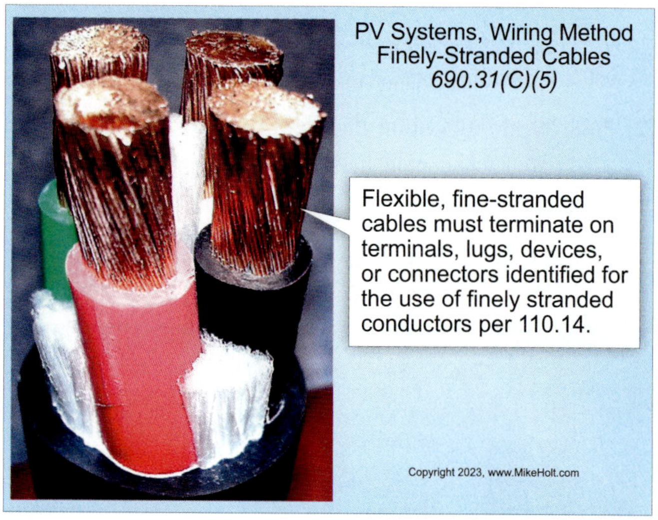

▶Figure 690–22

(D) PV System Direct-Current Circuits on or In Buildings. Wiring methods for PV system dc circuits on or in buildings must comply with the following additional requirements:

(1) Metal Raceways and Enclosures. PV system dc circuits on or inside a building must be installed in a metal raceway, Type MC cable that complies with 250.118(A)(10)(b), or a metal enclosure. ▶Figure 690–23

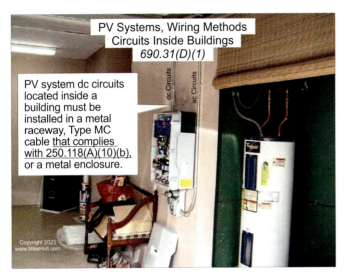

▶Figure 690-23

Ex: PV hazard control system conductors that are installed for a rapid shutdown application in accordance with 690.12(B)(2)(1) can be provided with (or listed for use with) nonmetallic enclosures, nonmetallic raceways, and permitted cable types other than Type MC cable, at the point of penetration of the building.

(2) Marking and Labeling. Unless located and arranged so the purpose is evident, the following wiring methods and enclosures on or in buildings containing PV system dc circuit conductors must be marked with a permanent label containing the words "PHOTOVOLTAIC POWER SOURCE" or "SOLAR PV DC CIRCUIT." ▶Figure 690-24

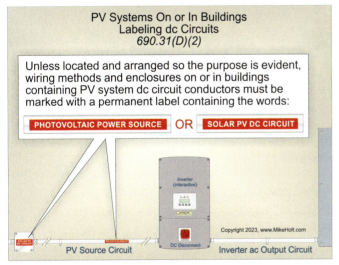

▶Figure 690-24

(1) Exposed raceways, cable trays, and other wiring methods.

(2) Covers or enclosures of pull boxes and junction boxes.

(3) Conduit bodies having unused openings.

The label must be visible after installation. The letters must be capitalized and be a minimum height of ⅜ in. in white on a red background. ▶Figure 690-25

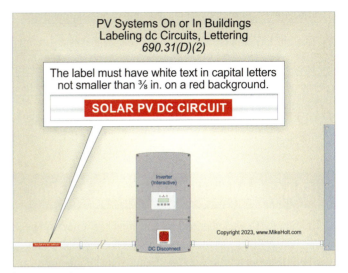

▶Figure 690-25

Labels must appear on every section of the wiring system that is separated by enclosures, walls, partitions, ceilings, or floors. Spacing between labels is not permitted to be more than 10 ft, and the label must be suitable for the environment. ▶Figure 690-26

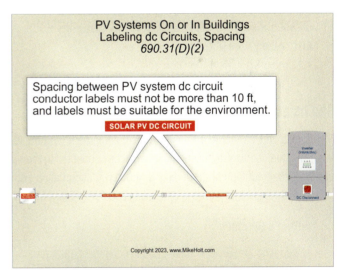

▶Figure 690-26

(F) Wiring Methods and Mounting Systems. Roof-mounted PV array mounting systems are permitted to be held in place with an approved means other than those required by 110.13. The wiring methods must allow for any expected movement of the array.

690.43 | Solar Photovoltaic (PV) Systems

(G) Over 1000V Direct Current. Equipment and wiring methods containing PV system dc circuits greater than 1000V must comply with the following:

(1) They are not permitted on or in one- and two-family dwellings.

(2) They are not permitted within buildings containing habitable rooms.

(3) They must be located not less than 10 ft above grade on the exterior of buildings and cannot be attached to the building surface for more than 33 ft from the equipment.

690.43 Equipment Grounding and Bonding

The title in (C) was changed to "Location" as it now specifies when EGCs can be run with circuit conductors and when they can be run separate from circuit conductors.

Analysis

CLARIFIED A change in the title and text clarifies that EGCs for PV system conductors within an array can be run separately from PV system conductors. But when they leave the vicinity of the PV array, the EGCs must comply with 250.134.

690.43 Equipment Grounding Conductor

Metal parts of PV module frames, electrical equipment, and enclosures containing PV system conductors must be connected to the PV system circuit equipment grounding conductor in accordance with 690.43(A) through (D) and in accordance with 250.134. ▶Figure 690–27

Author's Comment:

▸ According to 250.134, metal parts of equipment, raceways, and enclosures must be connected to one of the equipment grounding conductor types identified in 250.118(A). An equipment grounding conductor of the wire type for a dc circuit can be run separately from the circuit conductors when it is within the array [250.134 Ex 2].

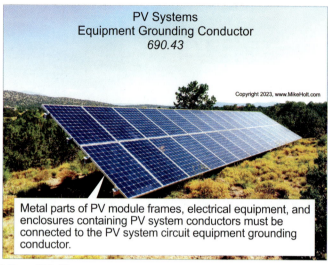

▶Figure 690–27

(C) Equipment Grounding Conductor Location.

Separate from Circuit Conductors. Equipment grounding conductors are permitted to be run separately from the PV circuit conductors within the PV array. ▶Figure 690–28

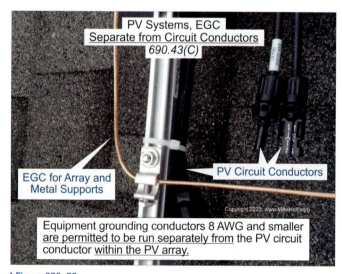

▶Figure 690–28

With Circuit Conductors. Where PV system dc circuit conductors leave the vicinity of the PV array, equipment grounding conductors must be contained in the same raceway or cable with PV circuit conductors [250.134]. ▶Figure 690–29

Solar Photovoltaic (PV) Systems | **690.56**

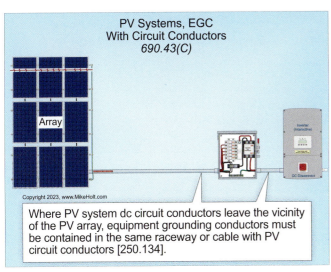
▶ Figure 690-29

690.56 Identification of Power Sources

As part of cleaning up redundant language, this section was condensed, and a reference to 705.10 informs us where we can find the information previously located here.

Analysis

REDUCED The requirements previously found here in (A) and (B) are in 705.10, so these requirements were replaced with parent text referencing 705.10.

690.56 Identification of Power Sources

A permanent plaque or directory must be installed in accordance with 705.10.

Author's Comment:

▸ Exposed equipment grounding conductors 8 AWG and smaller for dc circuits are permitted to be run separately from the circuit conductors where not subject to physical damage [250.120(C) and 250.134 Ex 2].

(D) Bonding Over 250V. The bonding requirements for metal raceways and cables containing circuits over 250V to ground [250.97] do not apply to metal raceways and cables containing dc circuit conductors.
▶ Figure 690-30

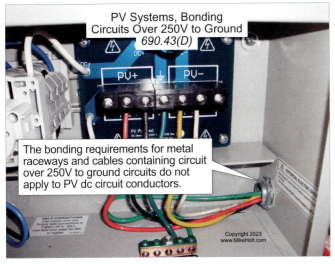
▶ Figure 690-30

Notes

ARTICLE 691 — LARGE-SCALE PHOTOVOLTAIC (PV) ELECTRIC SUPPLY SYSTEMS

Introduction to Article 691—Large-Scale Photovoltaic (PV) Electric Supply Systems

The general requirements for solar photovoltaic (PV) systems are covered by Article 690. This article defines what a large-scale photovoltaic system is and the additional requirements that must be met to take advantage of the alternative design and safety features unique to large systems. Large-scale PV systems are privately owned PV systems operated solely to provide electricity to a regulated utility as compared to the Article 690 systems that may be operated to provide power to the end user, utility, or a combination of both. Large-scale photovoltaic (PV) electric supply stations require a careful documented review of the design by an engineer to ensure safe operation and compliance with the applicable electrical standards and industry practices.

691.4 Special Requirements for Large-Scale PV Electric Supply Stations

Editorial revisions clarify how access is to be restricted to these sites and a requirement to monitor the site was added.

Analysis

EXPANDED **EDITED** List item (2) deleted the words "by fencing or other adequate means" and now references 110.31 which lists several methods by which access can be restricted to these systems.

NEW The new list item (6) requires the station to be monitored by a central command center.

RELOCATED List item (7) is new and contains information that was relocated from the scope. It tells us that a large-scale PV electric supply station must have a minimum inverter capacity of 5000 kW.

691.4 Special Requirements for Large-Scale PV Electric Supply Stations

Large-scale PV electric supply stations are only permitted to be accessible to authorized personnel and must comply with the following requirements:

(1) Electrical circuits and equipment must be maintained and operated by qualified person.

(2) PV electric supply stations must be restricted in accordance with 110.31 and have field-applied hazard markings that are permanently affixed and have sufficient durability to withstand the environment involved [110.21(B)].

(3) The connection between the PV electric supply and the utility system must be through medium- or high-voltage switch gear, substations, switchyards, or similar methods whose sole purpose is to interconnect the two systems.

(4) Loads within the PV electric supply station must only be used to power auxiliary equipment for the generation of the PV power.

(5) Large-scale PV electric supply stations are not permitted to be installed on buildings.

(6) The station is monitored from a central command center.

691.4 | Large-Scale Photovoltaic (PV) Electric Supply Systems

(7) The station has an inverter generating capacity of not less than 5000 kW.

Note: Some individual sites with capacities less than 5000 kW are operated as part of a group of facilities with a total generating capacity of much greater than 5000 kW.

ARTICLE 695 FIRE PUMPS

Introduction to Article 695—Fire Pumps

The general philosophy behind most *Code* requirements is to provide circuit overcurrent protection that will shut equipment down before allowing the supply conductors to overheat and become damaged from overload. Article 695 departs from this philosophy. The idea is that the fire pump motor must keep running no matter what! Since it supplies water to a facility's fire protection piping, which in turn supplies water to the sprinkler system and fire hoses, it is better to sacrifice the fire pump rather than the entire structure. This article contains many requirements to make certain an uninterrupted supply of water is maintained.

Some of these requirements are obvious. For example, locate the pump where its exposure to fire is minimized, which is usually in a separate space with fire-rated construction. It is important that the source of power is maintained for both the fire pump and its jockey (pressure maintenance) pump. Also, fire pump wiring must remain independent of all other wiring. Some of the requirements of Article 695 seem wrong at first glance, until you remember why that fire pump is there in the first place. For example, the disconnect must be designed to be lockable in the closed position. You would normally expect it to be lockable in the open position because other articles require that for the safety of maintenance personnel. But the fire pump runs to ensure the safety of an entire facility and for everyone within that facility. For the same reason, fire pump power circuits cannot have automatic overcurrent protection against overloads.

Remember, the fire pump must be kept in service even if doing so damages or destroys the pump. It is better to sacrifice the fire pump than to save it and lose the facility and/or its occupants. The intent of this article is to allow enough time for building occupants to escape and (if possible) to save the facility.

695.1 Scope

A new list item in (B) exempts one- and two-family dwelling unit water pumps used for fire suppression from the requirements of 695.

Analysis

REDUCED The new list item (B)(4) specifies that water pumps installed in one- and two-family dwellings for fire suppression are not covered by Article 695. The requirements for those pump motors are the same as for any other pump motor.

695.1 Scope

(A) Covered. Article 695 covers the installation of: ▶Figure 695-1

(1) Electric power sources and interconnecting circuits.

(2) Switching and control equipment dedicated to fire pump drivers.

(B) Not Covered. Article 695 does not cover:

(1) Performance, maintenance, testing, and the internal wiring of the components of the system.

(2) The installation of pressure maintenance (jockey or makeup) pumps.

Note: Article 430 governs the installation of pressure maintenance (jockey or makeup) pumps, whether they are supplied by the fire pump or not.

(3) Transfer equipment upstream of the fire pump transfer switch(es).

695.6 | Fire Pumps

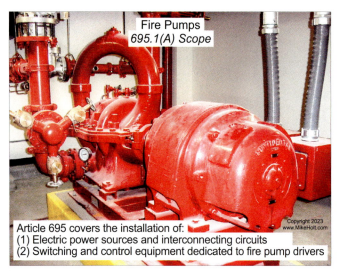

▶Figure 695–1

Author's Comment:

▸ Fire pump installations should be designed by qualified experts in the field due to the critical importance of professionally designed systems. Fire pump installations can interconnect with other systems such as backup power systems and sprinkler systems. Generally, the electrician or electrical contractor doing a fire pump installation will not be doing any calculations but following a set of specifications provided for the job.

(4) Water pumps installed in one- and two-family dwellings and used for fire suppression.

695.6 Power Wiring

Minor editorial revisions help clarify what a complete fire resistive cable system is. The text in (B)(1) was reorganized into a list, the method to determine full-load current was clarified, and raintight fittings are now required for EMT.

Analysis

 CLARIFIED Revisions to (A)(2)(4) clarify that cables and raceways listed as part of a fire-resistive cable systems or listed electrical circuit protective systems are only part of such a system but are not the complete protective system, as explained in the Informational Notes.

  REORGANIZED CLARIFIED The two conditions in (B)(1) were relocated from the subdivision text into list items. A revision to (B)(1)(1) clarifies that the full-load current found in the Tables in Article 430 should be used—not the motor nameplate. Also, the associated fire pump accessory equipment should be added at full-load current(s).

 REORGANIZED As we have seen in other long sections, (D) was split into subdivisions.

 CLARIFIED The permitted wiring methods in (D)(1) clarify the type of LFNC that may be used.

 NEW A new requirement in (D)(2) specifies that fittings must be listed for use in wet locations. This requires us to use raintight fittings for EMT installations.

695.6 Power Wiring

(D) Pump Wiring.

(1) Wiring Methods. Wiring from the fire pump controllers to the fire pump motors must be in rigid metal conduit, intermediate metal conduit, electrical metallic tubing, liquidtight flexible metal conduit, liquidtight flexible nonmetallic conduit Type LFNC-B, or listed Type MC cable with an impervious covering.

(2) Fittings. Fittings must be listed for use in wet locations.

(3) Connections. The connections in the motor terminal box must be made with a listed device. Twist-on, insulation-piercing type, and soldered wire connectors are not allowed.

695.7 Fire Pump Controller Voltage Drop

Editorial revisions clarify the meaning of the rule and correlate it with the corresponding language in NFPA 20.

Fire Pumps | 695.7

Analysis

The text was rewritten for clarity and for conformance with the requirements of NFPA 20. The general requirement did not change, but the Exception text was relocated into (B).

New rules in (C) permit the use of a variable speed pressure limiting controller but requires a means to bypass that device.

695.7 Fire Pump Controller Voltage Drop

(A) Motor Starting. The voltage at the line contact terminals of the fire pump controller is not permitted to drop more than 15 percent below the controller-rated voltage when the motor starts. ▶Figure 695–2

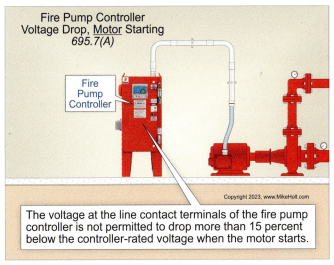

The voltage at the line contact terminals of the fire pump controller is not permitted to drop more than 15 percent below the controller-rated voltage when the motor starts.

▶Figure 695–2

(D) Motor Running. The voltage at the load contactor terminals of the fire pump controller is not permitted to drop more than 5 percent below the voltage rating of the motor when the motor runs at 115 percent of its full-load current rating. ▶Figure 695–3

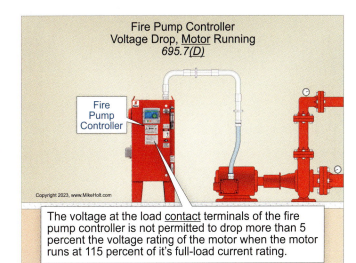

The voltage at the load contact terminals of the fire pump controller is not permitted to drop more than 5 percent the voltage rating of the motor when the motor runs at 115 percent of it's full-load current rating.

▶Figure 695–3

Author's Comment:

▸ Sizing conductors for fire pump circuits to account for start-up and running voltage drop because of low power factor during start-up must be performed by a qualified person—typically, an electrical engineer.

Notes

CHAPTER 7
SPECIAL CONDITIONS

Introduction to Chapter 7—Special Conditions

Chapter 7, which covers special conditions, is the third of the *NEC* chapters that deal with specific topics. Chapters 5 and 6 cover special occupancies, and special equipment, respectively. Remember, the first four chapters of the *Code* are sequential and form a foundation for each of the subsequent three. Chapter 8 which covers hard-wired telephones and coaxial cable is not subject to the requirements of Chapters 1 through 7 except where the requirements are specifically referenced there.

What exactly is a "Special Condition"? It is a situation that does not fall under the category of special occupancies or special equipment but creates a need for additional measures to ensure the "safeguarding of people and property" mission of the *NEC* as stated in 90.2(C).

- **Article 700—Emergency Systems.** The requirements of Article 700 apply only to the wiring methods for "Emergency Systems" that are essential for safety to human life and required by federal, state, municipal, or other regulatory codes. When normal power is lost, emergency systems must be capable of supplying emergency power in 10 seconds or less and be able to run loads for at least 2 hours on gasoline and 90 minutes on a battery.

- **Article 701—Legally Required Standby Systems.** Legally required standby systems provide electrical power to aid in firefighting, rescue operations, control of health hazards, and similar operations. They are required by federal, state, municipal, or other regulatory codes. When normal power is lost, legally required standby systems must be capable of automatically supplying standby power in 60 seconds or less and be able to run loads for at least 2 hours on gasoline and 90 minutes on a battery.

- **Article 702—Optional Standby Systems.** Optional standby systems are intended to protect public or private facilities or property where life safety does not depend on the performance of the system. These systems are typically installed to provide an alternate source of electrical power for such facilities as industrial and commercial buildings, farms, and residences, and to serve loads that, when stopped during any power outage, can cause discomfort, serious interruption of a process, or damage to a product or process. Optional standby systems are intended to supply on-site generated power, either automatically or manually, to loads selected by the customer.

- **Article 705—Interconnected Electric Power Production Sources.** It used to be that a premises having more than one electric power source was a unique situation, but as more and more facilities supplement their utility electric supply with alternate sources of energy it has become more commonplace. Alternate power sources, such as solar or wind turbines, that run in parallel with a primary utility source necessitate particular *NEC* requirements. Article 705 provides the guidance necessary to ensure a safe installation.

...

- **Article 706—Energy Storage Systems.** Energy storage systems can be (and usually are) connected to other energy sources, such as the local utility distribution system. There can be more than one source of power connected to an energy storage system and the connection to other energy sources must comply with the requirements of Article 705 which covers installation of one or more electric power production sources operating in parallel with a utility source of electricity. It might also be a good idea to be mindful of how this article correlates with other articles in the *Code* such as Articles 480, 690, 692, and 694.

- **Article 710—Stand-Alone Systems.** A "stand-alone system" is an electrical system that is self-sufficient and a completely "off the grid" source of electrical energy such as solar or wind. However, it still may be connected to a utility supply as part of an interconnected system. The fact that it can be self-sustaining is why Article 710 specifically addresses these systems.

- **Article 722—Cables for Power-limited Circuits, Fault-Managed Power Circuits, and Optical Fiber.** This Article combines common cabling requirements for Class 2 power-limited circuits [Article 725], fire alarm circuits [Article 760] and optical fiber cables [Article 770].

- **Article 724—Class 1 Power-limited Circuits.** This article covers Class 1 circuits that are power-limited and provides alternative requirements for minimum conductor sizes, overcurrent protection, insulation requirements, wiring methods, and materials. A Class 1 circuit is the wiring system between the load side of a Class 1 power source and the connected equipment [Article 100].

- **Article 725—Class 2 power-limited Circuits.** Article 725 contains the requirements for Class 2 power-limited circuits that are not an integral part of a device or appliance.

- **Article 726—Class 4 Fault-Managed Power Systems.** Article 725 contains the requirements for Class 4 Fault Managed Power Systems.

- **Article 760—Fire Alarm Systems.** This article covers the installation of wiring and equipment for fire alarm systems. It includes fire detection and alarm notification, voice, guard's tour, sprinkler waterflow, and sprinkler supervisory systems.

ARTICLE 700 — EMERGENCY SYSTEMS

Introduction to Article 700—Emergency Systems

Emergency systems are often required as a condition of an operating permit for a given facility. According to NFPA 101, *Life Safety Code*, emergency power systems are generally installed where artificial illumination is required for safe exiting and for panic control in buildings subject to occupancy by large numbers of people such as high-rise buildings, jails, sports arenas, schools, health care facilities, and similar structures.

The authority having jurisdiction makes the determination as to whether such a system is necessary for a given facility and what it must entail. Sometimes an emergency system simply provides power for exit lighting and exit signs upon loss of the main power or in the case of fire. Its purpose is not to provide power for normal business operations, but rather to provide lighting and controls essential for human life safety.

The general goal is to keep the emergency operation as reliable as possible. The emergency system must be able to supply all emergency loads simultaneously. When the emergency supply also supplies power for other nonemergency loads, the emergency loads take priority over the others. Those other loads must be subject to automatic load pickup and load shedding to support the emergency loads if the emergency system does not have adequate capacity and rating for all loads simultaneously.

As you study Article 700, keep in mind that emergency systems are essentially lifelines for people. The entire article is based on keeping those lifelines from breaking.

700.1 Scope

A new Informational Note, relocated here from the definitions, provides a great description of why emergency systems are installed.

Analysis

NEW Although the *Code* is not designed to be used by the untrained, sometimes giving a little context brings clarity to the reason behind a rule. A new Informational Note 1 added in the scope section provides just that type of information about where emergency systems are installed. It is important to understand that Article 700 does not tell you when these systems are necessary, only the requirements for their installation.

CLARIFIED Informational Note 5 was clarified and informs us that emergency systems are considered Level 1 systems, where an equipment failure could result in death or serious injury.

700.1 Scope

Article 700 applies to the electrical safety of the installation, operation, and maintenance of emergency power systems. These consist of circuits and equipment intended to supply illumination, power, or both within 10 seconds [700.12] when the normal electrical supply is interrupted. ▶Figure 700-1

700.3 | Emergency Systems

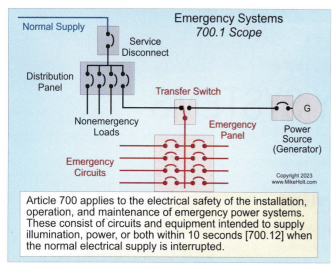

▶Figure 700-1

Some examples of circuits for which emergency power is required are those supplying egress lighting, exit signs, fire alarms, fire pumps, and voice evacuation.

Note 1: Emergency systems are generally installed in places of assembly where artificial illumination is required for safe exiting and for panic control in buildings subject to occupancy by large numbers of persons such as hotels, theaters, sports arenas, health care facilities, and similar institutions. Emergency systems may also provide power for such functions as ventilation where essential to maintain life, fire detection and alarm systems, elevators, fire pumps, public safety announcing systems, industrial processes where current interruption would produce serious life safety or health hazards, and similar functions.

Note 4: For specific locations of emergency lighting requirements, see NFPA 101, *Life Safety Code*.

> **Author's Comment:**
> ▸ According to NFPA 101, *Life Safety Code*, emergency power systems are generally installed where artificial illumination is required for safe exiting and for panic control in buildings subject to occupancy by large numbers of people. Some examples are high-rise buildings, jails, sports arenas, schools, health care facilities, and similar structures.

Note 5: For specific performance requirements of emergency power systems, see NFPA 110, *Standard for Emergency and Standby Power Systems*.

700.3 Tests and Maintenance

Changes to test and maintenance protocols now require emergency systems to be commissioned. Other changes to the rules for temporary power sources require listed interlocking equipment, and a permanent label outside the connection for temporary power.

Analysis

EXPANDED Revisions to (A) now require commissioning and not just testing of the emergency system. The term "commissioning" is defined in Article 100, in part, as the process, procedures, and testing used to set up and verify the operation of electrical devices and equipment, prior to it being placed into active service.

700.3 Tests and Maintenance

(A) Commissioning Witness Test. To ensure the emergency power system meets or exceeds the original installation specifications, the authority having jurisdiction must conduct or witness the commissioning of the emergency power system upon completion.

Note: See NECA 90, *Standard for Commissioning Building Electrical Systems*.

(B) Periodic Testing. Emergency power systems must be periodically tested on a schedule approved by the authority having jurisdiction to ensure adequate maintenance has been performed and the systems are in proper operating condition.

> **Author's Comment:**
> ▸ Running the emergency power system under its maximum anticipated load and making sure power is transferred within 10 seconds is often considered an acceptable method of operational testing.

(C) Maintenance. Emergency system equipment must be maintained in accordance with manufacturer's instructions and industry standards.

(D) Written Record. A written record of the acceptance test, periodic testing, and maintenance must be kept.

Emergency Systems | 700.8

Author's Comment:
▸ The *NEC* does not specify the required record retention period.

700.4 Capacity and Rating

Requirements were added to accommodate large transient loads when sizing emergency power sources, editorial revisions clarify the application of these rules, and a new subdivision provides rules for parallel power sources.

Analysis

EXPANDED The capacity of an emergency system is a life-or-death issue. Revisions to (A) require emergency systems to have adequate capacity to support the Article 220 load calculations, and now must also have sufficient capacity for any expected rapid load changes caused by equipment like a motor starting. A generator sized to the calculated load may not be able to start a large motor and this change addresses that fact.

CLARIFIED The phrase "load pickup and load shedding" in (B) was replaced with "load management" in both the title and text. This makes application of the rule broad and includes both load pickup and load shedding.

700.4 Capacity and Rating

(A) Capacity. An emergency power system must have adequate system capacity in accordance with Article 220 or by another approved method.

The system capacity must be sufficient for the rapid load changes and transient power and energy requirements associated with any expected loads.

(B) Selective Load Management. The electric power production system is permitted to supply emergency, legally required standby, and optional standby system loads where a load management system includes automatic selective load pickup and load shedding to ensure adequate power to the following:

(1) Emergency circuits

(2) Legally required standby circuits

(3) Optional standby circuits

700.6 Signals

An expansion to the rules in this section require network annunciation of fault signals, and the required battery charging signal was clarified.

Analysis

EXPANDED An expansion to this rule now requires network remote annunciation devices to be provided, where applicable, to indicate the system conditions.

CLARIFIED The title and text of (C) were clarified to tell us that only a battery charger "that is required for source readiness" must provide a signal when the charger is not working. This includes the prime mover start battery.

700.8 Surge Protection

Surge protection is now required for emergency system switchgear.

Analysis

EXPANDED The 2020 *Code* only required SPDs for emergency system switchboards and panelboards. This change recognizes that switchgear is also used for emergency systems and therefore require SPDs.

700.8 Surge Protection

A listed surge-protective device must be installed for all emergency system switchgear, switchboards, and panelboards. ▸Figure 700–2

700.11 | Emergency Systems

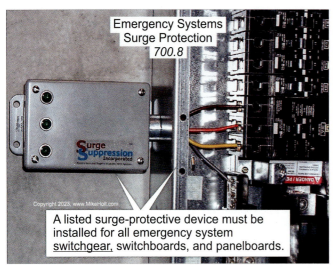

A listed surge-protective device must be installed for all emergency system switchgear, switchboards, and panelboards.

▸Figure 700–2

700.11 Wiring, Class-2-Powered Emergency Lighting Systems

Since the PoE lighting train is gaining momentum, a new section for Class 2 wiring provides the requirements for these systems. This is a great start!

Analysis

NEW — This new section addresses technologies such as PoE and other emergency lighting systems that utilize Class 2 power. The other rules in this article address line voltage systems and this new section provides requirements for low-voltage emergency systems. This section is a great start and I know we will see continued improvement to the rules as they mature.

700.11 Wiring, Class-2-Powered Emergency Lighting Systems

(A) General. Line voltage supply wiring and Class 2 power-limited emergency lighting control devices must comply with 700.10.

Class 2 power-limited emergency circuits must comply with 700.11(B) through (D).

(B) Identification. Class 2 power-limited emergency circuits must be permanently marked so they will be readily identified as a component of an emergency circuit or system by the following methods:

(1) All boxes and enclosures for Class 2 power-limited emergency circuits must be permanently marked as a component of an emergency circuit or system.

(2) Exposed cable, cable tray, or raceway systems must be permanently marked to be identified as a component of an emergency circuit or system within 3 ft of each connector and at intervals not to exceed 25 ft.

(C) Separation of Circuits. Class 2 power-limited emergency circuits must be wired in a listed, jacketed cable or with one of the wiring methods of Chapter 3. If installed alongside nonemergency Class 2 power-limited circuits that are bundled, Class 2 power-limited emergency circuits must be bundled separately. If installed alongside nonemergency Class 2 power-limited circuits that are not bundled, Class 2 power-limited emergency circuits must be separated by a nonconductive sleeve or nonconductive barrier from all other Class 2 power-limited circuits. Separation from other circuits must comply with 725.136.

(D) Protection. Wiring must comply with the requirements of 300.4 and be installed in a raceway, armored or metal-clad cable, or cable tray.

Ex 1: Section 700.11(D) does not apply to wiring that does not exceed 6 ft in length and that terminates at an emergency luminaire or an emergency lighting control device.

Ex 2: Section 700.11(D) does not apply to locked rooms or locked enclosures that are accessible only to qualified persons.

Note: Locked rooms accessible only to qualified persons include locked telecommunications rooms, locked electrical equipment rooms, or other access-controlled areas.

700.12 General Requirements

The reorganization and expansion of this section clarifies what the rules are for the different types of emergency supply sources, recognize that the normal power source may not be the utility, add ac microgrid systems to the mix, and clarify the rules for emergency power used for fire protection, suppression, ventilation, and separation systems.

Emergency Systems | **700.12**

Analysis

EXPANDED   REORGANIZED   Most of the requirements found in (C) were relocated here from 700.12(D)(2). These rules previously only applied to storage batteries, but now cover the supply duration for all types of emergency supply systems. Most of the references to batteries were removed and now simply say that the energy storage system must have the capacity to supply the required load. Other editorial revisions in list items (1) through (5) clarify the requirements for different types of supply systems.

CLARIFIED   The rule in (D)(1) was revised to say that a prime mover driven generator set must automatically start upon failure of the normal "power source." This recognizes that, in some cases, the utility service does not provide the normal power.

EXPANDED   Subdivision (E) was expanded to include stored-energy power supplies, other than a UPS. The rule goes on in (E)(1) to specify the different types of systems permitted, and (E)(2) details the requirements for fire protection, suppression, ventilation, and separation for the systems.

EXPANDED   In the 2020 *Code* the rules in (H) only applied to dc microgrids. Since there are both dc and ac microgrid systems, "dc" was removed from the rule title and text of this subdivision, and it was relabeled (G).

EXPANDED   The rules in (H) were relocated here from (I) "Unit Equipment" in the 2020 *Code* and only applied to self-contained battery-powered emergency luminaires. Changes this cycle expanded the scope to cover all types of battery-equipped emergency luminaires—not just unit equipment. This resulted in the section being retitled as "Battery-Equipped Emergency Luminaires." Other revisions include a new requirement for the product to be listed, removal of the battery capacity requirements, a new requirement that allows the luminaire to be cord-connected per 410.62(C)(1), and a clarification to the existing rule in (2)(3)(b) that permits the emergency luminaire to be connected to both a branch circuit and the switched conductor for the lights, if the emergency function of the luminaire works regardless of the switch position.

700.12 General Requirements

Emergency power must be available within 10 seconds in the event of failure of the normal power to the building. ▶Figure 700-3

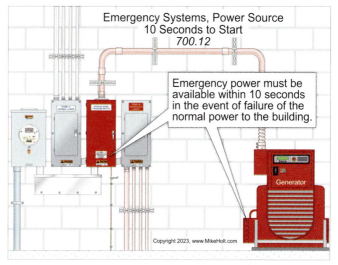

▶Figure 700-3

The emergency power supply must be any of the following:

(A) Power Source Considerations. In selecting an emergency source of power, consideration must be given to the occupancy and the type of service to be rendered, whether of minimum duration as for evacuation of a theater, or longer duration as for supplying emergency power and lighting due to an indefinite period of current failure from trouble either inside or outside the building.

(B) Equipment Design and Location. Equipment must be designed and located to minimize the hazards that might cause complete failure due to flooding, fires, icing, and vandalism.

(C) Supply Duration. The emergency power source must be of suitable rating and capacity to supply and maintain the total load for the duration determined by the system design. In no case must the duration be less than 2 hours of system operation unless used for emergency illumination in 700.12(C)(4) or unit equipment in 700.12(I).

Note: For information on classification of emergency power supply systems, see NFPA 110, *Standard for Emergency and Standby Power Systems*.

(4) Storage Battery and UPS Systems. Storage batteries and uninterruptible power supply (UPS) systems used to supply emergency illumination must be of suitable rating and capacity to supply and maintain the total load for a period of not less than 90 minutes, without the voltage applied to the load falling below 87½ percent of the nominal voltage. Automotive-type batteries are not permitted for this purpose. Automatic battery charging means must be provided.

> **Author's Comment:**
> ▸ Uninterruptible power supplies (UPS) generally include a rectifier, a storage battery, and an inverter to convert direct current (dc) to alternating current (ac).

(D) Generators.

(1) Prime Mover-Driven. A generator approved by the authority having jurisdiction and sized in accordance with 700.4 is permitted as the emergency power source if it has means to automatically start the prime mover when the normal power source fails.

(E) Stored-Energy Power Supply Systems.

(1) Types. Stored-energy power supply systems must be one of the following types:

(1) Uninterruptible power supply (UPS)

(2) Fuel cell system

(3) Energy storage system

(4) Storage battery

(5) Other approved equivalent stored energy sources that comply with 700.12

(F) Separate Service. An additional service is permitted as the emergency power source where approved by the authority having jurisdiction [230.2(A)] and the following: ▸Figure 700-4

(1) Separate service conductors are installed from the utility.

(2) The emergency service conductors are electrically and physically remote from other service conductors to minimize the possibility of simultaneous interruption of supply.

> **Author's Comment:**
> ▸ To minimize the possibility of simultaneous interruption, the service disconnect for the emergency system must be located remotely from the other power system's service disconnect [230.72(B)].

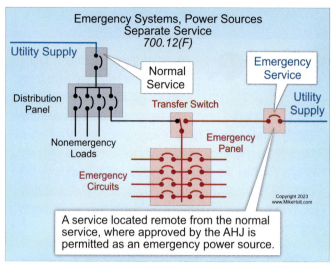

▸Figure 700-4

(H) Battery-Equipped Emergency Luminaires.

(1) Listing. All battery-equipped emergency luminaires must be listed.

(2) Installation of Battery-Equipped Emergency Luminaires.

(1) Battery-equipped emergency luminaires must be permanently fixed in place (not portable).

(2) Wiring to each luminaire must be installed in accordance with any Chapter 3 wiring method, or a cord-and-plug connection with a flexible cord not more than 3 ft in length. Flexible cord, with or without a plug, for unit equipment is permitted for battery-equipped emergency luminaires installed in accordance with 410.62(C)(1).

(3) The branch-circuit(s) wiring that supplies battery-equipped emergency luminaires must be one of the following:

  a. The branch circuit serving the normal lighting in the area, with a connection ahead of any local switches. ▸Figure 700-5

  b. The branch circuits serving the normal lighting in the area, if that branch circuit is equipped with means to monitor the status of the area's normal lighting branch circuit ahead of any local switches.

  c. A separate branch circuit originating from the same panelboard as the normal lighting circuits that is provided with a lock-on feature.

Emergency Systems | 700.27

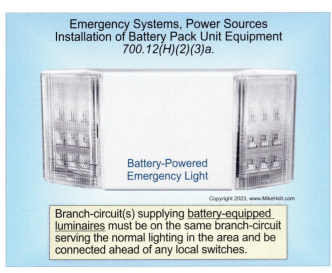

▶Figure 700–5

Author's Comment:

▶ There are two reasons why the battery-equipped emergency luminaire (battery pack) unit equipment must be connected ahead of the switch controlling the normal area lighting: (1) in the event of a power loss to the lighting circuit, the battery-equipped emergency luminaire lighting packs will activate and provide emergency lighting for people to exit the building, and (2) the battery-equipped emergency luminaire will not turn on when the switch controlling normal lighting is turned off.

(4) The branch circuit that feeds the battery-equipped emergency luminaires must be clearly identified at the distribution panel.

Author's Comment:

▶ Identification and marking must be in accordance with 110.22(A) and 408.4(A).

(6) Power for remote luminaries providing the exterior lighting of an exit door can be supplied by the battery-equipped emergency luminaries serving the area immediately inside the exit door.

700.27 Class 2 Powered Emergency Lighting Systems

This is a new section acknowledging the advances in PoE emergency lighting. We finally have "smart" Class 2 emergency lighting systems that are revolutionizing emergency egress lighting.

Analysis

NEW
Where a device combines control signals with Class 2 emergency power on a single circuit, the device must be listed as an emergency lighting control device. An Informational Note tells us that an example of this type of system is a Power over Ethernet (PoE) switch. UL 924 provides the listing requirements for this type of system.

700.27 Class 2 Powered Emergency Lighting Systems

Devices that combine control signals with Class 2 emergency power on a single circuit must be listed as emergency lighting control devices.

Note: An example of a device combining control signals with Class 2 emergency power sources is a Power over Ethernet (PoE) switch.

Notes

ARTICLE 701 — LEGALLY REQUIRED STANDBY SYSTEMS

Introduction to Article 701—Legally Required Standby Systems

In the hierarchy of electrical systems, Article 700 Emergency Systems receives top priority. Taking the number two spot is Legally Required Standby Systems which fall under Article 701. Legally required standby systems must supply standby power in 60 seconds or less after a power loss. Some examples of required standby circuits are those supplying fire command center power and lighting, ventilation and automatic fire detection, and egress elevators.

Article 700 basically applies to systems or equipment required to protect people who are in an emergency and trying to get out, while Article 701 addresses systems or equipment needed to help people responding to the emergency.

701.3 Commissioning and Maintenance

Changes to test and maintenance protocols now require legally required standby systems to be commissioned, resulting in a change to the title and text.

Analysis

EXPANDED Revisions to (A) now require commissioning and not just testing of the legally required standby system. The term "commissioning" is defined in Article 100, in part, as the process, procedures, and testing used to set up and verify the operation of electrical devices and equipment, prior to it being placed into active service.

701.3 Commissioning and Maintenance

(A) Commissioning or Witness Test. To ensure that the legally required standby system meets or exceeds the original installation specifications, the authority having jurisdiction must conduct or witness the commissioning of the legally required system upon completion of the installation.

(B) Periodic Testing. Legally required standby systems must be periodically tested in a manner approved by the authority having jurisdiction to ensure adequate maintenance has been performed and the systems are in proper operating condition.

Author's Comment:

▸ Running the legally required standby system under the loads of the facility to make sure power transfers within 60 seconds is often considered an acceptable method of operational testing.

(C) Maintenance. Legally required standby system equipment must be maintained in accordance with the manufacturer's instructions and industry standards.

(D) Written Record. A written record must be kept of all required tests and maintenance.

Author's Comment:

▸ The *NEC* does not specify the required record retention period.

701.4 | Legally Required Standby Systems

701.4 Capacity and Rating

Requirements were added to (B) that accommodate large transient loads when sizing legally required power sources. Other editorial revisions clarify the application of these rules, and a new subdivision provides rules for parallel power sources.

Analysis

EXPANDED The capacity of a legally required standby system can be a life-or-death issue. Revisions to (B) require these systems to have adequate capacity to support the Article 220 load calculations, and now must also have sufficient capacity for any expected rapid load changes caused by equipment like a motor starting. A generator sized to the calculated load may not be able to start a large motor and this change addresses that.

CLARIFIED The phrase "load pickup and load shedding" in (C) was replaced with "load management" in both the title and text. This makes application of the rule broad and includes both load pickup and load shedding.

701.4 Capacity and Rating

(A) Rating. Equipment for a legally required standby system must be suitable for the available fault current at its terminals.

(B) Capacity. The alternate power supply must have adequate capacity in accordance with Parts I through IV of Article 220 or by another approved method. The system capacity must be sufficient for the rapid load changes, and transient power and energy requirements associated with any expected loads.

(C) Load Management. The legally required standby alternate power supply can supply legally required standby and optional standby system loads if there is adequate capacity, or where a load management system includes automatic selective load pickup and load shedding is provided that will ensure adequate power to the legally required standby system circuits.

ARTICLE 702 OPTIONAL STANDBY SYSTEMS

Introduction to Article 702—Optional Standby Systems

Taking third priority after emergency and legally required systems, optional standby systems protect public or private facilities or property where life safety does not depend on the performance of the system. These systems are not required for rescue operations.

Suppose a glass plant loses power. Once glass hardens in the equipment (which it will do when process heat is lost) the plant is going to suffer a great deal of downtime and expense before it can resume operations. An optional standby system can prevent this loss.

You will see these systems in facilities where loss of power can cause economic loss or business interruptions. Data centers can lose millions of dollars from a single minute of lost power. A chemical or pharmaceutical plant can lose an entire batch from a single momentary power glitch. In many cases, the lost revenue cannot be recouped.

This article also applies to the installation of optional standby generators in homes, farms, small businesses, and many other applications where standby power is not legally required. ▶Figure 702–1

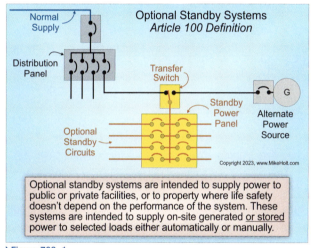
▶Figure 702–1

702.4 Capacity and Rating

A revision to the terminology in (A) allows the rule text to match the standard for this equipment, and a new Informational Note tells us what "nonautomatic" actually means.

Analysis

CLARIFIED The term "nonautomatic" was added to the title and text of (A)(1) to correlate with the product standards for this type of equipment. Also, a new Informational Note tells us manual and nonautomatic transfer equipment require human intervention.

EDITED The title, "Load Management System" was replaced with "Energy Management System (EMS)" in (2)(b) for consistency with Article 750 and throughout the *Code*.

702.4 Capacity and Rating

(A) System Capacity.

(1) Manual and Nonautomatic Load Connection. If the connection of a load is manual or nonautomatic, an optional standby system must be capable of supplying all the equipment intended to be operated at one time. The user of the optional standby system is permitted to select the load connected to the system. ▶Figure 702–2

702.5 | Optional Standby Systems

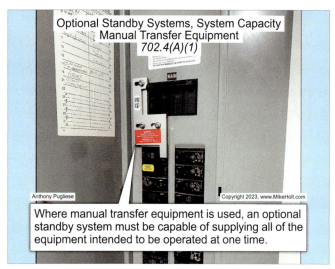

▶Figure 702–2

Note: Manual and nonautomatic transfer switches require human intervention.

Author's Comment:

▶ When a manual transfer switch is used, the user of the optional standby system selects the loads to be connected to the system, which determines the system's kVA/kW rating.

(2) Automatic Load Connection. If the connection for a load is automatic, an optional standby generator must be sized to the calculated load in accordance with Parts I through IV of Article 220 or by another approved method. ▶Figure 702–3

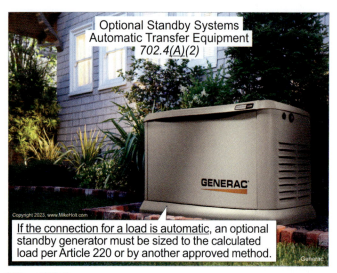

▶Figure 702–3

(a) Full Load. The standby source must be capable of supplying the full load that is automatically connected.

(b) Energy Management System (EMS). Where an automatic energy management system is employed in accordance with 705.30, the standby system must be capable of supplying the full load that will be connected.

Author's Comment:

▶ For existing facilities, the maximum demand data for one year or the average power demand for a 15-minute period over a minimum of 30 days can be used to size the electric power source [220.87]. ▶Figure 702–4

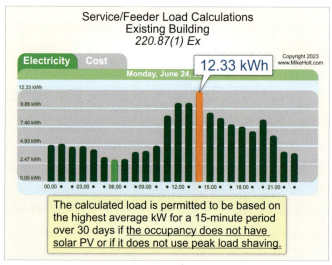

▶Figure 702–4

702.5 Interconnection or Transfer Equipment

A minor editorial revision officially adds interconnected equipment, and relocated rules made this section very user friendly.

Optional Standby Systems | 702.12

Analysis

CLARIFIED "Interconnection" was added to the title and text of (A) because the equipment used to connect multimode inverters and microgrid systems is called "interconnection equipment"—not "transfer equipment." On another note, the rules about inadvertent connection of sources previously located in (D) were relocated here.

702.5 Interconnection Device or Transfer Switch

(A) General. An interconnection device or transfer switch (manual or automatic) is required for the connection of an optional standby system. ▶Figure 702–5

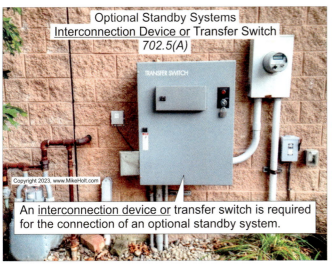
▶Figure 702–5

Interconnection devices or transfer switches must be suitable for the intended use and be listed, designed, and installed to prevent the inadvertent interconnection of all sources of supply in any operation of the equipment.

Ex: Temporary connection of a portable generator without a transfer switch is permitted where conditions of maintenance and supervision ensure that only qualified persons will service the installation, and where the normal supply is physically isolated by a lockable disconnect or by the disconnection of the normal supply conductors.

(B) Meter-Mounted Transfer Switches. A listed meter-mounted transfer switch is permitted to be installed between the utility meter and the meter enclosure. ▶Figure 702–6

▶Figure 702–6

Note 2: Manual and nonautomatic transfer switches use human intervention.

(C) Documentation. In other than dwelling units, the short-circuit current rating of the transfer switch must be field marked on the exterior of the transfer switch.

702.12 Portable Outdoor Generators

A change in (B) no longer permits the flanged inlet for portable generators to be in your garage.

Analysis

EXPANDED It is a common practice in many areas of the country to install the connection for a portable generator in the garage. A revision to (B) now requires the flanged inlet or other cord-and-plug-type connection for the generator to be located on the outside of the building or structure.

702.12 Portable Outdoor Generators

(A) Greater Than 15 kW and Permanently Installed. Where the disconnect of an outdoor generator is readily accessible and within sight of the building or structure supplied, an additional disconnect is not required for the building.

702.12 | Optional Standby Systems

(B) Generators 15 kW or Less. The flanged inlet for a portable generator rated 15 kW or less must be located outside a building or structure.
▶Figure 702-7

▶Figure 702-7

ARTICLE 705: INTERCONNECTED ELECTRIC POWER PRODUCTION SOURCES

Introduction to Article 705—Interconnected Electric Power Production Sources

Anytime there is more than one source of power supplying a building, safety concerns arise. In cases where a source such as a generator is used strictly for backup power, Articles 700, 701, or 702 require transfer switches and other safety measures to be implemented. When interconnected electrical power production sources, such as wind-powered generators, solar PV systems, or fuel cells are connected in parallel with utility power, there is no transfer switch. In fact, there will often be multiple sources of electrical supply connected simultaneously.

Article 705 covers the requirements for the interconnection of electric power sources that operate in parallel with a primary source. The primary source is typically the electric utility power source, but it can be an on-site source.

705.6 Equipment Approval

New Informational Notes were added that may be very helpful to AHJs.

Analysis

NEW The new Informational Note 1 identifies the standard used to evaluate interactive equipment and a new Informational Note 2 contains information that simplifies understanding the mandatory requirements.

Note 1: See UL 1741, *Standard for Inverters, Converters, Controllers, and Interconnection System Equipment for Use with Distributed Energy Resources*, for evaluating interconnected equipment. Sources identified as stand-alone, interactive, or multimode are specifically identified and certified to operate in these operational modes. Stand-alone sources operate in island mode, interactive sources operate in interactive mode, and multimode sources operate in either island mode or interactive mode. Stand-alone sources are not evaluated for interactive capabilities.

Note 2: An interactive function is common in equipment such as microgrid interconnect devices, power control systems, interactive inverters, engine generators, energy storage equipment, and wind turbines.

705.6 Equipment Approval

Interconnection and interactive equipment intended to operate in parallel with electric power production sources must be listed or be evaluated for the required interactive function and have a field label applied, or both.

705.11 Source Connections to a Service

There was a lot of reorganization here with a few technical changes and some clarifications. Clarifications about conductor sizing, line-side connection rules, and bonding and grounding requirements are just a few of the highlights. If you work in this industry, spend some time becoming familiar with the new layout. You will love it.

705.11 | Interconnected Electric Power Production Sources

Analysis

CLARIFIED Revisions to the title and text clarify that these rules apply to any connection to a service. Whether it be a new service dedicated to the power production equipment, or a connection to an existing building service, these rules apply!

NEW This revised subdivision, (A), allows an electric power production source to be connected to a service by one of three methods.

CLARIFIED The conductors indicated in (B), those between the power production source and the service, must have an ampacity equal to the maximum output current of the power production source and the conductors that connect the power production output to the service are service conductors. This clears up some long-standing confusion.

RELOCATED REORGANIZED The connection requirements in (C) are not new, they are just relocated rules from (D) from the previous *Code*, reorganized into a list format. In addition, the reference to 110.14 was replaced with references to 230.33 and 230.46 for splice and tap connections to service conductors.

NEW The new subdivision (D) adds the rules for a line-side connection of a power production source, makes it clear that the disconnect is a service disconnect, and says that the power production equipment connection must comply with Parts VI through VIII of Article 230. This clears up our long-standing confusion on what this disconnect really is.

NEW A new subdivision (E), covering the bonding and grounding of power production equipment connected to a service, simply requires the equipment to be bonded in accordance with Parts II through V and VIII of Article 250. This means power production equipment is installed just like any other service equipment!

RELOCATED Subdivision (F) contains a retitled and reorganized version of the previous (E) with a simplified version of (C) thrown in for good measure. It is titled "Overcurrent Protection" and includes ground-fault protection and overcurrent protection.

705.11 Service Connections

(A) Service Connections. Electric power production sources are permitted to be connected to:

> **Author's Comment:**
>
> ▸ An electric power production source includes electrical generating equipment up to the system disconnect supplied by any source of electrical power other than the electric utility [Article 100].

(1) A new service in accordance with 230.2(A).

(2) The supply side of an existing service as permitted by 230.82(6).
▸Figure 705–1

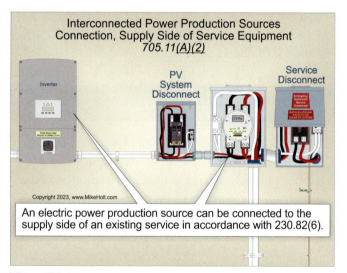

▸Figure 705–1

The connection must comply with 705.11(B) through (F).

(B) Conductor Sizing. Electric power production source connections must comply with all the following:

(1) Conductors must have an ampacity of not less than the sum of the power production source current as determined by 705.28(A).

(2) Conductors to the power production source disconnect must be sized in accordance with 705.28, but not smaller than 6 AWG copper or 4 AWG aluminum or copper-clad aluminum.

(3) The ampacity of any other conductors to which the power production sources are connected must not be less than that required in 705.11(B).

(C) Conductor Connections. Connections to service conductors or equipment must comply with the following:

(1) Splices or Taps. Service conductor splices and taps must be in accordance with 230.46.

> **Authors Comment:**
> ▸ According to 230.46, pressure connectors, devices for splices and tap connections, and power distribution blocks installed on service conductors must be listed and marked "suitable for use on the line side of the service equipment" or equivalent.

(2) Existing Equipment. Modifications to existing equipment to accommodate the supply-side connection must be in accordance with the manufacturer's instructions or the equipment modification(s) must be field evaluated for the application and be field labeled.

(3) Utility-Controlled Equipment. Supply-side connections within meter socket enclosures under the exclusive control of the electric utility are only permitted where approved by the electric utility.

(D) Service Disconnecting Means. Ungrounded conductors of a power production source must have a disconnecting means in accordance with Parts VI through VIII of Article 230.

(E) Bonding and Grounding. Metal enclosures, metal wiring methods, and metal parts associated with the service connection to a power production source must be bonded in accordance with Article 250, Parts II through V and VIII.

(F) Overcurrent Protection. The power production source conductors must have overcurrent protection in accordance with Article 230, Part VII.

705.13 Energy Management Systems (EMS)

This section has a new name and a new look, but it still covers the same applications!

Analysis

EDITED This section was retitled "Energy Management Systems (EMS)" and vastly simplified. It now only says that an EMS installed in accordance with 750.30 can limit the current and loading on busbars and conductors supplied by the output of electric power production or energy storage sources.

705.13 Energy Management Systems

An energy management system in accordance with 750.30 is permitted to limit current and loading on the busbars and conductors supplied by the output of one or more interconnected electric power production or energy storage sources.

Note: A listed power control system (PCS) is a type of EMS that is capable of monitoring multiple power sources and controlling the current on busbars and conductors to prevent overloading. See UL 1741, *Inverters, Converters, Controllers, and Interconnection System Equipment for Use with Distributed Energy Resources*, and UL 916, *Energy Management Equipment,* for information on PCS and EMS.

705.28 Circuit Sizing and Current

There are often language barriers between trade slang and the technical terms of the *Code*. Changes in this section attempt to bridge that gap with better technical language that reflects what is understood in the field.

Analysis

CLARIFIED Revisions to the text and the title of (A) clarify that the rule is about the maximum output of the of the power production source. The parent text is followed by three list items telling us how the maximum output current is to be determined. Other clarifications in (B) say the conductors being addressed are the power source output conductors. Three new Exceptions to (B)(1) provide relief to these rules under specific scenarios.

705.28 Power Production Source Circuit Current

(A) Power Production Source Output. The maximum power source output current from power production equipment is determined as follows:

(1) Equipment Nameplate. The continuous output current rating at the circuit nominal system voltage of the power production equipment.
▶Figure 705–2

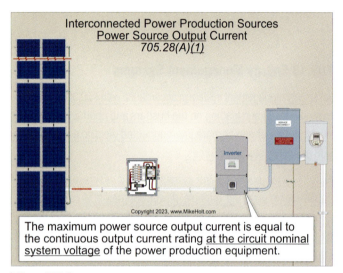

▶Figure 705–2

(2) Energy Management System. The current set point of the energy management system establishes the maximum power source output current for power production equipment.

(B) Power Source Circuit Ampacity. Power source circuit output conductors from power production equipment must be sized to the largest of the following:

(1) One hundred twenty-five percent of the maximum continuous output current rating of the power production equipment [705.28(A)] without conductor ampacity correction and/or adjustment [310.14].

Ex 1: If the assembly, including the overcurrent protective devices protecting the circuit, is listed for operation at 100 percent of its rating, the ampacity of the conductors can be sized at not less than the calculated maximum current of 705.28(A).

Ex 2: Where a portion of a circuit is connected at both its supply and load ends to separately installed pressure connections as covered in 110.14(C)(2), the circuit can have an ampacity of not less than the calculated maximum current of 705.28(A). No portion of the circuit installed under this exception must extend into an enclosure containing either the circuit supply or the circuit load terminations, as covered in 110.14(C)(1).

Ex 3: Neutral conductors that are not connected to an overcurrent protective device can be sized at 100 percent of the calculated maximum current of 705.28(A).

(2) One hundred percent of the maximum continuous output current rating of the power production equipment [705.28(A)] after conductor ampacity correction and/or adjustment [310.15].

(3) Power source circuit conductor taps for power production equipment must have an ampacity in accordance with 240.21(B) [705.12(A)(3)].
▶Figure 705–3

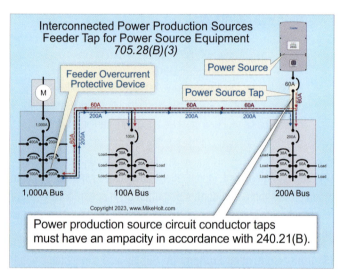

▶Figure 705–3

(C) Neutral Conductors. Neutral conductors may be sized in accordance with either of the following:

(1) Single-Phase Line-to-Neutral Power Sources. The ampacity of a neutral conductor to which a single-phase line-to-neutral power source is connected is not permitted to be less than the ampacity calculation in accordance with 705.28(B).

(2) Neutral Conductor for Instrumentation, Voltage Detection, or Phase Detection. A neutral conductor to power production equipment used solely for instrumentation, voltage detection, or phase detection can be sized in accordance with Table 250.102(C)(1).

705.30 Overcurrent Protection

Relocated rules from 705.12 make an appearance here where they belong, generator requirements were removed, a nagging question about which side of the transformer is the primary was answered, and a general reorganization of all the rules into a list format made the whole section easier to navigate and understand.

Analysis

RELOCATED The rules shown as new in (C), (D), and (E) are really relocated requirements from 705.12(C), (D), and (E). There were no technical changes, but this is where they belonged.

EXPANDED The rules in (F) were reorganized into a list format. Revisions in (F)(1) clarify that when a transformer has sources connected to both sides, the primary side is the one connected to the source with the highest available fault current. We finally know which side of the transformer is the primary!

DELETED Since there were no modifications to the generator rules in 705, (G) was deleted so we have less to step over in this section.

705.30 Overcurrent Protection, Power Source Output Circuits and Equipment

(A) Circuits and Equipment. Power source output circuit conductors and equipment must have overcurrent protection. ▶Figure 705–4

(B) Overcurrent Device Ratings. The overcurrent protective device for power source output circuit conductors and equipment must have an ampere rating of not less than 125 percent of the maximum current as calculated in 705.28(A).

Ex: Where the assembly, together with its overcurrent protective device(s) is listed for continuous operation at 100 percent of its rating, the overcurrent protective device is permitted to be sized at 100 percent of the maximum current calculated in 705.28(A).

(C) Marking. Panelboards containing multiple power source circuits must be field marked to indicate the presence of all sources of all power source circuits. ▶Figure 705–5

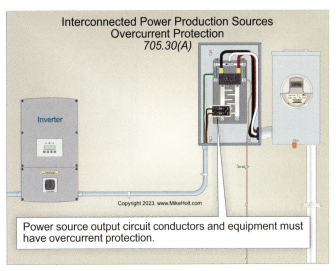
▶Figure 705–4

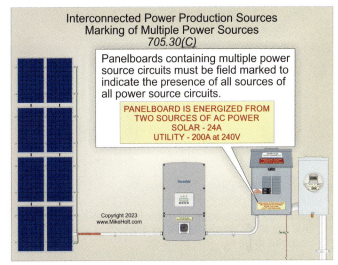
▶Figure 705–5

(D) Suitable for Backfeed. Fused disconnects and circuit breakers not marked "line" and "load" are suitable for backfeed. Circuit breakers marked "line" and "load" can be suitable for backfeed or reverse current if specifically rated for this application. ▶Figure 705–6

(E) Fastening. Backfed circuit breakers for electric power sources that are listed and identified as interactive are not required to be secured in place by an additional fastener as required by 408.36(D). ▶Figure 705–7

(F) Power Transformers. The following apply to the installation of transformers:

(1) For overcurrent protection, the primary side of transformers with a source of power on each side (inverter and utility) is based on the side connected to the largest source of available fault current.

(2) Transformer secondary conductors must be protected in accordance with 240.21(C).

705.82 | Interconnected Electric Power Production Sources

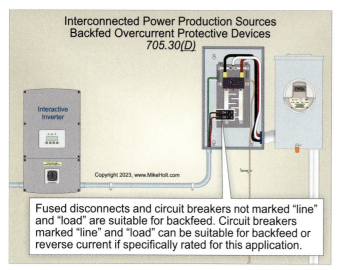

▶Figure 705-6

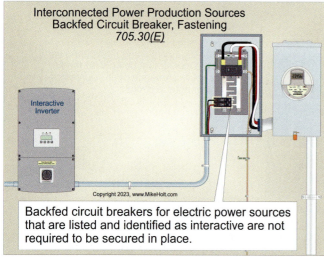

▶Figure 705-7

705.82 Single 120-Volt Supply

It is not uncommon for a small stand-alone system to supply only 120V loads. When this occurs, this new rule allows the use of standard 120/240V equipment.

Analysis

NEW This new section addresses systems operating in island mode to supply 120V to single-phase, 3-wire, 120/240V distribution equipment. In the past, there was no specific allowance for these systems. This new rule allows this type of connection if there are no 240V loads, no multiwire branch circuits, the total ratings of all power sources is less than the rating of the neutral bus in the distribution equipment, and a warning label that complies with 110.21(B) is posted.

Comment: The restriction on the neutral bus accounts for the system neutral current being additive since all the sources are on the same phase.

705.82 Single 120V Supply

Systems operating in island mode can supply 120V to single-phase, 3-wire, 120/240V distribution equipment where there are no 240V outlets and where there are no multiwire branch circuits.

In all installations, the sum of the ratings of the power sources must be less than the rating of the neutral bus in the distribution equipment. This equipment must be marked with the following words or equivalent:

WARNING: SINGLE 120-VOLT SUPPLY DO NOT CONNECT MULTIWIRE BRANCH CIRCUITS

The warning sign(s) or label(s) must comply with 110.21(B).

ARTICLE 706 ENERGY STORAGE SYSTEMS

Introduction to Article 706—Energy Storage Systems

It is important to understand to what Article 706 does and does not apply. The scope says it applies to all permanently installed energy storage systems "having a capacity greater than 1 kWh." They may be stand-alone or interactive with other electric power production sources. Although much of the original language used to create Article 706 came from deleted sections of Article 690 Solar Photovoltaic (PV) Systems, an energy storage system can store energy from any power source, there are no restrictions.

According to Article 100, an energy storage system has one or more devices installed as a system capable of storing energy and providing electrical energy to the premises wiring system or the electric utility supply. ▶Figure 706-1

Energy storage systems can include batteries, capacitors, and kinetic energy devices such as flywheels and compressed air. Energy storage systems can include inverters or converters to change voltage levels or to make a change between an alternating-current or a direct-current system.

An energy storage system might include (but is not limited to) batteries, capacitors, and kinetic energy devices (such as flywheels and compressed air). Some of these systems will have either ac or dc output available. They may also include inverters and converters to change stored energy into electrical energy. An energy storage system might directly power loads such as in a stand-alone system, or it might provide another energy management function like buffering energy produced by an intermittent source such as a wind or PV system.

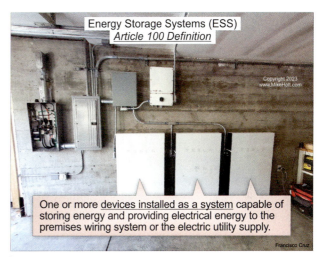

▶Figure 706-1

Energy storage systems can be (and usually are) connected to other energy sources, such as the local utility distribution system. There can be more than one source of power connected to these systems, and their connection to other energy sources must comply with the requirements of Article 705 which provides the rules for installations of one or more electric power production source operating in parallel with a primary source of electricity, such as a utility.

706.7 Commissioning and Maintenance

The section title was changed to incorporate "commissioning" and new rules require ESSs to be commissioned upon installation.

706.15 Disconnecting Means

A reorganization of the section's contents and some minor editorial changes to the title and contents, make this section much more user friendly.

Analysis

EXPANDED A new subdivision (A) requires ESSs to be commissioned upon installation. The commissioning requirement does not apply to one- and two-family dwellings. The maintenance requirements became subdivision (B), and new language was added to say that the maintenance requirements do not apply to one- and two-family dwellings.

Analysis

REORGANIZED The rules in this section did not seem to have a logical flow, so a reorganization of the existing rules and a cleanup of the language was a good choice. Subdivision (A) now requires a disconnecting means to be provided to disconnect the ESS from all wiring systems, and (B) now contains the requirements that were in (A) as well as the rules for remote activation of the disconnect.

NEW A new paragraph requires an ESS at a one- or two-family dwelling unit to have a readily accessible emergency shutdown switch outside that will cease power export.

NEW The new subdivision (E) specifies that batteries that are separate from the ESS, and subject to field servicing, must have a disconnecting means and marking that complies with 706.15(C)(1) through (C)(4).

706.7 Commissioning and Maintenance

(A) Commissioning. For other than one- and two-family dwelling units, energy storage systems (ESS) must be commissioned upon installation.

Note: For information related to the commissioning of ESSs, see NFPA 855, *Standard for the Installation of Stationary Energy Storage Systems*.

(B) Maintenance. For other than one- and two-family dwelling units, ESSs must be maintained in proper and safe operating condition in accordance with the manufacturer's requirements and industry standards. A written record of the system maintenance must be kept and include records of repairs and replacements necessary to maintain the system in a proper and safe operating condition.

Note: For information related to general electrical equipment maintenance and developing an effective electrical preventive maintenance (EPM) program, see NFPA 70B, *Recommended Practice for Electrical Equipment Maintenance*, or ANSI/NETA ATS-2017, *Standard for Acceptance Testing Specifications for Electrical Power Equipment and Systems*.

706.15 Disconnect

(A) Energy Storage System (ESS) Disconnecting Means. Means must be provided to disconnect energy storage system phase conductors from other power systems, utilization equipment, and its associated premises wiring.

(B) Location and Control. The disconnect must be readily accessible and comply with the following:

(1) The disconnect must be within the energy storage system.

(2) The disconnect must be within sight and within 10 ft of the energy storage system.

(3) Where not within sight of the energy storage system, the disconnect, or the enclosure providing access to the disconnect, must be capable of being locked in accordance with 110.25.

Where controls to activate the energy storage system disconnect are not within sight of the energy storage system, the disconnect must be lockable in accordance with 110.25, and the location of the controls must be marked on the disconnect.

For one- and two-family dwellings, an energy storage system must include an emergency shutdown function to cease the export of power from the energy storage system to premises wiring. An initiation device must be at a readily accessible location outside the building and plainly indicate whether in the "off" or "on" position. The "off" position of the initiation device must perform the energy storage system emergency shutdown function.

> **Author's Comment:**
> - It is important to note that the requirements in 706.15(A) can be met with disconnects that are integral to the listed energy storage system equipment. Since an energy storage system application may have multiple individual energy storage system units, each may require a disconnect, but this does not necessarily mean each will require a separate disconnect switch adjacent to the units. Many energy storage system manufacturers will choose to incorporate a means of disconnect into their energy storage system units. These disconnects will be evaluated during the system's listing.

(E) Disconnecting Means for Batteries. In cases where the battery is separate from the energy storage system electronics and is subject to field servicing, 706.15(C)(1) through (C)(4) apply.

Note: Batteries could include an enclosure, battery monitoring and controls, or other related battery components.

(1) Disconnecting Means. A disconnect must be provided for all ungrounded conductors. The disconnect must be readily accessible and within sight of the battery.

Note: See 240.21(H) for information on the location of the overcurrent protective device for battery conductors.

(2) Disconnection of Series Battery Circuits. Battery circuits exceeding 240V dc nominal between conductors or to ground must have provisions to disconnect the series-connected strings into segments not exceeding 240V dc nominal for maintenance by qualified persons. Non-load-break bolted or plug-in disconnects are permitted.

(3) Remote Activation. Where a disconnect is provided with remote controls to activate the disconnect and the controls for the disconnect are not within sight of the battery, the disconnect must be capable of being locked in the open position, in accordance with 110.25, and the location of the controls must be field marked on the disconnect.

(4) Notification. The disconnect must be legibly marked in the field. The marking must be of sufficient durability to withstand the environment involved and must include the following:

(1) Nominal battery voltage

(2) Available fault current derived from the stationary standby battery system

Note 1: Battery equipment suppliers can provide information about available fault current on any battery model.

(3) An arc-flash label in accordance with acceptable industry practice

Note 2: See NFPA 70E, *Standard for Electrical Safety in the Workplace*, for assistance in determining the severity of potential exposure, planning safe work practices, determining arc-flash labeling, and selecting personal protective equipment.

(4) Date the calculation was performed

706.31 Overcurrent Protection

New text was added to clarify where overcurrent protection should be located for conductors connected between an ESS and another source.

Analysis

CLARIFIED An additional sentence was added to (A) clarifying that overcurrent protection by an OCPD must be at the end of the conductor with the maximum available current. A new Informational Note provides some explanation for the logic behind this change.

706.31 Overcurrent Protection

(A) Circuits and Equipment. Protective devices for energy storage system circuits must be in accordance with 706.31(B) through (F).

A circuit conductor connected at one end to a supply with integral fault protection, where the conductor is rated for the maximum circuit current from that supply, and also connected to sources having an available maximum circuit current greater than the ampacity of the conductor, must be protected from overcurrent at the point of connection to the higher current source.

Note: Listed electronic power converter circuits powered by an energy storage system have integral fault protection. Where these circuits are connected to higher current sources such as a utility service, the overcurrent device is more appropriately installed at the higher current source end of the circuit conductor.

(B) Overcurrent Device Ampere Ratings. Overcurrent protective devices, where required, must be not less than 125 percent of the maximum currents calculated in 706.30(A).

Ex: Where the assembly (including the overcurrent protective devices) is listed for operation at 100 percent of its rating, the ampere rating of the overcurrent protective devices is permitted to be not less than the maximum currents calculated in 706.30(B).

(C) Direct-Current Rating. Overcurrent protective devices, either fuses or circuit breakers, used in any direct-current portion of an energy storage system must be listed for direct current and have the appropriate voltage, current, and interrupting ratings for the application.

Ex: Where current-limiting overcurrent protection is provided for the direct-current output circuits of a listed energy storage system, additional current-limiting overcurrent protective devices are not required.

(D) Current Limiting. A listed and labeled current-limiting overcurrent protective device must be installed for each energy storage system dc output circuit. ▶Figure 706–2

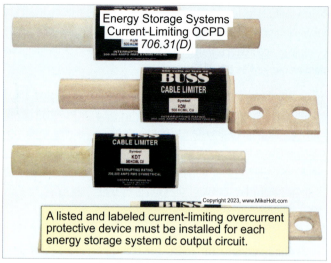

▶Figure 706–2

(E) Fuses. Means must be provided to disconnect any fuses associated with energy storage system equipment and components when the fuse is energized from both directions and is accessible to other than qualified persons. Switches, pullouts, or similar devices that are rated for the application are permitted to serve as a means to disconnect fuses from all sources of supply.

(F) Location. Where circuits from the input or output terminals of energy storage components in an energy storage system pass through a wall, floor, or ceiling, overcurrent protection must be provided at the energy storage component of the circuit.

Author's Comment:

▸ As with 706.15(D), this one will not apply to every energy storage system application where circuit conductors travel through walls, floors, or ceilings. This section is for those applications (typically large ones) where the battery is in one room and other equipment that is part of that energy storage system is in another room.

ARTICLE 710 — STAND-ALONE SYSTEMS

Introduction to Article 710—Stand-Alone Systems

Stand-alone systems are independent from the electric utility, or they can be interactive with other power production sources.

A "stand-alone system" is an electrical system that is self-sufficient and a completely "off the grid" source of electrical energy such as solar or wind. However, it still may be connected to a utility supply as part of an interconnected system. The fact that it can be self-sustaining is why Article 710 specifically addresses these systems.

Definitions. Terms contained in Article 100 that are important for the application of this article include:

Inverter, Stand-Alone. Inverter equipment having the capabilities to operate only in island mode [Article 100].

Island Mode. The operating mode for power production equipment or microgrids that are disconnected from an electric power production and distribution network or other primary power source [Article 100].

Stand-Alone System. An electrical power system that is not interconnected to the electric utility power system [Article 100]. ▶Figure 710-1

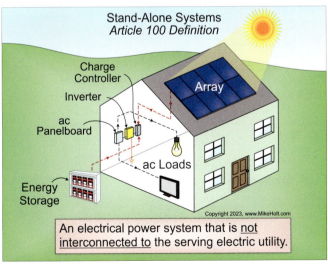

▶Figure 710-1

Author's Comment:

▸ Although stand-alone systems can operate independently of the serving electric utility, they may include a connection to the serving electric utility for use when not operating in stand-alone mode ("island mode").

710.1 Scope

The word "utility" was added to the rule text to clarify what determines when a system is a stand-alone system.

Analysis

CLARIFIED The scope of this section now states that stand-alone systems are those not connected to an electric utility or other electric power production and distribution network. The word "utility" was added in the scope to clear up any ambiguity.

710.6 | Stand-Alone Systems

710.1 Scope

This article covers electric power production systems that operate in island mode and are not connected to an electric utility supply <u>or other electric power production and distribution network.</u> ▶Figure 710–2

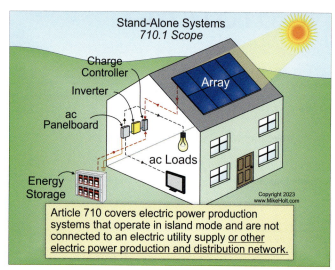

▶Figure 710–2

710.6 Equipment Approval

A minor editorial revision clarifies that power production equipment or systems are approved for use in "island mode."

Analysis

CLARIFIED — The revision of the parent text to include the word "island mode" clarifies for what the equipment needs to be approved. An additional revision clarifies that the equipment covered by this section includes all "power production equipment or systems."

710.6 Equipment Approval

Stand-alone <u>power production</u> equipment <u>or systems</u> approved for use in <u>island mode</u> must be: ▶Figure 710–3

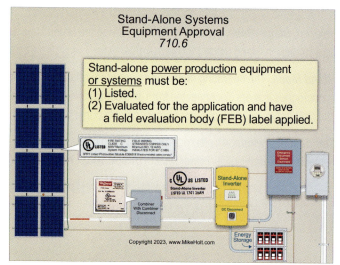

▶Figure 710–3

(1) Listed.

(2) Evaluated for the application and have a field evaluation body (FEB) label applied.

Author's Comment:

▸ An electric power production and distribution network is a serving electric utility that is connected to premises wiring and is not controlled by a system that operates in an interactive mode.

Note: Stand-alone systems <u>operate</u> independently from the electric utility, or they can be interactive with other power production sources. Stand-alone systems often include a single or an interconnection of sources such as engine generators, solar PV, wind, an energy storage system, or batteries.

Author's Comment:

▸ According to Article 100, "Island Mode" is the operational mode for stand-alone power production equipment, an isolated microgrid, multimode inverter, or an interconnected microgrid that is disconnected from the electric utility supply.

Author's Comment:

- A multimode inverter operates in island mode when it is not connected to an electric utility supply. Stand-alone inverters are not evaluated and are not intended for connection to export power in parallel with an electric utility.

- According to Article 100, a "Multimode Inverter" is equipment having the capabilities of both interactive and stand-alone inverters. ▶Figure 710–4

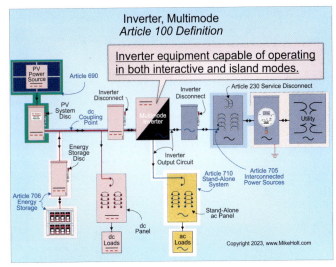

▶Figure 710–4

Notes

ARTICLE 722 — CABLES FOR POWER-LIMITED CIRCUITS AND FAULT-MANAGED POWER CIRCUITS

Introduction to Article 722—Cables for Power-Limited Circuits and Fault-Managed Power Circuits

This article combines common cabling requirements found in Articles 725 and 760 to remove redundancy and create better usability of the *NEC*. Part I covers the general requirements for the installation of Class 2 power-limited cables [Article 725] and power-limited fire alarm cables [Article 760]. Part II covers the listing and marking requirements for these power-limited cables. Specific requirements such as wiring methods, mixing of cables, and separation of cables must follow the requirements of the power-limited cables' respective Article [722.3(O)].

Article 722 Cables for Power-Limited Circuits and Fault-Managed Power Circuits

This article was added to combine the general requirements for all low-voltage cabling articles into one place, similar to what was done with Article 800 in 2020.

Analysis

 NEW This new article covers the general requirements for cables installed for installations covered by Articles 725, 726, and 760. Although in its infancy, this is a great start toward consolidating all these related rules. We will be seeing changes here for the foreseeable future as the language continues to be worked out and the rest of the common rules are moved into this article.

722.1 Scope

This new section provides the scope of this article.

Analysis

 NEW This new article covers the general requirements for the installation of single- and multi-conductor cables for Class 2 and 3 power-limited circuits, power-limited fire alarm circuits, and Class 4 fault-managed power circuits. Part I contains the general requirements for cables and conductors used for these circuits, and Part II contains the listing requirements for cables.

722.1 Scope

This article covers the general requirements for the installation Class 2 power-limited cables [Article 725], fault-managed power cables [Article 726], and power-limited fire alarm cables [Article 760].

722.3 | Cables for Power-Limited Circuits And Fault-Managed Power Circuits

722.3 Other Articles

Some rules from 725.3 and 760.3 were relocated here to remove some redundant rules across these sections.

Analysis

NEW This provides references to requirements in other articles that apply to installations of power-limited cables. This rule also tells us that only the sections of Article 300 specifically referenced in Article 722 apply to these installations.

722.3 Other Articles

In addition to the requirements of this article, circuits and equipment must comply with the articles or sections listed in 722.3(A) through (O). Only those sections contained in Article 300 specifically referenced below apply to cables for power-limited circuits.

(O) Specific Requirements. As appropriate, the installation of wires and cables must also comply with the requirements of the following:

(1) Class 2 cables—Part II of Article 725

(3) Fire alarm cables—Part III of Article 760

722.24 Mechanical Execution of Work

Although this entire article is new, most of these rules are a modified version of those from 725.24 and 760.24.

Analysis

NEW The second paragraph of (A) requires a bushing to protect cables where they emerge from a raceway used to provide mechanical support or protection. The third paragraph requires nonmetallic cable ties or accessories in plenums to comply with 300.22(C).

NEW The rules in (B) are not really new but are new in this section and should cause installers to pause. They specify that cables cannot be attached by any means to the exterior of a conduit or other raceway. There are also two Exceptions.

722.24 Mechanical Execution of Work

(A) General. Cables for power-limited circuits must be installed in a neat and workmanlike manner.

Cable Support. Exposed cables must be supported by the structural components of the building so the cable will not be damaged by normal building use.

Cable Securement. Power-limited cables must be secured by straps, staples, hangers, listed cable ties identified for securement and support, or similar fittings designed and installed in a manner that will not damage the cable. ▶Figure 722–1

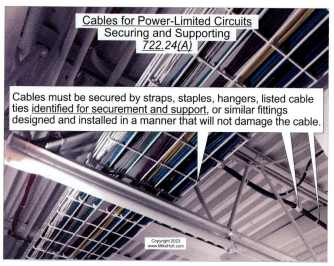

▶Figure 722–1

Protection From Physical Damage [300.4]. Power-limited cables installed through or parallel to framing members or furring strips must be protected where they are likely to be penetrated by nails or screws by installing the wiring method so it is not less than 1¼ in. from the nearest edge of the framing member or furring strips, or by protecting it with a $\frac{1}{16}$ in. thick steel plate or equivalent [300.4(A) and (D)].
▶Figure 722–2

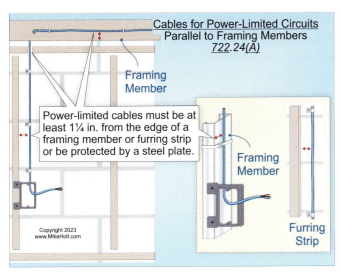

▶Figure 722-2

Securing and Supporting [300.11]. Ceiling-support wires or the ceiling grid are not permitted to support raceways or cables. Independent support wires secured at both ends can be used to support raceways or cables.

Protective Bushing at Raceway [300.15(C)]. A bushing must be installed where power-limited cables emerge from raceways. ▶Figure 722-3

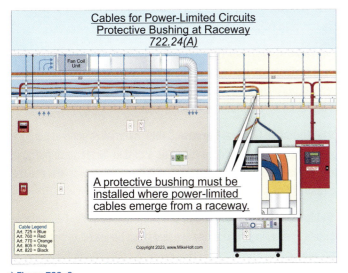

▶Figure 722-3

Cable Ties [300.22(C)]. Nonmetallic cable ties and other nonmetallic cable accessories used to secure and support cables in plenum spaces must be listed as having low smoke and heat release properties in accordance with 300.22(C).

Note 2: Paint, plaster, cleaners, abrasives, corrosive residues, or other contaminants can result in an undetermined alteration of Class 2 cable properties.

(B) Support of Cables. Cables are not permitted to be strapped, taped, or attached by any means to the exterior of any raceway.
▶Figure 722-4

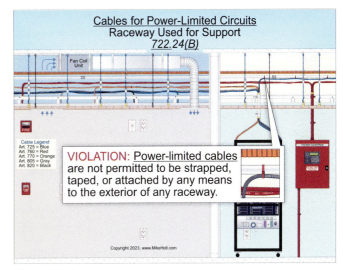

▶Figure 722-4

Ex 1: Cables can be supported by the raceway that supplies power to equipment controlled by a Class 2 power-limited circuit [300.11(B) and (C)(2)]. ▶Figure 722-5

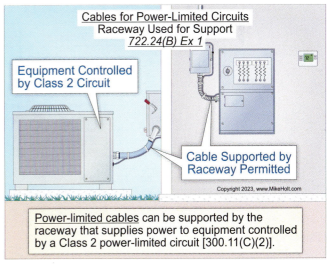

▶Figure 722-5

722.179 | Cables for Power-Limited Circuits And Fault-Managed Power Circuits

722.179 Listing and Marking of Cables

While it might be rare for you to need to reference the listing requirements for cables, having them all in one handy little list bears a mention.

Analysis

NEW This section contains the relocated and combined listing requirements for cables used with the systems covered in Articles 725, 726, and 760. There were no significant technical changes. One item of interest is (A)(11) which now requires all cables used in wet locations to be listed for such use and marked accordingly. That is going to cause some issues while the supply chain catches up with this change.

722.179 Listing and Marking of Power-Limited Cables

Power-limited cables installed in buildings must be listed in accordance with 722.179(A) and marked in accordance with 722.179(B) or (C).
▶Figure 722–6

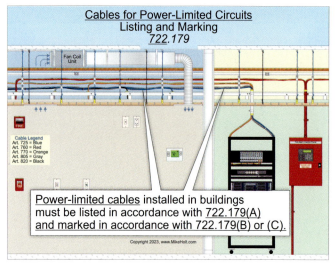

▶Figure 722–6

Ex: Optical fiber cables are not required to be listed.

(A) Listing. Power-limited cables installed as wiring methods within buildings must be listed as resistant to the spread of fire and other criteria in accordance with 722.179(A)(1) through (A)(16).

(1) Plenum-Rated Cable. Plenum-rated cable must be listed as suitable for use in ducts, plenums, and other space for environmental air. They must be listed as having adequate fire-resistant and low-smoke producing characteristics. Refer to Table 722.179(B) for plenum cable types. ▶Figure 722–7

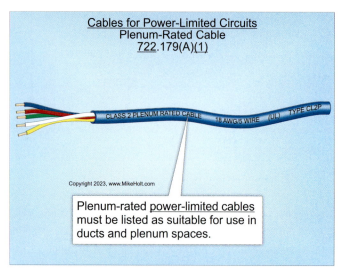

▶Figure 722–7

(2) Riser-Rated Cable. Riser-rated cable must be listed as suitable for use in a vertical run in a shaft, or from floor to floor, and must be listed as having fire-resistant characteristics capable of preventing the carrying of fire from floor to floor.

(3) General-Purpose Rated Cable. General-purpose rated cable must be listed as resistant to the spread of fire and as suitable for general-purpose use, except for risers, ducts, plenums, and other space used for environmental air.

(4) Alternative General-Purpose Cable. Alternative general-purpose optical fiber cable must be listed as suitable for general-purpose use, except for risers and plenums, and must also be resistant to the spread of fire.

(5) Limited-Use Cable. Limited-use cable must be listed as suitable for use in dwellings and raceways and must be listed as resistant to the spread of flame.

(6) Type PLTC. Type PLTC nonmetallic-sheathed, power-limited tray cable must be listed as being suitable for cable trays, resistant to the spread of fire, and sunlight- and moisture-resistant. Type PLTC cable used in a wet location must be listed for use in wet locations and marked "wet" or "wet location."

(9) Limited Power (LP) Cable. Limited power (LP) cables must be listed as suitable for carrying power and data circuits up to a specified current for each conductor. The cables must be marked with the suffix "-LP (XXA)" where "XXA" designates that the current limit is amperes per conductor.

Note: An example of the marking on a Class 2 cable with an LP rating is "CL2-LP (0.60A) 75°C 23 AWG 4-pair," which indicates it is a 4-pair plenum cable with 23 AWG conductors, a temperature rating of 75°C, and a current limit of 0.60A per conductor.

(11) Wet Locations. Cable used in a wet location must be listed for use in wet locations and be marked "wet" or "wet location" or have a moisture-impervious metal sheath.

Notes

ARTICLE 724

CLASS 1 POWER-LIMITED CIRCUITS AND CLASS 1 POWER-LIMITED REMOTE-CONTROL AND SIGNALING CIRCUITS

Introduction to Article 724—Class 1 Power-Limited Circuits and Class 1 Power-Limited Remote-Control and Signaling Circuits

This article covers Class 1 circuits that are power-limited and provides alternative requirements for minimum conductor sizes, overcurrent protection, insulation requirements, wiring methods, and materials. A Class 1 circuit is the wiring system between the load side of a Class 1 power source and the connected equipment [Article 100].

Article 724 Class 1 Power-Limited Circuits and Class 1 Power-Limited Remote-Control and Signaling Circuits

This is a new Article that covers Class 1 power-limited circuits. There are very limited applications for these rules, and in most cases those applications are mixed with nonpower-limited applications which negate most of the advantages of this article.

Analysis

NEW — This new article removes Class 1 circuits from Article 725. Article 724 says that Class 1 circuits must be supplied from a source with a rated output of not more than 30V and 1000 VA. This removes all 120V and nonpower-limited Class 1 circuits from either Article 724 or 725. Those circuits will be covered only by the applicable rules found in Chapters 1 through 4.

724.40 Class 1 Circuits

This new section outlines exactly what circuits are covered by these rules. As you can see, this is a very specialized set of rules.

Analysis

NEW — This new section limits Class 1 circuits to a maximum of 30V and 1000 VA. This makes all Class 1 circuits power-limited circuits for the 2023 *Code*, as there is no provision for nonpower-limited circuits. Previously, the *NEC* permitted nonpower-limited Class 1 circuits up to 600V. Those types of circuits will now simply be installed in accordance with the requirements of Chapters 1 through 4.

724.40 Class 1 Power Source

Class 1 power-limited circuits must be supplied from a power supply that limits the output to 30V at no more than 1000 VA. ▶Figure 724-1

724.40 | Class 1 Power-Limited Circuits and Class 1 Power-Limited Remote-Control and Signaling Circuits

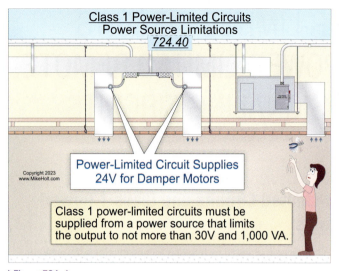

▶Figure 724–1

Author's Comment:

▸ Class 1 power-limited circuits are not that common. They are used when the voltage must be less than 30V (safe from electric shock in dry locations), and where the power demands exceed the 100 VA energy limitations of Class 2 circuits, such as for motorized loads like remote-controlled window blinds [Chapter 9, Table 11(A)].

ARTICLE 725 — CLASS 2 AND CLASS 3 POWER-LIMITED CIRCUITS

Introduction to Article 725—Class 2 and Class 3 Power-Limited Circuits

Class 2 power-limited circuits that are not an integral part of a device or appliance. This article includes circuits for burglar alarms, access control, sound, nurse call, intercoms, some computer networks, some lighting dimmer controls, and some low-voltage industrial controls.

Due to the power limitations of its power supply, a Class 2 circuit is considered safe from a fire initiation standpoint and provides acceptable electric shock protection.

The purpose of Article 725 is to allow for the fact that these circuits "are characterized by usage and power limitations that differentiate them from electrical power circuits" [725.1 Note]. This article provides alternative requirements for minimum conductor sizes, overcurrent protection, insulation requirements, wiring methods, and materials.

Article 725 Class 2 and Class 3 Power-Limited Circuits

First there were three, but now, there are two. Class 1 power-limited circuits are gone to the new Article 724, leaving only Class 2 and Class 3 power-limited circuits in Article 725!

Analysis

REORGANIZED — This article now only covers Class 2 and Class 3 power-limited circuits, since Class 1 power-limited circuits are now found in Article 724. In addition, "Remote-Control, Signaling" was dropped from the title of this article since all Class 2 and 3 circuits are covered no matter their function.

Notes

ARTICLE 726

CLASS 4 FAULT-MANAGED POWER SYSTEMS

Introduction to Article 726—Class 4 Fault-Managed Power Systems

Fresh to the market and new to the *Code* as part of the 2023 revision, Article 726, Class 4 Fault-Managed Power Systems, is a new classification standard dedicated to fault-managed power (FMP) systems and provides rules for their safe installation. Much like Power over Ethernet (PoE), FMP systems can intelligently transmit power at over 20 times that of PoE over extended lengths and still provide superior safety over a power system using traditional OCPDs. Class 4 fault-managed power systems are unique in that instead of limiting power source output, they limit energy and power available during a fault event. FMPs consist of a Class 4 power transmitter and a Class 4 power receiver connected by a Class 4 cabling system. These systems monitor the circuit for faults and control the source current so the energy delivered into any fault is limited.

Article 726 Class 4 Fault-Managed Power Systems

This new article addresses the likely future of smart power systems. The future is not here yet...but it is coming.

Analysis

NEW
There is not a lot to write about this new technology yet but it is coming soon. This new article covers the installation of wiring and equipment supplied by Class 4 fault-managed power (FMP) systems, also sometimes referenced as packet energy transfer (PET), and pulsed power, among others. These systems operate on pulsed dc power with a peak voltage of not more than 450V dc line-to-line. Communications between the power transmitter and the power receiver control shock and fire hazards.

Notes

ARTICLE 750 — ENERGY MANAGEMENT SYSTEMS

Introduction to Article 750—Energy Management Systems

This article applies to the installation and operation of energy management systems. These systems have become very popular and are used in electric vehicle supply equipment to adjust ampere settings, power monitoring devices for panelboards, as lighting controls for building automation, load-shedding systems for an alternate power source, and so on. Energy management ensures that the electrical system does not overload a branch circuit, feeder, or service and allows the electrical system to be sized based on the controlled/monitored current settings.

750.6 Listing

This new section requires energy management systems to be listed.

Analysis

NEW This new section requires energy management systems to be listed as either a complete energy management system, a field installable kit, or as listed individual components assembled as a system.

750.6 Listing

Energy management systems must be one of the following:

(1) Listed as a complete energy management system

(2) Listed as a kit for field installation in switch or overcurrent device enclosures

(3) Listed individual components assembled as a system

750.30 Load Management

Expanded requirements specify how an EMS should function when it is managing the load on conductors.

Analysis

EXPANDED These requirements were greatly expanded in (C) from the 2020 *Code*. Now an EMS used to manage the load on a conductor must have a maximum ampere setpoint that can be used for calculating the connected load in accordance with 220.70 or the maximum permitted source current. When the EMS malfunctions, it must automatically cease current flow. Adjustable settings for an EMS are only permitted if access to the settings is restricted and the equipment is marked according to (C)(4).

750.30 | Energy Management Systems

750.30 Load Management

Energy management systems are permitted to monitor and control electrical loads and sources in accordance with 750.30(A) through (C).

(A) Load Shedding Controls. An energy management system is not permitted to override the load shedding controls put in place to ensure the minimum electrical capacity for the following:

(1) Fire pumps

(2) Emergency systems

(3) Legally required standby systems

(4) Critical operations power systems

(B) Disconnection of Power. An energy management system is not permitted to cause disconnection of power to the following:

(1) Elevators, escalators, moving walks, or stairway lift chairs

(2) Positive mechanical ventilation for hazardous (classified) locations

(3) Ventilation used to exhaust hazardous gas or reclassify an area

(4) Circuits supplying emergency lighting

(5) Essential electrical systems in health care facilities

(C) Capacity of Branch Circuit, Feeder, or Service. An energy management system is not permitted to cause a branch circuit, feeder, or service to be overloaded. The EMS is permitted to limit the current on a conductor as follows:

(1) Current Setpoint. The maximum ampere setpoint of the EMS can be one or more of the following:

(1) The continuous load value in accordance with 220.70

(2) The maximum source current permitted by the EMS

(2) System Malfunction. The EMS must use monitoring and controls to automatically cease current flow upon the malfunction of the EMS.

(3) Settings. Adjustable settings are permitted if access to the settings are:

(1) Located behind removable and sealable covers over the adjustment means, or

(2) Located behind a cover or door that requires the use of a tool to open, or

(3) Located behind locked doors accessible only to qualified personnel, or

(4) Password protected with the password accessible only to qualified personnel, or

(5) Provided with software that has password protected access to the adjusting means accessible to qualified personnel only.

(4) Marking. The EMS equipment must be field marked with the following information:

(1) Maximum current setting

(2) Date of calculation and setting

(3) Identification of loads and sources associated with the current-limiting feature

(4) The following or equivalent wording: "The setting for the EMS current-limiting feature must not be bypassed"

The markings must meet the requirements in 110.21(B) and be such that they are clearly visible to qualified persons before examination, adjustment, servicing, or maintenance of the equipment.

ARTICLE 760 — FIRE ALARM SYSTEMS

Introduction to Article 760—Fire Alarm Systems

Article 760 covers the installation of wiring and equipment for fire alarm systems including circuits controlled and powered by the fire alarm. These systems include fire detection and alarm notification, guard's tour, sprinkler waterflow, and sprinkler supervisory systems. NFPA 72, *National Fire Alarm and Signaling Code*, provides the requirements for the selection, installation, performance, use, testing, and maintenance of fire alarm systems.

760.33 Supply-Side Overvoltage Protection

A new requirement for fire alarm control panels to have surge protection finally makes it into the *NEC*.

Analysis

NEW — This requirement has been around in some form or another in various other codes and has finally made it into the *NEC*. A listed SPD must now be installed on the supply side of a fire alarm control panel and comply with Part II of Article 242. Fire alarm control panels contain electronics that can be damaged by surges. Providing SPD protection can increase the reliability of the fire alarm installation and possibly save lives.

760.33 Supply-Side Overvoltage Protection

A listed surge-protective device must be installed on the supply side of a fire alarm control panel in accordance with Part II of Article 242.

Notes

CHAPTER 8
COMMUNICATIONS SYSTEMS

Introduction to Chapter 8—Communications Systems

Chapter 8 of the *National Electrical Code* covers the wiring requirements for hard-wired telephones [Article 805], radio and TV antennas, satellite dishes [Article 810], and CATV systems [Article 820]. ▶Figure 8-1

Communications systems are not subject to the general requirements contained in Chapters 1 through 4 or the special requirements of Chapters 5 through 7, except where a Chapter 8 rule specifically refers to one of those chapters [90.3]. Installations of communications equipment under the exclusive control of communications utilities located outdoors, or in building spaces used exclusively for such installations, are exempt from the *NEC* [90.2(D)(4)].

This material only covers the following articles contained in Chapter 8:

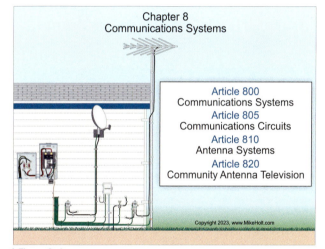
▶Figure 8-1

- **Article 800—General Requirements for Communications Systems.** This article covers general requirements for the installation of coaxial cable [Article 800], hard-wired telephones [Article 805], and radio distribution systems [Article 820].

- **Article 810—Antenna Systems.** Article 810 covers antenna systems for radio and television receiving equipment, amateur radio transmitting and receiving equipment, and certain features of transmitter safety. It also addresses antennas such as multi-element, vertical rod and dish, and the wiring and cabling connecting them to the equipment.

Notes

ARTICLE 800 GENERAL REQUIREMENTS FOR COMMUNICATIONS SYSTEMS

Introduction to Article 800—General Requirements for Communications Systems

Article 800 contains the general rules for, and applies to, installations of those systems covered by Articles 805 and 820. Note that the scope of this article does not include Article 810, Radio and Television Antenna Equipment. That article still stands alone from the rest of the *Code*, including the Chapter 8 articles. The specific rules in Articles 805 and 820 supplement or modify the requirements in Article 800. This is similar to the language in 90.3 that says the general rules in Chapters 1 through 4 may be modified by the specific rules in Chapters 5 through 7.

800.3 Other Articles

A clarification indicates that the definitions in Article 100 apply to Chapter 8, and new language specifies that Chapter 8 installations must comply with 800.3(A) through (I).

Analysis

CLARIFIED EXPANDED

This rule was expanded to say that the definitions in Article 100 apply to Chapter 8 installations. An additional clarification requires Chapter 8 installations to comply with 800.3(A) through (I) since nothing in Chapters 1 through 7 apply unless specifically referenced in Chapter 8. Article 800 contains the general requirements for Chapter 8 installations but does not apply to Article 810.

RELOCATED CLARIFIED

The rules in (A) are a combination of relocated rules from 830.3(B) and 840.3(B) to remove redundant text and eliminate references to complete articles.

800.3 Other Articles

Only those sections of Chapters 1 through 7 referenced in this article apply to Chapter 8. However, Article 100 definitions do apply to Chapter 8.

(A) Output Circuits. As appropriate for the services provided, the output circuits derived from a network-powered broadband communications system's network interface unit (NIU) or from a premises-powered broadband communications system's network terminal must comply with the requirements of the following:

(1) Class 2 power-limited circuits—Part II of Article 725 and Parts I and II of Article 722

(2) Power-limited fire alarm circuits—Part III of Article 760

(3) Optical fiber cables—Part V of Article 770

(B) Hazardous (Classified) Locations. For circuits and equipment installed in a location classified in accordance with 500.5, the applicable requirements of Chapter 5 apply.

(C) Wiring in Ducts for Dust or Vapor Removal. The requirements of 300.22(A) apply.

(D) Equipment in Plenum Spaces. Equipment installed in plenum spaces must comply with 300.22(C)(3).

800.24 | General Requirements for Communications Systems

Author's Comment:

▸ According to 300.22(C)(3), electrical equipment with a metal enclosure, or a nonmetallic enclosure listed for use in an air-handling space, can be installed in a plenum space. ▸Figure 800-1

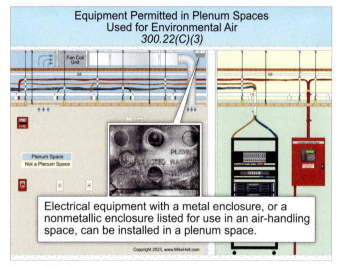

▸Figure 800-1

(E) Installation and Use. Communications equipment must be installed and used according to manufacturers' instructions in accordance with 110.3(B).

(F) Optical Fiber Cable. Where optical fiber cable is used to provide a communications circuit within a building, Article 770 applies.

800.24 Mechanical Execution of Work

Cable ties used in Chapter 8 applications are now required to be listed.

Analysis

EXPANDED The requirement for cable ties to be listed and identified for securement and support was added here to correlate with the requirements in the Chapter 3 cable articles, and the phrase "nonmetallic cable ties" was changed to "plenum cable ties." This is just a clarification since the requirement says cable ties must be listed as having low smoke and heat release properties.

800.24 Mechanical Execution of Work

(A) General. Coaxial cabling must be installed in a neat and workmanlike manner.

Cable Support, Damage. Exposed coaxial cables must be supported by the structural components of the building so the cable will not be damaged by normal building use.

Cable Securement, Fitting. Coaxial cables must be secured by straps, staples, hangers, cable ties listed and identified for securement and support, or similar fittings designed and installed in a manner that will not damage the cable. ▸Figure 800-2

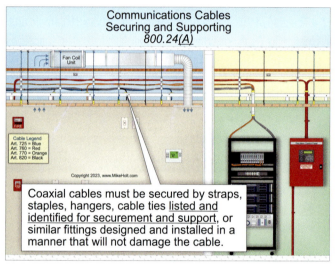

▸Figure 800-2

Protection From Physical Damage [300.4]. Coaxial Cables installed through or parallel to framing members or furring strips must be protected where they are likely to be penetrated by nails or screws by installing the wiring method so it is not less than 1¼ in. from the nearest edge of the framing member or furring strips, or by protecting it with a 1/16 in. thick steel plate or equivalent [300.4(A)(1) and (D)]. ▸Figure 800-3

Securing and Supporting [300.11]. Communications raceways and coaxial cable assemblies must be securely fastened in place. The ceiling-support wires or the ceiling grid are not permitted to be used to support coaxial cables [300.11(B)]. ▸Figure 800-4

Cable Ties, Plenum Rated. Cable ties used to secure or support coaxial cables in plenums must be listed for use in a plenum space in accordance with 800.170.

General Requirements for Communications Systems | 800.133

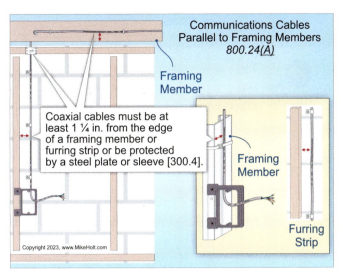
▶Figure 800–3

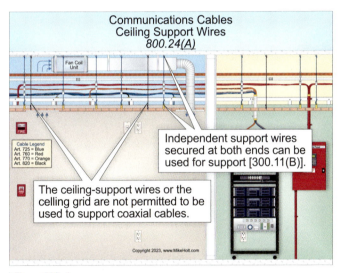
▶Figure 800–4

Note 1: Accepted industry practices are described in ANSI/TIA-568, *Commercial Building Telecommunications Infrastructure Standard*; ANSI/TIA-569-D, *Telecommunications Pathways and Spaces*; ANSI/TIA-570-C, *Residential Telecommunications Infrastructure Standard*; ANSI/TIA-1005-A, *Telecommunications Infrastructure Standard for Industrial Premises*; ANSI/TIA-1179, *Healthcare Facility Telecommunications Infrastructure Standard*; ANSI/TIA-4966, *Telecommunications Infrastructure Standard for Educational Facilities*; and other ANSI-approved installation standards.

Note 3: Paint, plaster, cleaners, abrasives, corrosive residues, or other contaminants may result in an undetermined alteration of wire and cable properties.

800.133 Installation of Coaxial Cables and Equipment

Although much of this looks new it is not!

Analysis

RELOCATED This section is another batch of material from 805 and 820 that was relocated here as a general requirement. There were no technical changes.

800.133 Installation of Coaxial Cables and Equipment

(A) In Raceways, Cable Trays, Boxes, Enclosures, and Cable Routing Assemblies.

(1) Permitted Other Circuits. Coaxial cables are permitted in the same raceway, cable tray, box, enclosure, or cable routing assembly with jacketed coaxial cables of any of the following:

(1) Class 2 power-limited circuits in compliance with Article 725

(2) Power-limited fire alarm systems in compliance with Parts I and III of Article 760

(3) Nonconductive and conductive optical fiber cables in compliance with Parts I and V of Article 770

(3) Separation from Power Conductors. Coaxial cables are not permitted to be placed in any raceway, compartment, outlet box, junction box, or similar fitting with conductors of electric power or Class 1 power-limited circuits.

Ex 1: Power conductors are permitted in the same enclosure with coaxial cables if separated by a barrier.

Ex 2: Power conductors that supply coaxial cable distribution equipment must maintain ¼ in. of separation from coaxial cables within the enclosure.

(B) Separation from Power Conductors. Coaxial cables must be separated by at least 2 in. from conductors of any electric light, power, and Class 1 power-limited circuits.

Ex 1: Coaxial cables are not required to have a 2-in. separation from a Chapter 3 wiring method.

800.170 | General Requirements for Communications Systems

(C) Support of Coaxial Cables. Coaxial cables are not permitted to be strapped, taped, or attached by any means to the exterior of any raceway as a means of support.

800.170 Plenum Cable Ties

The cable tie listing requirements found in 805 were relocated here so they became a general requirement for Chapter 8.

Analysis

RELOCATED This rule was relocated here from 805.170(C). Doing so made it a general requirement for Chapter 8.

800.170 Plenum Cable Ties

Cable ties intended for use in a plenum space, in accordance with 300.22(C), must be listed as having low smoke and heat release properties.

ARTICLE 810

ANTENNA SYSTEMS

Introduction to Article 810—Antenna Systems

Unlike other articles in this chapter, Article 810 is not covered by the general rules in Article 800. As a result, it stands completely alone in the *Code* unless a rule here references a specific rule elsewhere in the *NEC*.

This article covers transmitter and receiver (satellite dish and antenna) equipment, and the wiring and cabling associated with that equipment. Here are a few key points to remember about Article 810:

▸ Avoid contact with conductors of other systems.

▸ Do not attach satellite dishes, antennas, or other equipment to the service-entrance power mast.

▸ Keep the bonding conductor as straight as practicable and protect it from physical damage.

▸ If the mast is not bonded properly, you risk flashovers and possible electrocution.

▸ Remember that the purpose of bonding is to prevent a difference of voltage between metallic objects and other conductive items, such as swimming pools.

▸ Clearances are critical, and Article 810 contains detailed clearance requirements. For example, it provides separate clearance requirements for indoor and outdoor locations.

Article 810—Antenna Systems

Because of the change to the article title, we now know what this set of rules is actually about.

810.3 Other Articles

Revisions to this rule make it clear which rules apply to these installations.

Analysis

EDITED The title of this article was changed and now reflects what the requirements apply to. In general, the article applies to the installation of all antenna systems and the conductors and cables associated with those systems.

Analysis

CLARIFIED EXPANDED This section now has three list items that tell you what other *Code* rules apply to an Article 810 installation. The text in (2) clarifies that coaxial cables connected to antennas must comply with Article 800.

810.3 Other Articles

(2) Coaxial cables must be installed in accordance with Article 800.

Notes

2023 NATIONAL ELECTRICAL CODE CHANGES REVIEW QUIZ

1. A "special purpose ground-fault circuit interrupter" (SPGFCI) is a device intended for the detection of ground-fault currents, used in circuits with voltage to ground greater than _____, that functions to de-energize a circuit or portion of a circuit within an established period of time when a ground-fault current exceeds the values established for Class C, D, or E devices.

   (a) 30V
   (b) 60V
   (c) 125V
   (d) 150V

2. A "splash pad" is a fountain intended for recreational use by pedestrians and designed to contain no more than _____ of water depth.

   (a) 1 in.
   (b) 3 in.
   (c) 6 in.
   (d) 12 in.

3. In judging equipment, considerations such as cybersecurity for network-connected _____ to address its ability to withstand unauthorized updates and malicious attacks while continuing to perform its intended safety functionality shall be evaluated.

   (a) normal equipment
   (b) emergency equipment
   (c) standby power equipment
   (d) life safety equipment

4. The installation and use instructions for listed, labeled, or identified electrical equipment may be provided in the form of _____.

   (a) printed material
   (b) a quick response (QR) code
   (c) an internet address to download instructions
   (d) any of these

5. Electrical equipment shall be installed _____.

   (a) in a professional and skillful manner
   (b) under the supervision of a licensed person
   (c) completely before being inspected
   (d) all of these

6. In other than dwelling units, in addition to the requirements in 110.16(A), a permanent arc-flash label shall be field or factory applied to service equipment and feeder supplied equipment rated _____ or more.

   (a) 600A
   (b) 1000A
   (c) 1200A
   (d) 1600A

7. Electrical equipment servicing and electrical preventive maintenance shall be performed by _____ trained in servicing and maintenance of equipment.

   (a) qualified persons
   (b) manufacturer's representatives
   (c) service specialists
   (d) licensed individuals

8. Equipment servicing and electrical preventive maintenance shall be performed in accordance with the original equipment manufacturer's instructions and _____.

   (a) information included in the listing information
   (b) applicable industry standards
   (c) as approved by the authority having jurisdiction
   (d) any of these

Review Quiz | 2023 National Electrical Code Changes

9. Equipment that is reconditioned and required by the Code to be listed shall be listed or _____ as reconditioned using available instructions from the original equipment manufacturer.

    (a) identified
    (b) documented
    (c) field labeled
    (d) certified

10. Each disconnecting means shall be legibly marked to indicate its purpose unless located and arranged so _____.

    (a) it can be locked out and tagged
    (b) it is not readily accessible
    (c) the purpose is evident
    (d) it operates at less than 300V to ground

11. The grade, floor, or platform in the required working space about electrical equipment shall be as level and flat as _____ for the entire required depth and width of the working space.

    (a) practical
    (b) possible
    (c) required
    (d) none of these

12. All service equipment, switchboards, switchgear, panelboards, and motor control centers shall be _____.

    (a) located in dedicated spaces
    (b) protected from damage
    (c) in weatherproof enclosures
    (d) located in dedicated spaces and protected from damage

13. A listed Class A GFCI shall provide protection in accordance with 210.8(A) through (F). The GFCI protective device shall be installed in a(an) _____ location.

    (a) circuit breaker type only
    (b) accessible
    (c) readily accessible
    (d) concealed

14. In dwelling unit kitchens, GFCI protection shall be provided for 125V through 250V receptacles _____.

    (a) installed to serve the countertop surfaces
    (b) within 6 ft from the top inside edge of the bowl of the sink
    (c) installed to serve above or below the countertop surfaces
    (d) serving the kitchen

15. In dwelling units, GFCI protection shall be provided for 125V through 250V receptacles installed in areas with sinks and permanent provisions for _____.

    (a) food preparation
    (b) beverage preparation
    (c) cooking
    (d) any of these

16. In dwelling units, factory-installed receptacles that are not readily accessible and are mounted internally to bathroom _____ assemblies shall not require GFCI protection unless required by the installation instructions or listing.

    (a) surface-mounted luminaire
    (b) exhaust fan
    (c) electric baseboard heat
    (d) all of these

17. In other than dwelling units, GFCI protection shall be provided for receptacles and cord-and-plug-connected fixed or stationary appliances installed within _____ from the top inside edge of the bowl of a sink.

    (a) 3 ft
    (b) 4 ft
    (c) 5 ft
    (d) 6 ft

18. In other than dwelling units, GFCI protection is required for all 125V through 250V receptacles supplied by single-phase branch circuits rated 150V or less to ground, 50A or less, and all receptacles supplied by three-phase branch circuits rated 150V or less to ground, 100A or less in _____ areas of the basement.

    (a) unfinished
    (b) finished
    (c) wet
    (d) dry

19. In other than dwelling units, GFCI protection is required where receptacles are installed within _____ from the top inside edge or rim or from the conductive support framing of aquariums, bait wells, and similar open aquatic vessels or containers.

    (a) 3 ft
    (b) 5 ft
    (c) 6 ft
    (d) 10 ft

20. In other than dwelling units, receptacles installed within _____ of the outside edge of a bathtub or shower stall shall have GFCI protection.

    (a) 2 ft
    (b) 3 ft
    (c) 4 ft
    (d) 6 ft

21. According to Article 210, GFCI protection shall be provided for the branch circuit or outlet supplying _____ rated 150V or less to ground and 60A or less, single- or three-phase.

    (a) sump pumps
    (b) wall-mounted ovens
    (c) clothes dryers
    (d) all of these

22. At least one 120V, 20A branch circuit shall be installed to supply receptacle outlets, including those required by 210.52(G)(1) for _____ and in _____ with electric power.

    (a) attached decks, detached gazebos
    (b) attached garages, detached sheds
    (c) attached garages, unfinished accessory buildings
    (d) attached garages, detached garages

23. All 120V, single-phase, 10A, 15A, and 20A branch circuits supplying outlets or devices installed in areas designed for use exclusively as _____ in fire stations, police stations, ambulance stations, rescue stations, ranger stations, and similar locations shall be AFCI protected.

    (a) sleeping quarters
    (b) recreational areas
    (c) offices
    (d) all of these

24. If a receptacle outlet is not provided to serve an island or peninsular countertop or work surface in a dwelling unit, provisions shall be provided at the island or peninsula for _____ addition of a receptacle outlet to serve the island or peninsular countertop or work surface.

    (a) future
    (b) permanent
    (c) possible
    (d) none of these

25. Kitchen and dining room countertop receptacle outlets in dwelling units shall be installed on or above, but not more than _____ above, a countertop or work surface.

    (a) 12 in.
    (b) 18 in.
    (c) 20 in.
    (d) 24 in.

26. In dwelling unit bathrooms, at least one 15A or 20A, 125V receptacle outlet shall be installed within _____ of the outside edge of each sink.

    (a) 2 ft
    (b) 3 ft
    (c) 4 ft
    (d) 5 ft

27. In dwelling units, the required bathroom receptacle outlet can be installed on the side or face of the sink cabinet if not more than _____ below the top of the sink or sink countertop.

    (a) 12 in.
    (b) 18 in.
    (c) 20 in.
    (d) 24 in.

28. The required lighting outlet switch or wall-mounted control device shall not rely exclusively on a _____ unless a means is provided for automatically energizing the lighting outlets upon battery failure.

    (a) battery
    (b) solar cell
    (c) thermocouple
    (d) none of these

29. For feeders, barriers shall be placed such that no uninsulated, ungrounded busbar or terminal is exposed to inadvertent contact by persons or maintenance equipment while servicing load terminations in _____ supplied by feeder taps.

    (a) panelboards
    (b) switchboards or switchgear
    (c) motor control centers
    (d) any of these

30. Where a feeder supplies _____, a surge-protective device (SPD) shall be installed.

    (a) dwelling units
    (b) dormitory units
    (c) guest rooms and suites of hotels and motels
    (d) any of these

31. Surge-protective devices shall be installed in or adjacent to distribution equipment, connected to the _____ side of the feeder, that contains branch-circuit overcurrent protective device(s) that supply the locations specified in 218.18(A).

    (a) line
    (b) load
    (c) supply
    (d) line or supply

32. Where a feeder supplies the locations specified in 218.18(A), the required SPD shall be a _____ SPD.

    (a) Type 1
    (b) Type 1 or 2
    (c) Type 3
    (d) any of these

33. Where the distribution equipment supplied by the feeder in the locations specified in 218.18(A) is _____, the required Type 1 or Type 2 SPD shall be installed.

    (a) replaced
    (b) repaired
    (c) due for maintenance
    (d) replaced or repaired

34. Where the locations specified in 218.18(A) are supplied by a feeder, the required SPD shall have a nominal discharge current rating (In) of not less than _____.

    (a) 5 kA
    (b) 7.50 kA
    (c) 10 kA
    (d) the available fault current

35. When sizing a service or feeder for appliance loads in dwelling units, applying a demand factor of 75 percent of the nameplate rating load of _____ or more appliances rated ¼ hp or greater, or 500W or greater, that are fastened in place, and that are served by the same feeder or service, shall be permitted.

    (a) two
    (b) three
    (c) four
    (d) five

36. The electrical vehicle supply equipment (EVSE) load shall be calculated at either _____ or the nameplate rating of the equipment, whichever is larger.

    (a) 5000W (VA)
    (b) 7200W (VA)
    (c) 10,000W (VA)
    (d) 12,500W (VA)

37. If an energy management system (EMS) is used to limit the current to a feeder or service, the setpoint value of the EMS shall be considered _____ for the purposes of load calculations.

    (a) at 80 percent
    (b) at 90 percent
    (c) at 100 percent
    (d) a continuous load

38. For one-and two-family dwelling units supplied by an outside branch circuit or feeder, an emergency disconnecting means _____ be installed.

    (a) shall not
    (b) shall
    (c) shall be permitted to
    (d) none these

39. The emergency disconnecting means for one-and two-family dwelling units supplied by an outside branch circuit or feeder shall be installed in a readily accessible outdoor location on or _____.

    (a) within sight of the dwelling unit
    (b) at the source of power
    (c) in the panelboard
    (d) closest to the entrance of the branch-circuit or feeder cable assembly

40. If more than one emergency disconnecting means for one- and two-family dwelling units supplied by an outside branch circuit or feeder is provided, they shall be _____.

    (a) separated
    (b) adjacent to each other
    (c) grouped
    (d) away from each other

41. All services supplying _____ shall be provided with a surge-protective device (SPD).

    (a) dwelling units and dormitory units
    (b) guest rooms and guest suites of hotels and motels
    (c) areas of nursing homes and limited care facilities used exclusively as patient sleeping rooms
    (d) all of these

42. For one- and two-family dwelling unit service conductors, an emergency disconnecting means shall be installed in a readily accessible _____ location.

    (a) indoor location
    (b) outdoor location on or within sight of the dwelling unit
    (c) indoor or outdoor location
    (d) enclosed location with electrical power

43. The emergency disconnecting means for one- and two-family dwelling unit services is permitted to be a listed disconnect switch or circuit breaker that is marked _____ for use as service equipment, but not marked as suitable only for use as service equipment, installed on the supply side of each service disconnect.

    (a) suitable
    (b) appropriate
    (c) ready
    (d) none of these

44. Where equipment for isolation of other energy source systems is not located adjacent to the emergency disconnect required for one- and two-family dwelling unit services, a plaque or directory identifying the location of all equipment for isolation of other energy sources shall be located _____ the disconnecting means.

    (a) inside
    (b) on
    (c) adjacent to
    (d) within sight of

45. The markings for the required emergency disconnecting means for one- and two-family dwelling unit services shall _____.

    (a) comply with 110.21(B)
    (b) be located on the outside front of the disconnect enclosure with red background and white text
    (c) have letters at least ½ in. high
    (d) all of these

46. Remote access for an adjustable trip circuit breaker is permitted to be achieved by being connected directly through a _____.

    (a) secure network
    (b) local non-networked interface
    (c) hardwired ethernet cable
    (d) secure VPN

47. An SPD device used as an overvoltage protective device shall provide _____ that it is functioning properly.

    (a) indication
    (b) notification
    (c) a sign
    (d) a label

48. Grounding electrode conductors shall not be installed through a ventilation opening of a(an) _____.

    (a) enclosure
    (b) cabinet
    (c) motor control center
    (d) environmental air system

49. Metal enclosures shall be permitted to be used to connect bonding jumpers or _____ conductors, or both, together to become a part of an effective ground-fault current path.

    (a) grounded
    (b) neutral
    (c) equipment grounding
    (d) grounded phase

50. For the continuity of equipment grounding conductors and attachment in boxes, if circuit conductors are spliced within a box or terminated on equipment within or supported by a box, a connection used for _____ shall be made between the metal box and the equipment grounding conductor(s).

    (a) bonding
    (b) connections and splices
    (c) extending the length of the circuit
    (d) no other purpose

Review Quiz | 2023 National Electrical Code Changes

51. All conductors of the same circuit and, where used, the grounded conductor and all equipment grounding conductors and bonding conductors shall be contained within the same _____, unless otherwise permitted elsewhere in the Code.

    (a) raceway, conduit body, or auxiliary gutter
    (b) cable tray, cablebus assembly, or trench
    (c) cable or cord
    (d) any of these

52. Where raceways contain 4 AWG or larger insulated circuit conductors, and these conductors enter a cabinet, a box, an enclosure, or a raceway, prior to the installation of conductors, the conductors shall be protected from against physical damage by an identified fitting providing a smoothly rounded _____ surface.

    (a) fiberglass
    (b) plastic
    (c) insulating
    (d) gray

53. Where corrosion protection is necessary and the conduit is threaded anywhere other than at the factory where the product is listed, the threads shall be coated with a(an) _____ electrically conductive, corrosion-resistant compound.

    (a) marked
    (b) listed
    (c) labeled
    (d) approved

54. Raceways, cable armors, and cable sheaths shall be _____ between cabinets, boxes, conduit bodies, fittings, or other enclosures or outlets.

    (a) continuous
    (b) protected
    (c) buried
    (d) encased in concrete

55. Where the opening to an outlet, junction, or switch point is less than 8 in. in any dimension, the length of free conductor for each conductor, spliced or unspliced, shall extend at least _____ outside the opening of the enclosure.

    (a) 1 in.
    (b) 3 in.
    (c) 6 in.
    (d) 12 in.

56. _____ shall be installed so that wiring and devices contained in them can be rendered accessible in buildings and structures and, in underground circuits, be accessible without excavating sidewalks, paving, earth, or other substance that is to be used to establish the finished grade.

    (a) Boxes
    (b) Conduit bodies
    (c) Handhole enclosures
    (d) all of these

57. Type MC cable shall be supported and secured by staples; cable ties _____ for securement and support; straps, hangers, or similar fittings; or other approved means designed and installed so as not to damage the cable.

    (a) listed and identified
    (b) marked or labeled
    (c) installed and approved
    (d) any of these

58. Type NM cable shall be permitted to be installed in multifamily dwellings and their detached garages permitted to be of Type(s) _____ construction.

    (a) III
    (b) IV
    (c) V
    (d) all of these

59. In exposed work, Type NM cable shall be protected from physical damage where necessary by _____.

    (a) EMT
    (b) Schedule 80 PVC conduit or RTRC marked with the suffix -XW
    (c) RMC or IMC
    (d) any of these

60. In exposed work, where conduit or tubing is used for the protection from physical damage of Type NM cable, it shall be provided with a bushing or adapter that provides protection from abrasion at the point the cable _____ the raceway.

    (a) enters and exits
    (b) leaves
    (c) enters
    (d) none of these

61. The sheath on nonmetallic-sheathed cable shall extend not less than _____ beyond any cable clamp or cable entry.

    (a) ⅛ in.
    (b) ¼ in.
    (c) ⅜ in.
    (d) ½ in.

62. Self-contained switches, self-contained receptacles, and listed nonmetallic-sheathed cable interconnector devices of insulating material that are listed for use without a box shall be permitted to be used without boxes in _____.

    (a) readily accessible locations
    (b) locations protected from physical damage
    (c) hazardous (classified) locations
    (d) exposed or concealed installations

63. PVC conduit shall be permitted to be _____.

    (a) encased in concrete
    (b) used for the support of luminaires
    (c) installed in movie theaters
    (d) none of these

64. Where subject to physical damage, Schedule _____, and listed fittings for PVC conduit shall be used.

    (a) 20 PVC conduit and Schedule 20 PVC elbows
    (b) 30 PVC conduit and Schedule 30 PVC elbows
    (c) 40 PVC conduit and Schedule 40 PVC elbows
    (d) 80 PVC conduit and Schedule 80 PVC elbows

65. All _____ PVC conduit fittings are suitable for connection to both Schedule 40 and Schedule 80 PVC conduit.

    (a) listed
    (b) marked
    (c) labeled
    (d) identified

66. Expansion fittings for underground runs of direct buried PVC conduit emerging from the ground shall be provided above grade when required to compensate for _____.

    (a) earth settling
    (b) earth movement
    (c) frost heave
    (d) any of these

67. The use of EMT shall be permitted in concrete, in direct contact with the earth, in direct burial applications with fittings identified for direct burial, or in areas subject to severe _____ influences, where installed in accordance with 358.10(B).

    (a) corrosive
    (b) weather
    (c) sunlight
    (d) none of these

68. Receptacles shall not be installed inside of the tub or shower or within a zone measured _____ horizontally from any outside edge of the bathtub or shower stall, including the space outside the bathtub or shower stall space below the zone, and the space measured vertically from the floor to 8 ft above the top of the bathtub rim or shower stall threshold.

    (a) 3 ft
    (b) 4 ft
    (c) 5 ft
    (d) 6 ft

69. In bathrooms with less than the required zone, the receptacle(s) required by 210.52(d) shall be permitted to be installed _____ the bathtub rim or shower stall threshold on the farthest wall within the room.

    (a) opposite
    (b) vertically in
    (c) horizontally in
    (d) any of these

70. In a dwelling unit, a _____ receptacle shall be permitted for an electronic toilet or personal hygiene device such as an electronic bidet seat. The receptacle shall be readily accessible and not located in the space between the toilet and the bathtub or shower.

    (a) duplex
    (b) single
    (c) quad
    (d) any of these

Review Quiz | 2023 National Electrical Code Changes

71. All 15A and 20A, 125V and 250V nonlocking-type receptacles installed in _____, including their attached and detached garages, accessory buildings, and common areas shall be listed tamper-resistant receptacles.

    (a) dwelling units
    (b) boathouses
    (c) mobile homes and manufactured homes
    (d) all of these

72. All 15A and 20A, 125V and 250V nonlocking-type receptacles within clinics, medical and dental offices, and outpatient facilities in _____ shall be listed tamper-resistant receptacles.

    (a) business offices accessible to the general public
    (b) lobbies and waiting spaces
    (c) spaces of nursing homes and limited care facilities covered in 517.10(B)(2)
    (d) all of these

73. All 15A and 20A, 125V and 250V nonlocking-type receptacles installed in _____ shall be listed tamper-resistant receptacles.

    (a) residential care/assisted living facilities
    (b) social and substance abuse rehabilitation facilities
    (c) group homes
    (d) all of these

74. All 15A and 20A, 125V and 250V nonlocking-type _____ installed in areas of agricultural buildings accessible to the general public and any common areas, shall be listed tamper resistant.

    (a) receptacles
    (b) switches
    (c) overcurrent devices
    (d) none of these

75. Where tamper-resistant receptacles are required, receptacles located more than _____ above the floor shall not be required to be tamper resistant.

    (a) 4 ft
    (b) 5 ft
    (c) 5½ ft
    (d) 6 ft 7 in.

76. Every circuit and circuit modification shall be provided with a legible and permanent description to be located at each switch or circuit breaker in a switchboard or switchgear, and included in a circuit directory that is located _____ the panel door in the case of a panelboard.

    (a) on the face of
    (b) inside of
    (c) in an approved location adjacent to
    (d) all of these as applicable

77. All switchboards, switchgear, and panelboards supplied by a feeder(s) in _____ shall be permanently marked to indicate the identification and physical location of where the power supply originates.

    (a) other than one- or two-family dwellings
    (b) all dwelling units
    (c) all nondwelling units
    (d) all dwelling units and all nondwelling units

78. Where a replacement panelboard is not listed for the specific enclosure and the available fault current is 10,000A or less, the replacement panelboard shall be _____.

    (a) field labeled
    (b) identified for the application
    (c) approved only by special permission of the AHJ
    (d) not be used

79. Panelboards _____ be installed in the face-up or face-down position.

    (a) shall not
    (b) are permitted to
    (c) listed for such purpose may
    (d) approved for such use may

80. No parts of cord-connected luminaires, chain-, cable-, or cord-suspended luminaires, lighting track, pendants, or ceiling-suspended (paddle) fans with luminaire (light kit) shall be located within a zone measured 3 ft horizontally and _____ vertically from the top of the bathtub rim or shower stall threshold.

    (a) 4 ft
    (b) 6 ft
    (c) 8 ft
    (d) 12 ft

81. No metal parts of ceiling-suspended (paddle) fans in bathrooms and shower spaces shall be located within a zone measured _____ horizontally and 8 ft vertically from the top of the bathtub rim or shower stall threshold.

    (a) 2 ft
    (b) 2½ ft
    (c) 3 ft
    (d) 4 ft

82. The disconnecting means for air-conditioning and refrigerating equipment shall be located _____ from, and readily accessible from, the air-conditioning or refrigerating equipment.

    (a) within 5 ft
    (b) not less than 10 ft
    (c) more than 20 ft
    (d) within sight

83. The equipment grounding conductor terminal bar of a dry-type transformer shall be bonded to the enclosure in accordance with 250.12 and shall not be installed on or over any _____.

    (a) ungrounded conductor terminations
    (b) transformer coils or windings
    (c) vented portion of the enclosure
    (d) all of these

84. Areas designated as hazardous (classified) locations or determined to be unclassified shall be documented on an area classification drawing and other associated documentation and shall be available to the _____ and those authorized to design, install, inspect, maintain, or operate electrical equipment at these locations.

    (a) building owner
    (b) authority having jurisdiction
    (c) state fire marshal
    (d) all of these

85. Service equipment for a floating building, dock, or marina shall be elevated a minimum of _____ above the electrical datum plane.

    (a) 12 in.
    (b) 18 in.
    (c) 24 in.
    (d) 30 in.

86. When modifications or replacements of _____ are necessary on a docking facility, they shall be required to comply with the requirements of this Code, and the installation shall require an inspection of the circuit.

    (a) electrical enclosures
    (b) devices
    (c) wiring methods
    (d) any of these

87. Luminaires and their supply connections shall be secured to structural elements of the marina to limit damage from watercraft and prevent entanglement of and interaction with _____.

    (a) sea life
    (b) swimmers
    (c) fishing lines
    (d) tow lines

88. Luminaires installed at marinas below the highest high tide level or electrical datum plane and likely to be periodically submersed shall be limited to those luminaires that _____.

    (a) are identified as submersible
    (b) operate below the low-voltage contact limit defined in Article 100
    (c) are supplied by an isolating transformer or power supply in accordance with 680.23(A)(2)
    (d) all of these

89. All 125V, 15A and 20A receptacles for electrical hand tools or portable lighting equipment, supplied by single-phase branch circuits rated _____ or less to ground, installed in work areas where welders are operated shall have ground-fault circuit-interrupter protection for personnel.

    (a) 125V
    (b) 150V
    (c) 240V
    (d) 250V

90. The ampacity of the branch-circuit conductors and the rating or setting of overcurrent protective devices for electrically powered swimming pool heat pumps and chillers using the circulating water system shall be sized _____.

    (a) to comply with the nameplate
    (b) not greater than 35A
    (c) at 125 percent of its nameplate rating
    (d) at less than 60A

Review Quiz | 2023 National Electrical Code Changes

91. Rigid metal conduit, intermediate metal conduit, rigid polyvinyl chloride conduit, reinforced thermosetting resin conduit, and liquidtight flexible nonmetallic conduit shall be considered suitable for use as wiring methods for swimming pools, fountains, and similar installations in _____ environments.

    (a) dry
    (b) damp
    (c) wet
    (d) corrosive

92. Equipment listed for pool and spa use shall be considered _____ for use in corrosive environments.

    (a) suitable
    (b) appropriate
    (c) acceptable
    (d) any of these

93. Outlets serving pool motors for permanently installed pools shall have _____ protection complying with 680.5(B) or (C), as applicable.

    (a) ground-fault
    (b) overcurrent
    (c) shunt-trip
    (d) current-limiting

94. Where a pool pump motor in 680.21(C) is replaced or repaired, the replacement or repaired pump motor shall be provided with _____ complying with 680.5(B) or (C), as applicable.

    (a) new branch-circuit wiring
    (b) a new bonding jumper
    (c) ground-fault protection
    (d) GFPE protection

95. Metal piping systems associated with a fountain shall be bonded to the equipment grounding conductor of the _____.

    (a) branch circuit supplying the fountain equipment
    (b) bonding grid
    (c) fountain's equipotential plane
    (d) grounding electrode system

96. For the purpose of _____, the shell of a splash pad is bounded by the extent of the footing of the splash pad and rising to its exposed surface(s) and its collection basin area. The boundary of this area shall be considered to be the inside wall for the purpose of perimeter bonding.

    (a) lightning protection
    (b) equipotential bonding
    (c) ground-fault protection
    (d) current leakage prevention

97. Outlets supplying all permanently installed nonsubmersible pump motors for fountains shall have _____ protection.

    (a) AFCI and GFCI
    (b) GFPE
    (c) AFCI and GFPE
    (d) GFCI or SPGFCI

98. Article _____ covers the general requirements for the installation of single- and multiple-conductor cables used in Class 2 and Class 3 power-limited circuits, power-limited fire alarm (PLFA) circuits, Class 4 fault-managed power circuits, and optical fiber installations.

    (a) 722
    (b) 723
    (c) 724
    (d) 725

99. Article _____ covers Class 1 circuits, including power-limited Class 1 remote-control and signaling circuits that are not an integral part of a device or utilization equipment.

    (a) 722
    (b) 723
    (c) 724
    (d) 725

100. Article _____ covers power-limited circuits, including power-limited remote-control and signaling circuits, that are not an integral part of a device or of utilization equipment.

    (a) 722
    (b) 724
    (c) 725
    (d) 726

To check your answers, access the answer key at MikeHolt.com/MyAK23CC or scan the QR code.

WHAT'S THE NEXT STEP?
Follow the wheel and see how to take your career to the next level

Never stop learning...
To be a success, you have to remain current, relevant, and marketable. Your individual success is a function of your education and the key is continuous self-improvement, even if just a little each day. Here is a great map to make sure you have taken all the steps to complete your electrical education.

Mike Holt

MikeHolt.com/NextStep

LET'S GET YOU TO THAT NEXT LEVEL!
Call 888.632.2633 or visit MikeHolt.com/NextStep

Notes

ABOUT THE AUTHOR

Mike Holt
Founder and President
Mike Holt Enterprises
Groveland, Florida

Mike Holt is an author, businessman, educator, speaker, publisher and *National Electrical Code* expert. He has written hundreds of electrical training books and articles, founded three successful businesses, and has taught thousands of electrical *Code* seminars across the U.S. and internationally. His dynamic presentation style, deep understanding of the trade, and ability to connect with students are some of the reasons that he is one of the most sought-after speakers in the industry.

His company, Mike Holt Enterprises, has been serving the electrical industry for almost 50 years, with a commitment to creating and publishing books, videos, online training, and curriculum support for electrical trainers, students, organizations, and electrical professionals. His devotion to the trade, coupled with the lessons he learned at the University of Miami's MBA program, have helped him build one of the largest electrical training and publishing companies in the United States.

Mike is committed to changing lives and helping people take their careers to the next level. He has always felt a responsibility to provide education beyond the scope of just passing an exam. He draws on his previous experience as an electrician, inspector, contractor and instructor, to guide him in developing powerful training solutions that electricians understand and enjoy. He is always mindful of how hard learning can be for students who are intimidated by school, by their feelings towards learning, or by the complexity of the *NEC*. He's mastered the art of simplifying and clarifying complicated technical concepts and his extensive use of illustrations helps students apply the content and relate the material to their work in the field. His ability to take the intimidation out of learning is reflected in the successful careers of his students.

Mike's commitment to pushing boundaries and setting high standards extends into his personal life as well. He's an eight-time Overall National Barefoot Waterski Champion. Mike has more than 20 gold medals, many national records, and has competed in three World Barefoot Tournaments. In 2015, at the tender age of 64, he started a new adventure—competitive mountain bike racing and at 65 began downhill mountain biking. Every day he continues to find ways to motivate himself, both mentally and physically.

Mike and his wife, Linda, reside in New Mexico and Florida, and are the parents of seven children and seven grandchildren. As his life has changed over the years, a few things have remained constant: his commitment to God, his love for his family, and doing what he can to change the lives of others through his products and seminars.

Special Acknowledgments

My Family. First, I want to thank God for my godly wife who's always by my side and for my children.

My Staff. A personal thank you goes to my team at Mike Holt Enterprises for all the work they do to help me with my mission of changing peoples' lives through education. They work tirelessly to ensure that, in addition to our products meeting and exceeding the educational needs of our customers, we stay committed to building life-long relationships throughout their electrical careers.

The National Fire Protection Association. A special thank you must be given to the staff at the National Fire Protection Association (NFPA), publishers of the *NEC*—in particular, Jeff Sargent for his assistance in answering my many *Code* questions over the years. Jeff, you're a "first class" guy, and I admire your dedication and commitment to helping others understand the *NEC*.

ABOUT THE NFPA REVIEW TEAM

The National Fire Protection Association (NFPA) is grateful for the opportunity to partner with Mike Holt Enterprises to provide a technical review for this publication and to help further serve our collective community of electrical professionals, including electricians, electrical contractors, engineers, and inspectors, all who will find it to be a valuable resource for understanding the *National Electrical Code (NEC)*.

The NFPA technical review team consisted of multiple subject matter experts with varying backgrounds across the electrical landscape. At the NFPA, our electrical specialists work to provide accurate, relevant, and timely content and services. We combine our passion for the *NEC* with years of hands-on experience designing, installing, and inspecting electrical systems to connect industry professionals with the technical knowledge they need as they apply codes and standards in their everyday lives.

The NFPA is a global self-funded nonprofit organization, established in 1896, devoted to eliminating death, injury, property and economic loss due to fire, electrical, and related hazards. NFPA delivers information and knowledge through more than 300 consensus codes and standards, research, training, education, outreach, and advocacy; and by partnering with others who share an interest in furthering our mission. Our mission is to help save lives and reduce loss with information, knowledge, and passion.

NFPA 70, *National Electrical Code*, sets the foundation for electrical safety in residential, commercial, and industrial occupancies around the world. It is consistently reviewed and updated, with input from active professionals in the field, to stay ahead of the constant changes in technology and safety that affect your job daily.

ABOUT THE ILLUSTRATOR

Mike Culbreath—Illustrator

Mike Culbreath
Graphic Illustrator
Alden, Michigan

Mike Culbreath has devoted his career to the electrical industry and worked his way up from apprentice electrician to master electrician. He started working in the electrical field doing residential and light commercial construction, and later did service work and custom electrical installations. While working as a journeyman electrician, he suffered a serious on-the-job knee injury. As part of his rehabilitation, Mike completed courses at Mike Holt Enterprises, and then passed the exam to receive his Master Electrician's license. In 1986, with a keen interest in continuing education for electricians, he joined the staff to update material and began illustrating Mike Holt's textbooks and magazine articles.

Mike started with simple hand-drawn diagrams and cut-and-paste graphics. Frustrated by the limitations of that style of illustrating, he took a company computer home to learn how to operate some basic computer graphics software. Realizing that computer graphics offered a lot of flexibility for creating illustrations, Mike took every computer graphics class and seminar he could to help develop his skills. He's worked as an illustrator and editor with the company for over 30 years and, as Mike Holt has proudly acknowledged, has helped to transform his words and visions into lifelike graphics.

Originally from South Florida, Mike now lives in northern lower Michigan where he enjoys hiking, kayaking, photography, gardening, and cooking; but his real passion is his horses. He also loves spending time with his children Dawn and Mac and his grandchildren Jonah, Kieley, and Scarlet.

ABOUT THE MIKE HOLT TEAM

There are many people who played a role in the production of this textbook. Their efforts are reflected in the quality and organization of the information contained in this textbook, and in its technical accuracy, completeness, and usability.

Technical Writing

Brian House led the research team that created the text for the summary and the analysis of the *Code* changes that are the backbone of this book. He also coordinates the team that constructs and reviews our books and their supporting resources to ensure accuracy, clarity, and quality for our customers.

Mario Valdes is the Technical Content Editor and works directly with Mike to ensure the content is technically accurate, relatable, and valuable to all electrical professionals. He played an important role in gathering research, analyzing data, and assisting Mike in the writing of this book. He reworked content into different formats to improve the flow of information and assure the expectations were being met in terms of message, tone, and quality. He edited illustrations and proofread content to 'fact-check' each sentence, title, and image structure. Mario enjoys working in collaboration with Mike and Brian to enhance the company's brand image, training products, and technical publications.

Editorial and Production

Toni Culbreath worked tirelessly to proofread and edit this publication. Her attention to detail and her dedication is irreplaceable. A very special thank you goes out to Toni (Mary Poppins) Culbreath for her many years of dedicated service.

Cathleen Kwas handled the design, layout, and typesetting of this book. Her desire to create the best possible product for our customers is greatly appreciated, and she constantly pushes the design envelope to make the product experience just a little bit better.

Vinny Perez and **Eddie Anacleto** have been a dynamic team. They have taken the best instructional graphics in the industry to the next level. Both Eddie and Vinny bring years of graphic art experience to the pages of this book and have been a huge help updating and improving the content, look, and style our graphics.

Dan Haruch is an integral part of the video recording process and spends much of his time making sure that the instructor resources created from this product are the best in the business. His dedication to the instructor and student experience is much appreciated.

Video Team

The following special people provided technical advice in the development of this textbook as they served on the video team along with author **Mike Holt**.

Vince Della Croce
Business Development Manager, Licensed Electrical Inspector, Plans Examiner, Master Electrician
vincent.della_croce@siemens.com
Port Saint Lucie, Florida

Vince Della Croce began his career in IBEW Local Union #3, New York City as a helper, and progressed to journeyman and foreman electrician, before relocating to Florida. He's licensed by the State of Florida as a Master Electrician and Electrical Inspector and Plans Examiner.

He holds an Associate of Science degree in Electronic Engineering and Electrical Maintenance Technology from Penn Foster College and represents Siemens in the role of Business Development Manager with a focus on supporting electrical inspectors throughout the country.

Vince serves the IAEI Florida Chapter and IAEI Southern Section as Education Chairman. He was an alternate member of Code-Making Panels 7 and 12 for the 2017 *NEC*. He is an alternate member of Code-Making Panel 17 for the 2023 *NEC*. Vince is also a principal technical committee member of NFPA 73, 78, 99, and 1078.

Vince has two sons. The oldest is serving the community as a police sergeant and holds a Master's Degree in Business Administration. The youngest is working as a business developer and holds a Bachelor's Degree in Marketing.

About the Mike Holt Team

Daniel Brian House
Vice President of Digital and Technical Training
Mike Holt Enterprises, Instructor, Master Electrician
Brian@MikeHolt.com
Ocala, Florida

Brian House is Vice President of Digital and Technical Training at Mike Holt Enterprises, and a Certified Mike Holt Instructor. He is a permanent member of the video teams, on which he has served since the 2011 *Code* cycle. Brian has worked in the trade since the 1990s in residential, commercial and industrial settings. He opened a contracting firm in 2003 that designed energy-efficient lighting retrofits, explored "green" biomass generators, and partnered with residential PV companies in addition to traditional electrical installation and service.

In 2007, Brian was personally selected by Mike for development and began teaching seminars for Mike Holt Enterprises after being named a "Top Gun Presenter" in Mike's Train the Trainer boot camp. Brian travels around the country teaching electricians, instructors, military personnel, and engineers. His experience in the trenches as an electrical contractor, along with Mike Holt's instructor training, gives him a teaching style that is practical, straightforward, and refreshing.

Today, as Vice President of Digital and Technical Training at Mike Holt Enterprises, Brian leads the apprenticeship and digital product teams. They create cutting-edge training tools, and partner with in-house and apprenticeship training programs nationwide to help them reach the next level. He is also part of the content team that helps Mike bring his products to market, assisting in the editing of the textbooks, coordinating the content and illustrations, and assuring the technical accuracy and flow of the information.

Brian is high energy, with a passion for doing business the right way. He expresses his commitment to the industry and his love for its people in his teaching, working on books, and developing instructional programs and software tools.

Brian and his wife Carissa have shared the joy of their four children and many foster children during 25 years of marriage. When not mentoring youth at work or church, he can be found racing mountain bikes or SCUBA diving with his kids. He's passionate about helping others and regularly engages with the youth of his community to motivate them into exploring their future.

Eric Stromberg, P.E.
Electrical Engineer, Instructor
Eric@MikeHolt.com
Los Alamos, New Mexico

Eric Stromberg has a bachelor's degree in Electrical Engineering and is a professional engineer. He started in the electrical industry when he was a teenager helping the neighborhood electrician. After high school, and a year of college, Eric worked for a couple of different audio companies, installing sound systems in a variety of locations from small buildings to baseball stadiums. After returning to college, he worked as a journeyman wireman for an electrical contractor.

After graduating from the University of Houston, Eric took a job as an electronic technician and installed and serviced life safety systems in high-rise buildings. After seven years he went to work for Dow Chemical as a power distribution engineer. His work with audio systems had made him very sensitive to grounding issues and he took this experience with him into power distribution. Because of this expertise, Eric became one of Dow's grounding subject matter experts. This is also how Eric met Mike Holt, as Mike was looking for grounding experts for his 2002 Grounding vs. Bonding video.

Eric taught the *National Electrical Code* for professional engineering exam preparation for over 20 years, and has held continuing education teacher certificates for the states of Texas and New Mexico. He was on the electrical licensing and advisory board for the State of Texas, as well as on their electrician licensing exam board. Eric now consults for a Department of Energy research laboratory in New Mexico, where he's responsible for the electrical standards as well as assisting the laboratory's AHJ.

Eric's oldest daughter lives with her husband in Zurich, Switzerland, where she teaches for an international school. His son served in the Air Force, has a degree in Aviation logistics, and is a pilot and owner of an aerial photography business. His youngest daughter is a singer/songwriter in Los Angeles.

About the Mike Holt Team

Mario Valdes, Jr.
Technical Content Editor Mike Holt Enterprises,
Electrical Inspector, Electrical Plans Examiner,
Master Electrician
Mario@MikeHolt.com
Ocala, Florida

Mario Valdes, Jr. is a member of the technical team at Mike Holt Enterprises, working directly with Mike Holt in researching, re-writing, and coordinating content, to assure the technical accuracy of the information in the products. He is a permanent member of the video teams, on which he has served since the 2017 *Code* cycle.

Mario is licensed as an Electrical Contractor, most recently having worked as an electrical inspector and plans examiner for an engineering firm in South Florida. Additionally, he was an Electrical Instructor for a technical college, teaching students pursuing an associate degree in electricity. He taught subjects such as ac/dc fundamentals, residential and commercial wiring, blueprint reading, and electrical estimating. He brings to the Mike Holt team a wealth of knowledge and devotion for the *NEC*.

He started his career at 16 years old in his father's electrical contracting company. Once he got his Florida State contractor's license, he ran the company as project manager and estimator. Mario's passion for the *NEC* prompted him to get his inspector and plans review certifications and embark on a new journey in electrical *Code* compliance. He's worked on complex projects such as hospitals, casinos, hotels and multi-family high rise buildings. Mario is very passionate about educating electrical professionals about electrical safety and the *National Electrical Code*.

Mario's a member of the IAEI, NFPA, and ICC, and enjoys participating in the meetings; he believes that by staying active in these organizations he'll be ahead of the game, with cutting-edge knowledge pertaining to safety codes.

When not immersed in the electrical world Mario enjoys fitness training. He resides in Pembroke Pines, Florida with his beautiful family, which includes his wife and his two sons. They enjoy family trip getaways to Disney World and other amusement parks.

David Williams
Electrical Inspector, Instructor
daw1422@gmail.com
Delta Township, Lansing, Michigan

David Williams is an Electrical Inspector for Delta Township, Lansing, Michigan and has been an Adjunct Associate Professor at Lansing Community College in the Electrical Technology Program since 1995. He began his electrical career as an apprentice in 1974 at U.S. Steel, started inspecting for the State of Michigan in 1988, and has been inspecting for Delta Township since 1994.

Dave is a Licensed Master Electrician, Registered Electrical Inspector, Plans Reviewer, and Instructor. He holds a Certified Electrical Inspector—Master, Electrical Inspector General, and Electrical Inspector 1-2 Family through the International Association of Electrical Inspectors, IAEI.

He's served on a Technical Committee for the *National Electrical Code* since 2007 and is currently serving on the *NEC* Correlating Committee for the 2023 and 2020 *Code* and CMP-10 covering Articles 215, 225, 230, 240, and the new Article 242. Dave Chaired CMP-7 for the 2017 *NEC* and served on CMP-5 covering Grounding and Bonding for the 2008, 2011, and 2014 *Code* cycles.

Dave also serves on seven UL Standards Technical Panels; UL-111, Standard for Multi-Outlet Assemblies; UL-414, Meter Mounting Equipment; UL-1081, Swimming Pumps and Filters; UL-2200, Stationary Engine Generator Assemblies; UL-2201, Portable Engine Generators; UL-2743, Portable Power Packs; and UL-3001, Distributed Energy Generation and Storage Systems. He's served on the UL Electrical Council since 2010.

Dave is Chairman of the International Association of Electrical Inspectors, International Board of Directors. He's currently the IAEI Michigan Chapter Secretary and serves on the Western Section Board of Directors. He's past President of the IAEI Michigan Chapter and past President of the IAEI Western Section.

Dave and his wife Marie have two children (Christina and Aaron) and reside in Delta Township. He likes pickleball, golfing and they enjoy spending time at their family cottage.

Notes

Notes

INVEST IN YOURSELF

Save 25% On One Of These Best-Selling Libraries

Understanding the NEC® Complete Video Library

Learn from NEC® Expert Mike Holt, in this best-selling library where he captures all of his knowledge into one systematic training program. This library makes it easy to learn the Code and includes the following best-selling textbooks and videos:

Understanding the National Electrical Code® Volume 1 Textbook
Understanding the National Electrical Code® Volume 2 Textbook
Bonding and Grounding Textbook
Understanding the National Electrical Code® Workbook

General Requirements videos
Wiring and Protection videos
Bonding and Grounding videos
Wiring Methods and Materials videos
Equipment for General Use videos
Special Occupancies videos
Special Equipment videos
Special Conditions and Communications Systems videos

NEC® Online Quiz
Bonus video: **How to use the NEC®**

Plus! A digital version of each book and answer key

Product Code: [23UNDLIBMM]

Bonding and Grounding Video Program

Bonding and Grounding is one of the least understood and most important articles in the NEC®. This program focuses on Article 250 but also addresses grounding rules found throughout the Code Book. The textbook and videos are informative and practical, and include in one single place, all articles that relate to bonding and grounding. The full-color illustrations help break down the concepts and make them easier to understand. This topic is at the core of most power quality and safety issues, making this program a must-have for everyone in the industry. Order your copy today.

Program includes:
Bonding and Grounding Textbook
Bonding and Grounding videos

Plus! A digital version of the book and answer key

Product Code: [23BGMM]

Comprehensive Exam Preparation Video Library

A complete course designed for your success. In-depth instruction for electrical theory and Code, with step-by-step instructions for solving electrical calculations. The videos are a vital component to learning, and the practice questions are key to reinforcing what you learn.

Program includes:
Understanding the National Electrical Code Volume 1 Textbook
Understanding the National Electrical Code Volume 2 Textbook
Electrical Exam Preparation Textbook
Bonding and Grounding Textbook
Electrical Theory Textbook
Electrician Practice Exam Workbook

Videos for the following topics:
Code, Theory, Calculations

Plus! A digital version of each book and answer key

Product Code:
Master Library [23MACOMM]
Journeyman Library [23JRCOMM]

Call Now 888.632.2633
Discount code: B23CC25
or Order Online at MikeHolt.com/Products

 Mike Holt Enterprises

TAKE IT UP A NOTCH
Upgrade your learning tool box...

Do you have the digital products that accompany this book?

Videos

Mike's video recordings are dynamic. They feature a panel of industry experts that discuss the rules, explain why they are important, and provide insight as to how to apply them in the field. The best way to get the most out of this program is to watch the videos as you work through your textbook. Whether you're a visual or an auditory learner, watching the videos will not only help you process the information, but will also help your memory recall. Watch on your computer, tablet or phone!

Digital Book

Take your product on the road! The digital version of the textbook will allow you to use it on the job site or on the move!

SCAN NOW TO UPGRADE

Digital Answer Key

Wherever you've chosen to work on your program, you'll have access to the answer key readily available at your fingertips.

Did you buy the book from another seller?
Register to get a digital answer key at MikeHolt.com/MyAK23CC or scan the QR code to the right.

Did you purchase your product directly from Mike Holt Enterprises?
The digital answer key that comes with your product can be accessed in your account at MikeHolt.com.

Have questions? Call our team at 888.632.2633